CW01067039

THE WRONG SORT OF FISH OIL

THE TRIALS, TRIBULATIONS (AND TRIUMPHS) OF THE EARLY RAILWAY PASSENGER

Acknowledgements

Thanks are due to the staff of the Bridgwater Reference and Taunton Local Studies Libraries, where the bulk of the material from The Times and Somerset newspapers was found; also to the staff of the National Archives (ex-Public Record Office) at Kew, the British Library's Newspaper Library at Colindale and the House of Lords Record Office. John Gilmour, Dr John Gough and the late Bryan Wilson contributed points. The Railway & Canal Historical Society has kindly allowed me to re-use information from works published by them: Railway Stations in England, Wales and Scotland – a Chronology and articles from its Journal on luggage thefts (March 2004) and compensation (July 2005).

M. E. QUICK

THE WRONG SORT OF FISH OIL

THE TRIALS, TRIBULATIONS (AND TRIUMPHS) OF THE EARLY RAILWAY PASSENGER

AUSTIN & MACAULEY
PUBLISHERS LTD.

A CIP catalogue record for this title is available from the British Library.

ISBN 978 1 84963 174 7

www.austinmacauley.com

First Published (2012)
Austin & Macauley Publishers Ltd.
25 Canada Square
Canary Wharf
London
E14 5LB

Printed & Bound in Great Britain

Illustrations

Those from *Punch* come from these compilations:

Later Pencillings from Punch, John Leech, Bradbury & Evans, undated – mid/late 1850s?

Pictures from Punch, published by *Punch*, undated – Volume I about 1892, Volume III about 1900.

Punch Library of Humour: The Railway Book, Educational Press, 1910.

In the first two cases the books gave the year of the original cartoon. The last did not, but only cartoons whose content illustrates issues raised in the text have been used.

The rest come from early material owned by the writer, scanned in by Mail Boxes of Bridge Street, Taunton.

CONTENTS

INTRODUCTION

Most railway history tends to concentrate on companies and their major figures or to approach it geographically. This book is intended to give the worm's eye view – that of the passengers, in the first half of Queen Victoria's reign. It is an off-shoot of an earlier one which sought to give an exact factual record of the opening and closing dates of stations; initially, odd bits and pieces were collected for their own sake and the relief they gave from a pure diet of dates and somehow this gradually developed a life of its own. The idea throughout is to provide some idea of what matters were like for a railway traveller; it is not intended to be a comprehensive survey since that would require a far longer work. It also includes material that sheds some light on Victorian attitudes in general; at many points information about wider events has been included in order to show that faults described were not limited to railway companies.

Much information has been taken from *The Times* which then saw itself as the scourge of incompetent government of all types, not as a semi-official organ of the powers-that-were – thus its attacks on the Poor Law and lack of proper provision for Crimean wounded. It provided editorials, articles, advertisements and letters of complaint. The last are particularly useful for providing details of everyday travel, though a very one-sided one; letters of praise and approval were rare – a constant of human nature? Where material has been quoted in the original words the reader will find some spelling variations, such as *breaks* and *brakes*, and in the use of capital letters and hyphens; please assume that odd spellings in quotations represent what was found – repetition of '[sic]' would be wearisome. Interesting snippets from other papers also found their way in – perhaps via several intermediaries, though the origin was not always acknowledged.

Local newspapers have also provided material. This writer suspects that many editors of 'local' papers spent many working hours condensing national news from *The Times* and copying from others;. This provided much help since *The Taunton Courier* often contained information totally irrelevant to its locality; the hope is that journalists generally cribbed reasonably accurately.

The returns regularly made to Parliament by the Board of Trade (briefly replaced at one stage by the Railway Commissioners) are another prolific source of information. Important in themselves they also incidentally gave information about the habits of the time: Mr Hind, principal in a firm of silk-fringe manufacturers, living at Dalston, went for a walk on a Saturday afternoon in July 1846 and as he was passing Shoreditch station he saw a train about to start so he suddenly decided to take a ride to Ilford and back. We only know of this particular impulse to sample the new form of travel because his trip ended fatally in a crash at Stratford.

Most material comes from contemporary sources but some has had to be taken from works in modern print to fill gaps. Also, some that will be familiar to regular readers of railway history has had to be included in order to provide a coherent picture for anyone not so acquainted.

The approach is thematic, giving examples of particular issues. Thus some items used under 'Delays' could equally have been put under 'Accidents'; a few have of necessity had to be mentioned more than once but every effort has been made to avoid repeating detail.

For detailed coverage of standard railway history and locomotive technicalities the reader is referred to the many books already available.

Abbreviations have been avoided as far as possible; however, to give the full names of all companies would take up much space so those of most major companies are abbreviated but those that disappeared early by amalgamation and those content with one word names are given more fully, though in somewhat shortened form – e.g. 'the Caledonian' rather than 'the Caledonian Railway'.

Company Abbreviations Used; in all cases 'Railway Company' needs to be added:
GE = Great Eastern
GN = Great Northern
GW = Great Western
LBSC = London, Brighton & South Coast
LCD = London, Chatham & Dover
LNW = London and North Western
LSW = London & South Western
LY = Lancashire & Yorkshire
MS&L = Manchester, Sheffield & Lincolnshire (later Great Central)
NE = North Eastern
SE = South Eastern.

No attempt is made to convert Victorian prices. The goods then regarded as essential and the range available were so different that to apply the indexes sometimes used is nonsensical. What needs to be remembered is that a steady £1 per week kept many families going quite securely; when income-tax was introduced in 1842 it was only intended to be paid by the better-off and the starting point for payment was £150 per year. Furthermore, prices then were much steadier in the long term but could, especially before 1850, fluctuate over short periods as a result of, for example, poor harvests. The currency of the day is thus always quoted:
12 [old] pence (12d) = 1 shilling; 20 shillings (20s) = £1.

Similarly contemporary measurements are used:
22 yards = 1 chain; 10 chains = 1 furlong; 8 furlongs = 1 mile.

For an explanation of the title, please see the end of the chapter on 'Disruption'.

Chapter 1: HOAXES AND TALL STORIES

This chapter, which might be expected at the end, is put here to give some idea of the reliability of a main source used. Writers to *The Times* were allowed to use pseudonyms: *Viator* (= traveller) and *Constant Reader* were favourites. They were supposed to include their cards to guarantee genuineness but editors' ability to check was limited and some rogue items sneaked through. Railway officials certainly read the paper: letters refuting accusations appeared but it cannot be guaranteed that all of these were seen. Others which arouse grave suspicions, including pieces written by journalists, are included here as tall stories; a few, slightly less unbelievable, are included in relevant later chapters, with doubts expressed. It is possible that some suspects were genuine and that fabrications have crept into later chapters. The paper's editor certainly realised that invention and exaggeration might appear: in a leader of 14 August 1851 he wrote there was scarcely a day when he did not receive 40 or 50 letters complaining about railways, especially overcrowding, arrogance and indifference of management towards passengers and their interests, and the bullying of passengers; there were so many that there had to be a large measure of truth in them.

Accidents were a fertile source of exaggeration and error. *The Times* frequently prefaced accounts with a warning that early versions were likely to be unreliable. One early accident, on 22 June 1837, originally described in good faith, was on the London & Birmingham. A train had stopped near Chalk Farm to detach the rope which had hauled it up from Euston; it was so heavy that they added engines front and rear. The latter came on too fast and smashed the last carriage, killing Hallam, a footman to the Duke of Sussex (one of King George III's unlovely brood) and injuring several others. Affecting details were given of how the Duke ordered all care for Hallam but to no avail since he died in hospital. Next day it printed a correction: the stationary engine at Camden Town which operated the cable was out of action for repairs so the train was taken up the incline by the locomotive that was to take it on to Birmingham. Soon after starting the power was found to be inadequate because of the drizzle so another was sent to the rear; when it reached there, the wheels of the first slipped, causing a slight collision. No damage was done to the carriages; on visiting the hospital they found Hallam to be 'nearly quite recovered' but with some contusions to his head.[1]

One 'non-event' has appeared in several railway books down the years as if real. On 21 January 1842 an incident on the London & Brighton on the previous Tuesday was reported. A gentleman had had his carriage placed on the last truck and travelled in it, though advised against this. The truck somehow became disengaged and he was left in the middle of Balcombe Tunnel in the dark. He was frightened but decided it was safest to stay in place and thought his doom was sealed when he heard an engine coming, whistle screaming. In fact it was a pilot engine sent to look for him after his absence had been noted at the next station. Three days later they wrote that they had been assured from an official source that the story was a fabrication.[2]

On 14 November 1843 *The Times* gave an account of a serious and messy accident to a porter at Romford, after which he had been carried to Shoreditch by train. The next day, upon the authority of the Eastern Counties they said they were happy to state that there was no accident to a porter employed at Shoreditch, indeed no accident that day. The blame was now put on *The Globe*, from which the original had been copied. False accusations continued to appear from time to time. 'FK Robinson' (42 Fenchurch Street, EC) wrote that on 24 June 1870 there had been a sudden stop on the 5 p.m. London to Brighton express near Sydenham when they had nearly run into another train because a signal had jammed at clear. JP Knight, traffic manager of SE then wrote, asking him to send his details since he knew nothing of the incident, nor, on enquiry at the address given, could he find anything of writer.[3]

One entry not later contradicted but reading more like an episode from a highly-coloured melodrama appeared on 31 January 1842, headed 'Miraculous Escape'. A short time before a passenger train had been going towards Castle Eden, between Haswell and Hartlepool, when a rail was sprung so as to go diagonally through the floor of a coach. It was full but no-one was hurt. One man's hat was hit, and another thrown from his place by the shock, ending with his head in a lady's lap; if he had stayed in place, the rail would have gone through him. No later contradiction was seen, but it looks very suspicious, especially given its provenance: an accident in the north-east reached *The Times* via *a Cumberland paper.*

Hoaxes were not confined to events on the track. In March 1837 *Herapath* reported that several papers had said the whole of the Greenwich Railway had been seized at the suit of Mr Macintosh, its builder, for a debt of £300,000. It blamed the work of some mischievous imp of the Stock Exchange. The money column of *The Times* on 20 September 1844 included a copy of a letter sent to the Secretary of the LSW by John Julius Ramsden FRS, 22 Carlton Terrace, St Johns Wood, Westminster, who was praised for his selflessness: as a shareholder he had listed 12 points to be followed for the benefit of passengers, including faster trains, better carriages (especially 2nd and 3rd) and lower fares. However, on the 26th they included a facsimile of his signature, hoping that someone might help detect the writer of the fabricated letter. The much-battered Eastern Counties was the victim, 19 February 1845, of a fake advertisement for its Stock; next day an item said it was not inserted by the company nor authorised in any way by them.

Some letters seem to have been an attempt at what today would be described as 'dirty tricks'. In March 1860 a letter from Thomas Waddington M.D. of Wakefield described a serious, but fictitious, accident near Doncaster; the GN authorities suspected it had been sent to try and depress further their company's shares.[4] In the 1860s the SE and LCD were engaged in vicious rivalry including the cross-Channel trade. On 21 January 1864 George Roland (writing from 30 Gayfield Square,

Edinburgh on the 18th) made the unlikely claim that defective arrangements at Calais, in the dark, had caused him to walk into the sea and that the manager of the LCD had disclaimed responsibility. Next day TW Scott, writing for JS Forbes, the LCD's General Manager, said no accident had been reported and he could only suppose his letter was a 'weak invention of the enemy to bring our line into disrepute'.

Exaggeration was particularly likely where there was no means then available for accurate measurement. Notions of speed were hazy – trains were not fitted with speedometers so drivers had to learn to estimate speeds from the time it took to cover known distances. On 8 January 1838 *The Times* proclaimed that on the Grand Junction about 6 o'clock one night, *Caliban*, 'exercising' on the line near Stafford, came into violent contact with a mixed train coming from Penkridge. The intervening two tenders and two horseboxes absorbed much of the shock. The drivers were thrown out and injured and the engine of the mixed train became 'disengaged' and went off at the rate of nearly 100 mph, stopping after about twelve miles when it ran out of steam. This was taken from *The Staffordshire Chronicle* and the exact date of this unratified world speed record was not given. Exaggeration might also have crept into the figures given for the numbers of passengers on early excursions.

Some items were so bizarre that they defy belief. The paper of 22 January 1856 contained an item headed 'A Railway Romance'. On the Wear Valley Railway 'the other day' a gentleman from Birmingham had found himself seated after dark in a first-class carriage, the only other passenger in the compartment being a blooming lady answering to the description of 'fair, fat and forty'. They had hardly gone 100 yards before the lady leapt from her seat and said, 'How dare you sir, what do you mean?' and this was repeated at intervals. The man thought she was mad and decided to give her into custody at the next station but before he could do so, she opened the door and called very loudly for the guard. A crowd collected and she accused the man of improperly pinching her legs. Things looked bad for him but the guard then remembered he had put a basket containing a live goose under her seat and pulled it out, solving the mystery. This was one of those stories that did the rounds, appearing in *The Taunton Courier* eight days later.[5]

There were intermittent appearances of letters about madmen, some of which are used later. In two cases writers claimed two problems on the same train, which seems unbelievable. One was in 1847 when ED said he had recently travelled from Exeter by the express and was worried by the excited behaviour of a fellow passenger who took out a Testament and read it with 'eyes uplifted and strange grimaces'. At Taunton he moved to another carriage, as did others; they were congratulating themselves on their escape and exchanging stories about lunatics when they found that the lady in this carriage was insane and the gentleman accompanying her was afraid their conversation might send her into a frenzy.[6] The other was an item in 1859 which said that one of their readers, with a male and female friend entered a second-class carriage at

Canterbury. There was a drunk in one corner and once the train was on the move, he and another stranger started to chaff one another, stripped off, and threatened to fight. At Wye they moved into another carriage which contained two dragoons – a sergeant, asleep, and a private. The private took out a razor, looked wild-eyed and vigorously stropped it; he then pulled out a bundle from under the seat, cut off bread and meat and ate, and stropped the razor again. The sergeant woke up and dispossessed him, saying he was a maniac he was escorting to headquarters to be dismissed. When they complained about his having dozed off, he apologised but said he had been with prisoner the whole of the previous night and could no longer keep awake.[7]

It should be stressed that railways were not singled out by hoaxers. Shortly after the 1842 Brighton episode a letter copied from *The Morning Post* appeared under the heading *DREADFUL ACCIDENT AND EXTENSIVE LOSS OF LIFE*:

> ... Between 4 and 5 o'clock this evening, and when almost twilight, the entire surface of a very large piece of ground, more than seven acres at Combe-down, gave way, owing to the workmen having conducted their excavations in a stone quarry far beneath an angle, or rather street, of that populous village, of which above 18 houses, with its beautiful new church, school-house, &c., were thus completely undermined, and have been, by the instantaneous subsiding of their foundations, involved in ruin; and multitudes in the buildings and accidentally assembled on the spot have perished. ... the outlets of the city are thronged with anxious thousands crowding towards the scene of desolation. The bells of the Abbey and other churches are ringing violently, and the authorities are hastening to Combe to render what assistance they can to the surviving sufferers. ... Report speaks of hundreds slain and mutilated.

It was signed A. SISSON, giving his address as *Warden*-office, 53, Milsom-street, Bath,

The Times sent its reporter to see and his version appeared next day, headed *INFAMOUS HOAX*, BATH, TUESDAY EVENING, JAN. 11:

> ... the whole statement which we yesterday copied from *The Morning Post*, ... turns out, on enquiry, to be without the slightest foundation [an unhappy choice of word?]. ... there is no such paper as the *Warden* published here; there is no such number as 53 in Milsom-street; and every exertion has failed to make out whether in reality any such an individual as 'A. Sisson' is in existence. A personal visit, however, this day to Coombe-down ... confirmed the statement that the whole matter was a hoax.
>
> The village has through the day been thronged by anxious enquirers and the utmost indignation prevails against the miscreant who has been guilty of this mischievous and cruel fabrication [– particularly because most of the visitors showed their disappointment at not finding carnage?][8]

Finally, the most spectacular error of all: early in October 1854, *The Times* proclaimed 'THE FALL OF SEBASTOPOL'. This joyful news was copied by provincial papers across the country. Alas, the Allied troops did not capture the city until September 1855.

Chapter 2: CHANGE OR CONTINUITY?

It was the custom about a century and a half ago for persons intending to make a journey from London to York to arrange all their worldly affairs before starting on so dangerous and tedious an expedition; and now what would be the surprise and delight of our ancestors, could they but be permitted to glide luxuriously in cushioned vehicles over the smooth surface of the rails between the metropolis and the ancient city of York in less than one-seventh part of the time formerly occupied by them in the journey. *Francis Whishaw, 1842.*

Though the early traveller might grumble about the service provided by railways, it was far superior to what had gone before. People could now travel further, faster and more safely, for business, holidays and leisure.

An example of humbler new opportunities provided (and of contemporary journalists' style) is provided by this extract from a local paper of 1847:

The towns on the line of the Bristol and Exeter Railway are so favourably placed for the purpose, that a vast number of persons have arranged for a trip to hear the wondrous Vocalist, JENNY LIND, on Monday next at Bristol, and on the following night at Bath. The cost of a return ticket, the short time required for the journey, and the opportunity of hearing this delightful singer at an expence, the aggregate of which would be little more than that of a cab-hire in waiting at the Queen's Opera House, combined with the great advantage of listening within the convenient sphere of a provincial theatre to the finest voice that ever won unqualified and universal admiration, will no doubt create an irrepressible desire among many of this neighbourhood to profit by the opportunity thus presented; the concluding enjoyment of which will probably be further enhanced by the splendour of a moon-lit journey home.[1]

The Scots were not immune from this sort of writing. The opening of the line from Strathmiglo to Milnathort in 1858 prompted the local paper to write, 'as this is the day of the eclipse of the sun, we suggest a half-holiday to the working classes, as inaugurating an eclipse or extinguisher of the old modes of conveyance in this county.'[2]

Readers will note that some Victorian complaints are echoed today. However, it should soon become clear that in most respects railway travel has altered out of all recognition: it is far faster, trains are more frequent and more comfortable, information is much more readily available and the staff are far more polite and helpful than they appear to have been then.

Some odd ancient habits do resurface occasionally: *The Daily Telegraph* of 16 December 2006 mentioned a drunk who had chosen a line through Epsom station as a sleeping place and survived, illustrating one repetitive problem, others' misuse of railways. This did not usually directly affect passengers but could cause accidents and delays and shows that railwaymen were not responsible for everything that went wrong. At first many regarded railways as a straighter and less muddy route for pedestrians. The Stockton & Darlington had so much trouble that it even offered special services to try and eliminate this problem and the related one of unauthorised riding on coal wagons, particularly on the Middlesbrough line: in 1832 they provided what was effectively an annual season ticket for use on coal trains at 2s 6d and in 1837 a locomotive-hauled wagon that ran an as required service at 2d for the whole way and even cheap rides on engines were provided.[3] Railway companies were active in their efforts to cure this problem: one Board of Trade file at Kew records many prosecutions for trespass of various sorts. The Midland Counties provided several examples: in late July and early August Mary Painter was sent to prison for 14 days when she could not pay her 40/- fine for trespassing on the line near Loughborough, Thomas Tebbutt was fined £2 (with an option of one month) for being drunk on the line near Attenborough and Thomas Silvester (who had obstructed the 4.40 p.m. from Nottingham to Derby) was ordered to be taken care of in the workhouse. In November John Law even drove his sheep along the line near Beeston; he was only fined 20/- plus costs. Less lucky was William Winter, killed on 10 September 1842 while driving his horse and cart the shortest way home along the Pontop and South Shields despite having been turned back and warned several times previously; he had been to Sunderland market and was described as 'in liquor'. The Stockton & Darlington clearly had not solved its problem: as well as pedestrians it had to cope with James Johnson who rode his horse along the line (6d fine plus 6/6 costs) and William Robson his mule (1/- fine plus 7/6 costs). The returns made by the Wishaw & Coltness show Scottish lines facing the same problem.[4] It persists today: *The Daily Telegraph* of 8 July 2008 reported that figures released by the British Transport Police showed more than 1,000 people had been killed on the country's railways in the previous four years, level crossings especially tending to be treated with contempt by many road users.

The one apparently backward step is that many places with a station in 1870 now lack one. When a village was first served, its station, perhaps a mile or more away and served only by two or three trains each way per day, would have been regarded as a great advance; once a bus service direct to the village was started, the railway lost much of its attraction and what remained was destroyed by the advent of widespread private transport. The casualties have mainly been branch and wayside stations: the main lines that existed in 1870 are still mostly with us since a fair proportion of the big closures that occurred from about 1930 on were of lines built after 1870. All progress is liable to involve casualties. As early as 1838 *The Wolverhampton Chronicle* reported that the income from its local turnpike roads had decreased by more than £600 per year and the Stafford roads at £1,000 since the opening of the Grand Junction.[5] Next year the opening of the Arbroath & Forfar Railway caused the lease on the turnpike between the two to be knocked down at a much-reduced price.[6] The bankruptcy of Sarah Hayter, an elderly woman who had run a farriery business at Bagshot, was put down to the fact that the 45 coaches which had used to go through the town had been reduced to four.[7] In 1847 it was Andover's turn: the opening of railway from Salisbury to Bishopstoke (Eastleigh) caused the withdrawal of the only three coaches which ran through Andover out of at least 40 a few years previously.[8] Shipping services also suffered. In 1848 *The Scotsman* contained notices advertising 'Further reduction of fares between Edinburgh and London' as railways competed for their trade, and, eventually, destroyed most of it.

Chapter 3: FROM PRIMITIVE PASSENGERS TO A NETWORK

Primitive Passengers

There was a lengthy period of trial and error before the steam engine was reliable enough to be entrusted with the regular haulage of passengers but during this time some were able to make use of 'trains' over short distances. The first legal restrictions on the carriage of passengers only came in 1840 when the Board of Trade received supervisory powers, at first only advisory. Thus Trevithick was able to carry some passengers free on one of his experimental runs in 1804 and charge people for rides on his circular demonstation line in 1808. Present day health and safety zealots might have smothered railways at birth, confining mankind to horse power – but then would that temperamental beast, the horse, have ever gained certificates of rideworthiness and haulworthiness? However, even the most ardent critics of these zealots must admit that many of the habits described later are better not repeated.

The earliest railways, often called 'tramways' or 'tramroads', were short lines carrying minerals, complementing existing river and canal-borne traffic; some gradually allowed 'passengers' to travel on top of loads or in empty trucks. Little is known about these but in 1830 an Exeter paper described the Pentewan Railway, a 2 ft 6 in line near St Austell for carrying china clay, and said 20 persons were sometimes seen riding on the wagons at once.[1]

The earliest regular services were provided by contractors who paid to run a horse-drawn passenger carriage, picking up and setting down at any convenient point. The earliest known was in 1807, when Benjamin French contracted to pay rent for using the line between the Brewery Bank in Swansea and Castle Hill, Oystermouth; various contractors kept this service going, at times summer only, until about 1827.[2] Other examples included one run by William Wright on the Kilmarnock & Troon by 1818; when Parliament was seeking information about passenger traffic in 1838-9 the company said it did not run passenger services itself but allowed others to do so, charging them so much per ton, 'estimating so many persons to constitute a ton'. The Severn & Wye fixed a toll for Samuel Holder & James Ward to run a 'Pleasure Tram drawn by one horse' in 1821.

The Stockton & Darlington continued this tradition. Though steam was used on its promotional run, the first regular passenger service on 10 October 1825 was horse-drawn. Various contractors used convenient inns as termini and booking points; 'trains' consisted of one carriage, clearly of stage-coach ancestry, with space for 6 passengers inside and 20 outside (on top). This continued until 1833, when the company bought out the contractors and introduced its own steam-hauled services, though some Sunday services horse-drawn by private contractors persisted until 1856.[3] The Edinburgh & Dalkeith, originally using a 4 feet 6 inch gauge, followed the same pattern: MJ Fox began his service, from St Leonards, the company's Edinburgh depot, on 2 June 1832; it was so profitable that the company soon added its own and then took over completely. In 1847, after the North British had taken over, it was converted to standard gauge and steam haulage.[4]

Walton, who ran a service from Stockton to Coxhoe, where a road connection took passengers on to Durham, was let loose with steam power. According to Whishaw he paid 'the greatest possible attention to the accommodation and Convenience of the public' and his carriages were 'but little inferior to those belonging to passenger-railways generally'.[5] However, William Leathem's letter written two years earlier had given details of two accidents in which he had been recently involved: in the second, on 28 August 1840, he was returning from the British Association when a wheel of the tender broke; when he examined the wreckage he saw four old rusty fractures in addition to the new break.[6]

The Whitby & Pickering, opened in 1835, included a rope-worked incline in the middle of horse-drawn sections. Normally one horse was enough for most of the way but part of the route required two, and extra horses had to be sent to help in bad weather and contrary wind conditions. Since speed would obviously be limited, they kept costs down, thus including sharp curves. Its Board of Trade return for 1840 listed fares to several places which would never have a station in steam days, including Fen Bogs and Raindale. After conversion to locomotive-power in 1847 some straightening was achieved by agreement with local landowners but many tortuous curves remained so a maximum speed of 20 m.p.h. was recommended, at least until drivers became fully acquainted with the course of the line.

Rope haulage worked by stationary engines was used by the London & Blackwall at its opening in 1840, one consequence being that travel between certain pairs of stations was only possible by going to a terminus and thence back to the desired destination; it converted to locomotive power in 1849. The Durham & Sunderland, another to use this form of power, did not impress Whishaw: 'The difficulty of starting the trains, the numerous detentions on the way, and the great uncertainty of the time that a journey will occupy, added to the jolts experienced by passengers when reaching a bank-head, or when making a false start – a thing of very frequent occurrence – all present themselves as serious objections to the stationary system' When Parliament was discussing new railway legislation Mr Crawford of Sunderland sent an impassioned letter, claiming that frequent accidents on the line were 'a matter of great notoriety in its immediate neighbourhood, although from the influence exercised by the Directory over the local press the public at large remain ignorant of the fact'. The line was totally unsuited for passengers; he even claimed that one of the directors had admitted he had once travelled one way but been so terrified that he had returned by road in a friend's coach. In addition, there were dangers to other travellers because the road between Sunderland and Durham, thirteen miles long, was crossed by four tram roads from coal pits, none of which had any gates; one even had pointwork placed on the turnpike itself. Only in 1857-8 did the company start to replace rope haulage.

The Stanhope & Tyne illustrated how a service might evolve. It started carrying goods in 1834, without intending to carry passengers but local requests led to them being allowed to travel free on top of coal wagons. Soon a wagon was attached at the back just for passengers; this was followed by a locomotive-hauled separate passenger coach on fortnightly pay days, and in 1836 by a full service. This started from South Shields, where passengers boarded trains in sidings after buying tickets in a nearby inn and ran to a point on the Durham Turnpike near Chester-Le-Street, where road connections could be made. The company answered Parliamentary enquiries by saying that it ran this as a service to the public, not to make a profit for itself.[7] More convenient routes provided by other companies soon led to its demise. Somewhat similar were developments in the Monklands, where various lines built to carry minerals developed passenger services; some were incorporated in later and lasting projects but others soon lost their passengers.

Another whose early years showed how primitive services could develop was the Bodmin & Wadebridge. 'Passengers' travelling against the engineer's wishes on a trial run on 16 July 1834 were injured when the carriage was derailed.[8] The first fare-paying passengers were carried on Wednesday, 1 October 1834.[9] A note in the Board of Trade return for 1840-1841 said: 'There is not any separate passenger train; the staple traffic is sand, and to the train is attached a single carriage. On market and fair days there is one or more carriages attached to the train for passengers' and in 1844 it resolved to run steam trains only on Saturdays, Fair Days, Bodmin Assize Days and other public occasions plus occasions when a special goods cargo warranted it.[10] Only in September 1869 did it appear in *Bradshaw*, no intermediate stops being shown; the service was meagre – one train each way Mondays, Wednesdays and Fridays, two on Saturdays (Bodmin market day); in 1870 they only carried 4,689 passengers, 37 of them first-class.

Some primitive characteristics persisted on lines clearly built to higher standards. The limited power of early locomotives meant that haulage by stationary engine and rope was used on inclines such as the lines up from Liverpool to Edge Hill, Euston to Camden and Glasgow to Cowlairs. Sometimes progress was undone, at least temporarily: *The Times* reported on 24 January 1850 that the Tewkesbury branch had reverted to horse-power, which had originally run the line, owing to the need for economy. It referred to 'the now almost strange apparition of a railway train (1st, 2nd and 3rd classes in one carriage) drawn by a single horse'.

Another form of primitive travel occurred on lines before they had received Board of Trade approval; this was not illegal as long as no charge was made but sometimes the law was broken – without, as far as this writer knows, any penalty being inflicted. On 6 September 1866 an excursion train left 'Port Madoc' for a great religious gathering at 'Carnarvon'; those running the line had at first demurred but gave into pressure, charging 3s each for the trip; about 800 went and on the way back the engine derailed at points, five being killed and a sixth dying later. There were no proper carriages, only ballast waggons, and one 'passenger' rode on the tender.[11] The official report listed occasions when the line had previously carried passengers free and safely. These included taking the Portmadoc and Pwllheli companies of Volunteers to Carnarvon in ballast waggons with plank seats, excursionists from Carnarvon to Barmouth, a party of children from Portmadoc to Criccieth for confirmation, Sir Watkin and Lady Wynn and a large party from Barmouth to Carnarvon and several picnic parties at different times.[12]

Passengers could enjoy a spectacular free ride on the West Somerset Mineral Railway in the late 1860s, complete with views across the Bristol Channel. This consisted of a 'normal' railway from Watchet to Combe Row, at the foot of the Brendon Hills; from there an incline, 1,100 feet long with a vertical rise of 800 feet, similar in many respects to a cliff railway, linked it with the upper section. The company could not afford the safety measures necessary to satisfy the Board of Trade so passengers, mostly iron miners and their families, were taken free of charge.[13]

Some mature railways stopped for passengers between stations. The Maryport & Carlisle's timetable for 26 September 1842 included a note that 'Passengers set down between any two … Stations will be charged the same as if they were taken to the next Station'.[14] Francis Worsley complained in 1858 that he had gone from Buckingham to Bedford and arrived half-an-hour late having stopped about a mile before the station, opposite the racecourse, to let off passengers who, men and women, were left to 'stride, straddle and leap' from the high step of the carriage down to the rails and cross these.[15]

An early practice companies found it difficult to stop was that of taking free rides on goods wagons. About 300 yards beyond Wetheral there were coal staiths belonging to the Earl of Carlisle; a train derailed there on 3 December 1836 and on clearing the debris they found the bodies of two brothers who had secreted themselves under the cover of a grain wagon.[16] The Wishaw & Coltness, a primarily mineral line, clearly did its best since in September 1841 it had one offender fined £5 under its Act of Parliament.[17] However, a few months later two wagon-drivers took a couple of relatives on their wagons which were returning empty in January 1842. At a passing-place on the single line four wagons went one way, the following four another; the passengers were thrown off the first four and run over and killed by the others. The company then put forward bye-laws to prohibit, on pain of fine of £5, any driver from taking others – the 1841 prosecutions had been for trespass, which could not be proved against people invited onto the line by its servants. The official accident reports carried a stream of similar events throughout this period. For example, in 1854 a trespasser was killed in June trying to get onto a moving goods near Simpasture Junction on the Stockton & Darlington and in September a man who had secreted himself on top of a carriage on the Midland was injured when his head hit a bridge. A passenger without a ticket was killed trying to get onto a Midland wagon in motion at Holbeck in 1869.

Some primitive travellers went lawfully, accompanying animals. The Traffic Committee of the LNW recommended in 1841 that a groom in charge of 'an entire horse' should travel free.[18] Another group were drovers accompanying livestock, who travelled in guards' vans or 'carriages' (usually very flimsy) attached specially for their use and suffered more than their fair share of casualties since goods trains had an unfortunate record of being hit in the rear. In 1851 one was killed and three injured near Whitmore on the LNW when an engine ran into the back of their cattle train. On 9 September 1867 a Midland cattle train ran into a ballast train and broke in two, the rear part running back and colliding with an oncoming passenger train; four cattle drovers were killed and five injured. Three were killed when a heavy passenger engine ran into the back of their cattle train near Bullo Pill, on the GW's South Wales line in November 1868. In September 1852 one had been killed when his head hit a bridge while he was riding on top of a cattle truck.

A network develops

The success of the Liverpool & Manchester, opened in 1830, and usually regarded as the first 'modern' line stimulated others, though deciding on a route, raising the large capital sums, gaining Parliamentary approval and building the line, meant that at the end of 1835 railway travel was still limited to a few widely separated short lines. However, by the end of 1840 London, Birmingham, Liverpool and Manchester were linked and the West Coast route had been extended to Lancaster; York had been reached, via Derby and Nottingham, and Southampton had its route from London. Thereafter progress was rapid and has been described in many books now in print. By the end of 1870 the northern limit of continuous travel had reached Golspie; beyond there was an isolated stretch from Dunrobin to West Helmsdale, built privately by the Duke of Sutherland which would soon be incorporated into the line to Wick and Thurso. Important cross-country lines had been completed from Carlisle to Newcastle in 1839 and Manchester to Leeds in 1841.

Many separate companies were involved, each building a relatively short length; however, many were planned from the outset to complement one another and soon were amalgamated into larger concerns. The LNW emerged in 1844 to run the West Coast Route, and the Midland in 1846 from lines centred on Derby.

Delayed openings

Unsurprisingly not all developed smoothly so there were often delays in opening. Shortages of money and materials were often to blame, the former too commonly to warrant giving details. In the latter case, the London & Greenwich gave a shortage of iron as its reason. It had initially opened from Spa Road to Deptford and then advertised that its trains would start from London Bridge on 10 October 1836 but had to delay until 1 December; even then passengers had to buy their tickets at London Bridge and walk along the line to Bermondsey Road, where they boarded from ground level. The Aberdeen line to a temporary terminus at Limpet Mill, south of the city, was supposed to open on 30 October 1850 but was delayed, though only by one day, because the contractors and navvies refused to give up possession until their bills were paid.

Physical problems were often underestimated when lines were planned – there was, for example, little reliable geological information. Early on the Kilsby and Box tunnels held up progress on the lines to Birmingham and Bristol and there were many similar examples later. When the Southampton & Dorchester opened on 1 June 1847 they had hurriedly to provide a temporary terminus just west of the tunnel at Southampton because the latter had been found to be defective; for the first few days a restricted service was operated by an engine and carriages that had been horse-drawn through the tunnel and an omnibus was used to ferry passengers over the gap from the main station.

Falls of earth, usually caused by heavy rain falling on ground not yet consolidated were another cause of delay. The line between Norwich and Brandon had been advertised to open on 9 July 1845 but a slip caused a delay to the 30th.[19] The Whitehaven & Furness suffered a more spectacular loss when it planned to open between Bootle and Ravenglass on 1 July 1850, and had issued notices to this effect. At the end of June part of the viaduct across the River Esk was burned down (arson was suspected); it was rebuilt during the following week at a cost of £600 and they were able to open on 8 July.[20]

By far the commonest cause of disappointment was the over-optimism frequently displayed by directors. *The Times* of 2 January 1863 said of the Metropolitan: 'It appears that arrangements have been made for the opening of this line on the 10th inst., but as the 1st October, 1st November, the middle of December and the 1st inst. have been announced from time to time as the probable date of opening, it is presumed that no one will feel disappointed if a further postponement should take place'. It did actually open that day. The opening of the Tewkesbury to Malvern line on 16 May 1864 led the local paper to say that although it had announced the opening in its previous issue, 'many persons, after so much disappointment, refused to believe that such would be the case'. Even so the resited Tewkesbury station was not quite finished, having neither refreshment room nor a good approach road.[21] Linked to this was a tendency to put lines forward for government inspection before they were really ready so they were ordered to delay opening until deficiencies had been rectified.

Outsiders could cause delay. A dispute over the crossing of Northam Road by the railway meant that Southampton had initially to make do with a temporary station short of the road when the line from Winchester opened on 10 June 1839 (the line from London to Basingstoke opened the same day, with a connecting road service).[22] On 15

July *The Hampshire Chronicle* confidently predicted that the permanent station would be open by the end of the month but on 16 September it said the directors had decided to leave the opening to next spring; eventually, it and the missing middle section were opened on 11 May 1840 and even then workmen were in action until the last moment because of legal wrangles with the turnpike authorities.

The most spectacular delays resulted from disputes where those directing companies insisted on pursuing their own arguments and vendettas with complete disregard for the interests of would-be travellers. This is in marked contrast to public announcements often couched in such terms as 'the Directors of X humbly beg to inform the public that...' These disputes, which were usually legally very involved, are fully covered in existing works so only a few examples are given here, without much detail.

Both Parliament's reluctance to intervene on the passengers' behalf and the difficulties the GW created by its adoption of the broad gauge were shown when the LSW was able to exploit this to delay the opening of the Exeter & Crediton line, in which it had gained a controlling interest by underhand means and a line ready for opening in 1848 was left mouldering for three years. Elsewhere the Oxford, Worcester & Wolverhampton infuriated its locality until it finally opened throughout in 1854; here, the dictatorial ambitions of local directors seem to have been at the root of its failure to co-operate with the GW.[23]

The longest-running series of disputes resulted from the LNW's attempts at keeping others out of the area north of Birmingham; these centred on lines from Shrewsbury to Chester and Birmingham. Captain Huish was an effective driving force as Secretary of the LNW but at times his behaviour was better suited to the running of an East End protection racket than a railway company. A booking-clerk was forcibly thrown out of Chester station in 1849, connections were made as inconvenient as possible so that travellers wanting to go to Liverpool via Birkenhead and the ferry had to go a longer way round by LNW trains, and the Stour Valley line was left unopened for some months after it had been passed for opening. Even when it did open, the LNW deliberately made connections as awkward as possible.[24]

A prolific cause of friction was at junctions where two companies met before sharing a stretch of line into a major station, as happened at Havant. The first travellers from London to Portsmouth had to use the LBSC line to Brighton and then go west along the coast. When a direct line, from Guildford to Havant, was built the LSW gained control of it, though they needed to use the Brighton's line to run on from Havant to Portsmouth. This would divert traffic from the Brighton line and the latter's owners decided to use its control over the vital stretch to extort compensation for its losses; the usual ploys of removing rails, and bringing up gangs of men and blocking engines followed and it was impossible for the LSW's trains to get through so when the line opened on 1 January 1859 the LSW created a temporary terminus of its own at Havant, north of the junction, and carried passengers on in omnibuses. On 24 January through traffic began but was suspended again from 9 June to 8 August as a result of temporarily successful legal action by the Brighton company. Eventually the rival warriors reached a compromise which involved pooling and sharing certain revenues.[25]

The brutal approach sometimes worked: the LNW successfully killed off a service intended to provide a link between the GN (another of the LNW's enemies), Chester and London, using the Warrington & Stockport. After six months of hassle on 30 August 1858 the Warrington & Stockport told the public that because of the obstructions and false information constantly given to passengers, it had decided to suspend the service between Warrington and Chester; it never resumed. [26]

Some teething problems

Many lines were opened in instalments, sometimes starting at both ends at once, and road coaches were provided to complete journeys. The London & Birmingham initially opened from Euston to Boxmoor (now Hemel Hempstead) on 20 July 1837, extending to Tring on 16 October. On 9 April 1838 it opened to Denbigh Hall and from Rugby to Birmingham, and on 17 September 1838 right through. By the standards of many lines, this was rapid progress: the GW took from 4 June 1838 to 30 June 1841 to open fully from Paddington to Bristol, the short line from Maryport to Carlisle was opened in six portions (1840-45), involving the use of two temporary termini, and the Edinburgh & Northern used three of these in its progress from Burntisland to Perth (1847-8). A Welsh example of instalments was the Taff Vale, which opened from Cardiff to Navigation House (Aberdare) in 1840, providing a coach link to Merthyr until the line opened through next year.

Some of these openings in instalments resulted from the physical impossibility of opening a complete line in one go. Tunnels obviously took longer to build than surface lines: Kilsby Tunnel was the last section to be opened on the London & Birmingham, Box Tunnel the GW's last section and the Summit Tunnel that of the Manchester & Leeds. Bridges also caused delay: on 1 August 1848 the Chester & Holyhead, already open to Bangor, was opened across Anglesey but the Menai Bridge was not yet ready and omnibuses took passengers across the road bridge until the railway one was opened on 18 March 1850. The line from Elgin to Keith opened on 18 August 1858 with temporary platforms on either side of the river at Spey Bridge, between Mulben and Orton, pending completion of a permanent bridge early 1859.

The use of omnibuses meant passengers and luggage had to be transferred from train to coach, sometimes either side of a gap. Clearly all was not fully prepared when the London & Birmingham opened: it was reported in 1838 that at Rugby the road was so 'unsettled' and the omnibus so burdened with luggage that even with six horses it took half an hour to reach the highway from the station.[27] The following year 'TJL' complained about an early connecting service: 23 going from Slough to Windsor were crammed onto a bus licensed for 16.[28] In 1841 'A Bagman' left London by the 5 o'clock for Steventon, then the terminus, assured that he would be immediately conveyed on to Oxford. They arrived at Steventon at 6.55 where there was no porter to carry his luggage and when he reached Waddell's coach, it was already occupied by 11 outside and four inside and unsafe from the quantity of luggage and merchandise on its roof. He was told there was no place, but there was a second behind so he entered this with two others but they remained there one and a half hours, waiting for another train; coaching in Oxford was Waddell's monopoly and he chose to provide insufficient accommodation.[29] Earlier that year there had been a complaint that at Faringdon Road only coaches belonging to certain proprietors were allowed within station limits to collect passengers, others being turned away by a policeman, even if the passenger had made prior arrangements for the coach concerned.[30]

The only transport provided for the connection between Birmingham and Cofton, then the northern terminus of the Birmingham & Gloucester, consisted of two coaches and an omnibus. One day these were full long before they were due to leave Birmingham at 2 p.m. so many of the highest respectability, some of them ladies in a delicate state of health on the way to Cheltenham, were forced to travel on the tops of the coaches in the rain and others had to wait in Birmingham.[31] In 1846 a Worcester correspondent complained that the nearest station was then Spetchley, four miles of hilly road away; however many passengers and however much luggage, there was only one omnibus for the connection. One day he was one of 14 inside, four outside plus nearly a ton of luggage, drawn by two horses. After several attempts at the first hill, all had to alight into the snow and walk half-way up, where they were rescued by the empty omnibus from another train. On the Gloucester line there were so few porters that passengers had to move their own luggage or leave it to fate while they grabbed a place in the omnibus, whose driver was often too eager to start before the load became too much for two horses.[32]

Arrangements could also be dangerous. On 11 September 1841 when the 4 p.m. train from Bristol arrived at Bridgwater, then the terminus, and the passengers had alighted, the engine was used to move the train from one line to the other, ready for its return; it had to move the carriages 150 yards beyond the station, over a road crossing. It had already moved some and was coming back, tender first, for the rest when the *Exquisite* coach from Exeter tried to cross the line. The engine hit the front of this and wrecked it; passengers were scattered in all directions, six being injured.[33]

Some refinements

Initially many wanting to travel from London went a longish way round, but any sort of link was a welcome novelty. Immediately before the opening of the last section in 1844, *The Times* said 'the entire distance between London and Newcastle, upwards of 300 miles, [would] be accomplished, it [was] calculated, in 12 hours, including all stoppages'. The route consisted of:

83 miles along the London & Birmingham from Euston-square to Rugby;

49¼ miles along the Midland Counties to Derby;

63¼ miles along the North Midland to Normanton;

23¾ miles along the York & North Midland to York;

45 miles along the Great North of England to Darlington;

27¼ miles along the Newcastle, Darlington & Durham Junction to Worhington [= Washington];

5¼ miles along the Pontop & South Shields (formerly Stanhope & Tyne) to Brockley Whins;

6¼ miles along the Brandling Junction to Gateshead on the south bank of the Tyne.

For a few years it would still be necessary to catch a ferry across to Newcastle.

Gradually shorter routes were developed. In 1847 the LNW's Trent Valley line allowed some trains to Liverpool and Manchester to bypass Birmingham, so allowing businessmen wanting to go to Liverpool or Manchester, to transact business there and come home the same day. The GN's opening to Retford in 1852 cut the distance from London to York by 20 miles. The Midland originally depended on others to get its passengers to London: the earliest arrangement involved travel via Rugby but in 1857 it provided a shorter route via Bedford and finally it opened its own London terminus at St Pancras in 1868. The GW was the poorest provider of such improvements, though the journey between Bristol and South Wales was shortened in 1863 by providing a ferry connection between short lines to New Passage south of the Severn and Portskewett on the north.

More conveniently sited stations were another development. In 1844 the lines from Liverpool and Leeds were linked through Manchester's new Victoria station. The side-by-side termini at Birmingham Curzon Street were replaced by the through New Street in 1854. Edinburgh's first line from Leith ran to a station of its own but on 22 May 1868 it was diverted to Waverley, providing a much more convenient arrangement for passengers needing to change. A joint line and through station replaced the earlier termini and gap at Aberdeen in 1867. Originally Carlisle had three stations in use at any one time but by 1870 all its services had been concentrated on one, to the great benefit of those who had to change there as well as the locals. However, York was still a terminus which required reversal for through trains and Dundee had separate termini to the east and west.

London was served by termini scattered around outside the central area; some progress was made by extending lines towards the centre but links across the middle were then out of the question. The LSW originally terminated at Nine Elms and was extended to Waterloo in 1848, Victoria replaced an earlier terminus at Pimlico in 1860 and Charing Cross was added in 1864; Cannon Street and Broad Street had been added by 1870 for the benefit of travellers to the City. At the eastern end services were gradually extended, eventually reaching Fenchurch Street in 1841; however, Liverpool Street was yet to be added – the terminus was still at Bishopsgate. Various services were provided to try and overcome the problem. One success was the North London whose links enabled people from northern suburbs to reach many destinations west and east of central London. However, a service which initially ran from Euston via Willesden, Kensington, and a through platform at Waterloo to Cannon Street began in 1864 but suffered various reductions before expiring at the end of 1867; it was too indirect to be an improvement on crossing London by road and was handicapped by inter-company squabbles.

Too many cooks

At first passengers often had to buy separate tickets for each part of a journey; this was gradually reduced, by the amalgamations which simplified the network and by arrangements between companies. By September 1839 the London & Birmingham and Grand Junction trains were going into each others' stations at Curzon-street to make interchange easier.[34] A report of an accident 13 January 1841 showed that the Birmingham night mail train generally took two carriages for the Midland Counties which were handed over at Rugby. Details given of an accident at Harrow on 26 November 1870 concerned 19 carriages drawn by two engines; they were listed in order as luggage van, composite, first-class carriage and guard's break van for Manchester; one composite for Rochdale; one luggage van, three composites and a guard's break van for Liverpool; one composite for Birkenhead; two composites and a break van for Holyhead; one composite for Shrewsbury; one composite for Leamington; one composite, one first-class and one break van for Birmingham.[35] However, many shortcomings were not remedied for some time and complaints about the arrangements for through booking arose from time to time.

Where companies in the course of their power struggles set out to be deliberately awkward, suffering could be far worse. It would have been of great benefit to the public if Parliament had been far more willing to knock a few heads together occasionally. Those who created the system were undoubtedly men of drive, able to achieve progress despite great difficulties but they often believed they could not possibly learn anything from anyone else. They failed to realise that usually it would have been more sensible to work together to provide a smoothly-functioning network to encourage even more travel and provide a greater revenue that could be shared amongst companies; this, after all, was essentially what Adam Smith advocated in his treatise supporting free trade. Authority was remarkably supine, preferring to stand by and let rivals fight it out. The result could be infantile behaviour that caused problems for passengers. Ironically, many squabbles occurred between companies that later amalgamated. In many cases, relatively small amounts of money spent on connecting lines would have saved large amounts spent on competing ones, admittedly much of it after 1870, and left railways somewhat less vulnerable in the mid-twentieth century.

Few would deny that in at least some respects Brunel was technically a great engineer but his mule-headed arrogance, combined with the failure of the GW directors to control him and Parliament's reluctance to put an early end to the Broad Gauge farce meant that travellers to the west from the Midlands and the North faced problems at Bristol for many years – at times deliberately exaggerated by other companies. Whatever technical advantages might have been claimed for the broad gauge, it was clear that no-one else was going to use it and persisting with it was thus absurd.[36] 'Achivus' complained on 16 June 1845 about the feud between the GW and Bristol & Gloucester (eventually to join the Midland). He had arrived the previous Tuesday from Birmingham at 12.55, on time but there was no train to Exeter until 2.45. A friend came by the train due at 9.50, the Exeter train being supposed to leave at 10.10, but found the latter had gone. In addition, the Bristol & Birmingham kept Bristol time (though they did not announce this), the GW London time.

An early northern example of lack of co-operation involved passengers wanting to go from Leeds to Newcastle. At first they had to travel via York but in 1848 the Leeds & Thirsk provided a 'cut-off' giving a route 19 miles shorter. This company had its own 'Town' station at Thirsk but on the way there its trains ran into and out of the East Coast station of the York, Newcastle & Berwick. The latter made life as difficult as possible for the newcomer, which sent a dossier of letters of complaint to the Railway Commissioners in 1850: there was no shelter for passengers on the east side of the main line, carpet bags were dumped on the wet platform despite requests to protect them from the damp, the staff were extremely rude and unwilling to help, passengers bound for Leeds were prevented from changing here because the guard slammed the door and sent the train on as soon as he heard their destination and, unless specifically asked, booking-clerks issued tickets by the longer route. The Commissioners refused to intervene; in due course all did work together, both using the main line station at Thirsk and becoming part of the NE. In more recent times the cut-off has been closed and passengers again travel via York.

The south east suffered its share of company spats. The Caterham company opened its branch from Purley to the main line used by SE and LBSC in 1856. Both major companies were unco-operative, fearing that the new line might be extended in some way that would siphon off some of their trade. Trains ran but both companies made difficulties; connections were poor, fares high and no shelter was provided at Purley. Things briefly improved somewhat in 1859, when the line was sold to the SE but trouble was resumed in 1862 when the LBSC made connections deliberately difficult. One traveller to Caterham found the branch train had left three minutes before his train from Haywards Heath arrived at the junction; he walked six miles rather than wait four hours. On his return he could only obtain a ticket from Caterham to the junction and there found there was no train to Haywards Heath for five hours. He then decided to go north to East Croydon and catch a train home from there but was told that the next train, twenty minutes later, was not available to him because passengers from the junction could not be booked by it. In desperation he forced his way onto the train he wanted, despite the attempts of officials to stop him; one accompanied him to East Croydon, where his offer to pay the fare was refused and his name and address taken with a view to prosecution, though no further action seems to have resulted.[37] 1869 saw some relief in this area. In January both the SE and LBSC issued notices that from and after 1 February return and season tickets would be issued that would be available by both companies' trains between any of their London stations, Croydon and various other places such as Redhill, Tunbridge Wells, and Hastings whose residents had made similar complaints.

Scotland did not escape the madness. In 1859 an argument between the Scottish North Eastern and the Scottish Central about how much the former should pay for using the latter's station came to a head; it was complicated by the fact that the Central owned the section of track north of the station. On 8 August trains stopped at the boundary, 320 yards north of Perth General, collecting and dropping passengers at Glasgow Road. Emergency arrangements were made by other companies to provide a service over the disputed stretch but, meanwhile, hapless passengers had to make their way, with their luggage, between the two points, entailing a journey through the streets of about half-a-mile.[38] Eventually all became part of the Caledonian.

Problems that persisted

Some awkward arrangements still existed in 1870: the GW continued to send passengers for South Wales via Swindon and those to the south-west via Bristol. Newport in South Wales was a multiple sufferer; there were still three stations in 1870, although the GW now controlled all the lines involved, and only in 1880 would rationalisation occur.

Some idiocies would never be cured. To reach Weymouth the GW opened a line from Chippenham (later diverted along a shorter route via Westbury) and the LSW one along the south coast. They agreed to reach Weymouth along a joint line from Dorchester but built separate stations there even though it would have been easy to provide a joint one. In 1858 'A frequent traveller' complained that on 1 September he went from Poole to Taunton by train. Since it was impossible to do the journey in one day by ordinary trains he travelled by the luggage train, to which only one passenger carriage was attached, from Poole at 9.10 a.m., to Dorchester which he reached at 10.30 and left at 12.45 p.m., arriving at Yeovil at 1.25; he left there at 3.05 for Durston, where he was detained one hour and reached Taunton at 4.50, overall 67 miles in 7 hours 40 mins. He felt there was a conspiracy between companies to make life difficult for passengers. The LSW train arrived at Dorchester from Southampton at 1.10; one GW train left Dorchester at 12.45, the next 5.25[39] For anyone wanting to go from Exeter to Weymouth arrangements were even worse: Yeovil had three stations and would-be passengers had to change at all of them.

Others' actions could also harm passengers' interests. Railway Acts of Incorporation gave powers of compulsory purchase but wealthy landowners could be obstructive, conducting lengthy haggling over price and demanding features such as cuttings and tunnels to preserve their views. Lord Harborough's opposition to the Midland's line through Stamford caused the company to include an unwanted sharp curve at Saxby. The Admiralty displayed its customary refusal to agree with anyone else about anything. Greenwich was still a terminus in 1870, passengers for Woolwich and further east having to make a detour via Blackheath owing to its refusal to agree to passage along the obvious route. It also insisted on keeping the River Arun navigable and the result was a single-line drawbridge near Ford, where a collision occurred on 13 January 1861 when a pointsman sent a passenger train onto the wrong line as it left the bridge, sending it head-on into a waiting cattle train. Ironically, the LBSC, after much difficulty and opposition, had just gained power to replace with a fixed bridge and double line.[40]

Co-operation with other forms of transport

Railways did kill off stage-coach and some sea-borne services as the network spread but this was a gradual business and in compensation many new opportunities were created. Some of these were only short-lived as further rail openings made them uncompetitive but overall there was a vastly increased demand for road services for travel to stations from villages still not on the railway map and from people within towns and cities who needed to reach the nearest station. From the outset railways publicised links by sea and road: the Liverpool & Manchester timetable for March 1831 issued from the Liverpool office disposed of the railway service in one page but devoted two pages to steam packets from Liverpool and five to road coaches from the two termini.[41]

At first some stage coaches were carried by train, on flat trucks at the back; the passengers moved to the train but the guards and their luggage stayed with them. A couple of weeks after the opening of the GW's first stretch some of the Bath, Bristol and Reading stage-coaches were taken from London to Maidenhead, then on by train and by the end of 1839 Stroud and Gloucester were also so served. In November a train involved in an accident near Maidenhead was made up of four railway carriages, two stage coaches and a private carriage. By then, further south, Exeter coaches were being taken to Winchester and Salisbury ones to Woking by rail.[42] A guard was killed in 1839 when his head hit against a bridge as he sought to secure luggage which had shifted on the roof of the *Subscription*, being carried on the central Basingstoke to Winchester part of its journey from Southampton.[43]

When the Bristol & Exeter reached Bridgwater in 1841 a 'New Light Coach' was advertised in connection, running from Lyme via Axminster, Chard, Ilminster and Taunton; this took passengers to catch the noon train to London and collected them from the train arriving from London at 2.30 p.m. Even a short line such as that from Redruth to Hayle was provided with connections: from the outset in 1843, Crotch, the contractor running the passenger service for the company, advertised that coaches to and from Penzance, Truro and Falmouth would connect with his trains 'at a low rate of charge'.[44] Late in 1844 there were scuffles when a pirate coach firm tried to capture some of the passengers; next day the locals turned out to see a repeat of the fun but were disappointed because the forces of law and order were present to prevent this. In at least one case a coach service seems to have acted as a feeder to trains by serving intermediate places lacking stations; in 1853 a three-day-a-week coach service was advertised from Doncaster to Rotherham, where it connected with trains to Sheffield; amongst other places this called at Thrybergh and Hooton Roberts.[45] Coaches could even connect different lines: Whitmarsh & Co advertised that their *Prince Albert Coach* would provide a link between Taunton (GW) and Dorchester (LSW), serving Ilminster, Crewkerne and Maiden Newton on the way, then running on to Weymouth, which would enable passengers from Taunton to go on to Southampton and Portsmouth. It ran from Taunton to Weymouth on Tuesdays, Thursdays and Saturdays and returned the following days.

There were direct links to travel by water also. The Paisley & Renfrew, opened in 1837, ran its trains onto the wharf at Renfrew so passengers could board Clyde steamers. At opening in 1840 the Preston & Wyre advertised that the *Express* steamer would ply daily between Fleetwood, and the opposite side of Morecambe Bay near Ulverston, in connection with the railway.[46] That same year the opening of the Slamannan's line to Causewayend, near Linlithgow, connected with canal barges, allowing passengers from Glasgow a complete route to Edinburgh; road coaches later replaced the barges but that provided no defence against competition when a full railway route opened. On the west coast a route to London was provided by train from Glasgow to Troon, steamer on to Fleetwood and rail on from there; this was made redundant when the Glasgow & South Western opened its line right through to Carlisle. The Sheffield, Ashton-under-Lyne & Manchester offered a Fly Boat connection between Stalybridge and Ashton in 1843 (first-class 2d, second 1d).[47] In June 1868 the Furness opened a route to Windermere via Morecambe Bay and its Leven Valley line; trains ran onto the steamboat pier so passengers could walk on board direct from railway carriages.[48]

Many ferries worked in conjunction with railways, some actually being owned by them. The Thames was crossed by the Woolwich and Gravesend–Tilbury services, the Humber could be crossed from Grimsby to Hull and neither the Forth nor the Tay was yet bridged. On the western side travellers between Birkenhead and Liverpool still had to rely on the ferry. A 'Steam Packet' waited in 1841 at St George's Pier Liverpool and Monk's Ferry, Birkenhead to carry passengers and produce across the river; since the railway had not yet reached Monk's Ferry an omnibus was provided from the station in Grange Lane. Here class distinctions took over – the fares quoted included this for first and second-class passengers only; whether third-class passengers could use it on extra payment or were left to walk is not known.[49] Later many businessmen living in the Wirrall travelled to work in Liverpool by train to Birkenhead and thence to the ferry by omnibus. The last was known to be inadequate but, despite complaints, no action had been taken so as the train due at 8.35 a.m. arrived many regularly jumped out before it had stopped in order to get seats; on 8 July 1868 Mr Urquhart, son of the senior partner in a cabinet-making firm, fell between platform and train as he tried to join the rush and was injured, one of his legs having to be amputated.[50]

The various British islands were well served. The LSW provided a new route to Ryde from Stokes Bay in 1864, advertising that railway carriages would arrive and depart from the pier.[51] In Scotland steamers to Portree and Stornoway were available from 19 August 1870 when the Dingwall & Skye opened to Strome Ferry.[52] In 1848 the Chester & Holyhead ran 'The Admiralty's and the Company's splendid steam packets, 670 tons, 370 horse power', from Holyhead to Kingstown in connection with certain of its trains. The GW advertised arrangements in 1852 including use of the Bristol & Exeter and South Devon to allow passengers to book through from London to Cork via Plymouth; it improved its connection on 1 June 1868 with a new express at 4.50 p.m. running to New Milford, arriving at 1.40 a.m.[53] Meanwhile, the year before, the Midland had sought to improve its prospects by transferring its Belfast steamboat service from Morecambe to Barrow-in-Furness.[54] However, not all were successful: the Portpatrick's short-lived services from Stranraer to Larne made a loss and ceased at the end of December 1863.

Overseas links were also provided. Newhaven's Harbour station opened in 1847, Folkestone's in 1849, Harwich's in 1854 and Dover's Admiralty Pier in 1860. Further north the MS&L advertised the opening of a new dock at Grimsby for steamers on 27 May 1852: the railway had been extended to the edge of a landing-stage where a passenger station had been built. By mid-August steam packets were running to Hamburg, Rotterdam and Antwerp.[55]

Information

The earliest information was usually provided in sheet form, published by the company concerned; advertisement in *The Times* and the local press was also normal. Specialist timetables soon followed. George Bradshaw gained an early overall dominance though Scotland had its own timetable, published by *Murray*, and there were other local issues. An early problem Bradshaw faced was that of getting accurate information from companies; then he repeated the latest known times with some such warning as 'Accuracy uncertain, no recent information received' or left the spaces for times blank. At first some tables were only outlines, showing times at the termini and major points in between, with other stations in fare tables or notes only; others did not even list intermediate stations. However, the standard format which continues in use today was evolved fairly rapidly.

Alterations in times were inevitably made frequently as new lines and extensions were opened. Promises were often made that changes would only be made on the first of a month, but these could not always be kept: from time to time companies put apologetic notices in *The Times* giving details of changes ordered by the Post Office. However, that could not be blamed for all mid-month changes. 'A Sufferer' wrote in November 1849 to complain that changes had been made to the Eastern Counties timetable on 1 October, 15 October and again on that day; clerks often did not have copies until days after alteration and clocks along the line were not kept to the same time by 10 minutes.[56]

On Good Friday 1843 'a vast number' of passengers on the Eastern Counties arrived at Shoreditch to find that, without notice, trains ran to Sunday time, so there was no 11 a.m. to Colchester (the next at 3 p.m.). They included Mr Babington Macaulay MP, who claimed to have sent a servant the day before to ask if times would be altered and had been told they would not.[57]

The Times explained on 8 January 1846 that not all timetabled trains ran: one was advertised to leave Rugby for London at 4 p.m., taking passengers assembled from Lincoln, Nottingham, etc, booked through to London but it only ran if it suited those in charge at Rugby – if there were only a few passengers, they had to wait until 5 p.m.

Time

Previously people set their clocks by the local noonday sun. This did not matter when travel was leisurely: anyone going from Bristol to London would reset his watch to the capital's time when arriving or make the necessary mental adjustment. A Grand Junction notice in August 1844 warned that clocks at stations were set according to the longitude of each.[58] Early short lines from Manchester advertised that they would take their time from the Manchester Infirmary Clock.

When the LNW diverted its traffic over the shorter Trent Valley line in 1847, it warned that clocks would be set to Greenwich time which was:

Before		
	Birmingham clocks	7 minutes
	Liverpool clocks	12
	Manchester clocks	10
	Preston clocks	10
	Chester clocks	12

The Manchester Courier approved, suggesting that the Board of Trade could usefully recommend the public authorities of every town to adopt uniform time. 'In Manchester the change would be perfect and quite imperceptible, if, on the evening of the 30th inst. [November], every correct timepiece were put forward nine minutes. The only inconvenience would be the loss, for one night, of nine minutes' sleep'.[59] LNW and paper were apparently not agreed on exact Manchester time.

Other places tended to come into line when their first railway arrived, though not always immediately. The railway reached Taunton in 1842 but it was early 1848 before those responsible set the market clock at Greenwich Mean Time, 'at the request of many influential residents'.[60] Bristol had had its own peculiar solution in 1341, when the authorities arranged for an extra minute hand on the Exchange clock, but many church clocks persisted with local time and only on 14 September 1852 did the council resolve to regulate them by Greenwich time; by then the spread of the telegraph had made uniformity even more desirable since messages from London were apparently reaching Bristol ten minutes before they had been sent.[61] People at Langport were even less lucky: their station opened on 1 October 1853 but some months later it was reported that the old town clock was 'determined to set its face against innovation' so many travellers were to been seen 'rushing upon the Parrett bridge out of breath, just in time to see the train off, and to receive the congratulations of the boatmen who loiter there'.[62] However, some acted more promptly: the GW provided Tavistock with its first station on 22 June 1859 and a couple of days later *The Tavistock Gazette* reported that a vestry meeting had passed a resolution to keep the Church Clock by Railway time.

Summary of progress: Mileage open and passengers carried

All from Board of Trade/Railway Commissioners' Reports. Presentation varied over time so exact comparisons are not possible. Initially no separate figures were given for the constituent parts of the United Kingdom, so 1840 and 1845 figures include Ireland. From 1845 lines carrying goods only were included in the mileage total, no separate figure being given.

Miles open at the end of the year		Passengers carried (millions) #	
1840	1,330	6 (last 5 months only)	
1845	2,536	33(for year ending 30 June 1845)	

	Miles		**Passengers**	
	England &Wales	Scotland	England & Wales	Scotland
1850	5,130	952	58	8
1855	6,217	1,091	99	12
1860	7,583	1,626	136	16
1865	9,251	2,200	216	21
1870	11,043*	2,519*	288	27

* = miles constructed; not all yet open

= excluding season ticket holders; in 1870 there were 118,110 of these in England & Wales, 23,462 in Scotland.

Chapter 4: STATIONS

General

According to rumour the Fleet prison is to be a railway terminus. We are sure that there was no reason to have removed a brick of the old place for that purpose. Punch, quoted in The Times, 27 *November 1845*.

Some early services continued stage-coach practices, using inns as their terminal 'stations'. As late as 1837 the Stockton & Darlington's directors authorised acceptance of an offer of a waiting-room at the Mason's Arms at Shildon for £6 per year, including fire and cleaning, to save building a station of their own.[1] The Liverpool & Manchester seems to have set the tone; it had its own terminal premises but with intermediate stops there was much variation. RGH Thomas described its early practice thus: 'Passengers wishing to alight told the guard when joining the train, and if any were to be taken up, the policeman [signalman and often level crossing keeper as well] signalled the driver to stop ... There were no platforms or buildings apart from the gatekeeper's cottage, and this served as a waiting room for passengers in cold or wet weather and at night'. Gradually such facilities as name-boards, platforms and separate waiting-rooms were introduced. When Crotch, whose own hotel was described as the Hayle terminus, advertised his service to Redruth in 1834, he listed his 'stations' but press reports of the opening suggests that his 'stations' were like modern bus stops; proper stations seem to have been added after the company started running its own trains next year.

The Stockton & Darlington behaved similarly. In 1840 the level-crossing gatekeeper at Aycliffe Lane, one of the regular stopping places, was authorised to 'ticket passengers' but no station as such seems to have existed. In 1847 orders were given for the painting of name-boards for several stations already in use. Etherley got its board now and its platforms were lengthened in 1853 but only in 1855 was its clock ordered. This company was also expert at reusing facilities, suggesting that many were of a very basic nature. In 1848 they ordered a wooden station at Middlesbrough to be removed to the ancestor of what is now Thornaby, which was later altered and slightly re-sited several times in its early years.[2]

Variations

Whishaw's descriptions of 1842 revealed much variation in styles of architecture, size and facilities. Euston's grandeur and Gothic arch was acceptable to him since it was the 'key' to all railways north of London. At Arbroath the station (in Catherine Street) was sufficiently 'architectural' to provide a pleasing appearance; it contained a ticket-office, general waiting room and adjoining room for ladies but he felt the last should have had a separate entrance. He was also critical of arrangements at Gateshead which forced passengers to walk across an open courtyard in all weathers to reach the booking-office. Worse was the terminus of the Leeds & Selby at Marsh Lane, Leeds, where passengers had to step up into carriages directly from the ground; inevitably, he described this as particularly troublesome for ladies. He believed companies should provide intermediate stations as cheaply as possible so he was happy that no buildings existed on the intermediate stations on the Garnkirk & Glasgow where traffic was so small. He described that at Carnoustie as a small cottage, a building suited to the traffic of the place, and commended the Manchester & Bolton and Stockton & Darlington for their cheap stations. The Manchester & Leeds was criticised for providing 'Elizabethan villas' on a scale nearly sufficient for termini. Even worse was the North Midland from Derby to Leeds, where, 'Instead of cottage-buildings, which, for the traffic of most of the intermediate stopping-places on this line, would have been amply sufficient, we find the railway literally ornamented with so many beautiful villas, any one of which would grace the sloping lawn of some domain by nature highly favoured', though even here there were deficiencies: water-closets and urinals were provided on both platforms and arrangements for cleaning them were better ordered than on most lines but the doorways were 'in so exposed a situation as naturally to shock the female portion of travellers, who, while the trains are stopping, cannot fail to observe the constant bustle about these buildings'. He fully approved the iron railing on the platform at Ayr which separated first and second-class passengers on their way to trains.

Stations often opened incomplete. The *Northampton Mercury* of 26 September 1838 said many stations were unfinished: Blisworth was little more than a wooden shed and a tremendous flight of steps. *The Times* itself described the line the following year: Tring was incomplete and there was mention of a junction at Cheddington (for Aylesbury) but not of a station. An inspection report on the Taff Vale in 1841 said that at the two termini (Cardiff and Merthyr) 'ample accommodation, it is understood, will be provided; and at the intermediate stations there are, at present, sheds which are, perhaps, under all the circumstances of the probable traffic, as convenient as the passengers can reasonably expect'. Much of the line was already open and the extension to Merthyr would open next day. The SE's extension to Dover was inspected on 1 February 1844 and the recommendation was that it should be allowed to open 'as soon as they shall have erected a temporary station for the accommodation of passengers, ... which will be probably be finished in a few days'; they opened on the 7th and clearly not much could have been done by then.[3]

Even major London stations suffered. When Waterloo opened on 11 July 1848, the description read like that of a building site. The first train, the mail, arrived at half past four in the morning with about 40 passengers. Although workmen had been employed day and night, they had not yet prepared a clear entrance into Waterloo Road so passengers were obliged to make their way among masons and labourers to the road and considerable work remained before the booking offices would be completed.[4]

Some early primitive provisions provoked complaints. In 1842 'Lorgnette' complained she had accompanied a lady in rather delicate health to Greenwich and it had poured in torrents all evening. On arrival they were obliged to remain in a wretched bare brick hovel, called the terminus [London Bridge], with a door at each end continually open and a sulky fire that sent more smoke into the room than up the chimney. However, they were told that they had only five minutes to wait, so they made the best of it. When the train came, they paddled in the mud to the platform; and after much jostling among the passengers, were told there were no more places in the first-class carriages, for which they had taken tickets. The guard cried 'All right', and jumped into his seat, as the train moved on, leaving many in the pouring rain. They retired under a miserable canvas booth to wait a quarter of an hour for the next train, the ladies complaining bitterly of cold and wet feet.[5]

A piece mainly about fares in 1846 said complaints were loud and general in the north about poor accommodation on Hudson's lines; the station for such an important town as Sunderland was a trumpery wooden shed, in which all classes and both sexes were placed in the same waiting-room, with an apple-vendor and a bookseller plying their trade in the middle.[6] Years later 'W.G.S.' described the earliest station at New Cross as 'consisting of a full-sized watch-box, labelled "ticket-office", a Lilliputian wooden shed for a waiting-room, and two short wooden platforms, which were lengthened from time to time'. Waiting-rooms were not necessarily provided for all, at least at first. In October 1848 'Third-class passenger' complained about the lack of one for second and third-class passengers at Reading so that on a cold day he and about 50 others had to wait on the platform, exposed to a cutting wind, for one and a half hours since the train was late, as it frequently was.[7] The Newcastle & Carlisle was originally built as a single line. When it was doubled they did not at first provide platforms on the new line so as late as 1851 passengers had to climb in and out of the carriages on that side from the ground.[8] A station opened at Halifax in 1850, admittedly according to modern historians only intended to be temporary, was described in a local paper as a 'miserable, dirty, disagreeable shed' and a 'filthy doghole of a place'.[9]

Not all the blame lay with the companies. The authorities of Eton College prevented the GW from building a station at Slough but it stopped trains there nonetheless. 'One of the Public' complained about the lack of accommodation for second-class passengers, saying that those waiting were herded into a small space like cattle at Smithfield; when the train arrived they were released in a rush. On one occasion an elderly lady had been pushed across the line; fortunately nothing was coming the other way.[10] A proper station was opened soon after but did not always provide satisfaction. 'An Eye-Witness' complained in 1844 that a lady relation, in a delicate state of health and *enceinte*, was travelling 2nd class and when she asked at Slough for the waiting room she told it was for the first-class class only.[11] In 1867 'A Chilled Traveller' said that there had been no fire the day before in the ladies' first-class waiting-room on the down platform at Slough. The only waiting-room with a fire was a common thoroughfare from booking-office to platform which boasted a door which was being perpetually opened.[12]

On the Eastern Counties there was a lengthy and acrimonious dispute between the company and Lord Petre, the local landowner, over the siting of Ingatestone station. He wanted it in Hall Lane, the company favoured Stock Lane, which it regarded as more convenient for the locals but the deed of arrangement between Petre and the company said that no station could be built within a mile of his house without his consent. On his refusal to agree to Stock Lane, the company, with the locals' agreement, went ahead anyway and provided one there in July 1843. It only consisted of steps leading down into a cutting and two simple platforms; a nearby almshouse acted as a booking office. Legal actions by both sides led first to a cessation of trains using the station then to a partial restoration – trains stopped but passengers had to scramble up or down the slope since they were not allowed to use platform or steps; its dangerous nature meant a further short period out of use. Eventually Petre won and a replacement station was built in 1846 on land he gave at Hall Lane.[13]

On the other hand, it was not unknown for some public-spirited individual to provide a station. Burneside, in the Lake District, had its closed about the beginning of 1855 because it did not pay. Two years later Mr John Steele advertised that he had taken a lease of it for one year, to give people a chance of showing their support; additionally, on Saturdays 'for the benefit of the working classes' return tickets to Kendal were issued at 4d.[14] The station remained open so he presumably received the support needed.

Preliminaries

A would-be passenger's first task was to find the booking-office, making sure of being there in good time. The earliest Liverpool & Manchester timetable stated:

> In order to insure punctuality in the times of starting, which has frequently been prevented by Persons claiming to be booked, even after the appointed time of departure, no Passenger, *unless previously booked*, will be admitted into the outer door of the Railway Stations after the clock has struck the hour of departure; and Passengers too late to take their Seats, or otherwise prevented going, may receive back half the fare paid, if claimed not later than the day after that for which their places were booked.

Buying a ticket could be a problem, even some years later. 'Irritated traveller' complained about the short time allowed at termini and even shorter at roadside stations for buying tickets and by the time clerks opened up, crowds of flustered travellers were often besieging their office. 'ARC' added that it was especially awkward if the booking-office was on one side of the station, the platform you wanted on the other over a footbridge. The usual time allowed seemed to be 10/15 minutes.[15]

43

Early practice was to ring a series of bells to indicate that passengers still had five minutes to book and join a train, that the gates were closing and no one else would be admitted to the station and so on. The practice in some places of keeping people outside the station until the appropriate bell rang could lead to desperate scenes. On 12 October 1844 *The Times* reported that at Gloucester, when it was time to return, 1,500 or 1,600 of those who had arrived by a special train were shut out until almost the last minute. There was a tremendous rush to get the best places and one man was thrown onto the buffer of an engine, breaking his thigh. Other problems concerned the detailed application of the system, especially before passengers had become used to it. 'A Surgeon to whom the above loss of time was important' complained in 1841 that the previous Friday morning he had enquired at one of the LSW's offices about the time of a train to Woking. He was told 11 a.m.; he had arrived at the station about 4 minutes before 11, at the same time as three or four others. They found the doors closed and were informed that the doors always closed 5 minutes before a train was due to leave. The next train was at 1 p.m.[16] In 1843 'A Daily Reader' complained about similar treatment at Brighton, where the clock in front of the station gave a different, later, time from that in the yard by which the staff operated.[17]

Though passengers might have to be ready in time, others could disrupt schedules. 'A Constant Reader' complained in 1845 about the night mail from Nine Elms. The train was due to leave at 8.30 and passengers were warned to be there five minutes earlier, when the doors were closed – 20 minutes earlier if they had a lot of luggage. Thus most were there at 8.15 but they had to wait because the mail arrived 10 or 12 minutes later in two huge vans not adequately horsed. It was loaded on the up line, porters holding lanterns to read labels and sort sacks and then the carriage was moved to a gap left in the train on the down line.[18]

Quality of provision

The quality of stations could leave much to be desired. On 21 August 1850 the roof of Bricklayers Arms fell when a goods waggon was driven against one of the pillars holding up the roof. Fortunately one passenger train had just left and the next arrival was at a safe distance, though several railway workers were not so lucky; this station seems to have been jinxed since an earlier roof had fallen even before they had completed it. *Herapath* of 5 December 1846 reported that 'Last week' the roof at Fletton, near Peterborough, fell in with a tremendous crash and several people narrowly escaped with their lives; the station had been built too close to a river and with inadequate foundations. Six people were slightly injured when a portion of the platform at Hampton Court collapsed on 15 June 1859 and a Mr Walker was awarded £250 for injuries resulting from falling through a hole in a rotten wooden platform at Lea Bridge in August 1868.[19]

One recurring theme was that of lack of space. 'E.S.' arrived at the wharf of the Blackwall line by steam-boat at 7.20 p.m. on a Sunday in September 1843, expecting a saving of at least half an hour by changing to rail instead of continuing the passage by boat through the Pool but he did not arrive at the London end until 9.15. On his arrival the part of the office assigned to passengers waiting for admission to the train was densely crowded. Half-an-hour elapsed before the door was opened to admit so many as one train would contain; in the meantime the crowd outside the office, consisting of those who had arrived from Gravesend, 600 to 800 in a boat, accumulated to an extraordinary number and, as the inner office was relieved by those admitted to the train, these forced their way in by main strength. Consequently ladies were frightened and screaming, children trampled on and pockets relieved of their contents; the respectable portion of those whose money had been taken for first-class fares were compelled to allow this mob to pass before them.[20]

The Board of Trade regularly listed fatalities resulting from crowded platforms, though the blame did not always lie with the railways. There were at least two such in 1855: George Truman was 'incautiously' standing amongst a crowd waiting for the train to draw up at Epsom (LBSC) when he was pushed off and fatally injured and later that year a young woman anxious to get into a train as it ran into Perth station on a market day either fell or was pushed to her death. In 1858 Stephen Seward was drunk when he fell off the platform at Broughton, on the Furness line, on 6 October. Two passengers standing on the platform at Denton, on the LNW, were pushed onto the line by the press behind: one was killed and the other severely injured on 3 December 1864.

Length as well as breadth caused problems. At times passengers were decanted before a station. One reason was the length of the train, itself often the result of combining more than one; an example in 1842 was probably the result of the failure of an engine and the lack of a ready replacement so that one had to do the work of two. 'A Traveller' wrote that he had paid for a first-class class place on the 5.45 from Cirencester which should have reached Swindon at 6.35 and London at 9.20 but the train had come to a dead stand before Swindon, the engine was detached, took the luggage on, came back for the passengers and arrived at Swindon at 8.5. where they were detained until 9.10, when their train was mixed up with a luggage train on its way to London. They arrived at Paddington at 3 a.m. and then had to walk a quarter of a mile, with no-one to carry their luggage, before they could actually reach the station, with the chance of breaking their necks as they picked their way between carriages and other obstacles in the dark.[21]

John Smith wrote to the Railway Commissioners on 15 January 1850 complaining about:

> ... the danger attending passengers who alight at the Sutton station on the Croydon and Epsom line, owing to the shortness of the platform (which will only accommodate six carriages and the engine), being built on an incline, and beyond which, towards Epsom, there is a hole or ditch ... below the steps of the carriages. I was put out at this place in June last, and injured my back in such a way as to deprive me of the use of my hands for

three weeks, and to lay me up for three months. Although the Directors have been informed of the danger of this place, it is still left in the same state, and passengers have been put out twice in the last week, to my own knowledge. I also beg to call your attention to the Carshalton station, where parties were put out last evening on two planks joined together, about 18 inches wide, without any protection, and where there is a drop of three or four feet at least.

Captain Wynne investigated and confirmed that the dangers were as reported. In both cases, because of the inclines, trains were inclined to overshoot the stations; they were supposed to set back 'but the impatience of the passengers' was usually too great. He recommended filling in the ditch at Sutton and providing a railing at Carshalton, where the planks mentioned were really part of a ticket platform immediately beyond the station.

'A proprietor of North-western Stock' was in Shrewsbury, a joint station, on a Saturday in 1869 to catch the 12.30. He was at the station five minutes early and found a scene of indescribable confusion. The train came 20 minutes late from Aberystwyth; no anxiety was shown about punctuality and they left at 1 p.m. 'After starting we loitered on, and at last, after half a dozen trumpery stoppages, arrived at Stafford. Here we were quietly shunted into a siding – perfectly safe, certainly, while trains passed and re-passed and were made up and sorted in a wonderful way.' They were told they were waiting for the Holyhead train, much overdue. At last it came up and they were shunted on to the end of what he afterwards found was 23 carriages of various sorts. Owing to its length at Euston a mass of ladies and children had to alight in the ballast and amidst the wires of the numerous signals, as well as telegraph wires.[22]

This defect might have been why some passengers seem to have found difficulty in distinguishing between features at stations: Board of Trade reports gave several instances of people going off bridge parapets. In 1853 one hurt his back falling over that at Wreay. A man and the child in his arms were injured when he fell from the ledge of a bridge at Auchterarder, having mistaken it for the platform in 1855 and the same year three were killed when their train was held on Dinting viaduct because there was another in the way; they thought they were in the station and alighted, only to fall over the low parapet. Next year William Mitchell jumped out of a train which had slightly overshot Shadwell station and was still in motion; he went over the parapet of a viaduct and fell into the street with fatal results. Later that year Mr D Wooley was less himself to blame. He was in a special train too long for the platform at Basingstoke and, in the dark, he also went over a viaduct parapet; he survived but broke his leg.

Clutter on platforms was another source of danger and complaint. In 1853 M'Leod fell over a band-box at Northampton, rolled over onto the line and was killed. Mrs Mary Absalom, 70 years old, fell over the switch handle at Pontypool and injured her head in 1856. 'DCR' complained in 1858 that he had left Bristol on 4 October by the 3 p.m., due at Worcester at 5.01, intending to proceed to Oxford by the train leaving at 5.10. He believed that nine minutes would be enough to transfer himself and his bag to the isolated strip of wood from which the Oxford train started. His (Midland) train arrived there nearly half-an-hour late but the Oxford train had not left so he thought he might still have time to get his ticket and gain the isolated platform without being knocked down (the main tracks had to be crossed to reach the Oxford platform). At first he seemed lucky but then The Fates were against him – the narrow platform was blocked by luggage piled 6 feet high. After a struggle he got to the train side of the pile, only to see his train leaving.[23]

One unfortunate suffered a broken leg at Swinton when the blast-pipe of a passing goods engine broke off and flew onto the platform. At Lower Norwood on 25 September 1861 a passenger received serious injuries when he fell against a train after being struck by a board blown from the fence. 'A Season Ticket Holder' and 'X' both complained on the same day about the danger as they went to catch trains in October 1863 at London Bridge, where a new iron bridge was being built over the approach; no protection was provided against sparks and red-hot bolts falling from the workings and there had been several close calls to persons and their clothing.

Some had unusual fatal accidents that could not be blamed on station inadequacies. On 8 August 1858, Elizabeth Baldwin was seeing off a soldier at Guildford and walked along the platform beside the train holding his hand as it moved off, her clothing was caught up and she was dragged under the wheels. A woman shaking hands with a passenger through a carriage window as a train was leaving Deepdale Road, on the Fleetwood & West Riding Junction, suffered a similar fate in December 1866. In between, on 19 March 1860, 'A lady, from want of caution, came in contact with a pillar supporting the roof of the Reading station, and, falling from the platform, was run over and killed by a train which was entering the station.'

Another repetitive issue was the means available for crossing the lines. Some companies had realised from the outset the dangers involved in crossing the tracks: Whishaw referred to 'tunnels' through the embankments at some stations on the Birmingham & Derby Junction and a footbridge at Cheltenham on the Birmingham to Bristol line. He commended these but accepted that the cost of providing similar facilities at all stations would not be justified; indeed, many stations would never be so provided. Conditions at Accrington in 1849 were so bad that the magistrates sent a complaint to the Railway Commissioners; Captain Wynne was sent to report and agreed that the complaints were justified. The booking-office, waiting-room and other facilities had been built on the line to Manchester, with a convenient door to the town, but when they found that most of their passengers wanted to use the east-west route from Preston to Colne, they had closed the original facilities and put up temporary ones, requiring access via a wooden staircase up a steep bank. This meant that passengers destined for some places had to cross the lines in order to buy their tickets and cross back to reach their trains; those going to Preston had to cross and re-cross if they wanted shelter whilst waiting on a wet day. All this was made worse by the peculiar arrangements operated there: trains from Manchester, Preston and Colne were timed to arrive at about the same time so each could be split in two, one part for each of the other two; the halves for each destination were then joined as one and sent on their way. This saved passengers from having to change trains but it involved much shunting and an elaborate lay-out so passengers from Accrington to Manchester had to cross several tracks to reach their trains. Inevitably, some lost their sense of direction in all this and joined the wrong train. However, the problem was probably short-lived because Wynne was shown plans for a new station that would solve the problems, though it seems odd that a station opened in June 1848 should have required replacement so soon.

At Old Trafford, on the Manchester, South Junction & Atrincham line, the booking office was perversely on the side used by trains to Manchester, although 196 out of 204 passengers wanted to go the other way on the day whose records were shown to the inspector in January 1858. An accident a couple of months later led to strictures on the LY's station at Wigan, which was also the subject of a memorial from the mayor and corporation. It was approached from both directions by sharp curves which gave limited visibility; on the south side there was only a shed for shelter; the north side held the booking-office, a waiting-room of 'the most wretched description' which could hold only a limited number of people and 'other requisites'. As a result passengers had constantly to cross and re-cross the line. The company's excuse was that it was only intended to be temporary – but it had been thus for ten years already.

On 11 February 1861 a woman alighted from a train at Crystal Palace and attempted to cross to the booking-office in front of an approaching train; both she and the porter who tried to save her were killed. A grandfather and the child he was carrying were killed crossing to the booking-office at Nuneaton on 4 January 1868; passengers were supposed to cross at the ends of the platforms but the low nature of these meant it was easy to cross anywhere. A similar need was at St Boswells, a junction station between Edinburgh and Carlisle on the North British, where the booking-office, waiting-room and refreshments were all on the southbound platform, with only a shed on the other side. This entailed much crossing from side to side and a passenger was killed doing this on 6 November 1868.

Sometimes notice was taken of passengers' needs. An accident report in 1868 described arrangements at Torquay. Although the station was on a double line, platforms both sides, most trains both ways used the eastern platform, nearer the entrance, because many invalids used the station and passengers carried unusually large amounts of luggage; this way saved crossing the line.

Lighting was an obvious problem, though clearly much was done to deal with this. The tunnel between Liverpool (Crown Street) and Edge Hill was lit by gas from the opening of the line to Manchester in 1830. Whishaw reported in 1842 that the

Newcastle station from North Shields (in Carliol Square), although only a temporary one, was lit by seven gas burners and the company was hoping to extend this facility to other stations. On 10 May 1852 *The Times* reported that the GN had lit one portion of the station at Kings Cross by means of an electric light placed at the southern end of the departure side; this, however, was only an experiment. In 1870 gas was still the standard, and had been provided in many places for a long time; it was readily available since most towns had their gasworks.

Refreshment

Travellers were used to refreshment facilities at coaching inns and from the start inns close to stopping places on the Liverpool & Manchester and other early lines did their best to profit from waiting travellers. The earliest recorded railway provision was the Gartsherrie Inn on the Garnkirk & Glasgow where by July 1832 the company built an inn in response to complaints from pleasure trippers about the lack of accommodation. Later advertisements referred to milk, fruits in season, snacks, wine and the like but it seems to have ceased to operate by 1843, when travellers were able to travel further.[24] The Hull & Selby timetable bill for September 1841 said refreshments could be obtained at Hull in the house adjoining the booking-office.[25]

One of the first refreshment rooms in the modern sense was provided at Curzon Street station in Birmingham in 1838. Short breaks were built into the timetable, one being at Wolverton; in 1838 the facilities were described as inadequate but steps were being taken to remedy this. It was run by a 'generalissima' with seven 'very young ladies' to wait on the passengers and various other helpers. Their work involved hectic bursts of activity and the need to rush from one side of the station to the other to deal with trains both ways. The effect on the digestion of these rapid meals has not been recorded. When this company first provided third-class travel, 5 October 1840, it offered those using it 'ample time' at Roade, about half-way along the line; this was 75 minutes, presumably allowing travellers time to visit local inns.[26]

Excursionists could make use of the long delays they sometimes suffered. On one from Oxford to London in September 1850 they learnt that they would have to wait at least 20 minutes at Reading: 'hundreds rushed from the train and besieged all the houses of entertainment within reach ... At length the railway bell rang, and there followed a rush up the embankment and summersets over the rails to regain the carriages'.[27] In many cases, but not this one, which was only first and second-class, an extra motive would have been that third-class passengers were not admitted to many railway refreshment rooms though Manchester Victoria provided one for them in its basement.[28]

A GSW notice of 9 April 1851 said passengers by the 8.45 pm from London would get an extra 10 minutes for breakfast at Carlisle. When the Midland opened a new station at Trent in 1862 it allowed a ten-minute break there for principal through trains between London and the North. Excursionists might also be catered for – the report of an accident that occurred on 24 June 1841 said an excursion from Stirling to Aberdeen had stopped at Forfar for 15 minutes and in July 1858 a SE excursion notice included a note that London Bridge refreshment room would open at 6 a.m. The LNW advertised that certain fast London to Scotland trains would stop for a 20 minute refreshment break at Preston on and after 2 March 1863. In 1867 the SE advised passengers by the mail and early morning trains that breakfasts were served from 6.30 in the restaurant opening onto the platform at Charing Cross.[29]

What was available did not always satisfy. The most famous (or infamous?) was the GW's at Swindon. According to MacDermot's history it caused complaints from the outset, apparently not improving much even once the original temporary accommodation had been replaced by grand permanent rooms on both platforms.[30] On the other hand, there were even rare letters of praise. In 1842 following complaints in *The Times* Isaac Smith of Holloway, said he had been to and from Bristol, had his full 10 minutes at Swindon and the best of refreshments and the utmost and promptest attention had been paid to his wishes. It was far superior to the old stage-coach days. He ended with a disclaimer, perhaps fearing that others would regard his letter with suspicion: 'I have no interest in the railway or the station at Swindon'.[31] Measom's 1852 Guide to the line waxed lyrical about the speed and efficiency of service as well as the great variety of food and drink on offer – but it was an 'Official' guide. Many refreshment rooms were normally let out to caterers so railways were not strictly to blame for shortcomings but passengers tended to feel they should have exercised greater control over those to whom they let contracts. The SE was the target of a piece copied from *The Examiner* in 1854 after its spokesman, Mr Mangles, had spoken in praise of English railways, compared with French ones: French 'waiting rooms at stations are not shabby, dirty sheds, but handsome, well-furnished apartments and the refreshments are not mouldy hams, stale pastry, and detestable compounds under the deceptive names of tea, coffee, beer, and wine'.

Prices also caused complaints. In 1846 'GW' of Stockwell, asked whether the London & Birmingham directors had given their sanction to prices charged at Birmingham refreshment rooms for passengers coming to London? He had been charged 1/- for a cup of cold and villainously bad coffee. Yet the day before at the down refreshment room he had had an excellent dinner of soup, hot or cold meat, bread, vegetables, cheese and butter for 2/-.[32] 'One famished in railway travel' (third-class) had gone from York with a number of men travelling to the Paris Exhibition in 1867; at Peterborough some were charged 3d for a glass of bitter beer (not ½ pint), and 6d for three small squares about 1½ inches called by some misnomer 'sandwiches'.[33]

'A Traveller' lost his break altogether in 1843 when late arrival at Birmingham from Lancaster for a connecting train deprived him of his 20 minute refreshment break.[34] 'A Penny-a-Miler' suffered similarly a couple of years later when he was held at Rugby for 30 or 40 minutes, so at Roade the need to make up time meant that the stop was too short for them to get anything.[35] In the course of a complaint about the lack of punctuality on the LNW in 1851 'WS' made a similar point. To try to avoid delays he had chosen the 'express' from Glasgow due at Euston at 11 p.m., but it was past 1 a.m. before they arrived. In the whole 14 hours the only break was 10 minutes at Carlisle (which was of little use since it was only 3 hours from Glasgow). Not even 5 minutes were possible elsewhere though at Preston, Stafford and Rugby they were detained 10 to 20 minutes; passengers dared not leave the train since porters, when asked, invariably said they would leave in two or three minutes.[36]

Conveniences

Travellers, particularly long-distance ones, faced potential problems later solved by the provision of lavatories in corridor coaches. *Bradshaw* carried advertisements for such as Walters' Railway convenience for gentlemen, ladies, invalids, and children which could be 'worn imperceptibly with the greatest comfort and security'; an India rubber convenience for male and female railway travellers, invalids and children was offered by Sparks and Son, who claimed to be the original inventors. How many used these devices is not known. The general answer seems to have been to make a dash at intermediate stations as outlined in this instruction of 15 March 1842, from Charles Saunders, Secretary of the GW (which then locked passengers into their carriages):

> Complaints having been recently made of the refusal by attendants on trains to open the carriage doors to enable passengers to alight, when they may from unavoidable causes require to do so, I am desired to give the most strict orders to all conductors and guards that they instantly comply with any application from a passenger who may be desirous of getting out for such purposes, whenever the stoppage of the train will permit it, and more especially at the Stations where the engine may have to take in water, or where delay may from any other cause be likely to take place; while [they] act with the utmost promptitude in opening the door ..., they may of course represent to the passenger the necessity of his resuming his seat as quickly as possible to prevent delay to the train, or the loss of his journey.

More than eighteen months after the LNW station at Bedford had opened, the company's superintendent reported a great nuisance from the lack of a privy there; one was ordered at an estimated cost of £27. The following year it ordered repairs costing 35/- at Pinner (now Hatch End) after a complaint from the local magistrates had caused them to investigate the state of the closets there. The urinals at Tring were said to be offensive so a supply of water was to be laid on for £3 10s.[37]

The Midland was accused in 1849 of having at Bingley (7,000 inhabitants) a wooden station of the most wretched and disgraceful description. At one end, there was a clerks' room about three yards square, in the middle a small open shed and at other end a Ladies' Waiting Room, similar in size to the clerks' room. During wet

51

weather the clerks transacted business holding umbrellas to protect themselves from the rain dripping through the roof. In the open shed all classes, male and female, were huddled together for up to an hour – the trains were frequently late. The Ladies Room was being avoided for dread of the cholera; the stench coming from the conveniences, which had only thin board partitions, was dreadful. It was expected that the Improvement Commissioners would indict the station as a public nuisance.[38]

When most days' papers carried information about cholera then afflicting the country, 'A commercial traveller' wrote in 1851 that on a journey from Newcastle he was induced at Darlington to enter a doorway over which was 'Gentlemen'. 'Pigs' would have been more appropriate. Three privies were nearly full of soil – at any rate to within 15 inches of the seats; the urinals looked as if it was a long time since water had been poured over them. The stench was such that though he was only there two minutes and nine hours had passed since, nausea was still with him.[39] The same theme was followed nearly 20 years later by 'A Lady' who wrote about the disgraceful condition of the ladies' first-class waiting-room at Swindon, the only place where travellers to Devon were expected to alight. 'The smell is so offensive, even one room off the requisite apartment… that it is almost unbearable, and enough to turn one sick.'[40]

However, not all bad smells originated on the railway. Passengers using the Commonhead station at Airdrie complained in 1858 about foul water that was running down onto the platform from a nearby pig farm.[41]

Other facilities

Newspapers and books could be bought on major stations from an early period and passengers soon found that trains, unlike stage coaches, provided a smooth-enough ride to make reading possible. By 1839 the former were certainly being sold at Liverpool Lime Street; the earliest known bookstall was provided at Fenchurch Street by William Marshall in 1841. Others soon followed, often run by ex-railwaymen disabled in accidents, or their widows and at first these bookstalls had a reputation for trashy novels and even pornographic material. This gradually changed as W. H. Smith in England and John Menzies in Scotland came to dominate; the former, famed for his alleged prudishness, opened his first stall, at Euston, in 1848 and the latter his earliest at Perth, Stirling and Bridge of Allan, in 1857.[42] On Christmas Day 1848 *The Times* reported that a Reading Room had been opened at Rugby, to which passengers could gain access for 1d: London and provincial papers and periodicals were available. *The Taunton Courier* of 9 May 1849 reported that letter-boxes had been installed at all major stations as a result of orders issued by the post-office. In April 1852 there was a notice that various companies had resolved on permitting advertisements at stations. Increasingly, stations became places where people could send their own telegraph messages. In 1870 the Bristol & Exeter was reported to be brightening up its waiting-rooms and had started at Exeter St Davids: in the first-class there were paintings of Cheddar Cliffs, scenes of Dartmoor, etc and in the second-class various lithographs.[43]

Hotels were provided at many stations, some of those at leading termini being amongst the most opulent of the age. The earliest was built beside the station at Crewe in 1837 by Lord Crewe and leased by the LNW in 1864 (it later became outright owner); the London & Birmingham provided the first by a company, at Euston two years later. Many others followed, the GW's at Paddington in 1852 being particularly grand. Ports such as Newhaven, Dover and Harwich were also served.

Friends and relations

One early argument concerned whether people should be allowed into stations to meet and see off relatives and friends. 'A Father of a Family' complained in 1838 that railway companies were trying to justify their depriving female travellers of the protection of their relatives and friends, on their arrival at, or departure from, Euston by alleging the need to prevent confusion and plunder. However, he might have been in error. Eight days later 'HCD' said it was possible 'Father' had gone to the wrong side. He himself had gone to meet his family there, going first to the departure side of the station and was then directed to the correct place most helpfully and civilly. He defended the regulation on the departure side – if 200 or 300 passengers were leaving and all were accompanied by well-wishers, they would be difficult to control and a danger to property. On the arrival side there was a 'strangers' room', comfortable and heated, in which the respectable could wait for their families' arrivals though they needed to enter their name and address in a book.[44]

On 14 July 1842 *The Times* announced that the GW had just given staff instructions to allow friends to go onto platforms with passengers; discretionary power was given to superintendents to keep mere idlers off platforms; one wonders how they would have regarded train spotters, if there had been any such then. However, exclusion clearly continued in some places since in 23 September 1851 'A Visitor' complained that 'this company' had ordered that people not travelling should not be admitted to the platform; he agreed it was reasonable to exclude those with no business but not those wishing to escort wife, daughter, and sister to carriage, together with the numerous little packages that ladies will take and he alleged it was because a director had been incommoded by the crowd there.

A related problem occurred in 1864 at Dover once both the SE and the LCD were running trains onto the pier to connect with cross-Channel steamers. On 13 December 'A Sufferer' complained that barriers were put up about an hour before a steamer's arrival and kept closed until both trains had left; the public were thus confined to an inconvenient gallery or platform from which it was impossible to recognise arriving travellers or attract their attention. He quoted instances where people had sought to meet arrivals and had missed them altogether. On 30 December *The Times* reproduced correspondence between the Town Clerk of Dover and the Admiralty, which owned the pier. On 16 September the Clerk had written to the Admiralty about the inconvenience caused by their new regulations but received no reply. He wrote again 17 November; the reply dated 27 December was that they saw no reason to modify their rules.[45]

Luggage

Well-to-do Victorians depended heavily on servants; they often travelled with much luggage and railway companies employed large numbers of porters to carry this, even actively discouraging individuals from carrying their own. Thus they had to rely on railway staff to ensure that they and their baggage arrived at the same station. It is safe to assume that this usually happened and that complainants were exceptional in their misfortunes.

From the start, passengers were generally allowed to take so much luggage free. Amounts initially varied – the Liverpool & Manchester allowed 60 lb. per passenger, with 3s per cwt. for anything in addition; the GW's offering in 1842 was 112 lbs first-class, 56 lbs second and a miserly 14 lb third. Fairly soon most standardised at 150 lb, 120 lb, 100 lb. The companies' responsibility for luggage tended to be a small-print affair. Often notices just specified how much was free and what the charges would be for extra. Slightly fuller versions added after the 'free' part that no responsibility would be taken unless items were booked and paid for. The South Devon did spell things out: their bills offered insurance at one-half-penny for each pound sterling's worth of luggage for up to 50 miles, reducing to one farthing per 50 miles over 150 miles. When Parliament legislated on behalf of third-class passengers it specified a minimum of 40 lbs for them and a question concerning this was settled at a speed that today would seem impossible. Mr John Sandle of Chichester wrote to the Board of Trade on 26 October 1842, with a copy of the London & Brighton's time-bill; this showed that it restricted third-class passengers to 14 lbs. The next day Mr Laing wrote a letter to the company on behalf of the Board and on the 28th the company's secretary acknowledged the mistake and promised to correct it.

Methods of handling luggage varied. At termini passengers were sometimes kept outside until the train was ready for them; delays were reduced by sending porters out to collect luggage and put it on the train. In 1842 'SB' travelled to Blackwall with a carpet bag and a very small portmanteau, which, immediately on arrival at Shoreditch (later Bishopsgate), were seized by a porter, who assured him he would find them 'all right', and disappeared with them. As soon as the gates opened, he went upstairs for his seat. Previous to getting in, he was asked by an official if the luggage were his. When he said it was he was presented with a ticket for 1/- for carriage, wharfage and porterage. As the train was just about to start, he had no option but to pay, but it was twice the amount company prescribed for 30 lbs of luggage.[46] When 'Philo-Steam' left Bristol in 1845 his luggage was hoisted up through a trap-door so he could not see where it was placed on the train. At London there were two pens: one labelled 'Cirencester and

Cheltenham', the other unlabelled. [The train would have started in two portions, combined at Swindon.] As fast as the luggage was taken out, it was piled into the pens so that until the upper parcels were claimed, the owners of the rest had no chance. The sides of the pens were covered with swarms of passengers. At last he spied his luggage, in the wrong pen, had the strength of lungs to attract the notice of a porter 'haymaking' in it and received his luggage, which he carried to a cab himself. It had taken 30 minutes. He contrasted this with Euston where there were no pens and no scramble.[47] Other letters suggest that at times it was a single free-for-all at Euston.

At first the usual method of carrying luggage by rail was copied from stage coach practice; it was put on the carriage roof. There was soon not-very-effective pressure for it to be put in vans immediately behind the engine and tender, not only for greater convenience, but also to act as a buffer in collisions.

Commercial travellers were regular users of the railways and inevitably carried large quantities of luggage. Since this often exceeded the amount allowed free, it could lead to disputes. One writing from Lichfield on 31 May 1845 gave details of the varying weights given by scales at different stations: 'Railway scales, like church clocks, never seem to agree'. A small shopkeeper with his scales half an ounce against his customers was heavily fined and his weights confiscated but Inspectors of Weights and Measures allowed a public company to defraud their customers, though he assumed it was carelessness not intentional fraud. Another complained in 1851 about the same problem on the SE.

Victorians were as forgetful as moderns and 'lost property' made an early appearance. On 13 March 1845 an item in *The Times* explained that on the London & Birmingham Railway lost property was forwarded to Euston, where it was daily registered in a book, and kept in warm rooms and after a certain time unclaimed articles were sold, the proceeds of which could be collected by owners providing proof. The normal later practice was for companies to put in a simple notice that unclaimed luggage would be sold, after keeping it for a year. In 1853 the Caledonian provided a very detailed one, occupying about three-quarters of a column, two items per line, in very small print; umbrellas (129) were inevitably the most common. This approach does not seem to have been copied or repeated.

In theory companies employed porters to deal promptly and courteously with passengers and their luggage and forbade them to accept tips. 'JLR' complained in 1843 about 'that parcel of vagabonds that infested entrances to railway stations, self-styled "porters"', almost to the exclusion of men authorised. They bullied and badgered travellers; he and another had come to rescue of a lady surrounded and pushed about by them and received a mass of gratuitous abuse and insolence. That that super-excellent body the police were never to be found when wanted was universally acknowledged.[48] Official ones were not always an improvement: 'FGM' had had to meet a lady in 1851 who had three small boxes, all of which he could have been carried across the platform to the cab in which she was waiting in five minutes but there were upwards of sixty passengers and only two porters so ten minutes elapsed between the delivery of each because they were trying to satisfy all by bringing a little to each. He blamed the GW company for its niggardly provision of porters.[49] This was another hardy annual: 'RYS' complained 18 years later about the lack of porters at Waterloo: he had to carry his own baggage or risk being left behind.[50]

One possible reason for the shortage of porters was suggested by 'Precaution' in 1855. He had written from Cheltenham but did not specify the station he was writing about. After seeing a letter from 'Commercial Traveller' about railway servants constantly drinking in station refreshment-rooms, the previous Friday he had counted five porters in the public bar of an inn 100 yards from 'the station', drinking spirits and malt liquor at 11 a.m. On the ringing of the bell, 'sundry forcible anathemas escaped from them, and the pack left surlily for the platform'.[51]

Arrival at the station and escape from it

Cab fares to and from stations were a fertile source of grievance. In 1843 the directors of the railways terminating at London Bridge had posted at Greenwich, New Cross and more distant places, a table, alphabetically arranged, of coach and cab fares to 370 different parts of the metropolis and *The Times* hoped that others would follow this example.[52] Waterloo later became a favourite target of those complaining about porters and cabs. In 1856 'A South-western' said he constantly travelled via Waterloo where he always found a line of empty cabs waiting, but was told by their drivers that they were already engaged, even when he was first there. If they carried more than two passengers they could charge an extra 6d and 2d per parcel so they waited for parties of three or more with plenty of luggage. Three days later 'NE' joined in. He had been told that a 6d tip to a porter would secure a cab though he had not done this.[53] There was another burst June/early August 1859, when the holiday season was in full swing.

A recurring problem was that companies seemed to give a monopoly to favoured individuals at stations, a question touched on earlier. A Board of Trade report gave details of a lengthy correspondence (May 1842 to February 1843) with the LSW over Woking station. Guildford had yet to receive its own station so its residents had to go by road to Woking but only one coach proprietor was allowed to take his coach into the yard and others had to wait in the road outside – unusually, the yard at Woking was enclosed and gates could be used to shut out traffic. The company argued that it was acting in the best interests of passengers because allowing rival coaches into the yard might lead to a repetition of events elsewhere where 'passengers are impeded and insulted by the effects of rival coach proprietors and their servants' and magistrates had refused to act where this had happened on private premises. The station-master claimed he had 'a duty to perform to the nobility residing in the vicinity ... to take especial care that they may be enabled to approach their [own] carriages without any sort of molestation'. They also argued that there was only room for one coach in their yard and that there were not enough passengers to keep more than one firm in business. The Board was unhappy about the monopoly but the limitations of its powers were exposed. Even when Major-General Pasley reported that there was room in the yard for two coaches, the company refused to budge; at no point in its lengthy self-justifications did it answer a particular point, that the favoured coach did not meet all trains but its rival was still kept outside. The LSW was under attack again in 1857 when Mr Marriott gained a victory in the courts to enable him to send his omnibuses into Kingston station.

In 1863 Lord Talbot de Malahide complained that no cabs were allowed to wait for hire at Rugby. People who had not arranged in advance for a cab had either to be crammed into a small omnibus or walk a mile to the town centre. He understood it was the result of an agreement between the LNW directors and some private persons. His complaint was endorsed the following day by Theodore M Wratislaw, Clerk to the Local Board of Health, which had made a request for a cab stand and for the omnibus to be thrown open to competition but the railway directors had declined to act.[54] However, the LNW seems to have managed better at Euston. By about 1860, 65 cabs had the right to go onto the platforms to meet arriving trains and if more were needed, a porter fetched some from a neighbouring street. A man was stationed at the exit to take down the number of each cab and its destination as it left, in order to protect passengers from overcharging. Any cab-driver misbehaving had his licence to use the station withdrawn.

Connecting bus services sometimes provided an alternative: on 14 May 1852 *The Times* said the GW had established an omnibus which took passengers and luggage without stopping to the City for 1/- in connection with all trains. However, not all were immediately impressed. On 14 June 'Cerebrosus' said that only one bus and one cab had been provided to accommodate 200 pleasure seekers attracted by cheap return tickets.

Finally

Stations might be places where you encountered someone you would rather not have met. The Rev Roberts had earlier been a curate in Leicestershire and had compiled some pamphlets based on a diary kept while there. One of these, *Frowlesworth, a Dark Village in an Enlightened Age*, included a paragraph about the conduct of Mr J Spencer, a Leicester bookseller, and his brothers, referring to their 'filthy, low, vulgar and impertinent language'. Spencer met Roberts on Leicester station on 18 April 1865, called him a villain and slanderer and horsewhipped him. Roberts claimed £50 in damages but received scant sympathy in court: the jury awarded him a mere £5 and the judge suggested that in future he should find a better use for his time.[55]

In August 1869 *The Newcastle Chronicle* reported that shortly after the end of a day's racing a large number of Irishmen went into Stockton and made their way to the North station [present day Stockton]. Many were drunk and on reaching the platform they started kicking and striking all they met; numerous English workmen were not slow to retaliate. Mounted police had followed them from the course and went into action. There were broken heads and bloody faces on all sides.[56]

However, all cannot have been bad. 'A Slumberer', writing from the Railway Hotel at Taunton in 1843 seems to have found the waiting-room comfortable enough; his complaint concerned the failure of the GW staff to wake him up. He had arrived 20 minutes early by cross-country coach to catch the 12.32 London train and retired to the waiting-room as soon as he had bought his ticket. He had not been to bed the previous night and so fell asleep and was woken by the whistle of the engine starting; there was a nearly four hour delay to the next train.[57] An item in January 1845 said that the previous Wednesday evening Swindon station had been appropriated as a ballroom for the recreation of the country gentry of Berkshire, Wiltshire, Somerset and Middlesex. Passengers by the 5 p.m. from Paddington had been surprised to see the decorations put up ready in the refreshment room. The company began to arrive at 9 p.m., brought by special trains from various destinations; about 400 in all attended.[58]

Chapter 5: FARES; CLASSES; SPEED

Introduction

Early practice was varied: some passengers were carried in trains with only passenger carriages, others by mixed trains consisting of proper passenger carriages plus goods wagons; the latter were often described as luggage trains. There were other complications: additional fares were charged for travel in mail trains and many added surcharges for 'express' trains. Workmen's services are also covered here. The idea is to give an indication of what was available since any attempt at full treatment would result in a nightmare mass of statistics.

Early provision

The operators of the 'Elegant New Railway Coach' on the Stockton & Darlington, *The Union* charged 1½d per mile inside, 1d per mile outside in 1826. Clearly modelled on stage-coaches these were designed to hold 6 inside and 15-20 outside but on at least one occasion, when Stockton Races were being held, 9 inside and 37 outside were somehow fitted in, a second horse being added.[1] As other lines opened bewildering variation resulted. The earliest Liverpool & Manchester timetable, for March 1831, offered the traveller a wide choice. By First Class Train (only one intermediate stop) it was Coaches with four inside (6s for the whole journey, 31 miles) or six inside (5s); in addition, 'The want of a superior description of Carriage, at a higher fare, having been frequently represented to the Directors, they have caused one Four inside Coach, in each First Class Train, to be fitted up in superior style, for which an extra charge of 2s. is made'. By Second Class Train they could travel in Glass Coaches (5s 6d) or Open Carriages (3s 6d).

The Grand Junction's initial offering, from Birmingham to Liverpool or Manchester, was first class coach, six inside (£1 1 0d); Mail Coach, four inside (£1 5 0), Bed Carriage in Mail Coach (£2); Second Class Coach (14s); not long after it added third class open carriages for one train each way per day.[2] When the London & Birmingham opened to Boxmoor, its first-class coaches carried six inside and each seat was numbered to coincide with the ticket number; second-class carried eight inside, were covered but without lining, cushions or divisions and were not numbered. When third-class carriages were provided they carried four on each seat and were not covered.[3]

At least amongst major lines, the bargain basement seems to have been provided by the Newcastle & Carlisle (60 miles). In 1839 it charged 11/- for closed carriages and 8/6 for open ones in 'quick trains', 8/6 and 7/6 for travel in mixed trains. In 1850 it was essentially the same, though thirds at 1d per mile had, of necessity, been added.

Given some of the details that will be given later, it may be that its patrons did not consider its service to be such a bargain.

Information provided for Parliament in the 1830s showed that companies' classifications were inconsistent; what some were describing as seconds were others' thirds. To the end of July 1836 the Dundee & Newtyle only provided first and second but it then added 'extra first' (no explanation was provided) and on 1 November 1836 it added third; from 13 May 1837 it was extra first (only one carriage in each train), first (formerly second), second (formerly third) – what had happened to the previous first? The Manchester, Bolton & Bury added open waggons on 13 June 1838 but took them off again on 1 December; by mid-1839 first, second and second open were the normal provision. Only the Sheffield & Rotherham admitted to operating third-class carriages. The Liverpool & Manchester had only one description of second-class: 'partially open at the sides, but with close tops'. The Stockton & Darlington still listed 'inside' and 'outside', while a couple of companies (Ardrossan & Johnstone and St Helens & Runcorn Gap) only listed first-class and the Wishaw & Coltness only second open. The London & Birmingham was the only one that gave a fare for mail trains; this was shown from October 1838 and was 0.2d per mile above the ordinary first-class fare. It, the GW and the London & Greenwich were the only ones whose first-class fares were more than 3d per mile; at the other end the Monkland's charges for its one class were only 0.7d per mile.

> A description given on the opening of the London & Blackwall in 1840 said that:
> The carriages are of a deep blue colour, picked out with gold, and the panels bear the city arms, surmounted by a steam vessel, the whole encircled with the words 'The London and Blackwall Railway Company'. The first class carriages are of the usual description, except that there are no elbows to the seats. They are each divided into three compartments, and are intended to hold 32 passengers. ... The second class carriages are of the same construction as those on the Manchester and Leeds Railroad, and are termed by engineers 'Stand-ups' ... These carriages have been adopted in order to save space, as it is anticipated a great number of persons will travel by the second class in consequence of the low fare.[4]

Whishaw called the 'Stand-ups' 'Stanhopes' and was astonished to see 'several most respectably dressed persons' riding in them since they were intended 'especially for those who cannot afford to pay for better accommodation'; the fare for the whole journey (nearly 3½ miles) was 6d seated, 4d standing. He also described their use on the Manchester & Leeds, where they were provided with four doors and divided into four compartments by wooden bars lengthwise and crosswise and holes bored in the floors to let the rain out; the number contained depended 'on the bulk of the respective stanhopers'. However, the Eastern Counties, which opened a few days before the

Blackwall used the three class standard that would become the norm.[5] Whishaw approved of its arrangements: the thirds were open and consisted simply of truck platforms but had eight seats fixed across them, each holding five people. He also praised the Newcastle & Carlisle's first-class carriages which were fitted with spring seats, lined and stuffed throughout and had glass sashes that were entirely free from the 'chattering noise so annoying in most railway-carriages'. In contrast, the seconds on the Newcastle & North Shields presented 'as dirty an appearance as those of the Greenwich Railway, shewing the description of persons who are glad to avail themselves of railway-conveyance'. An 1840 complaint that the Greenwich had heavily advertised its 6d fare for third-class but there had only been one third class carriage, and that was overcrowded and filthy, would seem to support his verdict.[6] The original third-class carriages on the Taff Vale were trucks with sides about 4 feet 6 inches high which were let down to enable passengers to get in and out; they had neither seats nor covering.[7]

The Board of Trade return for the first half of 1841 showed that of the major companies only the Newcastle & Carlisle and North Union provided no third-class trains; the GW and LSW only took third-class passengers by luggage trains. Most consigned them to mixed trains which, on the whole, carried the lighter sort of goods, cattle and the like. Fares were mostly between 1d and 1½ per mile; the Birkenhead was cheapest at 0.82d and the London & Greenwich dearest at 1.6d per mile. A large third-class traffic was carried by most lines in the manufacturing districts of Yorkshire and Lancashire and the coal districts of the North and Scotland; the manager of the Manchester & Leeds, Captain Lawes, said his line

> ... passes through or near 15 towns, between which there were
> formerly several carts, waggons and vans passing every hour of the day
> and night, with manufacturing and market produce, of which the
> humbler classes could avail themselves at a trifling expence of money
> and a considerable sacrifice of time. These are now almost entirely
> swept away, and the market-people load one or more of the market
> trucks among them, paying 3d or 4d per ton mile for their goods, and
> in many instances less than 1d per mile for themselves. The effect has
> been to bring a supply of fruit, fish, and vegetables within the reach of
> those who could never obtain them formerly, and to afford very great
> advantages to the market-people and towns.
>
> In fine weather respectable tradespeople, clerks, &c., avail
> themselves of the third-class carriages to a considerable extent; but the
> great bulk of the half a million of third-class passengers who are carried
> on this railway in the course of the year are strictly the working-classes,
> weavers, masons, bricklayers, carpenters, mechanics and labourers of
> every description, some of whom used formerly to travel by carts, but
> the greater number on foot.

The fare from Manchester to London by railway and steam-boat *via* Hull is 14s; and many of the labouring classes will avail themselves of this mode of conveyance. In one respect a remarkable use has been made of the facilities afforded by railway communication. On the occasion of several strikes, when there was a press of work, bodies of workmen have been engaged in London and carried to Manchester and *vice versa*.

However, on longer lines with much through traffic to London there were far fewer third-class passengers. The Arbroath & Forfar, where Whishaw saw parties of reapers going to their work by train in September 1841, carried more than travelled between London, Manchester and Liverpool; seven times as many went by the Newcastle & North Shields as were carried between those three. The Board doubted that it would ever be in the interests of the long-distance lines to encourage third-class passengers but did express satisfaction over the increasing disposition to provide at least one train per day which the poorer classes could afford, though the advantages were reduced where more than one company was involved: third-class passengers from London to Manchester or Liverpool were detained at Birmingham from three in the afternoon until six the next morning.

Parliamentary intervention

Various concerns about the treatment of third-class passengers, especially an accident on the GW, described in a later chapter, led to a circular sent on 1 January 1842 from the Board of Trade asking companies for details of their arrangements. A bewildering array of answers resulted; even the height of the sides of carriages varied from 2 feet 8 inches to 4 feet. The Preston & Wyre explained theirs contained no seats, 'on account of the shortness of the journey, and to make a greater difference between them and the first and second class, for even without seats great numbers of people in affluent or comfortable circumstances go by them, and at all seasons'.

Not everyone was sympathetic towards the poor traveller. During the course of the 1844 debate about the need for change 'Justice' claimed he should be satisfied: the old expenses of travelling outside on stage-coaches were about the same as first-class railway fares now yet there was then no protection and the cheap travel provided for second- and third-class travel now offered was unknown so the poor had to walk or travel by waggon. The working population were not great travellers; seldom could they leave home on pleasure, and business requiring locomotion had they none.[8] 'R.Y.S.' put the other side: a gentleman going to Exeter first- or second-class took 7¾ hours and could travel at any time he pleased but a poor man, third-class, had to leave Paddington at 9.30 p.m., arriving at Exeter 11.55 a.m. next day (15 hours 5 minutes, much at dead of night). On his return he had to leave Exeter at 2 p.m., arriving at 7.45 next morning.[9]

That year Parliament decided for the 'poor' and passed what is often called 'Gladstone's Act'.[10] From 1 November every line would have to run at least one train serving every station each way per weekday, at a speed of at least 12 m.p.h. including stops, in carriages with seats and roofs and a fare of no more than 1d a mile; each passenger would be able to take half a hundred weight of luggage free. Children under 3 would travel free, 3 to 12 at half fare. The sop was that passenger duty would no longer be levied on fares of 1d a mile or less.

The Eastern Counties was blunt in its implementation: it advertised that 'Third Class Trains, for the poorer classes, in pursuance of Act of Parliament' would run on and after Monday, 21 October 1844.[11] The standards demanded by the Board of Trade for companies to be regarded as complying with the Act included complete protection from the weather, through the closing of apertures by curtains, shutters or Venetian blinds and provision for the admission of light when they were closed. It said most had complied with the 'utmost alacrity'; some had gone beyond the minimum by providing windows and even lamps at night. However, the GW did not enthusiastically adapt. One sample complaint was that of J Williams, living by daily labour in London, who could only by great exertions get a holiday once in a year or two. To visit his aged mother at Swansea, he had gone on a Friday night in August 1845, by the third-class train from Paddington for Bristol, for the packet sailing at 10 o'clock Saturday morning. The train ought to have reached Bristol at 5.20 a.m. but it did not arrive at Bath until 10 o'clock, where his brother joined him. They were too late for the packet; his brother had lost the chance of going while he himself was detained there until Tuesday for the next packet.

The running of seatless and open carriages was not banned. In 1852 LSW notices advertised cheap fares in open carriages to Windsor, Twickenham, Richmond, Hampton Court and intermediate stations. Timetables also sometimes included references to fourth-class provision. The North British advertised from 1 March 1850 'Cheap Trains for the Working-Classes': these were actually fourth-class carriages attached to the goods train leaving Burntisland at 11.30 a.m., reaching Perth 'about' 4.30 p.m. and Dundee 'about' 7.40 p.m., with one train the other way. The *Intelligible Guide* of June 1858 included a Thursdays-only, presumably market-day, fourth-class from Nottingham to Mansfield. Trains run in accordance with the Act generally became known as 'Parliamentary Trains' but the distinction between them and others taking third-class passengers was often blurred in the minds of the public.

One carriage provided on the Greenwich line in 1850 had been a covered one but the roof had rotted and been removed, leaving the framing of the ends and sides; a passenger who climbed onto a corner of this and sat there was killed when his head hit the roof of Spa Road station, which had been fitted into a narrow space with projecting eaves only 12 feet above the rails. A boy who had seated himself on the edge of one on the York & North Midland in August that year lost his balance and fell, resulting in the amputation of an arm. The report of an accident in 1854 in the Bramhope Tunnel, between Arthington and Leeds, said that the train was a third-class one of eleven passenger carriages, the centre one being an open one, full of Irish reapers. Also among the passengers were a number of respectable persons who were returning from 'Harrogate' where they had been for the benefit of their health.[12] The full danger run by those travelling in open carriages was exposed by a collision at Lewisham on 28 June 1857 when one passenger train was hit in the rear by another: a brake-van was pushed over the top of an open carriage whose buffers had been somewhat depressed by the weight of 30 or 40 people in a relatively flimsy carriage and twelve died.

'A passenger' complained in 1850 that his train from Croydon had three third-class carriages, two of which were open, one covered; all were refused entry to the closed one though it was raining in torrents and they arrived drenched to the skin.[13] That year 'A Railway Traveller' rode third-class from London to Tottenham and found his seat was wet; this was dried by a porter but did not help because the roof leaked. One passenger put up an umbrella but took it down because others complained that they were getting the drips from it.[14]

Finally, separation by class was not confined to trains. *The Taunton Courier* of 5 October 1853 described the opening from Durston to Yeovil. For the celebration at Langport some 'wiseacre' had arranged for champagne at one end of the room and small beer at the other. A wag had advertised a quantity of hurdles for keeping groups apart.

Fares: variations and fluctuations

Inevitably comparisons were made between companies. On 11 September 1839 'Viator' wanted to know why the London & Birmingham charged £5 0 6d for his carriage, 2 horses and a servant from Tring (31¾ miles), but the GW only £1 16 6d from Maidenhead (22½)? There were regular protests about increases; a piece copied from *The Birmingham Advertiser* on 29 September 1838 complained that the Grand Junction had put up intermediate passenger fares without notice (to Coventry from 2/6 first, 3/6 second to 3/6 and 5/-). In 1841 'A Heavy Sufferer' complained about recent increases in LSW fares. Second-class fares had been increased in such a way that the highest increases were part way along line, at Weybridge (his station), but much less either side of this. Weybridge fares had increased by 50% but Southampton 16%, Woking 14%, Farnborough 10%, and Walton 25%. Fares to Kingston, Wimbledon and Wandsworth, where coaches were still running had not been increased.[15]

Protest could be effective. At Brighton a meeting was convened in 1843 by the High Constable to protest against recent alterations in fares and times; they appointed a deputation of five to see the directors of the London & Brighton. A town meeting to consider deputation's report was satisfied when told that after 1 August prices by mixed or slow trains would be 12/-, 8/-, 5/-.[15a] An item on 1 August confirmed that a new list, reducing fares, had been issued and that in addition the timetable had been altered so that six trains each way would carried third-class.

In 1844 the trend was downwards, helped by Gladstone's Act. On 13 July it was reported that since the London & Croydon had cut their fares, they had gained: receipts in the previous week were greater than any since 14 September 1841 and the number of passengers carried only exceeded earlier in Whitsun weeks. On 1 October the reduction of the third-class fares to 1d per mile took place from Birmingham to Liverpool and Birmingham to London. Crowds thronged the gates at Birmingham in the morning for the Liverpool train; long before the 2.30 departure to London some hundreds assembled. Despite heavy rain, 10 carriages laden with about 400 passengers started; at Wolverton and Roade extras were added so that 12 plus luggage vans arrived at Euston, about 10 p.m. Passengers were chiefly of the working class and appeared to enjoy the ride although delayed one hour at Roade to allow two fast trains to pass. By the end of the year the success of 1d per mile on the Eastern Counties was shown by the need to put on two large omnibuses, which were usually filled, and a coach to provide a connection between Ipswich and Colchester.

The returns for 1850 show that overall fares on Scottish lines were somewhat lower than those in England: the highest was 2½d per mile charged by the North British and Edinburgh & Glasgow for first-class. There patrons of the North British vigorously pursued a complaint about overcharging. A public meeting at Stow resulted in a petition to the Board of Trade which included an accusation of a breach of the law over third-class fares. This had already been to the Court of Sheriff Arkley of Edinburgh when Mr Reavely, a woolsorter from Stow, had unsuccessfully tried to recover the amount of an overcharge: he had sued for 1¼d. The Board of Trade argued, however, that the opinion of the English Law Lords in a similar English case had gone against the company concerned and the Scottish Lord Advocate now agreed with them. The argument dragged on from late October 1855 until the end of April 1856, when the Company finally stopped wriggling and gave in; the Board had advised the Inland Revenue that the trains concerned did not qualify for remission of passenger duty, thus in effect fining the North British. The complaint was that the people of Stow had been charged 7d for the 6¾ miles to Galashiels and 5d for the 4 miles to Fountainhall. The company argued that since the actual distances were 259 and 108 yards respectively more than those shown in their timetable, it was entitled to round up the fares to the nearest penny but ultimately it had to alter its charges to the nearest farthing below.[16]

The 1857 Board of Trade Report showed that demand was for first-class accommodation by those willing to pay and cheap third-class; second-class, 'which is generally as little comfortable as third-class, is used by those who must travel and cannot obtain convenient third-class trains'. Already in Scotland 73% travelled third-class. However, some companies were still only providing the bare minimum of third-class trains and there was still a widespread feeling that some were deliberately being awkward. *The Observer* pointed out in 1861 that every Monday a succession of reasonably comfortable, fast and profitable excursion trains, running at a convenient hour, took trippers to Brighton for 2s 6d return. However, if an ordinary traveller needed to go the same distance, about 100 miles in all, it would cost 8s 4d and 'the only carriage in which he could travel would be a vehicle purposely and ingeniously constructed in such a manner as to be wholly unfit for the conveyance of a human being', at an awkward time of day and at a speed little better than that of the stage-coach. 'Equally intolerable is it that the humbler class of travellers should be subject on all occasions to a systematic roughness and insolence of treatment on the part of railway officials and servants, as if they were of no greater account than a herd of the lowest order of animals'. However, the LBSC's half-yearly report in February 1865 boasted of five thirds a day to Brighton at 4/2 single, return same day 6/6 and an item on 4 June 1866 said that Bristol & Exeter third-class passengers were now conveyed by four trains each way daily instead of one.

The 1860s were a mixed time for the passenger, with various reductions and 'revisions', though by modern standards fares were stable throughout the decade; full coverage would involve an indigestible mass of statistics.

Variations were particularly dramatic when companies went to war, which could be fun for the passengers while it lasted but ruinous for companies if continued. The LNW was particularly vulnerable to competition because its main line faced competition on both flanks as far as Manchester. Captain Huish, its Secretary, sought to protect its interests by making agreements with other companies, usually preferring the bludgeon to diplomacy; he wanted all to charge the same, regardless of any advantage one might have – a shorter distance, for example. However, the GN, the chief intended victim, which opened a new route to the north in 1850, was not prepared to co-operate. April 1851 saw tit-for-tat actions on fares. From 4 April the LNW and Midland greatly reduced their fares to York and the GN retaliated by saying its charges would in no instance exceed these. In January 1852 they reached agreement for the division of traffic and equal charges to and from Lincoln, Doncaster, Sheffield, Wakefield, Leeds and York.[17] This was only a truce. In 1856 the GN gave notice that on Monday 11 February passenger fares would be greatly reduced. Three days later the LNW offered a reduced fare from London to Peterborough: first-class 3/-, second 2/-, the same as the GN. On the 23rd the LNW, MS&L and Midland proclaimed that on and after 25 February fares would be further reduced – e.g. Peterborough 2/-, 1/-; again the GN retaliated with a similar offer. Alas for the passenger, on the 27th all four shared a notice that on March 1 the reduced fares would be withdrawn.

Manchester London Road was the seat of battle in 1857-8, with alliances somewhat reshaped. The GN made arrangements with the MS&L to run its trains from London to this station, which the latter shared with the LNW and this service began on 1 August 1857, with the added incentive of capturing some of the Art Treasures Exhibition traffic. The war saw fares reduced at one stage to 12s 6d, and then to 5s return for excursion tickets in closed carriages on two days of the week. Eventually peace was made: agreed ordinary fares were 33s first- and 24s second-class single.[18]

Concessionary fares

According to the 1838-9 Returns, only the Bodmin & Wadebridge gave a discount on return fares: first-class was 1½d per mile forward, half price backward if the same day, but not less than 4½d; second-class 1d, ½d, not less than 3d. In 1845 the London & Birmingham introduced a scheme which let persons travelling on Saturdays buy tickets at reduced or day ticket price which would 'free' them back again from the same station on Monday, e.g. Watford 4/- first class, 5/6 day ticket, thus 'holding out every facility and inducement to avoid unnecessary Sunday travel'.[18a] Others gradually followed, though inevitably the details differed. In 1849 the LY was going to charge families and children half-price during the summer, the directors believing it would encourage wives to compel [sic] their husbands to take them on excursions more frequently.[19]

Season tickets were an early development, though under different names. In 1834 the Canterbury & Whitstable advertised Family and Personal tickets, at five and two guineas respectively, from Lady Day to 1 November.[20] The London & Greenwich (then open only to Deptford) advertised its (single) fares as first-class 1/-, second- 9d, third- 6d and quarterly tickets for £5, £4 and £3 in 1837. It also stated that non-transferable free tickets could be obtained from its offices at 26 Cornhill.[21] Its 'free' tickets were probably annual seasons – the Stockton & Darlington was using the same term in the 1830s – holders were free to use them as often as they liked.[22] By 1838-9 the Dundee & Newtyle's 'seats contracted for' were about 20% below the standard fare. The London & Greenwich seems to have been brought more or less to order by a protest late in 1846; there had been rumours that it would cease issuing annual tickets but a public meeting was held and the company then said it would issue on the usual terms. However, at the start of 1847 passengers found they had to sign a stringent set of conditions and give 10/- deposit as security for returning the old at expiry.[23] In 1851 'Londoner' complained that the GW was then the only major company not offering seasons and its ordinary fares were outrageous for the daily traveller: someone living at Reigate paid £30 per year, someone the same distance from London on the GW would pay £122 4 2d, the Brighton resident paid £50 and the GW equivalent £328 10s.[24] In July 1851 the GW started to issue annual tickets but only as far as Maidenhead.[25] In February 1852 these were provided for travel between London and Reading, after at least two requests had been made by the town clerk of Reading; the annual cost was £50 first- and £36 second-class.[26]

From time to time other inducements were offered. On 18 April 1849 the LBSC was reported to be about to reduce its scale of charges for periodical tickets in order to encourage building near the Croydon and Epsom lines, with the promise that rates would not be increased once the houses had been built and the occupants committed to commuting; an LSW notice of April 1852 said that to encourage the erection of houses at moderate rents, £20 – £50 per annum, for clerks and similar classes on their suburban lines, the directors were prepared to offer a 20% discount for 7 years for Residential Tickets (first or second-class) to persons erecting 20 houses or more, for the use of occupiers of such houses and their families.[27]

Sharp practice was at times alleged. Season ticket holders along the GN held two meetings at the Victoria Hotel, Kings Cross, in October 1861, complaining that on the 1st of the month the company had taken off the 11.30 p.m. train and an earlier one, replacing them with one at 10.00 p.m. and they considered that this was a breach of faith since they would not have taken up residence along the line if they had known. At the second they appointed a delegation to present a memorial and were later able to report that the 9.20 p.m. and 11.35 p.m. had been reinstated for November.[28] In 1868 there was an argument about season ticket prices in the south-east where quarterly third-class seasons had originally been issued at a guinea but after 12 months were raised to 30/-. 'WGS' of Deptford said the guinea tickets had tempted hundreds of struggling porters, warehousemen and 'lower-class' travellers to take houses at New Cross. He suggested experimenting with 5/- monthly tickets (travel before 8 a.m., after 7 p.m.) and putting on extra trains from 5.30 using the oldest carriages. It was also pointed out that there were great savings by seasons but third-class passengers could not always put down a lump sum, and also had to consider the uncertainty of employment.

Workers' services

Some cheap travel for workmen was soon provided, though widespread provision had to wait until the later 1860s. The earliest services operated for workers living in isolated areas. Typical of these were a number in the North East of England. In 1845 the Stockton & Darlington began a service from Crook to Waskerley although it had not been inspected by the authorities prior to opening and when they found that two trains daily each way were carrying passengers Captain Laffan was sent in 1850. He wrote that it was essentially a mineral district, where previously few people lived and there was no or only very poor communication other than by railway so the company had come to attach some passenger carriages to mineral trains for miners, coke-burners and other workmen. The total revenue of the stretch for the last six months of 1849 was only £179. The only stations, at Tow Law, Cold Rowley and Waskerley Park had just rough platforms and lacked signals and there were also dangers from inclines so normally he would not have sanctioned passenger traffic. However, there was no other means of travel in the district and the revenue such that the company would not spend on improvements; an official ban would probably lead to men travelling free on mineral wagons, which would be even more dangerous. Thus it was left as it was until 1868, when this line was much improved by the elimination of the inclines. The same company ran a workmen's service from Eston Junction, on their Middlesbrough to Redcar line, to the Eston Depot of Bolckow Vaughan, owners of the line from the junction, for 10/- per day, agreement for which was reached on 17 February 1851. Market trips to Middlesbrough on Saturdays were first agreed on 10 May 1852; the initiative originally came from Middlesbrough tradespeople who paid the company 13/- per week for running the train (and it got the fares as well) but when the tradespeople pulled out in November 1853 the fare was raised from 3d to 4d. There were variations in the way the service was provided – at times Bolckow Vaughan ran it, using borrowed carriages.[29]

At one time the lack of cottages for workers at Whitworth Colliery near Spennymoor, somewhat to the north west of Stockton, meant trains were run from the main line along the Byers Green branch of the Clarence Railway which normally only carried passengers on market days; it is not known whether the costs were borne by the men or their employers. On 11 August 1853 their train ran head-on into a goods train; the smash was particularly bad because their wagon was being propelled from behind and all twelve in it were killed or badly injured.[30] This would suggest they were prepared to go to considerable lengths for just a few workers.

Later the attention focussed on London where the issue became increasingly pressing as the extension of lines towards the centre involved much demolition. W R Arrowsmith, incumbent of Old St Pancras, complained in 1865 about the damage to the poor from the Midland's activities. Overcrowding was being made worse as those evicted sought to stay close to their work and to that haven of temporary relief, the Parish Workhouse, but appeals to the company for help had met no response.[31] The extensions to Charing Cross and Cannon Street were other leading examples. Gradually, as a result of public pressure and Parliament's compulsion, workmen's fares were put on a firm footing. Unfortunately, practice did not altogether match theory since the poorest casual workers could not afford even these fares and in any case had to be close at hand to be available for jobs where they were engaged by the hour rather than paid by the week so overcrowding became even worse in some areas. The question of compensation, covered in a later chapter, caused some delay – or gave an excuse for delay to those unwilling to help.

A beginning had been made in 1857. On 27 June *The Illustrated London News* said the LSW had arranged to carry workmen for 1d from Waterloo to Nine Elms (presumably Vauxhall) at eight in the morning and back at eight-thirty in the evening, to allow those working in the central area to escape to homes in a more salubrious area.[32] The main stream of change was begun without compulsion by the Metropolitan in May 1864: it operated two early morning trains at 2d for the full journey, then Bishops Road (Paddington) to Farringdon, plus a return journey at any time after noon. Parliament first insisted on cheap provision with the passage in 1861 of the Act for the Moorgate extension, eventually opened in 1865; a 4d return from Hammersmith to the City became available in April 1865.[33]

The LCD began a service for artisans, mechanics and daily labourers (male and female) on Monday 27 February 1865, running once a day each way between Victoria and Ludgate Hill, calling at intermediate stations. Tickets were available at 1/- for six days' travel, one journey each way per day. The company provided this of its own free will but had taken the precaution of getting a special Act to limit compensation to £100 per person and have the amount decided by an arbitrator.[34] In August 1868 the SE began its workmen's cheap trains from Woolwich and intermediate stations; fares to/from any station would be 4d [return?] in covered carriages. At the start of 1869 the LBSC added workmen's trains between London Bridge, Norwood Junction, Streatham, New Cross and Wapping to ones already running between London Bridge and Victoria; at its half-yearly meeting in February it reported that it was running 18 suburban workmen's trains, return fare 4d for [up to?] 16 miles. An example of concessions outside London was provided later that year by a report saying the LNW's recently constructed line from Liverpool Lime Street to Bootle through the principal eastern suburbs would shortly be opened and morning and evening, workmen's trains at uniform rate of 1d any distance would run.[35] In March 1870 a snag in the arrangements was aired: poor women employed at a Pimlico clothing establishment were obliged to wait two hours in the cold before they could enter the works – they needed tickets available up to 9 a.m. It was also pointed out that in the north workmen were taken from Manchester to Liverpool (36 miles) for 3d; why not the same in the south?

Speed

In 1836 the fastest journeys to most places were those by mail coach though in a few instances slightly faster services were provided by other coaches. The times that follow are those from the General Post Office in London:

Birmingham	11 hours	08 minutes
Bristol	11	45
Dover	8	57
Edinburgh	42	23
Glasgow	42	00
Manchester	19	00
Southampton	8	30

Here the aim is to give a rough idea of how speeds developed in the earliest railway years. Companies (followed by many railway historians) tended to publicise the fastest, generally untypical, services. There were far more trains which stopped at every station than expresses designed to serve a few places. Cross-country and branch lines inevitably suffered slower trains.

It was generally accepted that newly-opened lines should be limited to 20 m.p.h. until the earthworks had had time to settle: Early speeds are difficult to determine since, even when timetables were published some companies were too coy to publish arrival times at the final destination, let alone at intermediate stops. In 1832 the fastest trains on the Liverpool & Manchester were supposed to take 90 minutes and drivers were ordered to take extra time in bad weather. In reality many managed the journey in anything up to 25 minutes less; far from being pleased, the officials threatened drivers with fines if they took less than 80 minutes because wear and tear on the engines was too expensive. Stopping trains were allowed two hours; these operated on a stop-where-requested basis and so intermediate times would have been impossible to predict as there were many potential stops.[36] By 1837 the timing was 15 minutes less for each type of train. It was felt worthy of note in 1838 when the *Sun* did the 31 miles from the mouth of the tunnel at Liverpool (to which point its train had been hauled by a stationary engine) to Manchester in the 'short space' of 41 minutes, representing 45 m.p.h.[37] The Stockton & Darlington also had problems with racing drivers on the Stockton to Middlesbrough section: in 1834 drivers were ordered to take 15 minutes, including stoppages over the 5 miles involved.[38]

Bradshaw's first known issue, dated 19 October 1839, was confined to the Lancashire-Yorkshire area. Only the Manchester & Leeds, open as far as Littleborough, gave full details of arrival times; it took 45 minutes for its 16 miles while the Sheffield & Rotherham offered '12 to 15 minutes' for its 6½ miles. An issue dated 25 October 1839 gave details of more lines as well. The fastest train on the London & Birmingham covered the 112¼ miles in 5 hours, Birmingham to Manchester (97¼ miles) took 4 hours (half-an-hour longer the other way) and Carlisle to Newcastle or Gateshead (60 miles) needed 3 hours.

In 1845 there was something of a competition between companies. In March faster trains began running on the GW: Exeter to London, 194 miles, was done in 4 hours 53 minutes to the ticket platform and passengers alighted at Paddington in the prescribed 5 hours while a down train reached Bristol, 118¼, in less than 3 hours, after stopping 10 minutes at Swindon (also calling at Didcot and Bath).[39] Towards the end of March the London & Birmingham said it would accelerate mail trains from 4½ to 3½ hours and also under consideration was the despatch of a train each way which would run the whole 112¾ miles in 3 hours.[40] Thereabouts a 'Liverpool paper' said swift trains were likely to be started very shortly which would cover Liverpool to London in 6 hours; the idea was that it would leave Liverpool about 3 pm, giving people the chance of doing a day's business before travelling.[41] The following year *The Liverpool Times* said the Grand Junction would put on a morning express to London from Liverpool, at 6 a.m., in response to a memorial from Liverpool merchants. They would also put back the express from London to 5 p.m., allowing businessmen to go to London and back in a day, doing business whilst there.[42]

Thereafter, progress was erratic though on most lines there was a significant increase in the number of trains running at or near the speed of the fastest. Other improvements in timing resulted from the provision of cut-off lines that reduced distances. In some cases there was regression. In the 1860s, in stages, the GW extended its Bristol timing to 2 hours 58 minutes (1867).[43] The LNW timetable for July 1852 included one train to Birmingham in 2 hours 45 minutes and one to Manchester in 4 hours 10 minutes but that for April 1870 showed fastest journeys (but more of them) at

3 and 5 hours respectively; on the other hand, Glasgow's fastest time had been cut from 12 hours 35 minutes to 11 hours 30 minutes. Elsewhere, Dover could be reached in 2 hours in 1869, Southampton in 2 hours 20 minutes (as opposed to 3 hours in 1840) and the time to Edinburgh via the GN was down to 10 hours 30 minutes in 1867.[44]

Chapter 6: TRAVELLING – COMFORTABLY?

Introduction

After complaints of insufficient accommodation on London & Birmingham trains *Herapath* came to the defence in September 1837, saying the public did not consider the difficulty of estimating how many would travel. It claimed the early problem had been overcome; at times as many as 40 carriages were being taken by one train. Such complaints resurfaced from time to time. One such resulted from a journey undertaken by 'Viator' in 1853.

> I took a second-class ticket this afternoon at Ashton-under-Line, to travel by the London and North-Western Company's 5h. 5m. p.m. train to Stockport, to save the express to Crewe. On the train's arrival at the Ashton station, I was surprised to find that it consisted of the engine and one solitary carriage ... Of course the passengers assembled on the platform made a rush for the solitary carriage, but they found no ingress, for the very sufficient reason that it was full already. In reply to the inquiry, 'what was to be done?' the guard coolly directed us to scramble over the shafts of the 'buffers,' to cling to the front of the carriage near to the guard's box (which was also full), and so to effect the transit to Stockport in a pelting storm of rain! ....[1]

At first all suffered a fair amount of bumping and jolting, which was rarely mentioned since most probably took it for granted, as they did in road vehicles. It took time to develop satisfactory springing, though the greatly improved methods developed on stage-coaches gave them a start. More seriously, braking depended on careful co-ordination between engine-driver, fireman, and guards scattered along the train so starting and stopping could be jerky. Charles Dickens complained in 1867 about rough riding on the Midland between Leicester and Bedford; the reckless fury of the driving and rocking of his carriage had caused him to give up his ticket at Bedford rather than go on to London. The authorities had said a thaw and the lightness of the carriage were to blame, but it was not the same on other lines and one of the loudest fellow complainants was in a heavy coach. His name resulted in an avalanche of letters. He received much general support; more specifically, William P Collins had about 12 months previously alighted from a Midland express before the end of his journey and resolved he would not again travel by one and MT Bass had travelled second-class on a mail so bumpy that his head bounced against the wooden carriage roof. 'Another traveller on the line' provided comfort of a sort: it was always like it so there was no need to be alarmed: Leicester to Hitchin was bumpy and on to London smooth so the fault must have been in the line's construction. On the other side, James Howard

(Britannia Ironworks, Bedford), a regular traveller on the Midland, was surprised by Dickens's letter and Alfred Ellis (Belgrave near Leicester) claimed to have been on the same train as Dickens, in a first-class carriage, nearer the engine, and had had no problem being able to read one of his books – he put the probable cause down to a faulty coupling.[2]

Another constant would have been the smoke emitted by the engines, which would have been especially irritating in stations with overall roofs. The Metropolitan's arrival provided a particular annoyance with its tunnels but Myles Fenton, its General Manager wrote in defence after some remarks had been made about the atmosphere there. He claimed the directors had asked three independent doctors, including the medical officers of health of London and Marylebone, to make a thorough enquiry. Their own physician, who also served the GW, had some time previously certified that the rate of sickness among their employees was less than half that on the GW.[3]

Locked doors

Locked carriage doors caused much early heart-searching. Locking needed to be done by railwaymen dealing with each compartment door individually, which, apart from anything else, took a fair time on busy occasions. Many felt it was ordered to prevent passengers from avoiding payment of their fares but companies argued it aided safety by preventing them from jumping out; some early passengers' antics show this claim had some justification. On 21 June 1837 the Eastern Counties suffered a fatal accident on only its second day of operation: near Stent's Bridge there was a 'sudden shaking and checking of the train'. Both men on the engine were killed but the passengers were only very frightened because they were locked in and could not break the glass to escape; the inquest jury blamed the accident on excessive speed and put the passengers' survival down to their being locked in and unable to jump out when the train started to rock.[4]

This question was given extra impetus after a serious accident at Versailles on 9 May 1842 which involved more casualties than any in Britain would do for some years to come: estimates of the dead varied from 40 to 100 – much to the disgust of *The Times* the French government gave no official figures. Some carriages were closed, with locked doors, making escape impossible. However, the force of the collision had caused so much destruction that rescue, at any rate of any seriously injured, would have been difficult given the speed at which the fire spread; some even argued that the carriages were so badly smashed that any not too badly injured to do so would have been able to escape.[5]

After this the Board of Trade circularised British companies about the practice here. The replies showed considerable variation, the London & Greenwich and GW being the only ones to lock both sides. The former claimed that it did so because their experience was that if their trains stopped between stations, passengers would alight and walk along the line if either side were left unlocked, risking falling over the parapet of its viaduct to London Bridge as well as being run over. Major General Pasley looked into this and pointed out that the London & Croydon, which shared the same stretch of line, left both sides unlocked. Since neither company had suffered any casualties and the space between carriages and parapets was so narrow that it would be physically difficult to get out, this did not help resolve the debate. The GW's response, far the longest, pointed out that the Board's own returns listed many examples of death and injury by falling out of trains and also argued that it helped passengers find the right carriage, since many were detached at various stations along the way. Others locked the off-side doors, some none. A couple of Midland companies gave as their reason for the last that at some stations, Derby, Leicester and Normanton for example, passengers had to board or alight on what was normally regarded as the 'wrong' side. Many stated the futility of locking uncovered third-class carriages and some ungenerously said this was the class most needing protection against its own stupidity; the exception was the Chester & Birkenhead, which gave no reason for its strange practice of only locking, and that on both sides, the doors of its third-class stand-up carriages. Possible compromises were suggested; some wanted a law to allow left hand doors to be locked, to stop fare-dodgers, and leave right hand ones unlocked as means of escape in an accident. In the Commons Russell opposed unlocked doors on grounds of danger, quoting Huskisson's death and in the Lords a bishop went so far as to say that it was worth some physical suffering if people could be prevented from committing the moral evil of fare-dodging. Sydney Smith made fun of the arguments that locking was safer because however many notices and warnings were given, people would still jump out of moving trains; in case of accidents, if carriages fell on the left side they could escape through an unlocked door, but on the right they were still trapped and, as for the bishop's view, 'To burn or crush a whole train merely to prevent a few immoral individuals from not paying, is I hope a little more than Ripper or Gladstone will bear'.[6]

Later that month 'Etoniensis' described some of the different approaches. On the London & Birmingham you paid your fare, took your seat in any carriage you pleased, and could be accompanied on the platform by a friend or servant to carry your luggage; at the end of the journey you gave up your ticket and that was that – no official pushed you into a seat whether you liked it or not and locked you in, so whenever the train stopped you could move to another carriage if you wished. The LSW locked the outer door to prevent passengers getting out on the wrong side. The GW left the outer door unlocked; after buying a ticket you were directed to pass to the platform, where you showed your ticket to a policeman who turned back all who did not have a ticket – husbands, wives and servants indiscriminately. When on the platform you showed your ticket again, some pompous gentleman unlocked a door, let you in and relocked it.[7] 'XYZ' complained in August 1845 about the locked doors and iron bars of the Gravesend & Rochester, which were to prevent people putting their heads out in a tunnel: what would happen if the train came off the rails and into the Medway Canal, along the banks of which it ran for about 3½ miles?[8] An accident at Maghull resulted in deaths because the train had been shunted onto the 'wrong line'; when five passengers jumped out, wrongly thinking there was a danger of a collision, the doors on the 'safe' side were locked and they landed in the path of the other train.

The practice continued erratically. T. Y. Jones wrote expressing his thanks to a lady and two young gentlemen who had risked their lives by helping several of his relatives through the window of their carriage which had been turned over on its side with the door locked in an accident at Rednal on 7 June 1865.[9] Apparently some passengers had their own answer to this: next day there was an accident between Saltford and Keynsham on the GW. The carriages were locked but in the last passenger compartment there was a 'commercial gentleman, happening to have a key in his possession'.[10] Soon after 'MA' complained that a GW train went on from Swindon with some doors locked, contrary to the company's rules: they were supposed to lock doors as tickets were checked, but unlock before the train left the station, a duty often neglected.[11] Lord St Leonards sent a copy of a letter from FG Saunders, Secretary of the GW, saying it was a general rule for both doors not to be locked at same time but it was necessary at Swindon for ticket checking; on the occasion quoted, the guard, in his anxiety to keep time, had signalled the train away before the porter had had time to complete unlocking.[12] This is one of those answers that leaves this writer sympathetic towards ordinary railwaymen: he suspects that they were under pressure from managers to ensure punctuality and not censured if they took a few short cuts as long as no outsider noticed. There were press criticisms following the 1868 accident near Abergele in which 31 passengers were killed in a fire following a crash. However, according to the accident report only some doors were locked, and in no case on both sides; while the inspector said the practice should be entirely discontinued, here it was irrelevant since fire had taken hold so fast that neither escape nor rescue would have been possible.[13]

Extraordinary provision

A special carriage costing £3,000 was fitted-up by the LNW for Queen Victoria.[14] Mr Towneley of Towneley Hall in Lancashire had his private carriage attached at his local station so that he could travel to London without a change; a train thus delayed was hit in the rear by a goods and he was one of those injured on 23 March 1858. For somewhat more general use the Manchester to Leeds had a 'Tourist' pleasure carriage, glazed all round and at the top, described in the report of an accident on 12 March 1847.[15] One special provision available on most lines by 1858, according to *The Intelligible Guide*, was the provision of invalid or bed carriages for those who had to travel lying down; three clear days' notice to the General Manager of the line concerned was advised. Presumably less luxurious was the Scottish prisons' board convict carriage involved in an accident at Southgate. The treatment of convicts caused the LNW second thoughts: initially they decided to charge the same as for soldiers, provided they were supplied in sufficient numbers but then decided on 1½d per mile each, to be 'forwarded' in a separate carriage attached to the Yorkshire Night Mail.[16]

Passengers could take their own carriages and horses by train and some trains billed as first-class only contained a few second-class compartments for the use of servants in livery accompanying their employers. Mr Greg and his daughter travelled from London in a first-class carriage in 1846 while his son and a servant rode in his carriage; at Chelford, the nearest station to his home, he went to arrange for the removal of his horse-box and carriage but he and the daughter had hurriedly to retreat when they saw a goods train approaching too fast to stop. The horse-box was shattered but the horses were able to gallop off; the carriage was thrown into the air and the glass broken so that son and servant were bruised and cut.[17]

First-class complaints

Even buying a first-class ticket did not guarantee comfort. In 1839 'WA' said he had bought first-class tickets at Slough for London but when the train arrived, there was no room and he was given the alternative of going second-class with a refund or waiting for the next train.[18] Ten years later 1849 'Zeta' complained that the London & Croydon still sometimes put eight into a compartment, contrary to its promise, which was particularly unsatisfactory because some had threatened to buy second-class seasons unless the practice stopped; the threat worked briefly but the practice had begun again on 1 January, after people had bought their tickets – his letter was published on the 3rd. Later that year the SE came in for much criticism and remained a favourite target for some years. According to 'A First-Class Man' their new first-class carriages ('vans' he preferred to call them) were constructed to carry as many passengers as could be crammed in, the windows were barred so that if an accident occurred they could not climb out and if the bars were removed their width was such that anyone leaning out would hit his head against a telegraph pole.[19] The carriages involved were the subject of continuing argument between local residents (particularly of Blackheath), the Railway Commissioners and the company. In 1849 the company gave an assurance that it would set back any obstacles to give at least 18 inches clear between walls, signals and trains but a further inspection in 1851 showed this had not been done everywhere.[20] Next year 'A Traveller by the SE Railway' had gone from Dover to London first-class when the rain came through the roof via the aperture made for the lamp; at the first stop they complained and the problem was partially mitigated.[21] This company was also the target of *The Examiner* in 1854 after its spokesman, Mr Mangles, had spoken in praise of English railways, compared with French ones. Its version was very different. 'A first-class SE carriage is a small box badly cushioned, and generally dirty, in which the passengers have scant room for their legs, and are altogether uncomfortably squeezed. A first-class French Northern carriage is spacious, handsomely lined, and almost luxurious in its style and furniture'.[22] Complaints about first-class travel became much rarer, though in 1862 Lord

Malmesbury wrote to agree with others about the LSW, arguing that firsts had deteriorated: originally there were six per compartment, with dividing arm-rests, now eight, without rests.[23]

Second-class complaints

There were frequent complaints about under provision of second-class carriages, commonly ascribed to a deliberate policy of seeking to encourage as many as possible to go first-class, a theme further pursued in the chapter on unwanted companions. The GW was the most consistently criticised; as early as 1838 'L.H.' was claiming that he and three friends had booked 3/- each for a closed second-class coach but when the train arrived at Slough, there was so little provision for second-class that the seats were soon filled; thus he got into a first but was ordered out when he refused to pay extra and eventually he travelled in a second open, for which the fare should have been 2/6 but he did not get a refund.

In a letter mainly about delays on the Liverpool & Manchester a writer early in 1839 said that during the hour they were waiting on Chat Moss he inspected the interiors of the second-class carriages, which were fitted up to a style of sordid meanness and discomfort which could hardly be surpassed; there was no intermediate provision between the monied respectable and pauperism.[24] However, in May 1844 this company was reported to be introducing an intermediate class in which passengers would be sheltered from the weather and the existing seconds would be used for the third-class at lower fares.[25]

In 1843 'A Constant Reader' bought a second-class ticket for London at Brentwood. There were only two second-class carriages, both crowded, and the passengers already seated protested loudly against his admission. He asked the official in charge to find him a seat or add an extra carriage of which there were some dozens in the station but was told there was plenty of room and he must make room for himself. After further argument he was told the train was about to leave so he boarded and travelled some miles to the discomfort of himself and fellow passengers.[26] Later in 1843 'R. Needy' wrote that he was a poor devil of an author whose wits often failed to procure him a dinner. He had come from Southampton second-class, with a roof but no side protection; his clothes were soon soaked by the rain which poured and the bottom of the carriage and seats soon became pools in which they had to sit for three hours.[27]

Problems could be worse for those having to undertake a journey involving more than one company, then the case with many journeys of any length That same year 'F.J.M.' (City) claimed he had returned from the North, travelling second-class. He left Derby at 4.40 in a carriage closed at the sides; on arrival at Rugby he was told, along with others, including women, that he would have to continue in one open at the sides unless he paid first-class.[28] The next year 'R' wrote that his son had business to transact in Liverpool and took the 6 a.m. from Euston-square, second-class. He arrived at

Birmingham at 10, expecting to go on by a Grand Junction train but when it appeared about 10.30, it was first-class only and the next, at 3.15, was the same so he arrived at Liverpool at 10 p.m., making it hopeless to expect to transact business then. Three days later he had support from 'A Commercial Man' who wrote that the GW and London & Birmingham provided a more plentiful supply of trains with second-class: the Grand Junction ran two per day, the London & Birmingham seven, the GW all. He understood that the London & Birmingham directors had tried unsuccessfully to persuade the Grand Junction to change its ways. A couple of months later 'Viator' complained that some weeks previously there were advertisements from the Grand Junction that it intended to attach seconds and thirds to all trains but it had not so far happened although the last dividend had been 11% and still left a considerable surplus.[29] Even with the same company there might be difficulties of this sort. In 1844 'A Constant Reader' wrote that he went to Shoreham to catch the 11.5 train to Brighton, and then on to London by the 11.30. The latter consisted of first and second-class closed carriages and the bills said passengers could book through from Shoreham but the clerk there said he could not: they had to go to Brighton and buy again. There he found only two second-class carriages, already full; since his business was urgent, he had to pay first-class.[30]

In 1844 'A Second Class Traveller' (a poor curate) asked that the GW, which now became the chief focus of complaints, should provide more shelter, though he was not asking for soft cushions. The fare was £1 1s from Bristol; outside a coach used to be 12s. Eight hours were saved, but would they compensate for many days' illness liable to be incurred from severe cold, which was never felt going at 9 or 10 m.p.h. as badly as it was at 30? 'A Poor Mechanic' complained of draughts which partial protection and partitions appeared to make worse than if carriages were completely open. 'Censor' (a London physician) went so far as to ascribe the death of a patient's husband to a chill caught while travelling to Bath in bad weather in a second-class carriage with unprotected sides. 'Viator' described a journey he had taken on 13 November when he had travelled second-class to Bath. It had rained incessantly and in an hour the floor flooded and the occupants of seats facing the engine were drenched by water dripping down their backs as well as driving in their faces; they had tried to protect themselves with umbrellas but the force of the wind broke them and they could not get railwaymen to mop the floor until they reached Swindon.[31] In December 'A frequent traveller by GW' claimed it had evolved a simple and cheap plan for driving second-class passengers into first-class. He had taken his seat in a second and found he had sat in a pool of water; he thought it accidental so he called a policeman who was near at hand. In reply to his inconsiderate demand to be put into a dry carriage, No 90 gauged the depth of water and finding it no more than two inches, said, 'That there wet ain't of no consequence at all' and warned him to get in or be left behind. This was no empty threat since the train started and he had to leap in. At Slough, where he alighted, he called the attention of the superintendent and he caused the little not already absorbed by their clothes to be removed, 'for which unguarded act of kindness I sincerely hope the directors will not deem it necessary to supersede him.'[32]

On 20 March 1845 it was announced that the improved seconds which were to have been used throughout the GW on Monday 10th of that month would not be introduced until June 1, by which time the weather would have reduced their value. Early next year 'An Old Subscriber' claimed he had gone to Bristol in one recently used as a fish van, judging from the effluvium and dirt; as it was a wet day, the windows were closed as much as safety from suffocation would allow. The doors did not fit, the floor was covered with nearly half an inch of water, his boots saturated, and as no porter would condescend to listen to a second-class man, no attention was paid until at Swindon a passenger found the superintendent, who had it mopped up.[33] In 1848 C Anderson of Bath claimed that on a recent Friday two female servants of his were put into a second-class carriage at Bristol and passengers were forced in, despite the remonstrances of those already there, until there were thirteen, on the plea that there were not enough people to require an extra carriage.[34]

However, the GW did not monopolise complaints. In 1845 'A Second Class Grumbler' complained about the London & Brighton's approach: they failed to see that they could expand business through cheaper fares on their day tickets and better treatment of seconds. A first-class day ticket saved one-third (9/- out of 29/-), a second only one-eighth (2/- out of 16/-). A Brighton tradesman going to London for a day's business needed to start at 7 or wait until 10. The second-class carriage then in fashion was a long caravan, with transverse seats, low backs and a series of windows made to slide open, which they did of their own accord. Compartments have been removed or discontinued – 'for no earthly reason unless one can imagine the railway company in a co-partnership with all the medical men of the place'.[35] About a month later 'A Traveller', who did not specify company/ies, complained about the lack of partitions in seconds: he had three times seen hats blown off and lost.

Improvements were on the way. In 1854 *The Times* announced that the SE's new seconds were being put on the line. There were stuffed leather cushions along the seats and backs and the carriages were well-ventilated and roomy, with windows from end to end on each side.[36] Certainly complaints seem to have faded away.

Third-class sufferings

The Manchester & Leeds was accused in 1841 of deliberately making life awkward to discourage all but the poorest from using third class. Their 'stanhopes', already described, were placed where their occupants were most likely to be hit by cinders from the engine – at least two had been burnt and there were allegations of bags of soot being thrown amongst passengers and some being made to travel in wagons containing sacks of flour. It was official policy (and Wishaw had seen notices to this effect) that porters should refuse help with luggage.[37]

The dangers faced by third-class passengers were shown by an accident on Christmas Eve 1841 on the GW. A goods train, the 4.30 a.m. from Paddington also carried 38 passengers. In the middle of Sonning Hill cutting it hit earth which had slipped from its sides, the engine derailed, the tender followed and the next truck, which contained the passengers, was thrown across the line and overwhelmed by those behind. The driver and the guard in the truck with the passengers saw the danger in time and jumped clear but eight were killed (mostly stone-masons working on the new Houses of Parliament) and 17 injured; the latter were taken to Reading hospital. By the end of the year another had died and nine were still in hospital, three of them in a precarious condition. Inevitably several letters arose out of this. 'JL' complained about the general GW treatment of third-class passengers and especially the barbarous practice of placing third-class passengers between the engine and goods – generally there were not less than 100 tons of goods behind the passengers. A particularly heart-rending piece appeared on the 27th:

> Often has my heart ached when I have seen these poor creatures, some but thinly clothed, exposed to dust, fire, the inclemency of the weather and the waterspouts of the tunnels, in an open truck, near the engine, sitting on a seat that holds the water like a dish, sometimes rushing through the air at 30 or 40 m.p.h., and sometimes standing for about an hour at the different stations. Often have I observed a goods train and some goods of all descriptions nicely covered with cloths through which the water cannot penetrate. I have seen the sheep, the cattle and the very pigs placed furthest from danger, in trucks whose sides stand high above their backs and shelter them from the cutting wind: but with shame be it told I have seen my fellow creatures in the situation I have above shown, and placed there by a body of men who I imagine profess themselves to be Christians.

Even after death the third-class passenger was apparently subject to inferior treatment; on 30 December 'THR' claimed that the friends of Hands and Clee, two of the victims, had heard on Monday night that all the bodies were to be buried at 8 next morning so they started by the 5 a.m. luggage train to demand them. At Reading, they saw the bodies but were not allowed to remove them. The eight bodies were then taken into the burial ground, where Hands's body and three others were demanded. After much parleying they were allowed to remove those, the others being buried in one hole. Hands's and Clee's bodies were then placed in the train, when word came that they were not to be removed. One of those involved went off with the superintendent to Paddington, where, after seeing the directors, and after much discussion, they consented to allow the bodies to be removed. 'Such is the plain unvarnished tale, and such is the humane conduct of the GW Railway directors.'[38]

'Vindex' complained in 1846 that the SE forced passengers in after all seats were occupied, so at one time there were 50 in a compartment on the way to Dover; some of those standing were women [so some Victorian men held onto seats?]. Some thirds were uncovered and many had to travel in the open in the rain because they had not provided enough Parliamentary carriages.[39]

After Lord Malmesbury's 1862 complaint about first-class accommodation on the LSW 'Parliamentary' retorted that he should try third. Leaving Christchurch by omnibus at 9 a.m., he might (if the train were tolerably punctual) reach Waterloo at 5 p.m., having travelled 100 miles in eight hours. One day at Brockenhurst, the ordinary third was full so he was politely asked if he would travel in the luggage van but he civilly declined and was put in a second. Others had accepted the offer: there were not many boxes in the van and probably they arranged carpet bags to represent first-class cushioned seats. Later that year 'Justitia' wrote about lack of third-class trains causing inconvenience for those attending markets near Exeter and also gave the example of a maid who wanted to come back to see old friends for a day but had to stay overnight.[40]

All was perhaps not as dire as some made it out to be. 'A curate' suggested in 1852 that many now travelled third since there was little difference in comfort from the second and the 'false shame' of travelling third was now a thing of the past.[41]

Lighting and heating

From an early stage oil lamps were placed in carriages, fitted through a hole in the roof, but this was erratically done and those provided gave only a feeble light. 'A Traveller' complained about the lack in a first-class carriage of the Northern & Eastern in 1845 which was particularly troublesome since they constantly stopped between stations and passengers could not be sure whether they were on a platform or not. Even when they were stopped for a station, passengers were often forced to get out onto the ground if the train overshot the platform: one woman and her child were only just saved by the husband from disappearing down a steep bank.[42] 'ER' complained that she and about 20 other ladies were amongst those on an Eastern Counties train in October 1853 when no lights were supplied for any part of train so at Audley End in the dark many got into the wrong carriages.[43] This would also suggest that some stations were either not lit or provided with only very poor lighting.

'Vindex' arrived by the 6.30 p.m. Parliamentary from Dover in October 1846. Prior to raising fares, the SE had had a lighted lamp in each carriage of 40 passengers but now they refused to provide. One brought his own candle; he was ordered to put it out by one of the 'railway Dogberrys' but all rallied round the candle and defied the authorities. Nearly a year later 'A Poor Man' claimed there were serious dangers from locking 40 people of both sexes together in dark hole for several hours; there was also the risk of fire since he had seen a passenger produce his own candle, which could easily have set a woman's dress alight.[44] 'All in the Dark' was a working man who had to travel as cheaply as possible: on the Eastern Counties he had to grope his way into a carriage and find an empty seat by touch. Some had to stand but still at the next station a guard with a lantern popped his head in, said 'plenty of room' and others rushed in so they were packed like sheep. It was very convenient for the 'light-fingered gentry'.

Some took advantage of the dark to talk obscenely and several women said they were shocked.[45]

Change was coming, slowly. On 16 September 1854 NE third-class carriages on local lines were reported to be lit up after dark since a clause making this compulsory had been introduced into the amalgamation bill through the influence of Sunderland Corporation. Various experimenters were at work: in 1857 Mr Knapton of Albion Foundry, York, was working on lighting carriages with gas, fitting a 'gasometer' under each carriage. The GN had directed him to fit up an experimental carriage; this provided a better light and the estimated cost York to London was no more than 2d as against 1/6 for a pint of oil.[46] The pace gradually increased: Mr Newall applied his method of gas-lighting to several LY trains, a successful experiment being reported in 1861 and by early 1862 gas was being used on some fast trains from Manchester to Bradford and Blackpool and the LNW was reported to be about to try it on its Holyhead express.[47] In December it was on trial with the Scottish Central, where a train had left Edinburgh for Perth with all carriages lit, giving a clear and steady light throughout the journey. That year, the North London was the first to install it on a regular basis. In late September 1863 the Metropolitan said new carriages lighted with gas would be ready in a few days.[48]

However in October 1863 'N', who paid first-class on a Parliamentary train, complained the lamp in his carriage from King's Langley was not lit; he was not impressed with the lamps on that line, even when lit, but, 'Bad as are those red, dull, fuliginous things called lights in the roof of the carriages, they afford some measure of protection' against thieves and ruffians. Next year 'Post Tenebras Lux' wrote that he was a regular second-class passenger on the LNW and never had a lamp: a friend going with children to North Wales asked for one at Rugby and was refused on the grounds that they were never given to second-class but when he said he would write to *The Times* one was speedily brought.[49] As late as 1868 'Viator' complained that for the previous year trains on the Mid-Sussex line had not been provided with lamps; there were fewer tunnels than when trains were routed via Brighton but there was the long Gatton Tunnel.[50]

Footwarmers, flat containers filled with hot water, were provided for first-class passengers at a small charge from the 1850s at some stations. There was much variation. In 1870 'A frozen traveller' complained he had travelled first-class from Brighton at 8 a.m. on Christmas Eve, with snow on the ground, but was not able to obtain one. The letter immediately after, from William C Ward-Jackson of Greatham Hall, near Stockton-on-Tees, said his thermometer had on a couple of days registered 12 and 13 degrees (presumably Fahrenheit) as the maximum temperature and at one point had been down to five degrees. Then 'K' wrote in praise of the Eastern Counties, 'which does not stand so high in popular favour': about three weeks earlier he had omitted asking for one on starting to Norwich but when he asked at Bishops Stortford, the first stop, one was instantly supplied and it was refilled with hot water at Ely without charge. Samuel Plimsoll M.P. wrote that he had travelled one day from London to Peterborough with a plentiful supply of footwarmers but next day (from Peterborough to his home near Sheffield?) none had been available and at every station the stamping of feet when the train stopped had been deafening. He had put forward a Bill to make companies provide such comforts but it had been defeated; he put this down to the power exercised by railway directors in the Commons – or was this as ill-thought-out as his famous, but totally ineffective, one on the loading of ships.[51]

Chapter 7: LADIES

From the outset some special provisions for ladies were made. Many early time bills stated that female attendants were stationed in the ladies' waiting rooms, though inevitably there were class differences; in 1847 'D' complained that there was no waiting-room at Newton [Abbot] for women travelling second-class.[1] Many who wrote to *The Times* seemed to think that ladies needed male protection, though perhaps they were often brought in to make complaints seem less selfish. Typical was the line taken by 'AB' whose 1840 complaint referred to the filthy state of the carriages of the London & Greenwich which deterred nearly all respectable females from using them.[2] There were, however, some instances of the chivalry preached by so many. One passenger, a third-class one at that, died in 1862 when he was leaning out of a carriage window as he tried to close the door which he had previously opened to free a lady's dress caught in it; his head hit against a bridge between New Cross and Forest Hill. On the other hand, some lady writers made it clear that they had travelled extensively on their own, or with female companions, in other countries, including the United States, as well as this one, and thus did not need protection.

A regular feature was requests for separate carriages for ladies, often linked to the need for some form of communication between passengers and railwaymen. 'A Barrister' had been alarmed the previous Friday in 1845 by the screams of a young lady standing on the steps of a carriage; she was with difficulty prevented from throwing herself off. Fortunately, the train at once stopped and she was removed from the carriage in which she had been alone with two men in the garb of gentlemen; the nature of their conduct was not revealed. Later that year 'C' described a Wednesday journey by two ladies who had taken day second-class tickets on the Norfolk Railway from Harling to Thetford. When they were returning in the evening, a few minutes after the train had started, two ruffians climbed over from another compartment and committed a gross and brutal attack, making their escape at Harling.[3] There was erratic provision: as early as April 1847 it was reported that the GW had arranged for one 'body' of a first-class carriage to be reserved for ladies travelling alone; how uniformly this happened in practice is not known.[4]

Some requests were clearly made from an ulterior motive. In 1861 'Paterfamilias', who had recently travelled 400 miles with his wife, two children, both under two, and their nurse, always first-class, complained about the lack of Ladies' compartments. Only on the broad gauge could he get one – at Bristol the Midland laughed at him for such a request and at Liverpool he was almost insulted. Anyone who travelled with children knew the trouble and annoyance they caused so it would be to everyone's interest to have carriages set aside for women, children and their attendants. [And leave fathers to travel in peace?][5]

A particular type of nuisance was described by 'Observer' in 1846 who described a set of ruffians and swell mobsmen who infested second-class carriages within 10-20 miles of London on return to town in the evenings. He and a friend were assailed on trying to enter a carriage on the 7.40 from Esher by shouts of 'no room' but they saw several empty places and insisted on entering, suffering coarse and insulting remarks from several well-dressed men. They worked out that the plan was to prevent any but ladies from entering, thus separating them from protection. One elderly gentleman, his daughter and a lad were allowed to enter the next division and had to endure most offensive conduct and language and many respectable-looking women were also compelled to listen to loud and indecent conversation. The custom was to distribute themselves in gangs or knots and if 'disappointed of plunder' to avenge themselves on passengers, especially female, by obscenity and insult. They were not drunk; it was calculated behaviour.[6]

More serious incidents were reported. A woman was killed when she jumped from a train on the York & North Midland on 18 January 1853 and it was 'supposed' she had done so to avoid an assault; the Board of Trade summary said a coroner's jury had given a verdict of manslaughter against a man, but the outcome was not found. Mr John Langdon, of independent means, residing in his own property at Upton, was prosecuted at Tiverton; on 3 November 1856, Miss Jane Baker, a respectable young woman, was in the same carriage and he insulted her in a most scandalous manner. She threatened to give him in charge when they reached Tiverton and he replied in the most disgusting language. She went home in tears and her father went to the railway authorities who tracked down the culprit and a witness. The magistrate imposed the maximum penalty under the company's bye-laws – a fine of 40/- for interfering with the comfort of other passengers plus £5 for common assault and costs.

In 1865 several cases came to notice. At the beginning of the year, William Whitehead, 36, of Wexham Rectory (presumably a servant), was charged at Marylebone police court with an indecent assault on Mrs Richardson in a GW carriage between Langley and Paddington – he had put his hands on her legs below her dress while drunk. Mrs Richardson had not wanted to proceed since she had heard he had a decent wife but the GW insisted and he was committed for trial; in the same court Thomas Daley was fined 10/- for being drunk in a GW carriage, so mere drunkenness was clearly seen as a minor offence. Once the prosecution had outlined the case, Whitehead changed his plea to guilty to save Mrs Richardson from having to give evidence – there were hints that rumour made his actions much worse and he wanted to put the picture straight. He was sentenced to two months in Newgate, fined £25 and on release would have to find his own surety of £200 and two others of £100, to keep the peace for 12 months. After the next case he was called back because the Common Sergeant had been advised he had no power to order him to Newgate so he would be sent to the House of Detention at Holloway instead.[7]

In 11 July of the same year 'HS' was on the 1.10 pm from Waterloo. After passing Kingston he saw a lady hanging by one hand to the outside handle of an adjoining carriage door when the train was travelling at about 40 mph. He had leant outside the carriage as far as he could, secured her by her wrist and pulled her onto the step of his compartment. She swooned and he had to hold her dead weight, fast losing his own grip, while the train travelled at least five miles until the guard's attention was drawn by people they passed. Her explanation was that a man was attempting to take liberties and she preferred jumping out, heedless of the consequences, to staying with him. At Farnborough he insisted on the man being given into custody. This seems highly unlikely melodrama but on 12 July *The Times* reported that at Aldershot Petty Sessions, Henry Nash, a middle-aged man of respectable appearance, a yeoman living at Hawley near Farnborough, was charged with indecent assault. The complainant, aged about 20, was accompanied in court by her father, the curator of Winchester Museum. Shortly after she had entered a second-class carriage at Waterloo the defendant joined her and tried to force a conversation but another woman entered, and the attempt ended. At Surbiton the other woman got out, the man moved to the seat opposite and questioned her again. Miss Moody went to the window, found a hand go down from her shoulder to waist, and felt her dress lifted in front. Then she opened the door ... and the rest of her story was as HS, now identified as Mr Stokes, military boot-maker of London and Aldershot, had given it. The case was dismissed, on the technicality that it needed to be tried by Surrey magistrates. On 30 July the case at Surrey Sessions was reported. Nash claimed he was afraid she would jump out and was trying to restrain her, but he was found guilty of common assault and sentenced to nine months in prison with hard labour. At the end of the year Henry Dibbles, merchant's clerk of Gainsborough, was charged at the magistrates' clerk's office at Retford with indecent assault. Miss Godson, a farmer's daughter, was travelling from Sheffield between 6 and 7 in evening, with no lights in the carriage, when he came close and put his hand up her clothes; she complained to her mother, who was with her, and the nuisance stopped but they mentioned it to the authorities at the next station. The Bench fined him 40/- plus costs.[8]

However, some were clearly not convinced that all allegations made were true. An official report from the Government Inspector of railways included: 'Gentlemen passengers, as well as railway officers of all classes, constantly refuse to travel singly with a stranger of the weaker sex, under the belief that it is only common prudence to avoid in this manner all risk of being accused, for purposes of extortion, of insult or assault'. The paper's comment: 'This may one day be thought a singular indication of the manners and customs of the English in the year of grace 1865'.[9]

Chapter 8: SUNDAY TRAVEL

THE RAILWAY MORAL CLASS BOOK
by the Bishop of London,
copied from *Punch* by *The Times* 15 August 1844

Morals for the 1ˢᵗ class.

The morals prescribed for this class are the same on all days of the week. An act which is moral on Mondays, Tuesdays, Wednesdays, Thursdays & Fridays, is moral also on Sundays. The reason is, that this class employs the best tailors, eats the best food, drinks the best wine, in short lives the best; and lastly and especially, pays the highest fare of all the three classes. Moreover, being accustomed to amuse themselves all the six days of the week, it would be cruel to deprive them of recreation on the seventh; and having little or no business on any day, they have as much business to travel on Sunday as on any other day.

Morals for the 2ⁿᵈ class.

It is not, strictly speaking, quite proper for persons of this class to do the same thing every day; so that a perfect system of morality would prohibit them from Sunday travelling. Many of them go to Holborn and the City for their clothes, dine upon two courses, and cannot afford hock, claret and champagne, or even good port and sherry. However, on the whole, they are pretty respectable. Thus, for the transgression, the rigid rule of right may be relaxed, and they may be permitted to travel on Sundays; but they are to understand this permission as a sufferance merely, and their conduct in availing themselves of it is by no means approved of.

Morals for the 3ʳᵈ class.

For this class of people to travel on Sundays is a heinous crime. They are meanly clad and live upon a coarse kind of food. Toil and hardship are their portion during the week, and enjoyment on the Sunday would make them discontented with their lot. The third class of railway passengers is formed of the inferior classes, and not being respectable, no respect whatever should be shown to its inclinations. Its fare is nothing like an atonement for the crime in question. The Legislature, therefore, has acted very improperly in compelling Sunday trains to run third class carriages; and the statute, if possible, should be evaded.

The main early issue concerned the propriety of Sunday travel for pleasure; there seem to have been no protests against the use of railways to take people to church on that day. John Taylor of Middlesbrough was granted leave at £10 per year to run a coach to Stockton and back on Sundays and Fridays so that he could take his family to worship and it is difficult to see what other purpose could have been involved in Sunday horse-drawn services on the Stockton & Darlington run for some time after steam had taken over on weekdays.[1] The earliest passenger service on the Hartlepool Railway & Docks line began in 1836 when Messrs. Wilkinson and Walker were given permission to run a passenger coach between Hartlepool and Haswell on Sundays for 6/- per day.

Some took Sunday observance very seriously; probably the advent of railways simply gave extra impetus to an existing desire to stop all Sunday activities, except church worship. In November 1839 a meeting in Bristol was held to found a Society for the Promotion of the Observance of the Lord's Day, to work in alliance with similar societies throughout the country. *The Bristol Times* devoted nearly two columns to this, the bulk of which was devoted to stressing the duty of Sunday worship; only towards the end were specific targets mentioned. Then there were no half measures: the aim was 'the discontinuance of all Sunday travelling by railway, steam packets or other conveyances; to procure a better regulation of inns and beer shops; to prevent the desecration of the Sabbath by the reading of Sunday or other newspapers on that day; to stop all mail-coach travelling, and to abolish the system of delivering letters all over the country on the Sunday; in short, to prevent the prosecution of any mercantile or commercial transactions, except where the most absolute necessity for them existed'. 'A reasonable company' was stated to have attended though there was some reluctance to put money into the project: what was presumably the national version was stated to be £500 in debt and at the end a collection at the door raised £8 13s, the proceeds of subscriptions, and donations £7 19s.[2]

To some extent the issue was out of the railways' hands since the Postmaster General insisted on the running of trains for the carriage of the mails and their duty to carry these was generally written into their Acts of Incorporation. One concession was made to church-goers in that several early companies, usually forced by their enabling Acts, ceased running during the hours of divine service. The Liverpool & Manchester initially ran no trains out of either terminus between 10 a.m. and 4 p.m. Later this habit mostly concerned short lines in the London area – such breaks would have been impractical on lines of any length. Thus *Bradshaw* for September 1846 showed that the Greenwich branch ran every 15 minutes but on Sundays there was a gap from 11 a.m. to 1.15 p.m.; the Croydon and Blackwall lines observed similar restraint.

Although the general view seems to have been either support for Sunday travel or indifference, there were implacables who persisted in raising the issue. At the half-yearly meeting of the London & Birmingham on 21 February 1838 Mr Sturge resigned as a director when his motion for preventing Sunday travel was defeated by 7,486 to 3,621.[3]

A Special General Meeting of the Edinburgh & Glasgow voted in favour of Sunday travel on 25 February 1841 though shortly after the minority was reported as intending to take court action, based on old Scottish laws.[4] On the first day of Sunday running at about 7 a.m. the Rev. Mr Burns appeared in front of the station at Haymarket (then the Edinburgh terminus from Glasgow), sang a psalm and commenced a sermon, which was not concluded until about 9. It was not known whether this had any effect on intending travellers but it did collect a crowd of 200 – 500; either he or someone of similar opinions preached at 5 p.m. The second day of Sunday trains passed off similarly: the total number of passengers carried was 841.[5] The same gentleman was in Newcastle on 29 August 1841 when a Sunday excursion was run to Carlisle and back: his placard and handbill claimed that the reward for Sabbath Breaking would be to be taken swiftly and safely to hell. He seems to have had as much effect as previously since the Brandling Junction almost immediately after started running Sunday trips from Gateshead to Monkwearmouth Baths and upwards of 2,000 travelled on the two trains on 19 September.[6]

Some opposition continued to be shown. In 1846 a petition against 'the increased and awfully increasing profanation of that Day, by Traffic on Railways' was circulating in Weston-super-Mare, with the evident approval of the editor of the newly-established local paper.[7] The advertisement section of the July 1848 *Bradshaw* contained a three-page item headed *The Railway and the Sabbath* which took the form of an alleged discussion in a railway carriage, culminating in a demand for strict Sunday Observance: 'a young man' claimed that 'Cheap Sunday trips were the ruin of the working men in Lancashire, two to three years ago. The men who were thus led away, were seldom at their work on Monday ... and though they had extravagant wages at the time, very few laid past anything, and they and their families are now in poverty and misery'. There were even attempts to see accidents as Divine Retribution for Sunday Travel. 'The More Haste the Less Speed' wrote in this fashion after an accident to a Sunday special to Newmarket.[8] However, a writer to the *Southport Visiter* of 22 July 1848 welcomed the prospect of a railway since the town's reliance on road and boat links had hindered its prosperity over the previous two years, but his pleasure was mitigated on hearing that some inhabitants were raising a petition against Sunday trains. He accepted they should not run during the hours of divine service but 'how is the shop-keeper, or the man of business, confined till late on Saturday to visit his wife and family, who may be staying here?' 'How is the poor working man, confined six days a week to incessant toil and a loathsome atmosphere, to escape from his imprisonment? ... Would they condemn him to his cellar, or confine him to the impure atmosphere of Liverpool ...?'

A meeting held in the Assembly Rooms at Bath decided in October 1850 to petition the GW against the running of Sunday excursions and agreed to collect subscriptions to further their cause. The GW was clearly not impressed because soon after an excursion from Frome and Westbury took about 2,000 to Bristol and Bath on a Sunday and it was planning 'express' excursion trains. The next Sunday one out of London took 600 to Bath, Bristol, Cheltenham and other places and on the same day

1,350 went to London from the west country. *The Times* described the continuance of these trains as 'a practical reply on the part of the GW to memorials from Oxford, Cheltenham, Bath and other places against Sunday excursions' and on the same day it reported that excursions to Brighton had averaged 600-800 during the last six weeks. It was clearly in the companies' interests to run these trains since the same items had said that a Monday excursion from Bath and Bristol had taken 800 or 900 while the Brighton Tuesday ones averaged 400 to 500. It claimed that larger numbers were taking advantage from places where meetings had been held against them than elsewhere.[9] In the course of this, it published a copy of a letter (perhaps written somewhat tongue-in-cheek) from CA Saunders, Secretary of the GW, to the Rev RA Taylor of St Werburgh's Bristol, who had been acting as co-ordinator of complaints on behalf of the Bishop of Oxford (Samuel Wilberforce). He defended the excursions on the grounds that workers only had Sundays for relaxation and it was better that they should be in the countryside than in taverns. Some who never attended church in London had been known to go to a country church with friends. 'It has been ascertained that persons resorting to those trains conducted themselves for the most part during the Sabbath with exemplary decorum and propriety'. As will be seen later, excursionists were not all angels.

Opponents were sometimes provided with opportunities at formal openings accompanied by banquets at which toasts were drunk to all and sundry, and suitable – and frequently lengthy – replies provided: one such was 'The Church'. At the opening of the Central Somerset line from Highbridge to Glastonbury in 1854, the Bishop of Bath and Wells was let loose. After a potted history of religion in England since the Tudors he concluded by saying that he had been asked to present a petition, in which he heartily concurred, 'that the sanctity of the town of Glastonbury might not be desecrated on the Sabbath day by the running of cheap excursion trains'. Apparently cheers greeted this – was there much agreement? Just relief that the Lord Bishop had finished? Or had they reached that mellow stage where they would cheer anything?[10] Similar futile actions were mentioned from time to time. A meeting of the town council of Selkirk in July 1856 condemned the local company for running trains on Sundays.[11] Company half-yearly meetings gave opportunities for opponents to try their luck. One regular was Captain Young, an LBSC shareholder, who regularly made his views known; in January 1858 he managed to get ten votes in favour of his motion to ban Sunday trains but in July 1865 he did not even get a seconder.[12]

Late in 1862 there was a mass attack on Sunday excursions when it looks as if a newly-appointed Archbishop of Canterbury felt he had to be seen to be doing something. On 30 December the text of a memorial from the Archbishops and Bishops of the Church of England to directors of companies running Sunday excursions was published. Sunday excursions were contrary to God's will, tempted many to make Sunday a day of dissipation and thereby tended to demoralise them and their contacts. They were anxious to secure the working classes the relaxation they needed but believed it could be done by cheap week-day travel. Railwaymen were deprived of their day of rest, 'which they all require[d], as accountable beings, with a view to preparation for eternity' and the more efficient, physically and morally, they would be for railway service. Sundry other religious groups added their support. Three days later 'A labouring man' pointed out that one who was married and had a family dependent on him, could only take them into the country on a Sunday. Did the bishops follow their own precepts? – did they expect a servant to light a fire before they rose on a cold Sunday? Cook breakfast for them? A coachman to get them to church? There was even an organised counter attack: a memorial in opposition was circulated and 'extensively supported' and a public meeting to protest against the bishops' attempt to diminish the innocent enjoyments of the working classes was planned for Cambridge Hall.

By then opposition to Sunday travel was really a cause lost beyond recovery and railways even advertised services designed to allow English people Sunday pleasures not available at home: the LBSC issued a notice for Dieppe Steeplechases, Sunday August 19 1860 which involved trains to Newhaven 17th and 18th and fast steamers to Dieppe. On 5 September 1863 a piece copied from the *Scotsman* said that the previous Sunday three passenger trains had run each way on the Edinburgh and Glasgow section of the North British with many passengers. Behaviour was orderly and the only symptoms of anything like disorder had arisen out of the denunciations of three street preachers, who collected a large crowd about 6 o'clock. The crowd was clearly not with them; at first they treated it as a joke but when a preacher got rather personal about some of onlookers, he was jostled and his hat 'ill-used'. A few years later *The Cardiff & Merthyr Guardian* said that 'Some years ago a few honest, but impetuous, individuals tried to stem the current of Sunday travelling'. To try now [in 1867] would be madness as the current had grown into a torrent. Merthyr was then 'tolerably deserted' on fine Sundays 'and the attendance at churches and chapels rather scant' as large numbers took themselves off to enjoy the mountains or visit friends in other parts of Wales. In July 1869 a Sunday excursion was advertised to Arundel and Littlehampton-on-the-Sea from London Bridge and Victoria at 8.25, calling at New Cross, Clapham Junction and Croydon; return 8.20 p.m.. Tickets 3/6, children 2/-, were obtainable at the offices of the National Sunday League, an opponent of the Sabbath Day observance faction, and at stations on the morning. His Grace the Duke of Norfolk (the premier English nobleman) would allow excursionists to go over his magnificent grounds while the Arundel band would play in the park.

Sunday travel was not always pleasant, largely it would seem, because of its popularity. The picture is sometimes of railways and their staff overwhelmed by the sheer masses confronting them; in some cases they did not dare to try and impose some sort of order but sought to get the hordes off their hands as fast as possible. 'JB' complained in 1850 about a Sunday journey on the London & Croydon. He and his wife had first class tickets at Sydenham to join the 8 o'clock train but there were no railway staff on the platform although many passengers were waiting. All pushed for seats regardless of class and he was just handing his wife to a first-class seat when it was taken by force by two young men while the guard took no notice. They were left behind and it was even worse with the next train so he saw the clerk who said he could not help and told him to look out for the guard. He saw him (No 27) deliberately filling firsts with second-class passengers and he was told that if he could pull people out he could have seats; they were left behind a third time. Next time they were luckier – they were shown to a seat after a third-class passenger, who at least had the decency to put out his pipe for his wife's sake. He was also sorry for the woman with a baby who had been there since six, continually pushed out of way, and a shop-girl afraid she would lose her situation through being late [presumably she was living-in at a store which imposed a curfew on employees]. 'A constant Traveller' came from Gravesend on a Sunday in a first-class carriage and was annoyed by the admittance at all stations of thirds, three of whom were intoxicated and used the most disgusting language. At London Bridge he enquired and was told it was the result of it being a Sunday and there not being enough third-class carriages.[13]

Similar complaints were made in 1851. In July 'Viator' had accompanied two ladies from Wandsworth to London the previous two Sundays. They bought first-class tickets but the station was so crowded that the first time they waited for four trains to pass without being able to get on, the second for five – and then they were hustled into a third-class carriage, being told if they waited for a first they would be there all night. The following month 'GDS' and some friends took places in a first-class carriage at Gravesend on a Sunday evening to return to town. At Greenhithe the carriage had 20 in it though built for 18 and at each station an attack was made to get more in but they held the door to prevent them. At Woolwich the station-master had allowed about 500 onto the platform; another attack was made and the station-master asked them to let more in to stand but they refused. Following another attack he (GDS) received a blow from an umbrella which drew blood. When the tickets were being taken officials were asked to let out one who had fainted but no notice was taken and he was carried out, not yet recovered, at London Bridge 20 minutes later. 'An Annual Ticket Holder' (Lewisham) had tried to get his friends onto a Sunday train on the North Kent line but after waiting some time amidst a perfect mob they were obliged to give up because trains were arriving already crammed to suffocation, quite unable to take up a single passenger.[14]

Finally, though the Scots are usually regarded as far stronger opponents of Sunday travel than the English, the criminal element there seems to have had no such scruples. In 1856 John Begg of Lochnager Royal Distillery Balmoral, complained that kegs of whisky were regularly tampered with, up to five gallons being drawn off and replaced with water – Sunday was the worst day for this.[15]

Chapter 9: MUCH SUCCESS AND A FEW FAILURES

Early novelty resulted in many items giving some idea of the numbers carried. The Stockton & Darlington, essentially a coal-carrying line, gained a mention for carrying no less than 158 passengers on one day in April 1826, the whole work being accomplished by two horses.[1] The directors of the Liverpool & Manchester were satisfied with their early traffic: their line opened fully to paying passengers on Friday, 17 September 1830 and up to Saturday 25th 6,104 passengers, average 763 per day had travelled and in October 1831 it was stated that since opening about 460,000 passengers had passed between the two towns.[2] The Glasgow & Paisley carried 36,864 passengers (average 85+ per trip) during the first 18 days it was open in 1840.[3]

Holiday time attracted large numbers: the Greenwich, then only open as far as Deptford, carried 62,802 over Easter 1837 (Friday to Tuesday, inclusive), and 67,270 Whit-Sunday to Wednesday, the largest number on the Tuesday. Most trains for special events are treated in a later chapter but a few are noticed here to show how numbers grew. In 1839 upwards of 30,000 were conveyed on the Monday for Greenwich Fair, the trains making 400 journeys in 20 hours to carry them all. Next year on a Paisley celebration day nearly 4,000 passengers were carried on the Glasgow line although canal boats were also crammed to suffocation and the Renfrew Railway and the Clyde steamers had a full complement. Shortly after, Paisley races were the attraction: the Joint line carried 14,700 on the two days and 17,000 came from Ayr and by the Renfrew Railway.[4] On Thursday, 14 July 1842, the 6 a.m. from Paddington carried the 'immense and unprecedented number of 2,115 passengers!', for an agricultural meeting at Bristol.[5]

Race meetings were the biggest revenue earners, with royal events close behind. In June 1844 the receipts of the GW on Cup day at Ascot, were a record so far: £4,100+ from 16,766 passengers, 229 private carriages and 551 horses. The previous day, nearly as many went to and from Slough for the Grand Review before the Queen, the Emperor of Russia and the King of Saxony; apparently the company was 'lamentably unprepared' for so many.[6] Numbers increased as the network grew: in 1857 36,500 passengers were passed through Chester Railway Station on Cup Day by the GW, LNW and Birkenhead lines without a single accident or unusual delay and in 1860 200,000 similarly cleared the station.[7]

There was a resurgence of interest in numbers after the opening of the first section of the Metropolitan. On a Sunday in 1863 38,000 passengers were carried and the interval between trains had to be cut from 15 to 4 minutes. The number on Whit Monday 1865 was 83,440, the largest for one day since opening and the total for the Whitsun week 370,843, while another 85,000 were carried over the Hammersmith & City.[8] In 1870 the numbers using the Metropolitan and associated lines had risen to 292,528 for Good Friday and Easter Monday and 216,573 for Whit Monday. Traffic in the provinces was understandably lighter but amazement was still being expressed: on

27 December 1866 a piece from *The Swindon Advertiser* said traffic on the GW had been unprecedented as on the Saturday alone 25,000 or 30,000 passed through Swindon station.

However, success was not uniform. The East & West Yorkshire Railway's half-yearly report in February 1850 said passenger revenue was so disappointing that trains had been reduced to two each way daily and Sunday trains discontinued – they had run at a loss from the start.[9] In June of that year the Duke of Devonshire opened Chatsworth for a day to visitors from London, though only 47 availed themselves of the offer. The train left Euston at 6 a.m., first-class only, at 15/- per passenger, the earliness of the hour being blamed for the poor response.

Accident reports sometimes provided evidence of low numbers: one on the Hull & Selby in August 1840 said four of the first seven carriages were empty and there were none at all on a Preston & Wyre train in December. In January 1843 the only passenger on the 5 a.m. Leeds to Derby train, who had three carriages to himself, was killed at Barnsley when his train was waiting in the station and was hit by a luggage train whose driver had failed to see or obey a signal. The 6 p.m. express from Leeds to Manchester on 22 August 1845 consisted of two first-class carriages and three of its eight passengers ended in Leeds Infirmary. Even at the end of the period there were examples of poor patronage: when the morning train from London arrived at Warrington on a Thursday in January 1869 there was no-one going on to Liverpool so it did not proceed; thus the London papers arrived in Liverpool about 3.30, and the delay caused some fear that an accident might have occurred.

One wonders how some stations managed to pay their way. Clevedon was the only station on a Bristol & Exeter branch line. An accident there on Christmas Eve 1852 was put down to the unusually heavy traffic on that day – 19 passengers had arrived on a train which was then shunted through a wall, demolishing a shed, because of wrongly set points; the only casualty was the unfortunate driver, bruised by falling bricks. There were seven trains each way daily, averaging about eight passengers but owing to the sudden upsurge in numbers, the policeman in charge of the points had been too busy helping the station-master and the porter (who was busy with parcels), the only other staff there, to pay proper attention to his own job.

From a very early stage some stations were closed. Indeed, some stations had only ever been intended to temporary: one such was Denbigh Hall, though at one stage the London & Birmingham did consider retaining it.

'The wooden offices are closed; the wattled stabling and greensward stable-yard, lately so crowded are empty; and the tarpaulin-roofed 'hotel' no longer offers the night traveller the attraction of a cheerful bonfire and a boiling kettle without and a ham sandwich and hot cup of tea within. All is tenantless and the train shoots by unheeded. The glory of Denbigh Hall is departed'.[10]

Other early casualties did include stations originally intended to be permanent: Bridg(e)ford and Coppenhall on the Grand Junction were closed in September 1840[11] and Winwick Quay, near Warrington, followed later that year. Much chopping and changing of minor stops on the Liverpool & Manchester occurred as alternatives to poorly patronised ones were tried. Several on the Eastern Counties had short lives in the 1840s; presumably traffic did not come up to expectation. Its successor, the Great Eastern, had a purge in 1866, when five stations were closed on 1 August: Bilney, Magdalen Gate, Redenhall, Starston and Eastrea had between them taken about £227 in a year while costing about £196 to run.[12] The GN built a station at Skellingthorpe, between Lincoln and Saxilby, in 1865 to serve those patronising Mr Footitt's manure works; three years later the works closed and so did the station.[13]

The West London Railway opened from the Willesden neighbourhood to Kensington on 27 May 1844, providing connections from the LNW and the GW, and was satirised as Mr Punch's line from nowhere to nowhere. It closed to passengers at the end of November. Its returns showed that from 1 July to 30 November (inclusive) it ran 1,452 trains and was rewarded with 2,208 passengers (209 first-, 1,999 second-class) and 1 dog (counted as third-class); the total revenue was £60 8s 9d. It was reopened to passengers by the LNW, without any passenger connection to the GW, on 2 June 1862, to a new station at Kensington, when the Exhibition there, forerunner of the South Kensington Museums, gave it a reason to exist.

There were also fiascos resulting from experiments with atmospheric propulsion. Brunel's on the South Devon line have been frequently chronicled elsewhere. Similar problems beset the London & Croydon, where 'A Passenger' described a journey in April 1846: two engines had taken his train, of about 18 carriages, as far as Dartmouth Arms (now Forest Hill), where one engine was replaced by the atmospheric and the other left to help it and he claimed that the five miles on to Croydon took 23 minutes, the performance being so poor that after two or three trains had been run this way they reverted to full locomotive haulage. [14]

Chapter 10: SOME SPECIAL SERVICES and STATIONS

Royalty

Queen Victoria was a frequent user of railways and various extra precautions were taken when she travelled, as an occasional caustic critic of normal railway practices pointed out. Her first railway journey was from Windsor to London on the GW on 13 June 1842; thereafter, until her husband's death, she used her travels as a way of letting herself be seen by far more of her subjects than any previous monarch. She (or at least her Household) paid for her travel, though whether the bills really fully covered all the expenses is not known; did the companies building special carriages treat them as prestige advertising? She had firm ideas about speed and trains carrying her were supposed to keep to 40 m.p.h.[1]

A number of special stations were built for her. One, about 600 yards long and costing under £8,000, was on a branch from Gosport into the Royal Clarence Victualling Establishment It was first used by a special which arrived from London at 10.45 on 13 September 1845 carrying cabinet ministers to a Privy Council held at Osborne House; it was apparently far from complete because in December it was reported that an elegant reception-room would be erected there.[2] Another was provided at Nine Elms, near Vauxhall.

Her trains sometimes used lines not available to the public. In 1865 she visited Germany, leaving Osborne on 7 August. The rail portion of the journey started from her private station at Gosport, leaving at 2.45, and she arrived at Waterloo at 5.30, where an SE engine took over, hauling her over the connection to the SE, and along the North Kent line to Plumstead, reached at 5.53, whence she was shunted into the grounds of Woolwich Arsenal along a single line laid during the Crimean War for carrying supplies; it had not been used much recently and was severely tested, a slight defect soon being remedied.[3] Clearly they still had misgivings for prior to her return various officials wanted to dissuade her from returning this way since the condition of the rails made it 'exceedingly injudicious to risk the chance of an accident'. However, they failed, probably because of the now-widowed Queen's obsession for privacy. Orders were given to police at the gates to bar the public, even officers in uniform; they travelled with blinds drawn through the Arsenal and along Plumstead Road and workmen were displeased at not being allowed to see her train pass.[4]

Particularly elaborate arrangements were made for the Prince of Wales's marriage to Princess Alexandra when she arrived in London on Saturday, 7 March 1863. He and his suite left Bricklayers Arms about 11 a.m. to collect her from Gravesend and came back about 2.10 p.m. Since Bricklayers Arms was then only a goods station much tidying up and erection of stage scenery was necessary: 'The day before painters, florists, upholsterers and a whole army of workpeople had possession of the Station' and managed to convert a heavy goods station 'into a perfect triumph of decorative art'. The married couple later left the GW station at Windsor for Reading, where an additional platform, handsomely decorated, had been provided nearby for spectators. Then they went on to Basingstoke and Southampton, where the train was late, which was hardly surprising since at each station mentioned they had stopped for presentations of loyal addresses from local dignitaries, some of whom waffled at length. At Southampton they were taken along the dock lines, lined with schoolchildren, direct to the ship.[5]

Private individuals

Lesser travellers could hire their own trains. The Whitby & Pickering offered this as early as 1835: parties could hire a horse-drawn 'train' from Whitby to the beauty spot at Beck Hole. From July to September 1842 the London & Greenwich table in *Bradshaw* carried a note saying anyone wanting to return from Greenwich after the last train had left at 10 p.m. could engage a special on application to the inspectors on duty; the price was fifty shillings plus one shilling (then the first-class fare to London) per passenger above fifty. The LNW was charging 5 shillings per mile for its specials in 1842; it also issued an order that they should be limited to 30 m.p.h. including stoppages except in extraordinary circumstances after the recent 'great speed' reached by a special used by the Duke of Buckingham in his journeys to and from Wolverton; had His Grace offered any inducements to the driver?[6]

Parties of the well-to going to race meetings made much use of specials. The Eastern Counties clearly wanted to impress the sporting world when they ran one for the Newmarket Craven Meeting; they undertook to run from Shoreditch, then their terminus, to Newmarket in four hours, which presumably would have included road travel from Chesterford, then the nearest station to Newmarket, on Sunday 12 April 1846. Two specially chosen engines were provided to draw, in order, five horse-boxes, a second-class carriage, three firsts, three more seconds and two trucks. The deputy chairman, secretary and locomotive superintendent travelled with them, on the footplates. The passengers included Lord and Lady Chesterfield, Lord E Russell and 'the elite of the sporting world'; the second-class carriages were for grooms and porters to help with the extra traffic. Unfortunately the second engine came off the rails, though the only human casualty was an injured guard.[7]

Family needs lay behind cases revealed in accident reports. Mr Cooley, a spirit dealer of Glasgow, was anxious to go to Edinburgh: he arrived at the Glasgow terminus of the Edinburgh & Glasgow between 5 and 6 p.m. on 19 May 1845 to find the next train was at 7.30 p.m. so he ordered a special. An engine and one first-class carriage were accordingly provided and sent off just before six but lost so much time that it was overtaken and run into by the 7.30; Mr Cooley was killed. On 8 January 1851 Mr Haviland urgently wished to go to Cambridge several hours before the normal service began to attend his father's death-bed; his train hit a stray goods wagon at Ponders End, killing a railwayman.

The Vale of Neath's advertisement in *The Times* of 5 April 1852 offered covered first-class and open excursion carriages, specially adapted for viewing 'the justly celebrated scenery of this valley and its tributaries'. Parties taking at least 12 tickets could have an excursion carriage attached to either of the ordinary trains, or a special engine upon giving due notice. Special trains could be stopped at the passengers' option; it is not clear whether the stop was just for a longer look at the scenery from the carriage or whether it would have been long enough for a ramble – since the ordinary traffic amounted to two trains each way, this could have been fitted in.

In 1855 the Stockton & Darlington advertised that it had built a handsome saloon carriage which could be hired by the day for pleasure parties. It was presumably added to scheduled trains since the charge for 24 miles and back was only £3 3s for up to 12 passengers.

A number of individuals had stations of their own, with varying rights of stopping trains; some were provided thus, some had opened as public stations but were kept for private use after they had failed to pay their way, some later became public. One early one was built for Hudson at Londesborough Park. Elsewhere they included one at Fallodon (or Falloden) for Lord Grey and several in Scotland, Castle Grant and Crathes Castle being examples; Sir Watkin Wynn had his at Glan Llyn in Wales.

Markets

Special provision for market people included extra trains on market days, extra stops on timetabled services or even trains on lines lacking a regular passenger service. Two early horse-drawn private colliery lines provided such services. The Brampton Railway was a network of services from Brampton to Lambley on Lord Carlisle's colliery line which had connections with the Newcastle & Carlisle at Milton (alias Brampton Junction) at the western end and the Alston branch at the eastern; in 1838-9 it was carrying about 2,000 passengers per month.[8] The Aberford Railway by 3 March 1837 was providing a market day service from Aberford to Garforth where it provided a connection with Leeds & Selby trains.[9] 'A Coach & Cattle Carriage' from St Helen's Auckland and Shildon on Wednesday mornings was advertised by the early Stockton & Darlington.

The earliest Liverpool & Manchester timetable carried a note that the last train from Manchester would leave half-an-hour later on market days (Tuesdays and Saturdays) and a GW notice in June 1838 said a train from Maidenhead would in future leave at 7.30 instead of 8 a.m. for persons attending London markets. By the end of 1840 the Hull & Selby was offering special tickets to second and third-class passengers, allowing them to travel from Selby by the 9 a.m. on Tuesdays and return free by the 3 p.m. from Hull. These were clearly popular: one witness claimed 400 travelled on one from Hull and in August 1841 they added an extra, market, train which left Hull at 4 p.m. Soon after extra stops were added to one train each way, market days only, at Broomfleet, Wressle and Crabley Creek; the first two eventually became ordinary stations but the last seems never to have been so served.[10] The Chester & Birkenhead offered a 'Market Luggage Train' on Wednesday and Saturday mornings from Chester at 6 a.m., returning from Birkenhead at 6.50 p.m.[11] The Byers Green branch in Durham carried passengers only on Saturdays in the 1840s and for some time after. The 1858 *Intelligible Guide* shows that the Morayshire was offering half-price returns from Lossiemouth to Elgin for 'Women with their fish, &c.' Four passenger carriages were attached once a fortnight to a luggage train from Yeovil to enable farmers to reach Salisbury market earlier than otherwise would have been the case; it was involved in a collision between Wilton and Dinton on the LSW in 1863.[12] A goods train left Peterborough at 2.30 p.m. and on Saturdays three or four passenger coaches were attached for the convenience of Holme and Ramsey market people. One day in July 1865 it left with about 100 passengers; a goods engine went on the loose without a crew, caught it up and stove in the last coach, where 40 or 50 passengers were injured, though all but seven were able to go on.[13]

Butchers were a particular group sometimes provided with specials. General Pasley wrote on 15 November 1844 that the Board of Trade had no objection to the Eastern Counties taking passengers by goods trains leaving Bishop Stortford at midnight and Colchester at 1 a.m., returning in the evening, for butchers and graziers attending Smithfield market. A service was offered in the 1850s for the New Metropolitan Cattle Market: most were directed to use Caledonian Road a few minutes' walk away but at one stage a special ran from Windsor LSW to the Cattle Market station in Maiden Lane and returned from the Cattle Siding there. The Newcastle & Darlington Junction provided one, of a single second-class carriage, at 5 a.m. from South Shields to Newcastle; in 1844 it was hit head-on by a stray engine.[14] An ordinary train from Bolton made a special stop for them at Windsor Bridge, near Salford, on Wednesdays and there in 1846 it was hit by a train from Bury; the butchers had already alighted from the last carriage, which was completely destroyed.[15] There was a fatal accident at Ordsall Lane on 23 March 1863 where a special carriage was attached to the 4.30 a.m. goods to Liverpool on Mondays for butchers.

Stoke Canon, near Exeter, received stops on market days ten years before a station was opened there; timetables in the local paper showed a Friday service to Exeter 1852 to 1856 and one to Tiverton from 1853 to 1856.[16] Oddly, two places of the same name appeared in *Bradshaw* served this way for the first time: Llangybi near Lampeter on the GW for markets and fairs in 1869 and Llangybi near Pwllheli on the LNW for a Tuesday only service next year.

Sometimes the demand on market days caught the authorities out. A train from Burntisland to Perth on 20 October 1848 contained seats for 114 passengers and was so full that at Newburgh two third-class passengers were put into second-class carriages and virtually no space was left. At Abernethy, the next stop, 150 third-class passengers, and a few others, were waiting; since no spare carriages were held there, somehow they were all crammed into the existing carriages and luggage-vans and two railway officials who were on the train transferred from first-class to the engine, though the driver repelled others who tried to get onto it. Before they could reach Bridge of Earn, where no doubt there would have been even more waiting, they were derailed by a broken tyre; the overcrowding caused most of the injuries since those hurt were in the luggage-vans and on the engine.

Funerals

By the middle of the century many London churchyards were literally overflowing, a danger to public health and offensive to sight and smell, so cemeteries were created outside London. The Brookwood Necropolis Railway ran a special train for its cemetery's consecration on 7 November 1854; the cemetery came into use six days later and the service was still operating at the end of 1870. Trains carrying coffins and mourners ran from a special station near Waterloo and at Brookwood there were separate Northern (Nonconformist and Roman Catholic) and Southern (Church of England) stations.[17]

Much shorter-lived was one at Colney Hatch, served from its own station at Kings Cross. A train for the consecration ran on 10 July 1861 and it opened to funeral parties next day. Initially it operated daily but the service was rapidly run down: from 1 August it was Mondays, Wednesdays and Fridays, from 14 February 1862, Fridays only and from 31 August 1862 Sundays (now allowed for working men's funerals) and Wednesdays, with occasional variations. After 1 January 1863 only occasional trains ran, the last known one on 3 April 1863, though it has been suggested that it might have operated again during the cholera epidemic of 1866-7.[18]

Chapter 11: GENERAL EXCURSIONS

Introduction

This morning the railways of the kingdom will disgorge, as usual, their countless swarms of excursionists at every terminus where novelty or amusement is to be found. The power of attraction is not confined to the Great Exhibition alone. Just now all England is on the move. ... The Crystal Palace secures a share, but only a share, of these extraordinary migrations. Windsor, Cheltenham, Southampton, Dover, the ports, the dockyards, the watering places, the universities, cathedral cities, manufacturing towns, every spot, in short, containing or promising an object of interest, is opened to visitors at a few shillings a head. Englishmen are beginning to live on railways like Chinese on rivers or Dutchmen on canals. ... Nor does our locomotion any longer restrict itself to trips of a few hours. The system of return tickets has been so rapidly developed that a man can frank himself for weeks together. Seven days is the period now commonly allowed for London. The South Eastern and South Western lines offer a month or more for Paris; the Lakes of Killarney are set for a fortnight, and the Scottish Highlands at half as much. Even the secluded regions of Scandinavia are now brought within the sphere of commercial speculation, and the Eastern Counties offers attractive excursions to Denmark, *via* Lowestoft and Hjerting. All this, too, be it remembered is over and above the usual amount of voyaging among the wealthier classes of our countrymen. The squares and terraces of the west end, the inns of court, and the houses of Parliament, dismiss their annual rovers as before; but the fancy, as well as the faculty of travel, has now struck wider root, and half the nation is on the rail. Leader, *The Times, Monday 18 August 1851.*

Excursions now-a-days are all the go, and it is a good thing that it is so. Our mining population, in place of hanging off their time about the fields, or worse still haunting the public houses, get up their band and have an excursion. The town is suddenly enlivened on a Monday forenoon by the military march of some of the bands belonging to our fellowmen of the collieries. ... A party of our townsmen the other day, impelled, we suppose by the spirit of the times, took an excursion to the Lomond Hills, *via* Blairadam and Kinross. Kinross is now accessible by railway, not only from Dunfermline, but, we may say, from London or the Land's End. Who would have been so hardy as ten years ago as to have prophesied such a result in so short a time, or such a result at all?

Item headed 'Dunfermline', copied from the *Fife Herald*, by the *Kinross-shire Advertiser* of 8 September 1860.

This chapter covers services that took passengers for leisure and enjoyment with no stated exact purpose; those to specified events are kept for the next chapter, with the exception of a few early ones included here to show how the idea developed. Typically, 'excursions' provided return fares at 1½ times the ordinary single, but this was not a cast-iron rule. Some even ran at higher than usual fares, especially those for the most important horse-race meetings where demand was so great that companies could exploit it fully. While most use was made by people going to attractions not available at home, those who had moved in search of jobs could also make brief visits to friends and relatives left behind.

The Liverpool & Manchester ran what is often described as an excursion the day between its formal opening on 15 September 1830 and its full opening on the 17th but full fares were charged; one train each way was run mostly for members of the Society of Friends attending their annual conference at Manchester though others could use it. At the beginning of October sightseers were taken from Liverpool to see the Sankey Viaduct in the train used to carry the Duke of Wellington at the formal opening, charging 5s return instead of the normal 8s. In May 1831 it let a private organiser take a party of 150 Sunday school children from Manchester to Liverpool and back for one-third of the usual fare.[1] Before it opened to the fare-paying public the Bodmin & Wadebridge 'treated about 150 of the Inhabitants of the latter place with a ride to Bodmin and back, in their waggons, drawn by the locomotive engine in September 1834. ... a band of music was placed in one of the waggons, and enlivened the party by playing favourite airs'.[2]

Widespread provision of reduced fares trips originated in the North East. In 1839 the Whitby & Pickering offered them from both ends to a bazaar held at Grosmont to raise funds for church building on 7 and 8 August. Next year, at the suggestion of the Mechanics Institute, the Newcastle & Carlisle offered cheap tickets for the Polytechnic Exhibition and on 14 June 1840 it ran the first known Sunday excursion, to Carlisle; about 320 are supposed to have travelled. Eight days later the Leeds Mechanics Institute ran a trip to York and on 9 August a second Sunday excursion took about 1,250 to Hull in a train of 40 carriages. Shortly afterwards the Newcastle & North Shields let the scholars and teachers of Gateshead Fell National School go at half-price to Tynemouth.[3] The Midland Counties ran one from Leicester to Loughborough and back for a temperance fete at ½d per mile for the return journey on 5 July 1841, organised by Thomas Cook, who would become known worldwide.[4]

As long as a line carried the minimum number of Parliamentary trains, others could be run without restrictions. Thus open trucks with basic, perhaps temporarily fitted, benches were sometimes used; with fares at less than 1d per mile many were happy to go for the day. Gladstone's Act helped because it freed these from passenger duty though previously some had used subterfuge to evade what, at one-eighth of a penny per mile regardless of class, was a considerable burden: they had halved their liability by charging full price one way, letting travellers come back free.

However, things did not always go smoothly. The first excursion from Oxford to London arrived so late that it had to return immediately and one from Leicester to York took nine hours on its outward journey; passengers were able to walk as fast as it was going and some spent an hour nutting in a wood when it stopped completely – the engine lacked the power needed to pull a heavy train.[5]

The main crop

Excursions continued until well into autumn: in 1850 the LBSC ran its last on 24 November and in 1854 the SE's last excursions ran Sunday and Monday 5 and 6 November, with other companies acting similarly but by 1870 they ended about a month earlier. Sundays and Bank Holidays were the big excursion days but many also ran on weekdays, so there was clearly a larger section of the population with leisure and money enough than many popular versions of Victorian life would suggest; Christmas Day was also an excursion day. Some were clearly aimed at the better off but even before regular holiday weeks many workers were able to manage the odd day to take their families on some treat for which they had saved. They seemed to take extended breaks after Bank Holidays: reports in the press referred to numbers travelling in Easter week and Whit-week. It seems that the first Monday in September was treated by many as a holiday, as was Michaelmas Day; on the latter day in 1842 a special train went from Bristol to Paddington with 700 or 800 who carried little luggage except a 'few goodly geese as presents to friends'.[6]

The gradual introduction of mid-day closure on Saturdays began in Manchester in the 1840s with banks, warehouses and public offices; others followed, including some in London in the 1850s. Employers could be helpful in other ways: one of those who died in the Nine Elms collision of October 1840 was a servant, who with another in the same employment, had been given a holiday to visit Hampton Court. Many Taunton tradesmen agreed to close their shops on Wednesday 7 June 1854 so that their assistants could go to Bath for the opening of the Bath & West Show.[7]

The poorest would not have been able to afford much, if any, excursion travel though there were occasional charitably arranged trips, especially for children, and Sunday School trips were sometimes subsidised by donations from richer people. The *Halifax Guardian* in August 1844 described one being organised: the aged, infirm, poor and really needy were to be treated to an early morning trip to Fleetwood on a Monday when there would be a good mid-day tide so many who seldom saw beyond their own cellars or street ends would be able to enjoy fresh air and sea bathing. Tickets made up in packets of about 40 for £1 would be offered to ministers of religion and other benevolent persons, for distribution to the really poor.[8] In Burnley it was the practice for Sunday School organisers to take their charges away for at least one of the days occupied by the horse and pleasure fairs thus removing them from 'the scenes of drunkenness and dissipation inseparable from the yearly fair of a large manufacturing place'. In 1852 the Church of England party went to York, the Wesleyan Methodists to Goole; each train carried about 1,000. That same year a 'Juvenile Excursion' from Taunton to Weston-super-Mare (1s children under 12, 1s 6d adults, in covered carriages) was advertised.[9] The Sunday Schools of Berwick filled 38 carriages with 700 children plus 400 adults in 1861: at 9 a.m. the children marched to the parish church for an address by the vicar and then processed to the station, accompanied by the Volunteer Flute Band. At the other end, refreshments were provided at Warkworth Castle before they separated; the majority visited the castle ruins and the Hermitage. Later there were races, cricket and other recreations before they returned home, reached at 8 p.m. Typically, the distance travelled (about 35 miles each way) was modest but doubtless it seemed impressive to those involved.

The early trips reaching the press were those that impressed by their size, as if some prize was offered for the most monstrous excursion. In August 1840 the longest train 'perhaps' ever known went along the Midland Counties from Nottingham to Leicester, arriving at about 12.30. This was the return visit by the committee and friends of the Nottingham Mechanics' Institute to the Mechanics' Exhibition of Leicester and was made up of four engines and 67 carriages, carrying nearly 3,000 passengers, most of whom were well and respectably dressed; the Duke of Rutland's band welcomed them and they left for home about 7.[10] The following month an 'immense' train ran from Leeds to Sheffield at reduced fares on a Sunday. The company in its innocence had let several firms have tickets to sell at 3/- and nearly 2,400 were sold. All turned up and threatened to tear down the station unless the contract was honoured. They were supposed to leave at 8 but it took until 9.30 to marshal the train – 63 carriages and four engines and reached Sheffield about 12; their return started about 6.45 with five engines and 73 carriages. Because of approaching darkness and the addition of extra carriages, progress was slow; at Woodlesford they were detained about an hour through lack of water for the engines (one had to leave the train, go to Leeds to fetch water and come back with it) so it was nearly 11 when they reached Leeds. There was a great bustle whilst they were in Sheffield and many inn-keepers had extra refreshments ready; another aspect of these early excursions was also mentioned – they were something of a spectator sport and 'vast numbers watched the passage of the train'.[11]

In 1844 the north did its best to retain the trophy for longest trains, though in the process the potentially dangerous nature of these monstrosities was revealed. On Monday 2 September one of about 170 carriages and 5,500 passengers left Sheffield for Hull and arrived safely (the Board of Trade report said, more believably, that four trains carried this lot). On the return some climbed onto the carriage roofs when the trains were going slowly, though before they had left Hull all had been cleared (temporarily).

At Swinton, about 12.30 a.m., a coupling on the first train broke, some carriages ran back and were hit by the second causing a minor shock which hurt no-one inside but was enough to dislodge some from the roof: one was killed and several injured. They soon set the record even higher: Thursday 12 September experienced an 'UNEQUALLED' train which ran in four sections to Hull, involving 10 engines and 250 carriages with 7,800 passengers from Leeds and Castleford. In the crush, a mother with a small child dropped her ticket and was nearly trampled as she tried to find it; it was some time before she could be rescued, frightened but uninjured. The infant was taken by its father to Hull in the special and the mother, who had lost her ticket, was permitted by Mr Thackray, the head station-master, to go free by the 10 a.m. ordinary train to join them.[12]

The excursionists of that era were a hardy breed. The Preston & Wyre ran Sunday excursions to Fleetwood and on 17 August 1845 more than 1,000 were packed into 21 open carriages. On leaving Preston they were hit in the middle by a train from Lancaster, whose line had to be crossed on the level. Two wagons were upset and the 80 or 90 people in them were thrown out but these immediately clambered into other carriages and as soon as the line was cleared they went on their way; only when they reached the coast was it realised that one man had a broken thigh.

Even economic difficulties could not dampen their appetite. In 1848 a number of European countries, including France, suffered revolutions. England faced various Chartist protests, some of which involved riots, making authority fear possible revolution here too, though in England the worst disturbances were in manufacturing districts, not the capital. On a Saturday in June people from Liverpool and Manchester took a trip to London which filled 54 carriages, of all three classes and on the following Monday nearly as many went from Liverpool and Birmingham. This information was given after an accident at Crewe on the intervening Sunday: by a supreme irony a train carrying troops to Manchester and Liverpool to help suppress disturbances there was hit in rear by an engine drawing empties which had been used by the excursionists, injuring a number of soldiers and destroying all the regiment's drums.[13]

The Brighton line was extremely popular: on Easter Sunday 1844 upwards of 7,500 travelled. The first down train contained 35 carriages, drawn by four engines and it arrived in Brighton at 12.20, instead of the usual noon. Three days later it was reported that excursion tickets issued from Monday to Wednesday were 5,720. Whit-Monday saw a similar effort when a train left at 8.30, having been delayed by nearly half an hour owing to the immense number of passengers. It started with 45 carriages and four engines and was joined at New Cross by six carriages and one engine, at Croydon by the same again. There were great worries at Brighton as 1 p.m. passed without its arrival so a pilot engine with a director on board was sent to find them and came back about half-an-hour later, heralding its arrival. It was closely followed by the Mail made up of 16 carriages. Earlier in the morning the Carpenters' Benevolent Society, 980 in number, had arrived by special train – 33 carriages, three engines. The first two ordinary up trains were also very large; the first had 22 carriages. Altogether 5,000 or 6,000 travelled on the London line and nearly 3,000 on the Shoreham branch.[14] The combination of the public's enthusiasm for these trips and the company's lack of experience in handling large numbers caused problems. *The Times* of 20 August described another extraordinary Sunday train which left London with 46 carriages holding 1,710 passengers, the whole ½ mile long. As early as 6 a.m. the office doors were literally besieged; the train was due to leave at 7, but owing to the scarcity of carriages, they had to add firsts, thus causing a delay. It reached Brighton at 11. Nearly 300 were left behind and most, to avoid complete disappointment, paid the regular fare by the 9.30. Next day 'E.W.T.' wrote:

> ... from an early hour the doors of the terminus were besieged by parties of people apparently determined for once in their lives (if no more) to visit Brighton. The moment arrived for the opening of the doors – the rush was tremendous, all crowding one upon the other (women at the risk of their lives) to secure good places. 20 or 30 are admitted; the doors are then closed until those inside shall have passed (at the rate of one at the time) through the check turnstile. The doors are again opened and another rush follows, and the same is over and over again repeated; at a certain time the train starts without any intimation to those waiting outside. ... Still the public are admitted as before, and find when they get inside that they have the option (instead of half fares) of paying full fares, or finding their way out ... ; many were, therefore, compelled to pay for their excursion about treble the amount they had expected; while others, who could not afford to do so, were compelled to submit to great inconvenience and disappointment.

They seem to have learnt from this because on the last day of the Brighton Sunday excursions matters were much better arranged. London-bridge was literally besieged by nearly 3,000. At 7 they began sending passengers off in batches: the first 700 in 25 carriages with three engines, immediately after another 500 in 20 carriages and at 8 a monster train of 40 carriages, containing 1,000, with 6 engines. All returned by 10 in evening in two monster trains without accident.[15]

The Board of Trade decided some sort of restraint was necessary and it sent a circular saying excursions should be divided into parts, no more than two engines with each. However, once a line had been passed for opening, its role was only advisory. Thus at Whitsun next year it was reported that as early as 7 a.m. the approach to London Bridge was a source of much confusion owing to the numbers waiting for excursions. The 8 a.m. to Brighton had 44 carriages with three engines and extended nearly half mile, with nearly 4,000 passengers.[16]

The passion for excursions had clearly caught on for in May 1845 a list of those coming up was published. The London & Birmingham, GW, LSW, Dover [i.e. SE] and Brighton companies were expected to send trains to London in the following week, as were the Hull & Selby and Midland from Leeds, York, Newcastle and Durham. On the

Liverpool & Manchester and Manchester & Leeds lines cheap waggons had been organised for Sunday Schools, the latter proposing to convey whole Sunday Schools from Manchester to Wakefield and other places in waggons at 6d per head, teachers 2/6 in seconds. The Manchester & Bolton would run cheap trains every 15 minutes to races on Kersal Moor. There were pleasure trips to Fleetwood for steamers. The Manchester & Birmingham had undertaken to carry members of clubs, charitable institutions and schools to Alderley and back at 6d each, parents and friends of children 1/- and would also run trains to Chester races. The Glasgow & Ayr would run specials to races at Eglinton Park. The Newcastle & Carlisle would convey passengers to Gilsland, Naworth Castle and Carlisle. The Chester & Birkenhead would concern itself with Chester races.[17]

Records continued to be broken by the year. In Whit-week 1850 the LNW carried 13,000 'holyday' excursionists between Liverpool and Manchester and 1,300 from Manchester to London. Pleasure traffic on lines out of Birmingham was unprecedented, being nearly 100,000. The Midland took 50,000 over its lines on Whit Monday and Tuesday.[18] Towards the end of September *The Times* issued a number of end of term reports. Upwards of 1,500,000 had been enabled to visit different parts of the country. On Sunday 22nd the GW ran to Windsor, Reading, Oxford, Bath, Bristol and Clifton [road connection provided?]; the SE from London Bridge to Gravesend, Margate, Ramsgate, Dover, Folkestone, Tunbridge, Brighton, Hastings, Portsmouth, Guildford, Reigate, Epsom, Croydon etc [with help from the LBSC?]; on the Saturday morning a special had started for Paris via Folkestone and Calais, to return Wednesday evening; the LSW ran to Portsmouth, Southampton, the Isle of Wight and Salisbury; the Eastern Counties to Cambridge.

The Great Exhibition did not claim all the patronage in 1851. *The Builder* claimed that provincial excursions were 'swelling extraordinarily, both in number and magnitude':

> Think of a single train with 3,000 excursionists! Such a train, comprising ninety-eight carriages, the other day conveyed the poor, hard-working, dust-breathing, close-confined cotton-spinners from nine or ten miles at [= within ... of?] Preston on a life-giving trip, through the fields and villages, to Liverpool, by Bamberbridge and Lostock. ... what life-giving medicine can compare with a light heart in pure air – could it only be taken in adequate doses regularly once or twice a day with a little nourishing food.

Perhaps the Liverpool of that era was not the most health-giving of places; however, the general sentiments made sense.[19]

Even if things were usually now managed better at the London end, there could still be shortcomings elsewhere. 'Scrutator' was on an excursion train on a Monday in August, which was supposed to leave Farnham at 6.50 a.m. and return from Waterloo at 7.30 p.m. It arrived tolerably punctually but on their return they were kept waiting at Waterloo for half-an-hour without explanation. At Guildford, where they had to change, no engine was ready to take them on so they reached Farnham at 11 instead of 9.30 and had some had 15 miles further to travel. This was not unusual: on a recent occasion a special excursion from his neighbourhood had carried nearly 1,000 and placards had promised closed carriages since it was known that many children would travel. They were kept waiting at Guildford, then sent down in sheep-pens and luggage waggons in less comfort than animals would have enjoyed.[20]

A cheap excursion from Southampton to London was advertised for a Monday early in September, due to start at 6 a.m., and return that night. At 6 upwards of 3,000 were assembled before Southampton station but the carriages had not arrived from London and the crowd was kept outside until they did, at 7. The doors opened and the crush was such that station windows were broken, several injured and a great number of hats, shoes etc lost; numbers of women fainted and children were in danger of being crushed to death. A large number of Southampton tradesmen and others had allowed their servants the day off to travel, paying their expenses. A large posse of 'maids of all work', dressed respectably, each with a little basket of provisions for the day, was amongst them; many had their clothes torn.[21]

An example of the effect on smaller places was provided by Kinross where excursions became a regular feature of life. On 24 July 1860, the day after the July Fair, upwards of 400 left at 5.30 a.m. on the Kinross-shire Railway, accompanied by the Kinross Instrumental Band; this was despite the rival attractions of a cattle show at Cupar and an alternative excursion on the Fife & Kinross to visit the grounds of Nuthill and Falkland. Soon after the town was visited by an excursion from Dysart when upwards of 200 spent the greater part of their day rambling around the grounds of Kinross House, kindly thrown open by Sir G Graham Montgomery, while others took advantage of the judicious arrangements of Mr Marshall, tacksman of Lochleven, to visit the castle famed for its association with Mary, Queen of Scots. The railways concerned were praised for their smooth running of these trips. [22]

By the 1860s companies had settled into a pattern that meant that throughout the summer a generous selection of seaside and other obvious pleasure places, near and far, were accessible. One May regular was provided by the LSW, which told the world that the chestnut trees in Bushey Park were in full bloom and providing an amazing sight; the nearest stations were Hampton Court and Teddington. There was an increase in notices concerning places of historic interest, including some stately homes. In 1861 the LCD offered excursions in covered carriages every Sunday to Sole-street (for Cobham Wood), Rochester (for the Cathedral, Castle Ruins, and Medway) and Chatham from Victoria for 2/- return. Five years later on a cheap excursion from Kings Cross for Nottingham Races on 17 July the GN provided a stop for passengers at Bottesford for visitors to Belvoir Castle; passengers presenting railway tickets (for the same fare as

Nottingham) would be admitted to the Castle for 3d and refreshments would be available at the nearby Belvoir Inn. There was also a trend towards ever more ambitious offerings. In August 1861 the SE combined offers for Deal and Walmer Regatta (26th) and Dover Regatta (27th) with one for the installation of Lord Palmerston as Lord Warden of the Cinque Ports (Dover 28th). The GW surpassed this in 1862 with an Eleven Days' excursion to the West of England, leaving Monday 18 August, which would allow people to visit the Royal Western Yacht Club Regatta and Volunteer Fete and Fancy Fair at Plymouth on 19th and 20th, All England Eleven cricket match at Plymouth 21st to 23rd, Torbay Regatta 22nd and Dartmouth Regatta 26th.

Some were clearly aimed at those of lesser means: at Easter 1851 both the LSW and GW offered open-seated carriages, attached to all trains, to Windsor for 2/- return, in May 1865 the LSW unashamedly offered cheap week-day excursions for the working-class to Hampton Court and Surbiton for 1/- from Waterloo Bridge, Vauxhall, Kensington, and Chelsea and by June 1868 such notices specifically included cheap trips into the country (which seems to have meant as far as Hampton Court) for school parties.

Excursions were not confined to this country. As early as 1844 a Caledonian notice in *The Scotsman* advertised a Whitsun excursion from Edinburgh and Glasgow to London and back, allowing a choice of 5, 10 or 15 days in London for 42s in closed carriages; in conjunction with this, Mr Marcus had arranged with the SE to run an 'Extraordinary Cheap Excursion' to Paris for £1 17s 6d third-class, £2 10s second and £3 10s first. Each passenger would be 'presented with a small Book of Instructions [containing] a vast deal of information respecting the various places of Amusement in London and Paris, and also a List of respectable Lodging Houses and Hotels, with their Charges &c.' This came free in return for 'Eight Postage Stamps' – penny ones?

Not popular with all

A stream of letters to *The Times* expressed the annoyance of non-excursionists at sufferings resulting from the proliferation of excursions. In June 1851 'A Passenger' complained about late starts from Waterloo where the excuse was that were so many excursions to Windsor that there were not enough carriages, which was unfair on men who had been working in an office all day. 'A Templar' complained in July that he was 1 hour 33 minutes late at Euston through having to wait for these extra trains and 'A Traveller' had come to London by a train due at 4.15 p.m. which was punctual to Rugby but then lost more and more time and was finally stopped at Camden Town by an excursion in front.[23] 'W' left London on the evening of 22 October 1858 for Halifax by a mixed express due at 11.35 p.m. All went well until Leeds where they were informed they should have to wait for and be attached to an excursion they had earlier overtaken. As usual, it was too heavy for the engine and soon came to a standstill so the guard had to walk back to Leeds for another engine; he finally got home over two hours late. E Ackworth, MD of Brighton, had had to leave by the 8 from Brighton, for

Gipsy Hill on a Friday evening in 1861. It was due at Norwood at 9.22, giving him a connection a few minutes later but it did not start until 8.15, because it had waited for excursionist children and he missed his connection. When he complained at Norwood, he was politely told that children had as much right to pleasure as anyone; he agreed, but his errand was important and the interval before the next train was such that he had to pay for a cab to Gipsy Hill, although he had already paid a rail fare. George S Jenkinson complained that the entrance to New Street Birmingham was blocked on 3 August 1863 by eight excursion trains so the express Irish Mail, with its high-fare passengers was kept waiting for 45 minutes and missed that day's boat.[24]

Excursionists did not always endear themselves to those they visited. The inhabitants of Weston-super-Mare described those involved in May 1856 as

A horde of savages making an excursion on a civilized settlement ... a mass of boys and girls and young men and women, comprising the lowest dregs of the more disreputable neighbourhoods of Bristol, who swarmed every avenue and invaded every quiet nook; the songs of the birds were hushed by the oaths of blasphemy; the ears of innocence shocked by the accents of obscenity; the air was polluted with the smoke of the noxious pipe, puffed forth by almost infant lips; gardens were robbed; drunken boys were to be seem staggering through every thoroughfare, fights were of frequent occurrence in the streets of the town, and scenes of lewdness met the eye of day. It was of course out of the question to expect our two policemen, aided by three special constables, to be able to watch the movements of some 5,000 or 6,000 persons roving at will over the town and suburbs.[25]

Later that year Weston had better luck. About 1,300 arrived from Glastonbury on the last Wednesday in July and the next day 1,000 from Taunton and Bridgwater. The former enjoyed themselves in boating, donkey riding and strolling about the beach and on both days they were described as being of 'a very respectable class'. In between times the first excursion over the newly-opened GW line to Salisbury had taken a large party from Bristol and Bath to Salisbury, who appear to have behaved responsibly. When this stopped at Wilton, Mr Sidney Herbert gave orders that his mansion should be shown to all who wished to see it. Those who took advantage went on to Salisbury by the next train and are reported to have been chiefly interested in the Cathedral and the Chapter House.[26]

Source of accidents

There was much concern about the frequency with which excursions were involved in accidents. Theoretically there might be very large numbers of casualties, though they often went so slowly that damage was very limited; in many cases where large numbers 'claimed injury' the official returns typically say 'mostly very slightly'.

There were, though, some serious episodes that justified the misgivings. In 1861 44 passengers were killed in England and Wales through no fault of their own and 762 injured; 38 deaths and 493 injuries were the result of only two accidents, one to an excursion train at Kentish Town and one to a collision between an excursion and an ordinary train in Clayton Tunnel on the Brighton line. When two Midland excursions collided at Market Harborough the following year one died and 142 were injured out of a national total of six dead and 426 injured for the whole year. An accident to a LBSC excursion at New Cross in 1869 did not immediately kill anyone but injured 357; the total for the year was 15 dead and 891 injured.

One source was the sheer numbers involved, effectively beyond the resources of the railwaymen to cope. At Mile End at Whitsun 1846 when a vast number got out of a very crowded train, which moved on again slightly, probably from its own momentum, a woman was hit by the flap of a carriage which was down and had to have a leg amputated; there were a number of 'frolicsome holyday folks' on the platform and it was possible she was pushed. At least, Mr Rooney, the company's secretary, visited her in hospital and directed that every comfort should be supplied to her and her family.

Two such accidents were reported in the same day's paper in 1856. At London Bridge on Derby Day, Wednesday 28 May, in an attempt to control the crowds the gates were only opened for a few minutes before each train departed. Despite this more pushed through than would fit one train so some were left on the platform and as the next came in would-be passengers ran alongside holding on to door handles to be sure of a place; one lost his hold and was fatally crushed as he fell between train and platform. On the following Monday an excursion train of more than 40 carriages from Derby stopped at Leicester to pick up more passengers. Four other trains were nearly due and there were several hundred people on the platform; in the rush for seats a young woman, only married that morning, was crushed between a pillar and the train, though it was hoped not fatally.

Lancastrians' appetite for excursions often overwhelmed the LY's resources. 1852 saw two particularly bad examples of its inability to cope. On 12 July two excursions were run from Burnley, chiefly for local schools. Both were far too long for the station which could hold only six carriages but the trains were made of 45 and 35, holding about 1,000 and 800 passengers respectively, so most had to climb on from the line. The arrangements for the return were left in the hands of a porter; the first returned safely from York, but the second, from Goole, was wrongly directed into a siding. Bolton was the scene on Monday, 23 August. As a result of the late running then endemic on that line: 'there stood in an uninterrupted line, reaching back upwards of a mile from the Bolton station, eleven engines and tenders, ten luggage vans, sixty-one goods waggons, and 156 carriages holding between 5,000 and 6,000 passengers; an accumulation of traffic perhaps unprecedented in railway history.' The sequence of stationary trains was ordinary (very late), excursion, luggage, excursion, luggage (mostly timber). A sixth, regular train, ran into the back of this lot; fortunately the timber absorbed most of the shock. The eventual blame was attributed to a signalman who had left his post so that no warning was given to sixth train; this was probably a mixture of stupidity and fatigue – he had committed suicide a couple of hours later so no-one could be sure of his reasoning. There was a further serious accident on this line in 1860 when part of an excursion train broke loose at Helmshore and ran back down the slope, colliding with another excursion: 11 were killed and 77 injured. Thereafter this company seems to have improved its ways.

A major problem was the lack of engines powerful enough to cope. An excursion to Southampton in July 1850 was so popular that it had to be run in two parts. The first part was taken by a goods engine, ironically called *Rhinoceros*, not up to the job of pulling 33 laden carriages. The second train left 20 minutes later and caught up with it. About two miles beyond Woking, the driver of the second train cautiously ran his engine against the rear of the first and helped push it up the incline that was causing the trouble. Once up the gradient, the second dropped back but another incline, just before Basingstoke, again slowed the leader, the second caught up and repeated the trick, a guard at the rear of the first using hand signals to help avoid a heavy impact. Unfortunately, despite warnings, some passengers persisted in sitting on the sides of their open carriages in order to get a better view and one was thrown off between carriages and killed. Races at Musselburgh the following month were so popular that several specials had to be run: a combination of slippery rails and an incline defeated the engine of one taking 11 carriages back to Edinburgh with as many passengers as each could hold so they split the train, the engine to take on the first half and come back for the second. They failed to scotch the wheels of the rear part adequately and this rolled back, derailing against an earth bank in a siding provided as an escape road for such an event. The passengers only suffered a few cuts and bruises, further harm being prevented 'by the close manner in which they were packed'. It was stated that the passengers in the last two carriages were 'very noisy', which cannot have helped the railwaymen deal with the problem in a calm and collected manner.

Another constant was the inadequate brake-power provided on many excursions. An excursion train from Uttoxeter to Liverpool in July 1850, consisting of 22 carriages with about 600 passengers, ran away down the incline from Edge Hill and collided with the stone wall facing Lime Street. There were three brakes; it was alleged that the guard in charge of one was 'unacquainted' with the incline and the other two were not able to control the weight on their own.

Passengers' own stupidity was also often exhibited. A boy on a Sunday School excursion from Manchester to Wakefield at the end of May 1844 persisted in sitting on the 'crib-rail' of his open wagon (about five feet from the wagon's floor) while the train was stationary at Miles Platting; the jerk as the train started threw him out, breaking his leg. A passenger on the Preston & Wyre insisted, despite warnings, in standing on the side, about four feet high, of a wagon and dancing there; he was killed by his fall. On Whit Saturday, 29 May 1858, 12,000 were taken to Liverpool by the LY and East Lancashire, 4,000 or 5,000 of them from Bury and Radcliffe. Outwards they were matched to seating capacity but when they were ready to return there was such a scramble that they were allowed to get on any train and one became very overcrowded; a combination of hot weather and 'excitement' caused many to climb onto carriage roofs. The head guard went along ordering them down but others climbed up behind him so eventually the train went off with some on top; others came out through windows and doors as they went along; one hit his head against a bridge – and was expected to survive.

Chapter 12: SPECIAL EVENTS

Royal events

In 1838 the GW advertised two extra trains from Maidenhead at 6 and 7, calling at Slough and West Drayton on Thursday 28 June, for the Coronation. The London & Brighton ran an extra express (first-class only) 'during the sojourn of the Court at Brighton' in February 1842 and in the same year, the GW advertised special arrangements for trains to Slough for the christening of the Prince of Wales.

In April 1849 the SE gave notice that:

> On Monday next, the 30th inst, His Royal Highness Prince Albert will Lay the Foundation Stone of the Philanthropic Society's Chapel and School of Industry for the Reformation of Juvenile Offenders at Redstone-hill, where there is a station on the South-Eastern Railway, three quarters of a mile beyond the Reigate Station. A SPECIAL FIRST CLASS TRAIN will leave the Bricklayers' Arms of the South-Eastern Railway at 1 o'clock p.m. on the above day, calling at [New Cross; Forest Hill and Croydon] to convey passengers to the Station at the Farm School, [returning at 6.0 p.m.].

It also ran two ordinary trains from London Bridge, and a first-class special from Maidstone, Tunbridge Wells and Tunbridge would also stop at the school. The station was a temporary one, perhaps on the site of the original SE station for Redhill.

Sandhurst, whose early station disappeared from *Bradshaw* after December 1853, was revived for specials for those going to see Queen Victoria lay the foundation stone of Wellington College on 3 May 1856; the SE again ran from Bricklayers' Arms, regarded as more convenient for the West End. The LBSC advertised specials from Brighton, Horsham and East Grinstead, adding that the ceremony would be in the presence of the Court, supported by 15,000 Troops, the Guards and Two Field Batteries. The GW ran its to Twyford and all offered conveyances from station to College. A month later there were further SE specials to Sandhurst for a fete. First and second-class passengers were taken on both occasions. In 1859 the College was provided with its own station (now Crowthorne); a special ran for those going to see the Queen open the College on 29 January, a day or two before the station was opened for general use. A special went to Wokingham on 12 July 1861 for Examination Day at Wellington College and the laying of the Chapel Foundation Stone by Prince Albert. The inauguration of the Albert Orphan Asylum at Bagshot and laying of the foundation-stone of the dining-room and chapel by the Queen on Saturday 29 June 1867 merited a special from Charing Cross and Cannon Street to Blackwater, 6/- return first-class with conveyances from Blackwater to Bagshot.

Important visitors to Windsor were another attraction: on 30 November 1855 special arrangements were made for those wanting to see the King of Sardinia. Even when royalty were not present in person there was still money to be made by the railways: after the marriage of Prince of Wales the SE ran extra trains from London Bridge to Woolwich up to 2 a.m. on 11 March 1863 ('Illumination Night') and both GW and LSW advertised trains to Windsor to view St George's Chapel and certain other state rooms, open to the public, free of charge, until the following Tuesday.

In due course the Prince of Wales (later Edward VII) and his wife took over much ceremonial, often meriting specials: they presided over a Grand Review of Volunteers in Hyde Park in May 1864, opened the Fine Arts Exhibition at Leeds on Tuesday 19 May 1868, attended the Earlswood Asylum Ceremonial and Summer Fete on Monday 28 June 1869 and laid the foundation-stone of Reading Grammar School in 1870. For the last event the notices specified cheap excursions, all three classes being provided.

Other odd events connected with the Queen brought revenue. On 10 June 1865 the LSW ran a special to Hampton Court for the sale of the Queen's Yearlings and they provided an extra stop at Surbiton for specified trains to and from Southampton.

Finally, this would seem to be the place to mention an event of state importance not strictly tied to the Royal Family. The Lying-in-State and funeral of the Duke of Wellington was treated with great pomp and many companies ran specials in November 1852.

The Army and Navy

The railways were bound by law to carry the forces of law and order:

> ... whenever it shall be necessary to move any of the officers or soldiers of her Majesty's forces of the line, ordnance corps, marines, militia, or the police force, by any railways, the directors thereof shall and are hereby required to permit such forces respectively, with their baggage, stores, arms, ammunition and other necessaries and things, to be conveyed at the usual hours of starting, at such prices or upon such conditions as may from time to time be contracted ...

said an Act of 1842. Two years later this was amended. Fares were now specified: not more than 2d per mile for officers, who were to travel first-class and not more than 1d per mile for others, including wives and children who were entitled to travel because their menfolk were being sent at the government's order and were to be provided with seats, protection against the weather and 'sufficient space'. How far they were carried in special, as opposed to timetabled, trains is not known.[1] The navy was only similarly covered in 1853; from the later 1860s it had its own, private, station at Keyham, near Plymouth. Here, though, the emphasis is on the part played by railways in letting the public see the armed forces at work.

1853 was the first year much of the army gathered in one place; the government was anxious that the public should be able to watch ceremonial and weapons practice in order to overcome a long-standing hostility to the existence of a standing army in time of peace (and to paying for it). From 16 June until mid-August there were frequent LSW and GW notices for trains to view the Grand Military Camp at Chobham. The LSW mainly used Chertsey – but Woking and Staines were also possible; the GW used Windsor. Omnibus and carriage connections were available and the LSW made arrangements for refreshments at Chertsey. At some point the SE joined in, with a connection from Blackwater. The outbreak of the Crimean War created a big surge in the army's popularity and in June 1856 the LSW offered trips to Farnborough, then nearest station to Aldershot, to see the militia in camp using huts of the pattern in use in the Crimea.

Thereafter Volunteers were often in the news. The Eastern Counties offered a special from London for the Grand Review of Yeomanry Cavalry and Volunteer Rifle Corps and Sham Fight at Hyland's Park near Chelmsford on Saturday 4 August 1860. There were special troop trains direct to Hylands, which lacked a normal station, but the return was from Chelmsford and a later report said that about 3,000 volunteers were collected.[2] Such affairs became regular events and one station was even specially provided for them. On 26 October 1860 facilities were opened for Volunteers and spectators on a siding at Hightown, near Southport, which served the practice ground for the Lancashire Volunteers and included not only butts for rifle practice and competitions but also scope for the volunteer Artillery. The local press reported that refreshment tents and spectators' places reserved for ladies were established there.[3]

These events became too popular for their own good. In August 1866 a large gathering was held at York; an item describing the arrangements said the total anticipated was 100,000 so that even horse-trucks and cattle-waggons were being converted to passenger use. York station was still a terminus and could not cope so some visitors used extra facilities, at least for the return. A report implied that all arrived in good order and said much about the decorations of York for the benefit of the Prince of Wales who had inspected the troops. However, according to EG Aycliff, Captain Commanding 16th Lincolnshire Rifle Volunteers, the return arrangements had broken down. They had departed from Sidings A & B, some of the general public using the same trains; they were kept waiting in the street outside from 8.15 to 9.30 p.m. and there was such a crush that it took 30 minutes to reach the 'platform' where there was a lack of information about which trains were going where. Eventually they left at 11.30 and arrived at Boston a little after 8 a.m. – they had been due at 1.45 and many anxious relatives were waiting, unable to get any information.[4] Something similar happened at Weymouth in September 1867: 'Squash' said all went well until departure, when there was no barrier, no officers to direct, no carriages allotted to troops, and no limit to the number on the platform so the whole speedily became one seething mass of men (armed and un-armed), women and children, babies and musical instruments.[5]

Spithead Reviews were the most important Royal Navy events which brought revenue to the railways. Specials merited by lesser events included one to Southampton for the visit of the steam frigates *St Lawrence* (British) and *Feizi Bahri (= Skimmer of the*

Seas) (Turkish) on 1 May 1851, one when the Baltic Fleet was anchored in The Downs in 1855 and others for the launching of the *Edgar*, a splendid screw-steamship of 91 guns on 23 October 1858 and the Man-of-War *Ariadne* on 4 June 1859.

A Great Passenger Liner

However, it was a passenger liner, *The Great Eastern*, which merited the most prolonged attention. On 15 October 1857 the SE said it was lying at Millwall ready for launching and the best view was from Deptford; its notice of 3 November said it would be launched that morning, and proceedings were expected to continue on the 4th and 5th; from 8 a.m. and as long as necessary trains would leave London Bridge every 10 minutes for Deptford. The Blackwall offered omnibuses from Limehouse and West India Dock stations to the ship, returning to Poplar station. No record was found of how they dealt with the delays; 'as long as necessary' was a hostage to fortune since only in January 1858 did it enter the river. In December the inducement was to have a look around it before it was fitted out for sea. Next year opportunities were provided to see it: at Weymouth, including steamboats from Weymouth Quay to the ship, at Holyhead and at Southampton. Even that was not the end: in July 1864 excursions were offered including a steamship trip around it at anchor in the Medway.

The Church

An LNW notice in 1850 advertised a special for clergy attending the Meeting called by the Bishop of Oxford (Samuel Wilberforce) for Friday 22 November. 'The station' used was a temporary one, not opened to the public until 2 December, some distance out of Oxford and needing an omnibus link. The meeting, one of many called by bishops across England, was to organise protests against 'Papal Aggression' – the Pope had appointed territorial bishops for England for the first time since the reign of Mary I.

Consecrations of Bishops also earned extras. In 1862 the SE and LCD ran specials on 12 December for the 'Enthronization' of a new Archbishop of Canterbury and on 4 February 1869 for the 'Enthronement' of his successor; this merited ordinary fares, first- and second-class. The LCD advertised a special to Canterbury on 29 June 1864 for the consecration of the Bishops of Peterborough, Tasmania and the Niger and there was also a special for the consecration of an unnamed collection on 1 February 1867.

Temperance

Temperance activities created excuses for excursions. On Whit-Tuesday 1849 a temperance excursion from Exeter to Bristol arrived at Taunton accompanied by a band of music.[6] Another such, engaged by the Committee of the Temperance Society, was advertised at '*very low charges*' for 31 May 1852. It would seem the organisers were not confident that temperance alone would fill their train for they added that the Grand Rural Fete at Bristol Zoological Gardens would take place on the same day and 'The company of any respectable Person is also invited'.[7] The LCD ran a special excursion train to Ramsgate on 1 May 1864 for a 'Great Temperance Demonstration'.

The real experts at this, though, were the Cornish. A sample of that county's activities was advertised in 1859 when J. F. Basset again allowed them the use of his Park and Grounds for A GREAT TEMPERANCE DEMONSTRATION, Monday, August 1st. Trains went from Penzance and Truro and then along the Portreath branch, not normally used for passengers, allowing visitors to be taken to and from Lovely Cottage near Tehidy. All fares quoted were third-class and included admission to the grounds; they varied from 1s 8d from Penzance down to 8d from the nearest stations. The following week's paper described the event:

> There were upwards of ten thousand persons on the grounds, and the respective processions were headed by their brass bands, five in number. There were three or four platforms at various distances, from which addresses were delivered by a number of local advocates; recitations and dialogues were given by children of the Bands of Hope, and there was also a Band of Hope drum and fife band, which highly delighted visitors. There was a street of booths and stalls, with fruit, non-intoxicating beverages and refreshments in abundance ... The whole affair went off in a most satisfactory manner, there being no accident, and the fact that not a shrub was injured, shows that when a sober assemblage meet for a holiday, they know how to conduct themselves properly, and be happy on such occasions.[8]

Cultural and educational

The Great Exhibition of 1851 is generally held to have led the way in accustoming a wide variety of people to what contemporaries might well have described as 'improving' excursions. This opened on 1 May; on the newly opened Buckinghamshire line an excursion left Oxford at 7.30 on 26 May to enable passengers to have a day there but most excursion traffic only began in June and on Whit Monday, 9 June the LNW alone ran nine trains to London. *The Manchester Examiner* claimed that a labouring man from Huddersfield left home on a Tuesday night with only a few sandwiches in his pocket and a shilling in his purse after paying his third-class fare of 5s. He paid his shilling next day to see the Exhibition, ate his 'grub' in the building, drank from the crystal fountain, returned home that night and resumed work on the Thursday morning, without having spent a farthing for lodgings, food or drink in the 40 hours he was away from home.[9]

The editor of *The Times* made an outspoken attack on the companies' behaviour in this year: 'For whole days, and even weeks together, there was scarcely a train on the

GW which either started or arrived at its appointed time'. Other long lines were no better and some of the smaller worse. No adequate provisions were made, so excursionists encumbered the line, disturbed the traffic, blocked up offices, and rendered stations almost inaccessible. Locally the GW received mixed reviews. From the Taunton area, at least, the start was hesitant. An excursion on 28 May was described as a complete failure, only two people from the town joining the train, with 'a corresponding indifference' shown during the rest of the journey; the previous week's edition had predicted this on the grounds of price (27s 6d first, 21s second-class), short notice and the fatigue likely (the train left at 4.30 in the morning and returned at 8.00 p.m., tickets only being available for that day). The company perhaps learnt from this: the excursion advertised to leave on 28 June provided for a week's stay in London, at 28s first and 19s 6d second-class. Later 'a Hampshire paper' was quoted as saying that trains from Southampton were very little patronised because the fares were too high – Londoners could go to Southampton for as little as 3s but the cheapest fare the other way was 18s, 12s 8d, and 7s. It alleged that the most recent Exhibition train had carried two first, nine second, and 110 third-class passengers – but at least the LSW did cater for thirds. The train on Saturday 27 July carried 500 from Taunton but a 'deficiency of water' caused a two-hour delay, the journey taking eight hours in all. Clearly there were continued problems because there was an obvious note of surprise in an item reporting that on Thursday 11 September a train of 39 carriages, three engines and 2,500 passengers went from Bath to Paddington and back; it reached London a little before 10.30 a.m. and returned to Bath twelve hours later: 'We did not expect anything so good of the GW Directors'. The last of the series from Taunton was advertised for 4 October.[10]

In 1857 an Art Treasures Exhibition was held at Manchester from 5 May, when it was opened by Prince Albert, to 15 October; it was given its own station, served trains on the line to London Road (later Piccadilly), and provided with connecting trains from Chester and elsewhere. A Grand International Exhibition opened at South Kensington on 1 May 1862 and for this the LNW revived the passenger service, abandoned in 1844, on the West London line.

Many other cultural events merited railway help. The Midland allowed people going to Gloucester Music Festival in September 1856 to travel free on the Dursley branch a few days before it was opened to the public.[11] Other music festivals were patronised: for example at Birmingham 27-30 August 1861, Norwich 14-18 September 1864 and Gloucester 5-8 September 1865. Eisteddfods held at Chester in September 1866 and Carmarthen in September 1867 received the same attention. Other artistic events included the Hastings Great Bazaar and Exhibition of Paintings in aid of funds for the completion of Holy Trinity Church, 3-5 April 1861 and the Stratford-upon-Avon Tercentenary Festival 23 and 25-29 April 1864, for which special trains returned patrons home after each evening's performance.

The Crystal Palace provided a wide range of attractions. The LBSC opened its first station on 10 June 1854; this soon became inadequate so on 14 March 1855 they opened extra accommodation, and the SE added its High Level station on 1 August 1865. On 18 June 1856 there was a special, first-class only, from Brighton at 10.30 to the Palace direct, returning thence at 7 p.m. for the Inauguration of the Great Fountain and the Water Cascade in the presence of the Queen. There were highbrow events such as Haydn's *Creation*, with 3,000 performers on 1 May 1861 and a Handel Festival in 1865. The notices of special trains in 1866 advertised Grand Displays of Fireworks, Grand Concerts, The Royal Dramatic College Fete and a Grand Christmas Festival. One out-of-the-ordinary occasion was on 16 April 1864 when Garibaldi, whom the mass of Englishmen regarded as a hero for his actions, up to that time in vain, against Italian despots, spoke there. The visit of Sir Robert Napier on 8 July 1868 allowed the LCD to advertise frequent ordinary and special trains from Victoria to the High Level station to enjoy a ballad concert at 4, fireworks and illumination of the fountain, the Palace staying open until 11. There were also specials organised by private parties, such as the brewers' trip which came to grief in June 1869, covered in the chapter on compensation.

As ever, arrangements were not always adequate for the crowds they should have anticipated. 'M.D.' described the scenes there on Boxing Day 1861 when he had taken his children to see the pantomime but been disappointed. On leaving to return they found thousands, presumably also disappointed, packed into a corridor, endeavouring to force a way out. Each time a barrier was raised there was a rush to get out and he only saved his children from being crushed by passing them under a barrier to the police, who behaved admirably all through. They entered the corridor at 5 and escaped into the grounds through a sliding door at 7.30, having only advanced 100 yards. The heat was such that many fainted; much glass was broken to get air – the windows would not open. Every carriage in returning had double the number of passengers it should have had.[12] In June 1868 'Once Caught' complained about the facilities for getting back from Crystal Palace after Handel and fireworks when he had taken 3 hours 10 minutes over 10 miles.[13]

A couple of GN offerings would seem to qualify as instructional. On 15 March 1858 an excursion went to Werrington Junction, and other trains stopped specially there, so those interested could view a total eclipse of the sun from a point the Astronomer Royal had predicted likely to give the best view; apparently 'upwards of 1,000' took the opportunity but Nature confounded them with a cloudy day.[14] In 1860 there was an excursion to Doncaster to see the Coal Mines: 'Descend into the Mines, to see the men at work' ran the advertisement. 'This will give a new interest to [your] cheerful winter's fireside.' One wonders how the miners reacted to this invasion.

Schools were a regular source of extras, Eton being particularly well served despite the authorities' initial opposition to the railway: special trains were run from Paddington and Maidenhead to Slough for its Montem on 5 June 1838, just after the line had opened and one on 28 June took boys to the Coronation.[15] The LSW advertised extra trains to Windsor in July 1850 for the Eton Election, Saturday 27th, and Vacation Monday 29th and in 1864, for example, it provided specials on 6 June to Windsor for the Commemoration of the Birthday of George III, a procession of boats, regatta and display of fireworks. Elsewhere in 1864 the LNW provided an extra stop at Harrow on 30 June for those going to speech day and the SE a train from Charing Cross to Wellington College and back for governors and visitors to speech day, July 3, for which first-class fares were charged.

Agricultural

The annual meetings of the Royal Agricultural Society called for special arrangements. These usually involved extra trains to the nearest station but sometimes special temporary ones were provided. As early as 1842 the GW ran additional trains on 13 and 14 July for the meeting at Bristol.[16] For the Edinburgh Agricultural Show on 3 and 4 August 1848 the North British advertised that, 'Farm Servants (having a certificate from their employers that they are so) will be taken to and from Edinburgh ... in Third Class Carriages for one Fare, a Penny per mile' – presumably 'one Fare' equalled 'return fare'. In 1856 the Eastern Counties provided a complex service of specials for the show at Chelmsford 15-18 July 1856 and the following year the LSW did the same for Salisbury. Arrangements for Canterbury in July 1860 were more ambitious; the first week was for the 'trade', with the concentration on machinery, and the second for the public. The show-ground occupied about 28 acres in front of the mansion and grounds of Hales's-place, a little east of the SE station but the only carriage approach from the city, through the Westgate, was very constricted so a temporary platform was erected near the ground. From 9 July there were extra trains direct to the Show-yard station; those by ordinary trains could alight at the City or Show-yard station but all had to return from the former. The LCD opened its line as far as its rival station on 9 July, just in time. The turn of Leeds came in 1861. For this the GN contented itself with extending the validity of day tickets but the Midland's offering suggested an eclectic occasion: it advertised trains from Leeds to Armley at frequent intervals for the Great National Exhibition of Sporting and Other Dogs and North of England Royal Horticultural and Floral Society's Floral and Musical Fete at the Show-ground within two minutes' walk.

Various local events were recommended to railway travellers: a cattle and Poultry Show at Birmingham in December 1853, the Cheltenham Flower Show in June 1854, a Dog Show at Agricultural Hall, Islington, in June 1865 and the Bath & West Show at Southampton in 1868. A SE notice of 13 June 1868 even advertised a special train (first-class) 'this day' for Mr Blenkiron's Sale, Middle-park Farm. Brighton was honoured with a special fast train on 24 June 1869 for the Grand Flower Show and Fashionable Promenade at the Royal Pavilion, Brighton.

Fairs

On Thursday 9 and Friday 10 September 1841 trains made an extra stop at Netteswell (eventually Harlow Town), not yet a scheduled station, for those attending Harlow Bush Fair; this became a yearly offering. Greenwich Fair was another regular: for example, in April 1851 the SE said that while it was open trains would run every five minutes until midnight; the fare was 6d, any class, and no return tickets were issued. The SE ran a special excursion to the fete of The Ancient Order of Foresters at Tunbridge Wells in July 1854, warning that passengers with luggage would be charged ordinary fares. In September 1859 the GN offered specials for Barnet Fair, on Monday 5th and Wednesday 7th; evening excursions would be despatched in accordance with the requirements of traffic. For October 1864 the SE suggested trips to the Great Pleasure Fair at Canterbury, the Maidstone Hop and Pleasure Fair and the Charlton Pleasure Fair. Earlier that year one such occasion had not gone to plan. In June the NE was overcome on the People's Day at the great York Gala since the numbers of would-be excursionists were far more than they could carry and hundreds from the North and East Ridings could get neither carriages nor tickets. The company limited tickets issued to the number of seats available, so people in country districts came to stations to find all had been sold, Malton and Pickering being particularly badly hit.[17]

A more exotic selection of events was sometimes offered. In March 1851 the LBSC invited people to go to the Grand Fancy Fair at the Royal Pavilion, Brighton and later that year the LNW ran a special from Euston-square on Tuesday morning June 24th at 8, returning from Coventry the same evening at 7, for Peeping Tom of Coventry, the Lady Godiva Procession. This event, a triennial one, that year attracted more than 60,000 spectators to see a procession more than half-a-mile long.[18] On 19 July 1855 the Eastern Counties put on a special from Bishopsgate for [Bishops] Stortford at 10.35, returning at 11 p.m. the same day for the presentation of the Dunmow Flitch by W Harrison Ainsworth Esq., plus a Grand Procession and Fete; the return fare was 6/- first, 4/6 second, 3/- third-class and coaches and other conveyances would run to and from Dunmow in connexion with every train.

Sport

Horse racing merited most extra trains and early provision of special stations: the Liverpool & Manchester opened one at Newton Bridge, on a branch from Earlestown in 1832 and when the line from Manchester to Bolton opened in 1838 it included a station at Agecroft Bridge which seems for some years to have been used on race days only.

In 1848 an Eastern Counties train carried second-class passengers at 6/-, and third-class at 4/- to Newmarket and back (130 miles) in 31 carriages, each containing nearly 50 passengers, total 1,537, drawn by two of the company's most powerful engines at an average speed of 23 m.p.h.; the experiment was so successful that the directors determined to repeat it for the Houghton meeting.[19] This company even sought to gain publicity for itself on the race track: the fourth race on the Tuesday's programme for the First October Meeting in 1860 was *The Eastern Counties Railway Handicap*, the company adding 100 sovereigns to the prize money. Perhaps the organisers had a sense of humour – the following race was *The Hopeful Stakes*.

The big meetings such as Ascot, Epsom, Newmarket and Doncaster were invariably provided with specials, not necessarily cheaply. In 1860 the LBSC notice for the Epsom Spring Races, 19-20 April, specified ordinary fares up to 11 a.m. from Pimlico (precursor of Victoria) and 11.15 a.m. from London Bridge, single 2/3, 1/9, 1s 2d; return, not available for return from Epsom until after 7.30 p.m., 3/-, 2/6, 2/-. Special expresses would run from London Bridge between 11.30 a.m. and 1.45 p.m. and Pimlico between 11.15 a.m. and 1.20 p.m., returning between 4.30 p.m. and 7.30 p.m., during which time ordinary traffic would be suspended; single 4/-, return 7/6, no particular class of carriage guaranteed. The LSW offered similar trains from Waterloo, identical in price. The same year the LBSC offered 'Free Transit Tickets' for a fortnight for £5 (first-class only), available 21 July to 4 August, to allow travel from Pimlico and London Bridge by any special or ordinary train to Goodwood, Lewes and Brighton Races. In earlier years, when these had started from London Bridge only, they had offered the extra inducement of the use of a private entrance there by those taking the special train.

The numbers involved were such that ordinary stations could not always cope and other sites had to be pressed into use. For example, a GN notice of arrangements for St Leger Day, Wednesday 16 September 1863, said cheap excursion trains would use the Shakespeare Sidings, Doncaster, 'to prevent crowding on the platforms'. Complex arrangements were needed for dealing with St Leger specials; in 1864 they had to deal with 74 trainloads and numbers continued to increase thereafter.[20] Not all worked smoothly: under the heading 'An errant railway train' *The Times* described a return from Doncaster on St Leger night in 1858. Since there were many extra trains, several drivers unfamiliar with the routes were engaged; one gave a wrong whistle or was misunderstood by a pointsman who sent him the wrong way and he was as far south as Ranskill before he realised his mistake and he then had to go back to Doncaster for the right line towards Sheffield. All was done safely and the passengers were highly amused, giving the driver much geographical and other advice while waiting to leave Doncaster the second time.[21]

Special provision was also made for many lesser events. Taunton races in 1852 attracted 'many hundreds' on an excursion from Weston-super-Mare; they were led to the course by the Mendip band.[22] Amongst the vast number advertised in *The Times* were Crewkerne National Hunt Steeplechases (April 1866) and West Drayton Summer

Races (August 1867). As early as August 1851 the LBSC was offering special terms for Dieppe races: return tickets were available for departure by any train 23 or 24 August, returning up to 1 September.

In October 1858 both GW and LNW were advertising hunting tickets for the Oxford/Leamington/Warwick area and the Midland's notice of alterations for September 1869 included: For the accommodation of gentlemen hunting with Mr Leigh's hounds a new train will leave London St Pancras for Luton at 9.10 a.m. calling at most of the intermediate stations. In between, the GW announced that Her Majesty's Staghounds would meet Friday 7 December 1866 at Winkfield Church and a special would run at 9.30 from Paddington to Windsor for gentlemen and horses riding with them.

In 1852 the LSW put on a special to Putney and Mortlake, for the Oxford and Cambridge 'Grand Eight-Oared Match' and thereafter there were annual arrangements for the 'Boat Race'. In 1868 they offered tickets to view from Barnes Bridge at 10/- each including the railway fare to Barnes and back, by when the normal service was being suspended, such was the demand. In 1869 the same arrangements were also made for the Oxford and Harvard Boat Race on 27 August.

Regattas were also catered for – in 1859 Henley (July) and Folkestone (August). The GE was more ambitious in 1864 for the Royal Thames Yacht Club Ocean Match from Thames to Harwich on Saturday 4 June; as a bonus the steamboat *Avalon* would leave Harwich pier on the arrival at noon of the 10 a.m. from London, steam up the Swin and return to Harwich with the competing yachts (tickets 5/- extra).

A wide variety of other activities were helped. On 30 June 1851 the LNW offered cheap trips for the National Archery meeting at Leamington leaving London at 8 p.m. Wednesday, back Thursday at Leamington 8 p.m.. By 1862 this event had clearly expanded because the LSW provided cheap fares for the meeting at Salisbury from 7 to 11 July. In May 1867 the LSW advertised trains for the Gold Medal of the Royal West of England Golf Club at Westward Ho!; no cheap tickets were mentioned but tourist tickets were given an extended life. Old Trafford, Manchester, was used for both cricket and association football.

Most contentious was the help railways gave to prize-fighting, by then illegal. The railway officials played the innocent, claiming they had not known the intention – and pocketed the proceeds, which were considerable since those running the specials charged higher-than-usual prices for tickets including admission to the fights. Preparations were elaborate and companies made sure that they had plenty of their own police on hand to keep undesirables away from stations. However, this was of limited use, for a description of a fight near Fulbourne in 1848 said those directly involved, about 300, came 'from the great nursery of gamblers, blacklegs, and pick-pockets, by express trains', though it added that the fight was witnessed by fifteen hundred 'well-dressed people, artists [artisans?] and labourers'; even the referee had his pockets picked, losing his watch and purse.[23] Mostly they seem to have carried three or four hundred passengers, though some of the thirty or more carriage 'monsters' are likely to have had about 800 to 1,000. They played a cat-and-mouse game with the police, keeping the destination secret and moving to a different one if the authorities caught up with them. Apart from anything else, the practice of stopping between stations created dangers for other travellers, often increased by having one of the organisers on the footplate to tell the driver where to stop and by the provision of a second special, closely following the first.

In 1860 some correspondence from a quarterly report by the Chief Constable of Kent to the Home Office was printed. Railway directors had assured the Home Office on one occasion that the arrangements he had complained about had been made without their knowledge and they had taken steps to prevent a repeat. However, six months later a magistrate reported a special to Etchingham for another prize-fight (Sayers v Brettle) and when the police at Etchingham applied there to use the telegraph to collect reinforcements, they were told it would be occupied for some hours. The directors claimed that applications for tickets for the scheduled train to Etchingham had been so great that they had had to divide the train, running a separate portion for there because the company had to carry by regular train all who presented themselves. The Etchingham telegraph was already in use between two other stations and once it was free, 37 messages were waiting to go out [planted by fighters' patrons, no doubt].[24] The SE was not deterred: in 1861 an excursion took patrons to Strood, whence a ferry carried them to an island in the Medway. The LCD took one lot to Meopham in the same year; when police interrupted them, they moved on to continue the fight near Sittingbourne.[25] The SE is supposed to have collected £3,000 from one fight, King v Heenan, in 1863; the carriages were speedily filled, left London-bridge soon after 6 a.m. and went direct to Wadhurst, stopping in the midst of the valley. One lot that year went to the lengths of going to Wootton Bassett on the GW, returning to London, moving to the SE and ending their journey by steamer.[26]

Miscellaneous

Railway building itself generated specials. Over Easter 1848, just before the Chester & Holyhead line was opened to Bangor, excursions were run to Conway for people to see the Tubular Bridge; the Britannia Bridge later received similar treatment. In 1857 this line offered special tickets to Holyhead Harbour Works where 18,000 pounds of powder would be used to create a monster blast expected to displace 130,000 tons of rock. The LBSC ran trips on 19 September 1850 to see a 'Grand Explosion at Seaford-Cliff' when officers of Her Majesty's Board of Ordnance would spend up to three hours using twenty tons of gunpowder to blast out 'a considerable portion of the cliff'. In comparison the GW's advice that the second tube of the Royal

Albert Bridge would be floated Saturday 10 July 1858 and return tickets to Plymouth issued on the 9th would be available for return on the 12th was tame news.

The viaduct at Crumlin attracted many sightseers on Whit-Monday, 1857. It had been in general use for a few days but the local press regarded the holiday invasion as the real opening.

> Into that secluded valley, 15,000 persons, at the lowest computation, landed from the several excursion trains from Hereford, Newport, Usk, Abergavenny, Pontypool, Blaina, Tredegar, Ebbw Vale, Abersychan, Blaenavon and the surrounding towns. ...

> Train after train continued to arrive, each laden with about a thousand passengers, and on reaching the platform they were welcomed by firing from nine cannons ...

> Towards evening the trains began to re-load and return to the different towns, but we cannot say much for official arrangements. None of the trains had on them any notification of their destination, and the rush to gain seats was terrific – men, boys, and girls, and even women with children in their arms, simultaneously rushed on the stopping of the train ... and on more than one occasion, we observed the mother loose the infant at her breast to save herself – fortunately, the children were saved by falling on the heads and shoulders of those beneath, and restored after a time to their mothers. About a thousand persons filled each train in less than two minutes, and many, for want of information as to the route of the trains, were taken far from their homes.[27]

Celebratory occasions called for specials. The London & Blackwall marked the end of the Crimean War by opening Victoria Park for the day on 29 May 1856 and running trains until 1 a.m. the next morning so people could attend the fireworks display. Most companies ran specials to London for celebrations such as Lord Mayor's Day. At a much humbler level, when Silverton's station opened on 1 November 1867, the Rev HF Strangways, Rector of Silverton, sent more than 70 boys of the school at his own expense to Exmouth and liberally supplied them with sandwiches and buns.[28]

Charity was not overlooked: in 1859 the public were offered an excursion to St Albans from Euston in aid of funds for the Railway Benevolent Institution. They were tempted by the promise of a band, large marquee and amusements in a field near the station, in addition to which there would be 'Refreshments on the ground at moderate prices'.

Legal occasions received their share. In August 1854 the LSW advertised a special train every day for Guildford Assizes; the same was done for Kingston Assizes in March 1855. Politics might usefully grouped with this: a special train, second as well as first-class, was run to Cambridge for each of the polling days, 7, 8, 9 and 11 February 1856 – this would have been for the benefit of those qualified to vote for the University's M.Ps. On 28 and 29 June 1859 the LNW made extra stops at Bletchley, with a special connecting train for Oxford University voters. The increased electorate created by the Second Reform Act was probably why the SE provided an extra train to Canterbury from each direction for the General Election of November 1868.

Even disaster could be turned to railway profit. The Earl of Carlisle's Naworth Castle was gutted by fire on 18 May 1844 and on 9 June the Newcastle & Carlisle ran an excursion to see the ruins.[29] An Eastern Counties notice in 1862 advertised a trip to see the floods following the bursting of the Middle Level Sluice and Inundation the Fen near Lynn. The burst had occurred at the junction of the Middle Level Drain with the Ouse, on Tuesday 13 May and by the 15th 20,000 acres were flooded and 80,000–100,000 more at risk.

Most grisly were specials for public executions. The Bodmin & Wadebridge ran three to Bodmin for the hanging of William and James Lightfoot on 13 April 1848; reputedly about 1,100 took advantage. The LY ran cheap trains, all densely packed, to Kirkdale for the execution of Gleeson Wilson on 15 September 1849 and there was also one to Norwich that year.[30] In 1860 many went by ordinary train to see a hanging at Carlisle but the way some were turning against public executions was shown by the advertisement of an excursion to take people away from the town at a time when it would be infested with many undesirables.[31]

Overseas

The early 1850s saw the railways profiting from improved relations with France, which would soon see two long-standing enemies as Crimean allies. In 1851 there were cheap return trips to Paris for the Grand Military Fete, 10 and 11 May, when Louis Napoleon would present new colours and a 'restauration' of the Eagle would be made. Later that year the LSW provided cheap trips for the Fetes at Havre, 8 & 9 August for a regatta (including some English yachts), the unveiling of a couple of statues and Louis Napoleon's presence. In 1854, when the Crimean war loomed, the SE advertised express tidal trains and steamers, to Boulogne via Folkestone, for the visit of Prince Albert, Napoleon III (now Emperor) and the King of Belgians to the great military camp of 80,000 at Boulogne. In 1856 sea-bathing at Dieppe and an excursion to Rouen were on the programme, as well as the LSW's 'Delightful Summer Excursions to Paris (28s first-class, 20s second, including French railways and steam-packet) and in September 1858 it was the turn of a Grand Music Festival at Boulogne.

These were not confined to the better-off. A Working Men's Excursion to Paris via Folkestone and Boulogne was advertised for Whit weekend 1861. For the 1867 Paris Exhibition very elaborate arrangements were made. The LCD offered Artisans' returns from Ludgate Hill or Victoria by the evening express at 5.40, arriving Paris next morning at 7, at the greatly reduced prices of 26/8 second-class, 20/- third (the SE was then charging 60/-, 40/-, 30/-) and tickets would be available for 14 days. The LNW and GW notices said artisans with their wives and families, factory hands and other workpeople could obtain cheap returns; all required certificates from employers, the forms for which could be obtained from them. The Society of Arts started a subscription with 100 guineas to assist British workers to visit and a public meeting convened by the Metropolitan Working Men's Exhibition Committee at the Whittington Club on 8 May had many employers on the platform: they had arranged with Mr Cook for the use of a building in Paris provided they could guarantee at least 200 per week and the first batch would go in the first week in June. It would cost 30/- for one week including railway fare and lodging; a guide and interpreter would be provided free so, allowing 30/- for living expenses and Exhibition tickets, it would total £3. For men taking their wives the arrangements would be of a more private nature so it would be £3 10s in all.[32] On Saturday 8 June the first batch left London Bridge at 10 p.m. To the end of August about 2,000 men had gone to the lodgings for workmen in Paris at £3 each.[33]

Afterwards it was back to more mundane events. In 1869 the LNW and Western Railways of France advertised a tour through Normandy and Brittany in July and the LCD and SE a joint venture for Lieges Fetes in September. However, foreign travel was somewhat impaired by the outbreak of the Franco-Prussian War in 1870. The SE's special tidal train ceased running on Sunday 18 September since Paris was now under siege but the day boat continued to run from Folkestone to Boulogne. In November travellers to Metz, Sedan, Woerth and Strasburg were informed that their best route was via Brussels and the Great Luxemburg Railway since the route via Dover and Brussels continued uninterrupted.

Chapter 13: UNWANTED COMPANIONS

Class distinctions

A persistent complaint was that of having to endure the company of those felt not to be proper travelling companions.[1] In 1850 letters from widely separated areas criticised a lack of third-class carriages which meant they suffered the company of lesser beings. 'A Railway Traveller' was blunt about why he paid first-class: it was not merely to sit upon cushions but also to avoid 'the rough companions likely to be found, especially in manufacturing districts, in the second and third-class carriages', especially when travelling with ladies. 'A Surbiton Season-Ticketholder' went to town from on a Saturday in October 1866. On his return he arrived at Waterloo for the 11.57 p.m. and found nearly every seat occupied. As a last resort he was getting into a first, which had no light in it, at the end of the train when he found it full of navvies and mechanics; he was told it was a temporary second because no regular ones were at hand. Eventually he did find a place but he maintained it was scandalous that firsts should have to travel in a carriage previously occupied by those whose garments must necessarily from their occupation leave behind a most unpleasant odour.[2]

Second-class passengers often accompanied their grievances with the charge that life was deliberately made awkward to encourage them to go first-class, the GW being a major target. 'A Railway Traveller', living at Reading, complained in 1844 that returning from Paddington by the Mail, he had been in a carriage with three other male and two female (mother and daughter) passengers. At Slough a number of workmen were put into their carriage and not only was the stench of their clothes intolerable from their being covered with the composition used to preserve sleepers, but their conversation was blasphemous and disgusting. His coat had been ruined by contact with one squashed in alongside him. 'Pliny' complained in 1847 about the way railway workmen were allowed to use second-class carriages on Saturday evenings and sit anywhere. 'I need hardly observe how abstemious some of the men are of water and how many of necessity are of clean linen and flannel.'[3]

In 1857 'MW' complained that his second-class carriage from Gloucester (GW) was as filthy as a dog kennel – cages under the seats were used as dog boxes and there was no room for bag or umbrella. Two or three dirty, half-drunk workmen with third-class tickets in their hands were thrust into the overcrowded compartment. There were no lights and in the long tunnel between Gloucester and Swindon they were reduced to a crawl – a child in the compartment was terrified; he was told by the guard that they had recently been told to withdraw lights from seconds as an economy measure – yet they had recently presented the managing-secretary with £5,000.[4]

If correspondents' letters were any guide, the companies serving the south-east were particularly bad lines for drunks – or was it that people there were more likely to complain to *The Times*? 'Viator', a third-class traveller, recounted a string of encounters with drunks on a Friday evening train from Canterbury (LCD) in 1861. Next day George Butler recounted his experience on the same line at Faversham. There were many drunken and quarrelsome navvies at the station; he told the station-master that they were too drunk to travel and might get killed but the reply was that they were not a bit too drunk, though the drunkest had obviously been fighting. He did not travel in the same carriage so he did not know how they behaved on the journey.[5]

In 1869 the *Pall Mall Gazette* produced a general summing-up: 'A man is not a bloated aristocrat because he dislikes travelling a hundred miles with a gang of reeking navvies, who disgust at least half his senses, or a party of half-fuddled shop boys, who, probably, disgust them all ... Perhaps the most barefaced trespass of the kind is the deliberate way in which their own workpeople are conveyed along the line in second-class carriages. It is quite a common thing on some lines in England to see half-a-dozen navvies fresh from their work, unwashed, half-drunk, obstreperous, and perhaps obscene, bundled in among a number of other passengers who have paid their money expressly to avoid such company'.[6]

Excursionists

'LCC' had agreed to accompany a lady and her child from Bath to Weston-super-Mare, then on a short branch from the main line, on a Tuesday in September 1854, but learning of an excursion that day, postponed the trip a day. On Wednesday when they reached Weston Junction on the way back they found that a heavy excursion had gone to Glastonbury and had been joined to their train at Highbridge for the return to Bristol. They entered the least full of 11 or 12 carriages laden with the 'tagrag and bobtail of Bristol and its neighbourhood', whom he described as not desirable fellow passengers at any time, and still less so after a day's 'pleasuring'. At Clevedon Junction (later Yatton) they found another 50 or 60 waiting and these were huddled into any holes and corners that could be found. One lady fainted with the heat. Earlier, the lady with him nearly did the same in terror of a drunken man who would keep addressing her.[7]

'MM' complained that as a first-class passenger on 16 November 1858 from Norwich to Yarmouth he had been troubled by rough types who had joined at Brundall after a prize-fight: 'four of the greatest blackguards you can imagine ... My immediate and opposite neighbour happened to be a mulatto. I have seen such in the coster-monger carts of Whitechapel. He had warmed himself by exercise ... even to perspiration. He had refreshed himself with gin, I fear without water – and had pocketed a half-extinguished pipe of strong tobacco.' He had changed to another carriage at Reedham, into the only vacant seat; those already present included a lady and three of the same sort though certainly more respectable than those he had left; a gentleman told him they had entered smoking tommy pipes and had been talking about the details of the fight, the lady hearing every word.[8]

Near the end of the period, 'M.P.' complained that his wife, little girl and maid had travelled on the Midland and at Hendon had found the station 'in possession of a howling mob of ungovernable roughs, who invaded the train, setting all regulations, classes and authorities at defiance'. The chaos made the train an hour late in London. His complaint to the general manager was answered with the excuse that the circumstances were exceptional, however, the event was an annual one, occurring when there were race meetings at Hendon which he called 'aggregations of Metropolitan blackguardism called a Suburban Meeting', accusing railway companies of being ready to earn a few pounds at the cost of the convenience and risk to their lives of terrified regular passengers.[9]

Convicts and madmen

'A Second-class Passenger' accused the Grand Junction of going to extreme lengths to try and drive travellers into first-class carriages in 1844. They had contracted with the County of Stafford for the conveyance of prisoners to gaol and threw strings of them, teeming with filth, among the second-class passengers. WA travelled one evening in 1848 in a second-class carriage from March to Cambridge and found, soon after he had taken his seat, that he was in company with eight convicted felons, in chains, six men and two women, being taken to Ely. 'Viator' complained in 1851 about the LSW's practice of sending convicts going for transportation by second-class on ordinary trains.[10]

A particularly worrying hazard was that of being shut up with a madman, with no chance of safe escape until the next station; letters describing such events usually included a plea for some sort of communication device. The result was episodes that would have provided material for the melodramatic chase sequences of silent films as participants clambered from carriage to carriage along the outsides of moving trains. An item 'From a correspondent' on 16 October 1846 related how on the Monday previous (12th) a gentleman called Parker (from Sydenham) was travelling by mail from Derby to London. His only companion, aged about 30, began an increasingly wild conversation: he had once had a vast fortune and lost it and had retired from the army. Then he went down on his knees to pray for the Dukes of Beaufort and Wellington and started to undress and became even more disturbed by the noise of a train going the other way – he said it was Hell. He put his head out of the window and it was covered in blood when he hit against something. Next, he started to hit Parker, who enjoined him to pray again. Parker then made his way to the next carriage, helped in by its only occupant who had heard much of what had happened; the madman followed and it required the united efforts of both to keep him out, so he retired to his own carriage, by which time they were near Watford. Repeated calls for assistance were made to the guard but he said could he not stop the train because one from Manchester was close behind. All Mr Parker knew further was that the guard of a following train saw a man in a state of nudity running by the side of the line so he must have thrown himself off. The genuineness of this was confirmed on 1 December, via *The Globe.* Mr Markham, the gentleman who had violently attacked a fellow passenger and made an extraordinary escape from a train in an attack of brain fever had been restored to perfect health and left town to rejoin his family.

Also fully publicised were the exploits of Scott, a man of respectable appearance, travelling third-class early next year. He talked increasingly wildly; at Folkestone he said other passengers were trying to stab him. He jumped out after the train restarted, the train halted, the guard pursued him, caught him and brought him back. Though now under the care of a porter and two fellow passengers, he managed to break a window with his head and shoulders and was only just restrained from jumping out again. At London Bridge he was handed over to the police and a magistrate returned him to the care of his friends. He was a student for the Catholic priesthood, on his way from Calais to friends at Liverpool.[11] In 1863, between Bletchley and Camden Town, Mr Michael Lyons, a teacher from near Dundalk with a history of mental illness, suddenly drew a knife and attacked two of his fellow passengers, badly wounding them before they were able to overpower and hold him down.[12]

Far less believable in 1847, was 'GD' who complained next year about a madman who had been taken by two keepers in an ordinary second. Suspicions are roused by the description of the man's attire, including a nightcap in the daytime, a standard cartoonist's device of the time to indicate a madman. As so often others then wrote similarly: 'A frequent traveller' complained that at Swindon he and another were put into a second containing a lunatic and his attendant.[13]

Other hazards

Sometimes people's property caused offence. 'Caller Ou's particular grievance in 1862 was that people bought cheap left-over fish which not only gave off a foul smell but exuded liquid which was absorbed by the 'voluminous flounces' of the ladies.[14] In February 1865 a master chimney-sweep sent one of his men to Walker (near Newcastle) to go by train to a job but he was refused a ticket on the grounds that it was against the rules to allow a sweep to travel by train. The master complained to a director who told him that only drunks could be banned but the General Manager gave a different opinion – any person in a filthy condition became a nuisance to others and dirtied the carriages to the injury of later travellers. The dispute was sent off to be settled by Newcastle County Court but the outcome was not found.[15]

One risk, which must have been far more common than indicated by the evidence seen, was that of contracting contagious and infectious diseases. In 1844 George Stephens, writing from Bristol, said that he had left London that morning by the 10.15 in a second-class carriage with seven others. One was a young man recently out of the smallpox hospital, still with six large pustules (healing) on his face. The young woman next to him was alarmed since she had not had the disease. He called for the superintendent, Mr Seymour Clarke, and complained. He offered to move the writer but this was not necessary since he had had the disease. He did move the woman but would not put the sufferer and his accompanying father in a separate carriage unless they paid for the whole of it.[16] One point he overlooked was that separate carriages would have been of limited effect unless these were removed from service for fumigation before others could use them. In fairness, it should be added that there were at about this time a number of items saying ordinary cabs were being used in towns to take sufferers to smallpox hospitals and put straight back into service. Another instance was reported twenty years later. 'G.A.' had travelled from Paddington to Cheltenham by an express train and, with two others had briefly left his carriage at Gloucester. When they returned they found 'a man who presented one of the worst cases of smallpox which could possibly be, and at that stage of the disease that no medical man would certify as being fit to travel'. They insisted upon being removed from the compartment they had been locked in with the sufferer and at Cheltenham had complained to the station-master, who claimed he could do nothing. Six days later, 'W.J., M.D.' wrote that he was surprised that no further notice had been taken of G.A.'s letter. He claimed criminal law would hold directors responsible for any ill consequences resulting.[17]

There were lesser annoyances. 'A nervous man' complained in 1854 that at a station between Stratford and North Woolwich a woman with an accordion had entered his second-class carriage and played tunes, ending with an appeal for coppers and he had suffered similar annoyance from a singer and fiddler about a year previously on the Blackwall.[18] 'An occasional traveller on the Metropolitan Railway' had wanted to go from Kings Cross to Portland Road on a Saturday night in 1863; he took his seat in a third-class carriage and just before the train left, a somewhat powerful man entered and showed by gesture and pushing that he wanted his seat. He stayed put since there were plenty of empty seats but the new arrival then said if the writer would not give up his seat, he would sit on his knee, and did so. He complained but was told guards were too busy to deal with this sort of thing; apparently there were some who frequently travelled on that line for no other purpose than annoying other travellers.[19]

If 'TW' is to be believed not all of the unwanted were alive; no denial or explanation from the company was seen though the story seems implausible. He, his wife and her maid had driven to Burton Salmon for a train to York, where he was needed for Grand Jury service, late in 1846. The train arrived about 7.15. when it was quite dark and there was no light in the carriage. The maid went to a second-class carriage, in which there were two other passengers, he and his wife to a first. When they arrived at York, they saw a full-sized coffin taken from beneath the seat of the carriage in which the maid had travelled and carried away by four porters. The maid said she had suffered the most extreme annoyance from some horrible effluvium and one of her fellow-passengers had been driven out part way by the smell.[20] Not quite so grotesque was the experience of 'Viator' who travelled second-class on 23 August 1869 from Plymouth to London by the 2.30 mail. At Bristol their carriage was detached as part of it was used by the Post Office but no other was added. There was a large rush for the vacant seats in the remaining carriages from passengers already waiting and those ejected; his group was among those left out. The inspector refused to add another carriage or to let them use first-class unless they paid the difference: there was room in the luggage van, or they could stay behind. Two compartments were cleared of luggage and planks attached to the sides were let down as seats; there were neither lights nor ventilation. While they were being urged to occupy one of the compartments a coffin was brought in by six men so all went into the other.[21]

Some of the live problems had more than two legs. In 1841 'A Victim' wrote that a small colony of fleas had established itself in the first-class carriages of the Southampton Railway. The previous Saturday, when he travelled by the night train, he and his fellow travellers were prevented from enjoying one moment's rest by these 'carnivorous kangaroos'.[22] Remarkably, this letter is the only one seen on a subject one might have expected to provide regular complaints; perhaps fleas were too common an affliction to be worth comment. It was reported in September 1852 that a few evenings previously, 'at a station', (in south-west Scotland?) a large mysteriously muffled-up package had been placed on the floor of a third-class carriage. The train went on its way in the dark: there was a sudden scream from a female passenger and others started hitting about with hands, shawls, anything available, at an unseen foe who seemed to be everywhere. The package was a bee skep whose inmates had been annoyed by the jolting of the train and angry at having been moved from home.[23]

'A first-class passenger to the Woking station' had his troubles from the other end of the animal kingdom; on the 9 a.m. from Nine Elms two elephants were fellow travellers. Before arriving at Wandsworth these showed an evident dislike of their treatment and caused the train to stop; though they were very 'restiff', neither guard nor clerk there detached them. By Wimbledon, where they were removed, they had given added evidence of their power by smashing their cages.[24]

Chapter 14: THE WORLD TURNED UPSIDE DOWN? – PASSENGERS AND RAILWAY STAFF

The railwaymen most in contact with travellers were recruited from those normally regarded as members of the servant class or on a level with clerks in commercial concerns and assistants in shops, all of whom were expected to show due deference to well-to-do Victorians; this led to conflicts and complaints and often it is impossible to determine who was to blame. It would seem sometimes passengers were arrogant and expected more than it was realistic to demand and on other occasions porters, ticket-collectors and ticket-clerks could not resist using their new-found authority to gain revenge on those who normally dictated to them; however, some victims of particularly tyrannical behaviour were third-class passengers. The possibility must also be considered that pressure applied, and the example set, by higher officials such as Huish, lay behind some high-handed acts. There were also more letters in defence of railway staff, relating acts of helpfulness of one sort or another, than there were otherwise in praise of railways.

Staff were generally provided with a uniform. Blackwall guards and servants were originally dressed in blue, braided with white though only in 1863 did the GE announce it would supply its station-masters with a uniform that would make them recognisable by the public.[1] Most employed their own police, though the Blackwall initially arranged with the metropolitan police to provide officers to keep order when necessary. Female staff were occasionally mentioned. In a piece copied from 'The Scottish Press' on 16 December 1858 a traveller had been pleasantly surprised at an Edinburgh booking-office to be waited on by a bonnie and blooming lassie who, along with an activity quite equal to, exhibited a politeness very rare in railway clerks of the literally ruder sex. All three in the department were women – two dealing with tickets, the third the telegraph.

In January 1839 *Herapath* said there had been many complaints about the insolent conduct of staff on the London & Birmingham; some were no doubt true, others not. A notice was now exhibited at all stations:

> The public are hereby informed that all the company's servants are strictly enjoined to observe the utmost civility and attention towards all passengers; and the directors request, that any instance to the contrary may be noted by the offended party, in a book kept at each station for that purpose, and called 'The Passengers' Note Book'.

On the Hayle & Redruth one of Crotch's notices assured that, 'Any incivility offered by any of the Servants connected with this Line of traffic, will be met by their instant dismissal'.[2]

Some complaints were so generalised that it is impossible to guess what lay behind them. A piece copied in 1838 from *The Birmingham Advertiser* said 'It may be as well if Directors would take some steps to render their servants more generally civil and communicative than they are. Among them are to be found some of the most insolent, disobliging and dogmatical persons we know' and in 1844 'A Subscriber' said that nowhere else than the SE would you find the same idle, gossiping, chattering and laughing servants instead of prompt and business-like manner of men on other railways.[3] Many others would seem to have found the servants on other lines far from 'prompt and business-like'.

In 1840 there were letters complaining that the Greenwich had taken fares without saying there had been an accident and would be delays; the Blackwall was similarly criticised, especially since it was subject to quite frequent delays caused by problems with the rope-haulage used initially. An 1841 complaint concerned failure to provide information. The writer had gone to Romford where he had asked for the time of the return train and was told 4.15. He arrived 10 minutes before that and 12 or 14 were already waiting; the clerk was asked when the train would start but said he knew nothing about it and at 4.30 he threatened to have another questioner thrown out of the station by the policeman, although he had paid his fare. Then the writer found an inspector, who was civil and explained that the train to Brentwood had been delayed for a reason unknown to him and they would have to wait for it to reach Brentwood and come back – probably about half-an-hour.[4]

On occasion ignorance seems to have been to blame; one potential trouble spot was at Parkside, about half-way between Liverpool and Manchester, where, at first, passengers from north and south had to come because there were as yet no short cuts to avoid a right-angled journey. 'FK's letter on 14 September 1842 told that he had begun his journey on the North Union, leaving Lancaster by the 1 o'clock for London via Birmingham and was informed at Lancaster that he would have to re-book from Parkside. There he left the carriage, to put his luggage on the Birmingham train and re-book but was told by the guard that the train he had left was the Birmingham one; he had only just retaken his seat and put his luggage back on when another told him that it was for Manchester. Finally he was accidentally seen by the 'gentleman who appeared to be directing trains' and just reached the right train before it started.

'An Old Subscriber' claimed that some rudeness inflicted on passengers was deliberate retaliation on people known to have made complaints. He had returned from Bristol in 1846 and, driven into a box pointed out by a policeman there, he had found all means of opening the windows removed. Another called to rectify said it was no affair of his. The superintendent was called and directed a man to open them with his knife; he tried, said it could not be done, called out 'Lock the doors' and 'Go on', and they did. A short time previously, going from Bristol to Bath, it had been raining in torrents and he had objected to being shut in a box with 11 others. He was told if did not like it, he might go in an open carriage where he would have plenty of room; he entered that and just before departure three drunken carpenters, with their tools, were put in as his companions, and they passed their time in swearing and singing all the way.[5]

Lack of anyone to take an initiative frustrated some. FT faced this problem in 1844 at the end of the excursion season, when about 1,000 had arrived at Shoreditch from Yarmouth and Norwich. The station was placarded with large bills saying they could return any day until Saturday by the 6 a.m. train only, but on Friday he had arrived to find the station shut and about 300 waiting, in the dark and in cold drizzling rain because the train had been retimed to 8; when they applied to the only railwayman about, a porter, for admission to a waiting room for the women, the reply was – 'I have no orders'.[6]

One instance of high-handed behaviour arose from the inter-company wrangling which was an intermittent feature of Victorian railways. 'A Solicitor' writing on 1 August 1844 claimed he had gone to Croydon on business at the Assizes and at London Bridge had taken a day return second-class ticket for 3/-, going by a London & Brighton train. About 4 p.m. he went to the London & Brighton station at Croydon and asked for the next train to London; he was told about 5 but there was a London & Croydon train at 4.20. He showed the ticket at the gate of the Croydon [Company] station, was told 'all right' and got in but at London the ticket collector said he wanted 1/- since it was a Brighton ticket. He referred the latter to the ticket which said on the back that it was available for any train except an express without any mention of a company and refused to pay; the ticket collector said he could not go unless he did. He offered his card with his name and address but it was thrown down; he was seized and when he resisted two or three policemen were called. He refused to go before their secretary so they hauled him off to the Metropolitan Police station house. A tradesman who had seen the incident gave him his name and address, though warned by the railway police to mind his own business. He entered a recognizance and was allowed home; next day he appeared at Union Hall, where the magistrate said they had no right to detain him after he had given his card, especially since no fraud was attempted; an unintentional error had been committed partly by the negligence of the officer at Croydon in allowing him to pass, but he thought the shilling had better be paid, leaving him to seek remedy for assault and false imprisonment elsewhere.[7]

Other legal points cropped up from time to time. Mr Chilton, a Queen's Counsel, travelled from Sydenham to London in 1847, losing his ticket on the way, and on arrival he was asked for the fare from Croydon, the starting point of the train; when he refused to pay more than the fare from Sydenham he was taken to a police station, in accordance with an 'alleged' [in his view 'illegal'] bye-law. After a few minutes he paid, but then brought an action for trespass and false imprisonment. At one point it seemed that counsel for the company, who had admitted it was bound to lose, was about to make an apology but was prevented by one of its officials so the case pursued its full course. After two hours' deliberation the jury awarded £500 compensation. The company appealed on the grounds that the amount was excessive and a new trial was granted. Both now and at the second hearing the judges were badly divided – should a jury's finding be sacrosanct? Their second failure to agree meant that the original verdict stood.[8]

For Wychwood Forest Fair on 13 September 1854 trains from Oxford to Charlbury, the nearest station to the fair, were advertised, day return trip at single fare, and 1,100 people took advantage; return trains at hourly intervals from 6 p.m. to 11 p.m. were promised. Four 'respectable tradesmen' from Oxford found themselves stranded and having to stay at Charlbury; when they returned next day, they refused to pay the fare (1s 1½d) demanded for travelling then. They were summoned and the magistrates unanimously threw the case out, giving costs against the GW: the Charlbury station-master admitted that only three trains had started back, instead of the seven [sic] promised.[9]

A couple of Irish merchants travelled from Preston to Manchester on the LY in 1855; for some reason not explained one had notched his ticket with a pair of scissors, without destroying any printing. At Manchester they were given into custody for defacing their tickets, searched, stripped of their money, put in company with felons and taken before the magistrates, who dismissed the case. The company refused compensation on the grounds that it was not responsible for its servants' acts but the Recorder found against it and each received £25 in damages. Later that year Mr Cridland bought a return ticket between Dudley and Kidderminster on the Oxford, Worcester & Wolverhampton, but lost it – this does not seem to have been disputed. However, at Round Oak he was taken into custody and put in a police cell on a charge of attempting to defraud the company and failing to give his name and address. Evidence given showed that the second accusation was untrue and that he had not been drunk, as was also claimed. The judge said the power of arrest given to companies was only meant to cover cases where there was an intent to defraud and he received £20 damages.[10]

Even children could find themselves innocent victims of inflexible adherence to rules. In 1862 'R' wrote that his son of eight had to come from Exeter to London by 10.30 express: he was brought to the station by a servant [the school's] and placed in the care of the guard, who took charge of his ticket. By mistake, the ticket involved was for an ordinary first, not the express. The station-master at Taunton allowed him to go on but at Bristol he was turned out, told to sit still on a bench and wait for the ordinary train so he arrived at 5.40 (the train was 40 minutes late) instead of 3 and had had to rush to Euston to catch a connection and save his mother from worrying.[11]

Similar arbitrariness was described by 'Q.Q.' In 1844 he had set off second-class by the mail for York. At a station near York, several with third-class tickets were waiting; there was no room in the third and no time to add an extra carriage so they were pushed into a second. He had clearly heard them say they had only thirds but the guard said never mind, get in. One compartment was so crowded that one was forced to sit on another's knee. The persons thus forced in were working men, cleanly dressed, and had probably left work early on Saturday to spend the Whitsun holidays with friends or families. When they arrived at York, the last two or three in were told to pay an extra 1/-; they protested and others expressed astonishment. He backed the workmen and called the station superintendent but the latter still insisted on payment and told him it was none of his business. He said he would lock the men up until they paid and they were taken off to another part of the building and two servants were ordered to turn him out. There was no point in further argument then but on Wednesday he had found one of the directors and was invited before a regular Board meeting arranged for the next day. This was a farce since both guard and inspector were vouched for as 'respectable' men, known to, or connected with one of the directors. The victims' treatment seems particularly reprehensible because so many letters seen included references to third-class passengers being pushed into first and second-class compartments that it must have been a regular practice on many lines.

One particularly annoying practice highlighted from time to time was the way doors were closed on passengers. On 17 September 1842 one complained that at Ilford the previous Sunday there was no-one to open the door so he did it for himself [strictly against the rules]; the men had alighted and one of ladies with them was about to do so when an official slammed the door and started the train. He was left at Ilford, his wife and child were taken on to Romford and had to pay the excess fare. 'Viator' complained that on Christmas Eve 1844 he had caught the 3.30 Northern & Eastern with his wife, child and nursemaid, intending to be put down at Ponders End but on arrival they were ordered out onto the road instead of being landed on a platform. Despite the most earnest remonstrance that their luggage was still on board, they were told the train could not be kept all night for them and off it went. Their luggage came later that night on payment of 2/- to those bringing it.[12]

A further instance of rough treatment was alleged in 1862 by 'Noli Me Tangere' (Croydon). A female relative had entered a carriage of the 3.0 pm to Brighton from London Bridge on 25 September, believing she could use the return part of a Croydon ticket, paying the difference – it was a local ticket and she was in a main line train. The officials refused and as the train started, an official and a porter pulled her out, fortunately with no greater damage than fright and a slightly torn dress. A threat to report them was treated with derision and a letter had been written to the secretary. The official reply was that she was in the act of obeying the request to leave the train when it started and the officials gave 'a little extra assistance' to secure her safety: bye-laws said passengers could be fined 40/- for getting out of carriages in motion but apparently that did not apply to an officer who assisted a passenger.[13]

This issue came to prominence in 1868 when relatives claimed Mr Jourdain had entered a second-class compartment at Kentish Town on the North London Railway, found it was a smoker and tried to move to another. He had begun to enter the latter before the train started and could easily have managed to climb in safely if he had been left alone but the station-master grabbed him; they had struggled and fallen between train and platform where he was killed while the station-master ended safely under the hollow platform. The railwayman claimed the train had started before Jourdain made his move and was going quite fast as he tried to climb in; he had told him to let go of the rail of the door and his aim in seizing him had been to steady him as he fell but

Jourdain had clung on and thus the accident. The inquest jury adjourned in the hope of obtaining further evidence, but nothing more was found.[14]

Next year, at Edgware Road on the Metropolitan, T Loving, 65, a licensed victualler of March, Cambridgeshire delayed getting into the third-class carriage until the train had started and tried to enter against the loudly expressed orders of the guard who supplemented the order by catching hold of his coat. After a brief struggle he fell between train and platform; the train went over his leg, which had to be amputated and he died as a consequence. At the inquest it was said that as he slipped he grabbed at a young woman's shawl but this came off and she tried to hold him but was not strong enough. The evidence was conflicting about whether the train was about to start or actually in motion and it was also argued that overcrowding in the carriage (the woman was standing) impeded him from entering. The verdict was accidental death.[15] Inevitably there were letters as a result of this. 'MJB' (38 Mincing-lane) said it was common to see guards and porters pulling men, and even women, back as they tried to join a moving train; he agreed that the latter was a dangerous practice but it was made more so by these actions of the guards.[16]

Action was sometimes taken against over-zealous railway officials. In 1851 a station-master and a guard on the Caledonian were fined £3 16s and £2 7s for taking into custody a passenger who had protested against the undue filling of a carriage beyond the number allowed by company regulations.[17]

A couple of writers, of 1845 and 1865, produced lists so lengthy that they provide a recap of most of the complaints seen.

'A [commercial] Traveller' writing from York, 5 August 1845, had left Leeds by the train due to leave at 7.20. It took him nearly 20 minutes to get his ticket (probably second-class) since there had been an immense influx of third-class passengers and there was only one clerk. There was very little luggage at Leeds considering the number of passengers so the two porters there should have been sufficient; he asked them six times to carry his luggage but to him and others they insolently replied 'take your seats'. On reaching the train he saw there was only one third-class carriage, nowhere near capable of containing all who wanted to travel third. It would have been easy to add a carriage or two; he was told the guard had asked but the station-master had refused, so the second-class was filled with the large overplus of thirds and they left 15 minutes late. Many were waiting at Castleford where, despite the addition of first and second-class accommodation, third-class passengers were introduced into first as well. Every carriage was crammed so that full-grown women were sitting on each others' knees and there were 13 in his 'department', intended for 8. They stopped at all stations but he was unable to hear the name at any; there was only one board at each, not conspicuously placed, so few could see it, especially in a crowded train. One woman wanted Ulleskelf but she received no help from the guard; he happened to see the board and called it out, but his pronunciation was so different from hers that she did not recognise it. The stops were so short that there was no time for enquiries and eventually several stations later she caught the attention of the guard, who pulled her out, screaming with fright; he told her it was a long way back and threw her umbrella after her – he did not know if she had any luggage. Another young woman wanted Church Fenton but was carried on to York where she was ordered to go back by the next train and so lost about two hours.[18]

Twenty years later 'A.J.D.' complained of insufficient and inefficient staff. His train was supposed to leave Euston for Staffordshire at 2.45 but did not do so until two minutes after 3 o'clock. His two items of luggage, weighing together half a hundredweight, were labelled at 2.20 but, although he asked porter after porter, they were not loaded until 10 minutes after the train should have left. They left with a coupling screw not properly fixed and so had a rough ride, especially since after Watford they put on speed to make up lost time. 'One passenger, a portly dignitary of the Roman Catholic Church ... crouched in a corner of the compartment, his hands firmly clinched, his teeth set, his face blanched with terror.' The one opposite 'attempted a recumbent position, which, however he was unable to retain, although to prevent being shaken off the cushion, he had tightly grasped the window strap'. At Blisworth they all called for a guard; one came, coolly told them he was a Cambridge guard and had nothing to do with their train, though another did come and fix it, and when he was asked for an assurance that all was right, he replied, 'Yes; hold your bothering noise' [or at least that was the version in *The Times*].[19]

In August 1851 a case received much publicity because of the social standing of those involved and suggests that sometimes the blame lay with the public. Viscount Ranelagh and Mr Michael Rowan, both living in Park Place, St James, were charged with violently assaulting two railway constables while they were in discharge of their duties at Greenwich. In court, as witnesses for Ranelagh were Lord Alfred Spencer Churchill, Colonel M'Dowell and Captain Jennings. William Price, No 7 Sergeant of the SE police said that at 10.30 on Sunday evening he was ordered to close the gates during the departure of the London train in order to prevent a rush – many were coming from the waiting-room. He desired them to stand back but the defendants and their friends, five or six in number, rushed forward. He told them the train was full but they forced their way on and Ranelagh struck him a violent blow on the eye. The others helped Ranelagh seize him and Mr Rowan held his collar. The magistrate could not give a verdict since the evidence was so contradictory and ended proceedings with ambiguous remarks. Two days later the paper said they had been acquitted and made a complaint as a result of which Mr Mallalieu, Superintendent of R Division, had brought the policemen before the court. After various other instalments on 19 August it was reported that a Grand Jury had returned a true bill against Lord Ranelagh and ignored others matters arising out of counter-charges preferred by his Lordship but no further result was seen.[20]

Another case pointing in the same direction involved an argument over a lost luggage ticket in 1852, when 'TER' complained about the 'tyranny of railway autocrats'.

He had travelled to Dover, accompanied by his wife, having previously sent most of his luggage and 'establishment' ahead and only took four packages with him, three of which went into the luggage van, for which he was given a small piece of paper of banknote consistency. On his arrival the porter was about to put his luggage into the fly when he demanded the ticket; this could not be found so even though his name and address was on the luggage, the porter and his immediate superior refused to give it to him and a long, involved and unsuccessful wrangle ensued. Even TER's version made it clear that the railwaymen were confronted by an overbearing passenger.[21] This was a particularly unwise complaint because there was much correspondence at this time about luggage thefts and many had been suggesting the introduction of some sort of receipt for items lodged in the luggage van.

A scattering of letters giving a different view followed critical ones; it is to be hoped these were genuine, not somehow planted by railway directors. The first seems rather difficult to believe but perhaps in the very early years they had time for such benevolence. 'GW', of Lower Rock Gardens, Brighton wrote in 1843 that he had paid 8/6 on Monday, his fare from Redhill to Brighton but on arrival could not find his ticket so he presumed he had lost it and felt obliged to pay again. He wrote to the Superintendent at Redhill stating the facts and the directors had sent an officer to him and repaid the cost. Three years later 'Sola Nobilitat Virtus' told a complicated story about buying a ticket to Birmingham which he had not used: he was surprised to get a refund without any fuss since he was used only to the SE, where they did not do such things.[22]

Consumer satisfaction was clearly implied by an 1866 advertisement put in by a committee requesting contributions to a testimonial for Mr Fisher, late station-master at Kings Cross, as a mark of esteem for the attention he always paid to travellers. The list of subscriptions already received was headed by the Dukes of Cleveland and Manchester at £5 each. However, one wonders whether all classes felt the same way and how common was the treatment accorded to the lady whose adventures were described by 'Your Constant Reader' in 1852? He had escorted her from Newcastle as far as York in 1852 but his train back was about to leave and in his hurry he returned to Newcastle with her ticket. The station-master at York had furnished her with a pass and the one at King's Cross escorted her to the best cab in the rank, assuring her that the matter would speedily be put right.[23]

There were stories of special arrangements. 'Civilis' of Whitchurch returned home in 1844 by a Grand Junction train from Birkenhead which was late, apparently owing to lack of engine power for an overweight train, so he missed his connection and would have had to stay in Chester all night but Mr Jones, the Grand Junction line superintendent, provided an extra train for those affected.[24] On at least one occasion attempted help went badly wrong: a girl who had missed her Midland train on 9 September 1867 was allowed to ride in a brake-van at the back of a cattle train which ran into a ballast train and broke in two, the rear part running back and colliding with an oncoming passenger train. The girl and four cattle drovers were killed.

There were cases of rewards being given to railwaymen. WHC Taylor wrote in praise of a driver and stoker suddenly faced with a ballast train on a sharp curve near Basford near Crewe in 1860. The stoker had crawled along the side of the engine and poured sand on the rail, staying there until they had hit the obstacle. Thanks to his and the driver's efforts the collision had only been slight, although heavy rain was falling. Next day it was stated that Mr Mc'Connell, the locomotive superintendent at Wolverton would receive donations; several had already been given, including one from the Marquis of Stafford, who had been on the train and helped rescue a woman (whose presence was not explained) from the wreckage of the ballast train.[25] The passengers on the express to Scarborough derailed just outside Leeds in 1868 were very impressed with the skill of driver Joseph Wright in gradually stopping the train so that they scarcely felt the shock, and made a subscription presented to him on the spot.[26] Authority presumably regarded these incidents as exceptions to the no tipping rule.

A down train from Ayr to Glasgow was waiting at Dalry Junction in 1851 when a Saltcoats grocer waiting for the Glasgow – Kilmarnock train suddenly remembered he had left a package in the other train. He crossed the rails, ignoring warning shouts about the approaching train and was only saved by the guard Auld who jumped down and pushed him out of the way; both were unhurt.[27] Other railwaymen paid with their lives when helping passengers. On 29 June 1846 Mrs Murphy slipped and fell when, despite being warned, she was crossing the line to catch an up-train train at Balcombe and was hit by a down-train; the station clerk, Shaw, attempted to rescue her but both were killed.[28] William Parker, a guard, and Mary Hurst, a passenger, were run over and killed at Liverpool on 28 November 1853 when he was escorting her across the line; she had missed her train at Ormskirk and been taken on by a goods train.

ILLUSTRATIONS

The Changeover – A Handbook for Travellers along the London and Birmingham Railway, R Groombridge, c 1840.

The starting train – Great Eastern, Measom 1865.
Note guard perched behind tender.

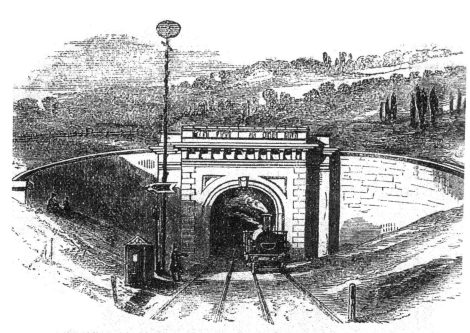

WESTERN FRONT OF BOX TUNNEL; HAZLEBURY HILL IN THE DISTANCE.

Entrance to Box Tunnel – Measom's Guide to the Great Western, 1861.
Note signalbox and signal.

VIADUCT TO RAILWAY STATIONS, BIRMINGHAM.

Viaduct to Railway Stations, Birmingham – Tuck's *Every Traveller's Guide*, 1843.

MOORSWATER VIADUCT, LISKEARD.

Moorswater Viaduct, Cornwall – Measom's Guide to the Bristol
& Exeter, etc Railways, 1860.

STRATFORD JUNCTION.

Stratford Junction – Measom's Guide to the GE, 1865.

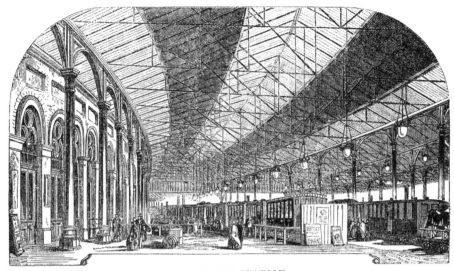

WATERLOO STATION.

Waterloo Station – Measom's Guide to the LSW, 1857.

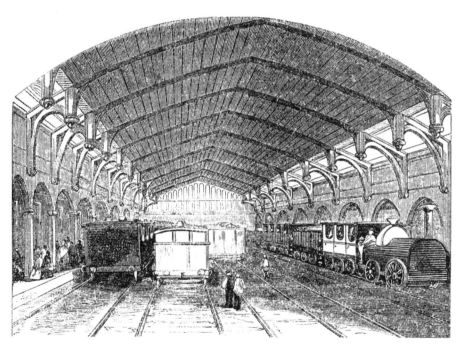

Original terminus at Bristol Temple Meads – Measom's Guide
to the GW, 1861.

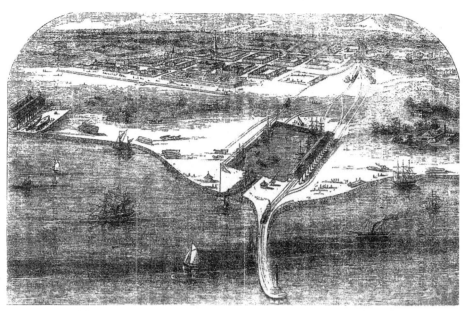

Silloth – Measom's Guide to the Lancaster & Carlisle, etc., 1859

PRATT'S
OLD LONDON INN
AND
GENERAL COACH OFFICE, EXETER.

GREAT REDUCTION IN FARES AND CARRIAGE OF PARCELS
TO
LONDON, BATH, and BRISTOL.
FARES!!

	INSIDE.	OUTSIDE.
FROM EXETER TO BATH, ...	**20s.**	**10s.**
FROM EXETER TO BRISTOL, ...	**20s.**	**10s.**

PARCELS to and from LONDON, under 8lbs. weight, ONE SHILLING EACH.

LONDON—"**TELEGRAPH**," every Morning, (Sunday excepted,) at FIVE o'Clock, performing the journey in FIFTEEN HOURS.

LONDON.—"**VIVID**," every Evening at SEVEN, a very superior fast conveyance.

JOSEPH PRATT AND Co., PROPRIETORS.

N.B.—Orders for Places by Letter punctually attended to.

Dated February 27th, 1839.

☞ AT VERY REDUCED FARES.

INSIDE ···················· 36s.
OUTSIDE ··············· 18s.

BY
THE "VIVID"

Superior Coach, Unrivalled for Speed and Regularity, to Exeter, Plymouth and Devonport, through

ANDOVER, WINCANTON, ILMINSTER, SALISBURY, ILCHESTER & HONITON,
EVERY AFTERNOON, FROM THE
CROSS KEYS, WOOD STREET, CHEAPSIDE, GEORGE AND BLUE BOAR, HOLBORN, 41, REGENT CIRCUS, PICCADILLY, AND GOLDEN CROSS, CHARING CROSS, LONDON.

B. W. and H. HORNE, Proprietors.

On the arrival of the VIVID COACH at PRATT'S OLD LONDON INN, Exeter, Coaches depart for TIVERTON, TOTNES, TORQUAY, and DARTMOUTH.

Dated Feb. 28th, 1839.

Conventional pictures of trains used in handbills and press advertisements

Norwich (Thorpe) station – Measom's Guide to the GE, 1865.

The Block System: the Board of Trade wanted all to adopt a system which allowed only one train into a section at a time; the *Punch* version had a garrulous woman holding up passengers desperate to buy tickets for a train shortly due. JP Atkinson, 1882, *Pictures from Punch Vol I.*

A Station on the North Staffordshire Line. Traveller, told by boy that he is the ticket clerk, asks for time of next train and is told 'No time in pertickler. Sometimes one time – and sometimes another'.
The Railway Book.

Manners and Cvstoms of Ye Englyshe in 1849, A raylway statyon.
Showynge ye travellers refreshynge themselves.

151

Behind the Scenes. Head barmaid: 'These tarts are quite stale, Miss Hunt – been on the counter for a fortnight! *Would* you mind taking them into the *second-class* refreshment room?' *The Railway Book.*

One of the perils of travel was broken couplings, leaving part of a train behind. *The Railway Book.*

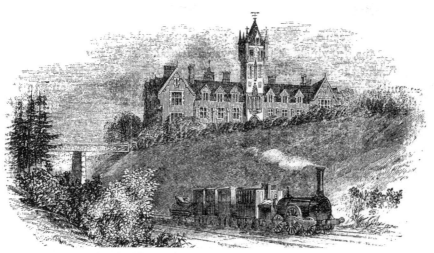

Freemasons' School, Battersea Rise (note carriage on last truck) –
Measom's Guide to the LSW, 1857.

A Reminder: old lady asks porter in detail if he has included all the
many items of her luggage and if he is sure she has not left anything
behind. Porter: 'No, mum, not even a copper'. *The Railway Book.*

Zoology: Porter (to old lady travelling with a menagerie of pets): 'Station-master says, mum, as cats is "dogs", and so's parrots; but this ere "tortis" is a insect, so there ain't no charge for it!' Illustrates complicated fare structure. *The Railway Book.*

A Branch Station: Miss Tremmles (who is nervous about railways generally, and especially since the last outrages) asks to be put into a carriage with ladies or respectable people. Porter: 'Oh, you're all safe this mornin' miss; you're th' only passenger in the whol' tr'ine, except another old woman.' *The Railway Book.*
Unlike most letter-witers to *The Times*, Punch cartoonists were never sympathetic towards the ladies.

For Ladies Only: an item in the *Daily News* had said that if you travelled in these reserved carriages you ran a greater risk than in an ordinary one. 'I have known railway officials allow men to jump into them at the last moment before the train starts, with a mutual wink at each other and a very objectionable grin'.
The Railway Book.

Behind Time: ticket collector challenges use of a half ticket by her son. She replies that he might be too big now but not when they started – an allusion to notorious delays on excursion trains. *The Railway Book.*

Pretty Innocent: Little Jessie: 'Mamma why do all the tunnels smell so strongly of brandy?' The Lady in the middle never *was* fond of children, and thinks she has never met a child she disliked more than this one. G du Maurier, 1865, *Pictures from Punch vol I.*

A Delightful Reminiscence of the Boat-race: Sweep (to a carriage full of light blue ribbons): 'Won't yer make room for a little 'un, ladies and gents? I'm for the Cambridge lot!' *The Railway Book.*

La Belle Dame Sans' Merci'. The Railway Book.

Traveller's Luggage: Elderly passenger: 'Going out fishing, I presume young gentleman'. Reply: 'No! It ain't fishing rods – it's sky rockets I'm taking down for my cousin's birthday. Have a weed?' J Leach, 1860, *Pictures from Punch vol I.*

In the Wilds of Suffolk: Gallant Volunteer: 'I hope you don't object to gunpowder smoke, sir. I've got four more blank cartridges. Charles Keane, 1861,
Pictures from Punch vol III

Things one would rather have left unsaid: 'I'm afraid we shan't have this compartment to ourselves any longer, Janet'. 'Oh, it's all right, aunty darling. If you put your head out of the window, I dare say nobody will come in!'
The Railway Book.

A Hint to Railway Travellers: By breathing on the glass – and holding a speaking doll by way of baby to the window – you may generally keep your compartment select. *The Railway Book.*

Easier said than done: Porter: 'Dogs not allowed inside the carriages, sir!' Countryman: 'What not a little tooy tarrier? Wall, thee'd better tak' un oot then, young man!' Illustrates one of the difficulties passengers could create for railwaymen; dogs were supposed to go in the luggage van. Charles Keane, 1863, *Pictures from Punch vol III.*

Quite Unimportant: Thompson (interrogatively, to beauteous but haughty damsel, whom he has just helped to alight). 'I beg your pardon?' Haughty damsel: 'I did not speak!' Thompson: 'Oh – I thought you had said thanks!' Not all the rudeness was on one side. *The Railway Book.*

A fact: Guard (putting in his head): 'There are two things not allowed on this line, gentlemen; smoking, and the servants of the company receiving money.' The result, a metallic pass from Gentlemen to Guard. Charles Keane, 1858, *Pictures from Punch vol III.*

Passenger: 'Well, you say you've put all my luggage safe, what are you waiting for? – I thought you were forbidden to take money!' Porter: 'So we is, sir. We never "takes" it – it's "given to us"!' *The Railway Book.*

Ticket Platform at Holloway – Measom's Guide to the GN, 1861. It is the open platform to the left.

Muddleby Junction. Overworked pointsman (puzzled): 'Let's see! – there's the "scursion" were due at 4.45, and it ain't in; then, afore that, were the "mineral", no! that must ha' been the "goods", - or the "cattle". No! that were after, – cattle's shunting now. Let's see! – fast train came through at– Con-found! – and here comes "the express" afore its time, and blest if I know which line she's on!!'. Board of Trade accident reports frequently highlighted companies' habit of endangering safety by employing staff inadequate in numbers and training.
The Railway Book.

Railway Undertaking: Touter – 'Going by this train, Sir?' Passenger: 'M? Eu? Yes'. Touter: 'Allow me, then, to give you one of my cards, Sir.' John Leech, 1852, *Later Pencillings from Punch*, published by Bradbury & Evans.

Railway Amalgamation – a Pleasant State of Things: From time to time company amalgamations were a major news topic. The *Punch* interpretation was somewhat different. The guard explains that they have run into an excursion train and reassures a passenger who knows that there is another train behind that a boy had gone down the line with a signal 'and it's very likely they'll see it!' John Leech, 1852, *Later Pencillings from Punch*, published by Bradbury & Evans.

Sonning Cutting – Measom's Guide to the GW, 1861. Scene of the serious third-class accident.

Risks. Shrewd clerk (with an eye to his percentage) sells an insurance ticket by telling passenger that the next smash is 'hoverdue exactly six weeks and three days'. *The Railway Book*.

Chapter 15: TWO RULES MADE TO BE BROKEN: TIPPING AND SMOKING

Tipping

Tipping was a deeply-entrenched custom so railway companies were giving themselves a very hard task when seeking to break the habit. The Liverpool & Manchester set the tone as usual, though some ambiguity crept in:

PORTERS

The Company engages to load and unload Passengers' Luggage, upon and from the Railway Carriages and Omnibuses, and to deposit it in any of the Coach-offices, free of charge; for any service in addition to this the Porters are allowed to make a reasonable charge.

GUARDS

No gratuity is allowed to be taken by any Guard, Engineman, Porter, Omnibus Driver, or other servant of the Company.

Others followed this lead, usually without qualification. In December 1841 the Hull & Selby added a bold note down the side of its handbill: 'Company's Servants are not allowed to receive Gratuities on any pretext whatever'.[1]

In 1838 'A Traveller' said that although the London & Birmingham made a great fuss about having no coachmen or guards to pay, the guard applied for a gratuity and, on his refusal, assailed him with abuse.[2] 'Saddlebags', a commercial traveller, complained in 1846 about charges on excess baggage. He argued that he and the railways had the same interest – if his samples resulted in extra sales, there would be more goods for railways to carry, so they should give commercial travellers reduced fares and rates; thus he considered it fair to use tricks of his own in return and since he had been tipping porters he had not been charged.[3] 'A railway director' replied at the start of 1849 to a letter 'most justly complaining about the growing practice of feeing railway porters', claiming that the fault was not with directors, who sought to stop the practice but with the public who did it out of sight. 'By their conduct they demoralize the men and do what they can to check civility and attention to those who will not give way to the practice of feeing'. As for those who bribe railwaymen to under-declare weight of luggage – 'I must leave them to their own consciences, if they have any'. Shortly after an item said the LNW was determined to stamp out gratuities, which, despite warnings, were still being given and solicited; in future men would be immediately dismissed for accepting, even if the money had been pressed on them by a passenger.[4] Even if the LNW had much success, which is unlikely, given the letters that appeared a couple of years later, others did need to act. Near the end of the year 'A Clergyman' complained that porters on the Eastern Counties at Shoreditch (then the terminus) expected tips and described an incident where a lady with a child had been politely escorted to a cab and her luggage placed in it. She was just about to close the door when the porter jumped in and said she must give him something – and make sure that no-one saw; she was so frightened that she gave him a shilling.[5]

There was a major burst of interest in 1863. On a journey from Lancashire to the West of England 'A Lancashire Lawyer' claimed that all had been in order until they were past Shrewsbury. They then came to

'a city' where fees, neglect and confusion seem to be the order of the day. On our arrival our luggage was seized upon in an officious and irregular manner by three porters (one being quite sufficient). I told them that we intended to stay in the city for three hours, and would have the luggage put in the 'Left luggage-office'. Two of the porters placed their burdens on the platform, and politely told me that it would be quite right. "We will take care of it for you, Sir". I pretty well understood what this meant, but insisted on having the usual receipt, and the consequence was that when we returned to the station, five minutes before the departure of the train, it was with the greatest difficulty that I could obtain the least attention, and we were very near being left behind. There was an amply sufficient supply of porters, and the reason from the first was obvious to me why I was neglected, and my suspicions were confirmed by the fact that a new comer, who had arrived several minutes after me, and who seemed to know the 'custom of the country', and was willing to comply with it, obtained for a shilling the immediate attention of one of the porters who would neither hear nor see me.

Various others joined in, often taking a highly moral tone; one indulged in complicated economic analysis of the distortion caused by tipping, enabling companies to employ their men at less than their true value and another even advocated treating the giving of a tips as a crime.[6] In the middle of this burst the editor brought the full weight of his heaviest artillery to bear, at more than a full column's weight of shot:

There are few breaches of social morality so indefensible in principle, yet so frequently committed in practice, as that involved in the custom of giving fees to railway officials. [Nearly everyone does it and argues that it does not really matter, but that is not so.] The shilling given to the railway porter must not be regarded as a thing by itself; it belongs to a genus of exactions which in past times flourished everywhere, to the utter corruption of public morals. Sinecure offices and pensions, lucrative and easy berths for agents of an inferior rank, perquisites for every one, high or low, who filled any public situation ... [have disappeared as fixed salaries had become the rule and hotels have adopted the practice of including a charge for attendance in the bill.] It is not pleasant to feel that one must purchase civility, especially when one has to compete with those who are sure to outbid oneself. This source of discomfort seemed to be effectually removed by the bye-laws of the new railways, and for some time the regulations insured first, second, and third class alike impartial attendance and assistance from the company's servants. By degrees, however, the old habit returned. People arriving late at the station with a quantity of baggage compounded with the porter so as to avoid its being weighed. Families accustomed to get a carriage to themselves readily gave something to the guard to keep strangers out. Smokers purchased the right of breaking the company's rules in the same way. Parties leaving luggage for a short time found it more convenient to let it stand on the platform under a porter's charge than to impound it in the cloak-room, which might be on the wrong side of the station. Others, in a hurry to get off from a terminus, thought it no sin to pay for having their luggage taken out and put on a cab before the van was unloaded. ...

It is not merely that the porter is induced to do what he knows to be wrong and what renders him liable to dismissal; it is not merely that the donor appropriates to himself time and labour which the recipient has no right to sell and which is due to other persons. Let this kind of bribery once become the rule, and not the exception, and all will suffer alike, unless the rich should raise the standard of their douceurs still higher, and so regain their advantage over the poor. There is really no limit to the disorder and unfairness which would be produced by such competition. ... The process of deterioration has already begun, but it may still be arrested if English gentlemen – for the ladies are not so much to blame – can but be brought to regard the matter in its true light. ...[7]

Given the correspondence that had appeared intermittently in his paper over many years, was he really justified in arguing that there had been 'deterioration'? Was it not always thus?

The issue resurfaced in 1868. 'An Old Railway Guard' asked passengers not to treat guards to drinks at refreshment stops because it was too tempting and had caused many to lose their jobs. On 9 September the editor joined in with another leader but some of his correspondents argued that the expectation of railwaymen was so deeply and universally ingrained that passengers had no alternative to follow the crowd. 'A Clergyman' went even further. A few years before he had secured a porter's job at a London terminus for a respectable young man. The official had told him the wages would be 17/- or 18/- per week but 'we' consider your place at a London terminus worth 10/- a week more; this despite the fact that the usual notice against tipping had been freshly painted. 'Another Railway Director' blamed public apathy for breaches of the rule – the clergyman should have told the directors [would his protégé have kept his job?].[8]

There were far more serious implications. People waiting at Kings Cross on 30 May 1860 were astonished to see an excursion from the Liverpool and Manchester area, containing about 800 passengers in 35 carriages, two of which were brake vans, come into the station at a speed which would not allow it to stop in time. The engine and leading carriages jumped over the platform end and were only stopped by a large heap of earth excavated during the creation of the Metropolitan line. A railwayman on the platform was sure the rear brake had not been applied and when he went to investigate he found the 'hind guard', who worked for the MS&L, helplessly drunk on the floor. The latter recovered sufficiently to stagger off to his nearby home but was followed, brought back, taken before a magistrate and despatched to prison. 15 passengers were injured. The Board of Trade accident report was highly critical: there had been barely sufficient brake power to start with and this had become inadequate after some passengers had treated the guard with ale at Hitchin, when he was already 'fresh'. After this accident, Ellis A Davidson, Head Master of the Chester School of Art, wrote that he had often seen the same railwayman brought into a refreshment room by different passengers and treated to a drink. This was even more undesirable than giving a tip, since 'a man would be unlikely to expend it in four glasses of ale and one glass of gin during the short stay of the train at one station'.[9]

As part of his general denunciation of railway companies following the Abergele accident, Lt Col Hutchinson included an attack on this practice:

> Guards of the highest class may be seen daily carrying boards to supply passengers with, for the purpose of enabling them to lie down in the carriage, on the secure understanding that they will be rewarded for their trouble; and the practice of treating railway servants in the refreshment rooms, which is fast increasing, will bring with it its chapter of accidents. Four or five porters may constantly be seen racing after one railway carriage door, where they have recognised a passenger well known to themselves to be liberal.

> The permitted breach of this regulation may at first sight appear trifling as regards the safety of the passenger, but it is not so. The guards are employed in looking after their own interests, instead of seeing after the organisation and fittings of the train of which they are about to take charge.

He went on to argue that these activities bore a major responsibility for the late running of trains, a contributory factor in many accidents.

Smoking

Whether smoking should be allowed was another hardy perennial. Inevitably, the Liverpool & Manchester deserves the first word, though to begin with it stopped short of the complete ban:

SMOKING

No smoking will be allowed in any of the First Class Carriages, even with the general consent of the Passengers present, as the annoyance would be experienced in a still greater degree by those who may occupy the same coach on the succeeding journey.

The Hull & Selby's early time bill was simpler: 'Smoking is strictly prohibited in any of the Carriages or on any of the company's premises'.[1]

There were attempts at enforcement. A passenger detected smoking in a GW railway carriage between Swindon and Chippenham in 1841 was given into custody on arrival at Chippenham, taken before a county magistrates and convicted in the mitigated penalty of 10/-. In 1855 Mr. Samuel Haycroft of Plymouth was prosecuted. He had been told by the guard to stop smoking his cigar when his train was at Durston and was again seen smoking when the train left Taunton; his reply to another challenge was: 'he should still smoke, and he [the railway official] might do his worst'. He was fined £3 10s, including costs. He was brazen enough to do this in the compartment next to the 'guard's box'; others were probably more prudent.[10]

At least two paid with their lives. Some lines (or at least their employees) allowed smokers to sit on the guards' seats outside carriages. A party of young men, apparently completely sober, were allowed to do this while travelling first-class from Chester races back to Birkenhead in 1842; they were warned not to leave their seats but one did stand up, with fatal consequences when they passed under a bridge. Another was Captain Watkins of the Northamptonshire Militia, in a troop-train on its way to Plymouth on 10 December 1857; he took out his pipe, filled it, leant out of the window to get a light from an officer in the next compartment, stretched right out so that he could wave his cape against the latter's window and was killed when his head hit a bridge at Aller.

Protests were frequent. In 1846 'Tobacco Stopper' came to town by a 'bran-new' carriage of the London & Croydon which reeked of tobacco smoke. Everyone knew smoking on trains was banned but in tobacconists' windows it was common to see 'railway pipes', adapted for instantaneous concealment.[11] CW highlighted one of the difficulties of enforcement when he complained that in a second-class carriage on the way to Brighton several ruffianly fellows whose poisonous fumes and offensive language caused the guard to warn them several times only to be answered with jeers and laughter.[12]

Particularly concerned were parents. 'A Parent' in wrote in 1855 that two of his daughters (elder 16) and son (a little boy) left Tonbridge by 11.20 a.m., second-class and also in the carriage were two or three soldiers, two common men, a 'half-and-half-gentleman' and a dog [whose presence was almost certainly against the rules]. All except the last smoked all of the way. Could this possibly have gone on unnoticed by company's servants? One of the children was made quite sick; they had wanted to change carriages but there was no room and bars prevented them from putting their heads out of the windows [just as well?]. Later that year 'A subscriber' wrote that his two eldest children, a boy 13, and a girl 11, in delicate health, travelled second-class in a LNW train from Birmingham. Two ruffians smoked, though his son had civilly asked them to stop on the grounds of his sister's health. The guard would not interfere: indeed, one of smokers was heard to say that the guard would provide them with matches. They had to open a window, though it was bitterly cold and they were thus likely to be ill over Christmas. No indication was given of the ruffians' reaction to opening the window.[13]

At least one non-smoker fought back. In 1853 Mr Buchanan sued the Edinburgh & Glasgow for £8 6 8d as restricted damages sustained by him from the danger he ran from fire and injury to his feelings since the company had not strictly enforced its anti-smoking byelaw. He held an annual ticket and had often remonstrated with guards, to no avail. The sheriff heard the case in his chamber and decided that the company was bound to enforce its rules. He said that if a guard smelled smoke and could not see the culprit, he should summon all the occupants of the compartment, but when asked if he would convict them all, he prudently declined to give his opinion. The company was fined 20s.[14] Would this have bound English railways too?

One story, found copied in a paper far from the GW, seems too good to be true. Allegedly the station-master of an un-named GW station vainly asked a man walking about on the platform to put out his cigar; when his increasingly insistent demands were ignored, he took direct action, seizing the cigar and throwing it away, an action that met with no response from the cigar's loser. Shortly after a carriage belonging to the Duke of Beaufort arrived and the culprit was carried off. Enquiry by the station-master revealed that his victim was Lord Palmerston, recently Prime Minister. The horrified railwayman went post-haste to tender his abject apologies. The answer he received was that Palmerston was not annoyed at the time because he considered the man had only being doing his duty but now had lost all his respect for him as a result of his fawning apology.[15]

Appeals for proper facilities to be provided were frequent, often a standard ingredient of letters protesting about smoking. In 1840 *The Railway Times* said an appeal had been made for cigar smokers to be allowed to smoke since the Belgians were about to introduce one carriage per train but it was clearly not sympathetic: 'The public taste is becoming fastidious in respect of travel accommodations; will "smoking diligences" be the next indulgence asked for and granted?'.[16] Towards the end of 1843 the North Midland was reported to have fitted up a large carriage for the accommodation of 'those gentlemen who were emulous of competing with the engine in the quantity of smoke that could be thrown off in a given period'; it was termed the 'divan' and first-class fares were demanded.[17] In September 1846 a smoking carriage was introduced on the Eastern Counties, aimed at the Cambridge and Newmarket traffic: it resembled the Royal Carriages of other companies in build, with leather seats along sides and a mahogany table in the middle and was first used when Hudson and a large party of directors went to Ipswich to the seat of Mr Bagshawe, lately MP for Harwich. Several others were under construction and they would be attached to all fast trains to Cambridge, available to those paying first-class fare.[18] However, provision did not become general for quite a long time.

In 1866 battle, at least in the columns of *The Times*, was joined with a vengeance. 'Socius' (writing from Brooks' Club) said the LBSC had recently issued a public notice expressly prohibiting smoking. His fellow passengers on the express had denounced this and were united in their determination to disobey. That provoked FHT and FRS into complaining about the non-enforcement of the rules but they did agree that separate carriages should be provided. Somewhat lengthier was the contribution from 'One who can't reach town until 8.40 nor leave it after 9.30', an annual ticketholder for many years, first on the LBSC, then on the LSW, who claimed that only the dogged obstinacy of some of the directors prevented the LSW from providing smoking carriages. On the same day 'A piper' claimed the consequence of the ban on smoking was like that of the Maine Liquor Law on drunkenness [an early form of Prohibition] – smoking took place under the noses of officials and all carriages smelled of stale tobacco smoke. Laurence Vanderpant said that he had at one time leased a house at Kingston-on-Thames and travelled daily to London to practise as a dentist. He always arrived thoroughly impregnated with tobacco smoke: 'My patients, I learnt, especially ladies, disliked the odour with which I was compelled to approach them … in the end I gave up my house at Kingston to avoid compulsory tobacco fumigation every morning I travelled.' 'A season-ticket holder on the Richmond and Windsor branch for upwards of seven years' said that when he had first taken a season ticket, which all had to sign, it had included a clause promising not to smoke; many signed and walked straight onto the platform with pipe or cigar in mouth but one, more scrupulous than the rest, had refused to sign and after a great hubbub the clause was removed and a modest notice merely printed at the foot of the ticket that smoking was banned. It had no effect and the habit was daily persisted in. At Waterloo porters did manage to keep a fair proportion of carriages for non-smokers but no such control was exercised on up trains. The directors had sporadically tried to enforce: they had gained convictions against several flagrant offenders and placarded carriages with notices but all had been in vain – in one carriage in use barely a month in which he had travelled the notices had been altered to give the opposite meaning, the ceilings were covered with scratches

171

where matches had been lit, holes had been burnt into the cushions and the carpet completely spoilt by a horrible mixture of saliva and cigar dust.

'HB' claimed that on a journey by an LCD train from Margate a delicate-looking young lady sat beside him. The person the other side was about to light a clay pipe; when appealed not to do so he unwillingly abstained for a minute or two but his friend opposite lit up and he followed. At Whitstable or Faversham he had complained to the guard; the smokers were told to stop and if they resumed he was to tell the guard at the next station. The result was that, with two friends, they abused him, continued smoking and varied their amusement with obscene language and dirty innuendoes. They insulted an old lady, who, as a result of the noise, was carried beyond Sittingbourne, her destination, to Chatham. The ring-leader alighted at Walworth Road and he asked the guard to get his name and address since he was determined to summon him but the guard sent the train off in a hurry, leaving him there. 'L' made a general attack on smokers for making others look misanthropic; he saw smoking as a growing habit; 'As for ladies, I presume they will soon take to smoking, too, so I say nothing about them'. The editor added a note that he had strayed from the point under discussion; however, he could not be faulted for his ability to predict the future. In December it was reported that the LSW had at length conceded the privilege of smoking in some compartments, which would benefit both sides.[19] Two years later Henry B Sheridan pointed out that non-smokers needed to show some consideration: recently the only second-class smoking compartment on a train from Brighton to Lewes was filled with ladies, whose well-being was one of the main aims of the act, though there was plenty of room elsewhere.[20] A law compelling railway companies to provide smoking accommodation was passed in 1868, though the Metropolitan was briefly excluded, apparently by an oversight.

The erratic nature of the problem was shown by 'WS', who complained in April 1870 that after some respite smoking was again widespread in all carriages. 'Persistent breakers of the law, like a lot of prairie-dogs, at once dived into their holes out of sight until the storm blew over'. He did not specify the line but he was clearly a London commuter. This pattern seems to have been repeated because 'A constant passenger' claimed in November that smoking had abated after the batch of letters published in July but then was common again.[21] This latest burst revealed another chink in the armour of those opposed to smoking. 'Another passenger' complained that at Charing Cross he had got into a second-class non-smoker and at Cannon Street several with pipes had joined him so he complained to the guard who said he had given permission. He had written to the General Manager whose reply was that that train did not have any smoking carriages so guards had discretion to give permission.[22]

Chapter 16: DISRUPTIONS and DELAYS

Introduction

This chapter deals with ways in which services were interrupted or delayed. Where accidents were concerned it concentrates on consequences, leaving causes as far as possible to a later chapter. Delays have always occurred in all forms of transport and are so common that fuller treatment beyond the examples given here would be tedious; most space has been given to early incidents, with enough later ones to show that some trouble continued.

Some delays were built in. At many stations water tanks on tenders had to be replenished; extra carriages, trucks carrying private carriages and horse-boxes had to be added or detached. There was thus much more flexibility than with today's fixed formations, but it meant frustration as sometimes complex shunting manoeuvres were carried out. In one, admittedly extreme case, a train arrived at Maghull on New Year's Day 1850 with only one carriage, normally sufficient, but it was a special day with good skating conditions nearby. An extra carriage had been sent along, to be kept in a siding (on the wrong side) until it was needed but there was only the station clerk, the worse for drink, to deal with everything there; his fuddled state meant six shunting movements, taking seven minutes, were required to add it.

Ticket platforms at the approach to some stations, especially termini, were another standard cause of delay; trains stopped for tickets to be checked or collected, making it much more difficult for people to sneak off without paying. 'A Traveller' returning from Birmingham was held in July 1837 for about half-an-hour near the extremity of Regents Park [probably Camden Town] by this.[1] By July 1839 some changes had been made to save time since passengers' tickets from Birmingham were being collected at Watford and those from London at Coventry. However, they seemed to have reverted to old habits at the London end. In July 1845 'A Penny-a-Miler' came from Wigston by the cheap train due at Euston at 9.50 but early delays made it late at the ticket platform. They were ordered to get their tickets ready but two fast trains, due at 10.15 and 10.30, were nearby and his train was backed onto the down line while they went through, detaining them nearly an hour.[2]

Following the Nine Elms accident in 1840, 'Testis' claimed part of the delay was due to a lengthy stop at Wandsworth for ticket collection; even though officials must have known that a fast train was on its way. In his carriage a passenger tried to save time by collecting the tickets for the inspector, but the latter was so deliberate about counting them that there was no gain.[3] 'A Professional Traveller' in 1844 blamed much of the SE's unpunctuality on stops about a furlong short of termini to collect tickets; it could be half-an-hour at busy times if there was only one collector for the whole train.[4] At Bootle Lane, the last stop before Liverpool, tickets were collected on the platform on the main line, used by two companies; an LY train, running late as usual, was hit in the rear on 15 July 1852 by two East Lancashire goods trains coupled together at a previous junction. The following month an excursion train stopped at Lostock Junction, near Bolton, for 20 minutes while about 1,200 tickets were collected, making it even later than it was already and contributing to another accident. In 1856 CR Weld found delays especially irritating on short journeys where they had just stopped at another station, suggesting that Waterloo tickets be collected at Vauxhall, and Brighton and Crystal Palace line tickets at New Cross. He concluded with what would then have been the ultimate insult: 'Even the Irish manage better'.[5]

Interruptions of service

An almost immediate stoppage could happen if a company 'forgot' to ask the Board of Trade for permission to open. One such was the branch to Hyde (Central) opened on 1 March 1858; when the Board found out it was inspected early in May and closed shortly after owing to the 'incompleteness' of the works; this was soon remedied, and it reopened, with approval, on 26 May. Other closures resulted from shortcomings in the line as originally built: the Halesworth, Beccles & Haddiscoe line was closed in 1858 so that it could be relaid.

The need to convert lines also resulted in short closures or provision of a poorer service for a while. The Blackwall changed from rope to locomotive haulage in 1849 and was able to keep trains running by dealing with one line at a time but this meant a reduction from a train every 15 minutes to one every 30.[6] The largest number of such conversions, lasting well beyond the limits of this book, resulted from the GW's need to undo Brunel's broad-gauge folly. His successors kept disruption to a minimum, in part through the practice they had. Where a line was double a service was kept going, converting one line at a time but with single lines there was no alternative to closure. In October 1868 the GW warned that the service from Aylesbury to Princes Risborough would be suspended from 5 a.m. Wednesday 14th until 6 a.m. Wednesday 21st for conversion; passengers would still be booked and omnibuses provided. This one actually took slightly longer but when in August 1869 they warned that Hereford to Ross would be closed from 10 p.m. Saturday 14th to 6 a.m. Monday 23rd the operation went so smoothly that they were later able to advertise resumption for Friday 20th.[7]

Some other scheduled breaks have been covered in the chapter on Sundays. In addition to the weekly ones, on Good Fridays the Croydon and Greenwich trains which should have started from London Bridge between 11 a.m. and 1 p.m. started from New Cross because the Greenwich's Act prevented its lines from being used then. Thursday 15 November 1849 saw service reduced, on some lines at least, to a Sunday one because the Queen had appointed it as a General Thanksgiving Day, following the end of a cholera epidemic, though the editor of *The Times* was more realistic: he suggested practical drainage improvements were needed, not a day of prayer. The Crimean War resulted in similar reductions, when Wednesday 26 April 1854, was appointed as a Day of National Humiliation and Prayer to mark entry into the war; Wednesday 21 March 1855 received similar treatment. Another occurred on 7 October 1857, the day appointed for Humiliation and Prayer after the Indian Mutiny.[8]

The most controversial interruptions occurred every time there were important race meetings. Trains running when most racegoers needed them ran at higher fares, had extra passengers crammed in, took longer over the journey and first-class tickets had 'First-class accommodation is not guaranteed' printed on them. A couple of examples from 1856 were an LBSC notice for Epsom races which said ordinary trains would not run on the Mitcham & Wimbledon and Croydon & Epsom lines on Derby and Oaks days (28, 30 May) but would be replaced by a special, more frequent service and an LSW notice for Ascot Races which said that on 10 and 12 June the ordinary service from London to Twickenham, Windsor and Hounslow would be suspended 'but trains will be run at intervals uncertain'. In July 1862 there were protests that passengers were seen during the day arriving with children, servants and luggage to find all arrangements thrown out.[9] None of this made any impact: the special traffic was far too profitable to be sacrificed for the interests of captive regular passengers. A further example was Saturday 20 June 1868 when the LSW's arrangements for the Volunteer Review in Windsor Great Park meant certain timetabled trains would not run or would stop short of their usual destinations and after 6.15 p.m. passengers would not be conveyed from Windsor or Datchet until all Volunteers had left. In 1869 the ordinary service through Barnes was suspended from 1 to 4 p.m. on 15 March for the Oxford and Cambridge Boat Race and on 27 August for the Oxford and Harvard Boat Race.

Financial problems sometimes caused difficulties. A particularly shambolic railway was the Potteries, Shrewsbury & North Wales, opened 13 August 1866. On 27 November bailiffs entered its Shrewsbury station and when a train arrived its engine and carriages were seized, despite the fact that many had bought tickets for the return journey. Ultimately it was allowed to go but at the time the news was sent to *The Times*, the Under-sheriff had refused to make further concessions and since it was a fair day at Shrewsbury many were stranded. On 3 December the Acting-sheriff relented and the service resumed but a bailiff travelled with the train and remained on it at night.[10] The Hoylake Railway suffered on 4 July 1870: a considerable length through the land of Mr Vyner, who had been unable to obtain settlement of a claim, was seized by sheriff's officers and taken up. It had to devise a makeshift station at Leasowe Crossing and take its patrons on to Seacombe by road.[11]

Awkward individuals could also inconvenience the majority. Captain Bacon objected to the use of locomotives on the Newcastle & Carlisle and gained a temporary stoppage of traffic on 28 March 1835, only a couple of weeks after the line had opened to Hexham, because the company's Act had only authorised horse-power; however the resultant public outcry caused him to relent, trains resumed on 6 May, and the company obtained a new Act.[12]

The Navigation station (now Abercynon) on the Taff Vale served its locality and acted as junction station for the line to Aberdare. The Company fell out with the landlord of the nearby inn and refused to sell tickets to people who had visited it, the only place of refreshment thereabouts; law cases had gone against it so on 1 November 1855 it stopped issuing local tickets there, though keeping it in use for exchange purposes. The publican's lawyer wrote to the Board of Trade, which claimed it was a private matter best left to individuals to resolve before the courts; even a petition drawn up at a public meeting in Merthyr failed to move it. Eventually sanity prevailed and the station was reopened fully on 1 May 1856.[13]

Constructional and Structural failures

Newly-built lines were vulnerable. The branch to Gosport opened on 29 November 1841, against the inspector's advice (the Board of Trade had yet to receive power to prohibit) and bad weather caused several slips in the earth works so on 4 December the service was suspended; it resumed on 7 February 1842. Two days after the Croydon, Mitcham and Wimbledon Railway was opened on 22 October 1855 the service was briefly suspended after an accident near Beddington, in which the driver was killed; all five passengers were travelling second-class in the last of three carriages while the one nearest the tender, a third, was smashed so none were seriously injured. The inquest verdict was 'accidental death' and the jury endorsed Colonel Yolland's suggested 20 mph limit. There are suggestions that the line had been badly laid, especially with regard to ballast, but blame was put on the driver, who had been told to ignore the timetable and keep speed down yet was going at an estimated 27 mph. Officialdom all had a vested interest in absolving the company and GP Bidder, the contractor operating the line: Yolland had passed the line fit for opening only a few days before and said the ballasting was no worse than on many new lines – it just needed time to settle.[14]

Tunnels sometimes failed. Part of the roof of the Bramhope Tunnel fell on a passenger train on 19 September 1854 and the line was not reopened until 1 January 1855. The Thurgoland Tunnel partially collapsed on 14 July 1855 when there were no trains in it; the hole was about 16 feet x 10 feet, the result of an old mine-shaft not being sufficiently filled. The line was closed and passengers were taken from Wortley through Mr Corbett's grounds in omnibuses; the delay being about 20 minutes. Repairs proceeded so fast that they were able to resume working through the tunnel on the 17th.[15] Nearly all the traffic on the GN main line was suspended from Thursday evening, 25 October 1856 to the Sunday owing to a considerable portion of Stoke tunnel, a few miles south of Grantham, falling-in, though no train was involved; all traffic from Grantham to Peterborough was sent by the 'Loop', 20 miles further while traffic between Peterborough and the damaged portion went by a special service. The company's handling of this drew a blast from 'WC', writing on behalf of a lady who, on the Saturday, had bought a first-class ticket for Nottingham by the 10.30 a.m. from Kings Cross. No indication was given of delays, though officials at Kings Cross knew the line was blocked. The first she knew was when she saw luggage being turned out at Peterborough and when she enquired, she was told she must wait for the 5 pm. No explanation was given – it needed a resolute enquiry to establish the cause, in the face of indifference amounting almost to rudeness. Eventually they went on and at the scene some passengers scrambled over the top of the tunnel on foot while those incapable of doing so or encumbered with children were taken slowly through it in an open carriage drawn by horses. It was probably dangerous; it was certainly terrifying for ladies and children. She could have travelled via the Midland if she had known of the problem.[16] A tunnel at Llangunllo on the Central Wales section of the LNW collapsed on 12 February 1868; there were no casualties but the line was blocked. Later in the day service was resumed: trains ran to the ends of the tunnel (about ¾ mile long) and passengers walked between them.[17]

Bridges were also vulnerable. That across the Dee collapsed on 24 May 1847, killing three passengers and injuring 17. On the night of 21 September 1858 a timber viaduct 150 yards in length carrying the Trent Valley line at Beswick over the River Penk and the Trent & Mersey Canal was destroyed by fire; through traffic resumed after a temporary bridge had been completed, trains going over slowly.[18] Near Saltley, on the GW line between Chester and Shrewsbury, sparks from an engine caught a hedge alight and the fire spread to the timbers of a bridge in April 1868. The fire was put out with water from an engine's tender and by spreading ballast on the sleepers; after an inspection (one suspects very perfunctory), a passenger train was allowed across.[19]

Sometimes it was the line's foundations that gave way. In December 1845 a portion of the Newcastle & Darlington, 50 to 60 yards long, running over Morden Carr, about 8 miles north of Darlington, gave way about 9 o'clock, and sank in the marshy ground on which the foundation had been constructed. It was necessary to transfer passengers and luggage across the obstruction to another train; one of the third-class passengers alighted on the wrong side in the dark and had a cold bath. The same transfer arrangement was in force next day while 200 workmen were engaged on repairing the damage but incessant rain meant little progress was made: as soon as ballast was added, the additional weight caused it to sink again. Thus they constructed a temporary line, avoiding the swamp and uniting the sound portions of the line; this was so far completed in two days that it was no longer necessary to transfer passengers and luggage: the carriages were pushed over one at a time and taken on by another engine, the original engine being left behind.[20]

Nature

Nature was the greatest disruptive agent. Heavy rain was the most frequent culprit but wind, frost and snow also played their part. In some respects railways have always been particularly vulnerable given their many embankments, cuttings, bridges and tunnels, all of which can cause trouble. However, there were items on the credit side: as early as December 1836 it was reported that Whitby had been cut off by road but trains on the line from Pickering, then horse-drawn, had been able to get through and in 1867 this line remained passable when others nearby were closed even though the drifts were so deep that the carriage steps were cutting through them.

An example of how both road and rail transport was affected was provided by events early in 1841. There was a heavy fall of snow, particularly in the south and west, which delayed many mail coaches though most battled through; the Lynn and Cambridge Mail arrived in London in time for the first delivery, but this was much later than usual, not starting until ten minutes to ten, the Worcester Mail only arrived just in time for the afternoon delivery at a quarter to three, and the Brighton Mail was only a little delayed but had had to go through so much water that it had not carried any inside passengers. A drift of fifteen feet stopped the Bath Mail so the guard took his mail bag on by horseback. Trains brought the Liverpool, Manchester and Birmingham mail in on time, but without the Edinburgh and Glasgow bags, which were brought on by midday; the Exeter mail, also taken part way by rail arrived after eleven. The LSW was the worst hit railway: one engine was so deeply embedded near Woking that the united efforts of six others could not shift it and workmen had to be sent to dig it out.[21]

Later that year there were widespread floods. On 6 December the Northern & Eastern warned some services would be discontinued and others shortened owing to the unprecedented wet weather. The worst sufferer seems to have been the London & Brighton, which had only opened throughout on 21 September. Early in October its drivers were ordered to take an extra quarter of an hour for every journey during the winter months. A fall of earth in the cutting at Merstham on the 30th interrupted services and travellers had to be taken four miles by road between Merstham and a temporary station at Hooley House. On 2 November they advertised that all obstructions would be removed that day, and trains would run throughout 'tomorrow'. Unfortunately, that very day there was a serious fall in the clay cutting north of Dartmouth Arms (now Forest Hill) which stopped both Brighton and Croydon trains. Thus on 4 November the London & Brighton said passengers were being conveyed between New Cross and Dartmouth Arms, 2½ miles, by coaches and the rest of the way by rail. Croydon passengers had to walk a short distance over New Cross Hill; one train left passengers at New Cross and another was brought close to the south end of the obstruction. On the 20th they were able to say the obstruction had been removed and a reduced service would run on and after Monday, the 22nd. The respite was only brief for on 7 January another extensive slip occurred near Finch's Bridge, essentially a continuation of the earlier one; the rails were covered for 140 yards to a depth of 9 feet. Men were immediately sent; by the end of the day 1,000 were employed there. A platform, which would be covered with an awning, was set up so that passengers could pass over the slip to a train waiting the other side and they would not be detained more than 10 minutes.[22]

1848 was another year of multiple trouble. For example the SE Canterbury branch was interrupted when floods broke down a bridge; a footway was carried across and trains operated from either side. Similarly floods temporarily cut the line between Swavesey and St Ives and a bridge or two was reported down on the Northampton – Peterborough line.[23]

Floods continued to be a nuisance (and sometimes still are – the line along the coast at Dawlish was a frequent casualty, then as now); only a few examples are given. Late 1852/early 1853 the effects were again widespread: in October 1852 floods caused the slip of several thousand yards of earthworks near Grantham and such was the damage that in January 1853 nearly 300 men were said to be still at work clearing the damage; they were then working over a single line laid on top of the displaced earth.[24] The main line to the west was so badly affected that on Saturday 13 November no train reached Taunton until 8.30 p.m. when 'three trains conjoined' arrived, one of which carried the London mail.[25] Later that month ingenuity was shown when floods affected the line two or three miles south of Oxford: at Kennington Crossing the engine was moved to the rear of its train, from where it pushed its carriages as far as it could, horses were harnessed to pull them through the flood and an engine waiting the other side took them on. This added about 20 minutes to the journey time.[26] An LNW notice warned that until the effect of recent continuous rains had ceased to have effect, the speed of fast trains would be reduced. Widespread flooding near Essendine, on the GN, loosened the earth under the line so that when 'a powerful and ponderous locomotive used for the mail trains' tried to pass through it found itself on the line without any support and zig-zagged into the mud; there were no casualties but traffic was suspended.[27]

A particularly vicious set of storms hit several parts of the country in August 1857. The rain was so heavy that nearly a quarter of a mile of the Midland's Nottingham to Lincoln line was washed away near Fiskerton. The worst damage was done between Newark and Retford; there the culverts beside the line were unable to take the water, which washed away the low embankment under the lines. Since it was dark the driver of a fish train from the north failed to see the danger and his train collapsed into the floods; before anyone had time to act a passenger train going the opposite way had followed into the ditch. Two days later they had already constructed a 'tramway of a single line ... in a sinuous form to afford a passage of the regular trains through the wreck'.[28]

In late August and September 1866 there were reports of much damage to crops, stock being drowned, and towns flooded in Yorkshire and other areas. The Malton &

Whitby line suffered the loss of a bridge over the Esk at Grosmont but when the floods lessened they succeeded in throwing a temporary bridge across and traffic resumed three days later. Nearby there was worse trouble on the North Yorkshire & Cleveland line: the last train from Whitby came off the rails near Trenholme Bar where it was believed recent rains had caused some settlement in a culvert under the line.[29]

Frost and snow also frequently caused problems though ingenuity was sometimes used to overcome this; in February 1844 engines on the Hull & Selby were reportedly being preceded by a waggon with brooms attached to clear snow. In 1838 a severe frost caused some of the tubes in the boiler of a London & Greenwich engine to burst; there was a temporary delay to some trains but the damage was soon repaired.[30] More serious consequences followed the freezing of some of the pipes on a Midland Counties goods train in 1841: while the problem was being sorted out, a passenger train ran into the back of the goods killing two and injuring another two.

Late 1846 'Frigidus' recounted a tale of woe occupying 1½ columns. He claimed that a Saturday 7 30 p.m. train from Newcastle to Durham, sent with insufficient power to cope with the snow, stopped shortly after Leamside and its fire was drawn out. He was on the Mail which came upon the failure and towed it back to Fencehouses, reached at 1 a.m., though they had sufficient power to have pushed the other onwards. They needed help from Gateshead, where the company boasted of having relief engines in readiness but the station-master at Fencehouses was inexperienced in using the electric telegraph and only resorted to it at the demand of the passengers. No answer was received until about 10, when they were told they would be reached in about 1½ hours, men being set down at intervals to clear the snow. At Fencehouses there was a small and dirty public house where scarlet fever was raging, three small cottages, two pigsties, a cowshed and a station-house; they had to cope with the passengers from two trains. They were only able to get poor coffee, a little bread, cheese and bacon at high prices, with some passengers having to rely on the charity of others; there was also one rabbit pie, of which his share was two ribs and a morsel of piecrust though the worst of the suffering was from cold. Most ladies and some gentlemen were able to procure beds but others, men and women together, slept on the waiting-room floor, and some in the booking-office where the favoured place was under the counter, sheltered from draught. One old lady unable to get a bed at night bought the privilege of turning into one in a cottage when its occupants left; at least she got a warm bed but was disturbed by five or six men who spent the day smoking and drinking in the room. On Sunday an engine from Belmont approached but it went away again, showing they could at least have got food and blankets to them. Monday about noon Mr Allport, superintendent at Gateshead, arrived with five engines; he refused to take them forward but suggested they should go back to Gateshead while he would go on a few miles to clear the line. After a lengthy delay Allport came back but would not provide an engine to take them on: they would have to wait for the next mail. They pointed out the danger from more snow but he said he did not want anyone to tell him his business; when they complained they had no food or blankets he told them to take the matter up with Providence or the company's solicitor. He brought a director, Mr Plews of Darlington, who said their hardships were nothing compared with his – though a director and colleague of a great King [Hudson] he had exposed himself on the tender since breakfast time. 'Wonderful devotion!'; he had sacrificed his lunch and was earning his fees while Frigidus had paid £3 4 6d and nearly froze and starved. Allport seems to have had second thoughts for he sent a relief train a few hours before the mail would have been due.[31]

In February 1847 it took four hours for a GW train to cut its way through snow between Bristol and Keynsham.[32] The temporary blocking by deep snow of the line between Huddersfield and Penistone in May 1853 meant the train was stopped about a mile after Penistone and the passengers (thirteen or fourteen) had had to be led back there, to find solace in the inns.[33]

In 1854 there was a spate of letters about incidents where wheels of their carriages had broken owing to frost, one on the GN near Hitchin, others on the GW near Slough and Pangbourne and one on the LSW between Winchester and Bishopstoke. In the Slough and LSW cases men who had seen part of a tyre fly past were able to lean out of their windows and attract the notice of porters to stop the trains. No serious injuries occurred in any of these cases.[34]

The line between Berwick-upon-Tweed and Dunbar was blocked for several days in December 1859, trains being sent meanwhile via Tweedmouth and Kelso.[35] The LCD and Eastern Counties felt it wisest to take precautions during the severe winter of 1860-1 when there were items about the hardship caused to those out of work as consequence of continuous frosts from December and many advertisements for contributions to relief funds. The LCD limited expresses to 24 mph, ordinary trains to 20 mph while the Eastern Counties was more general – express and fast trains would be allowed extra time, and they were also making extra stops so that wheels could be checked more often. Early 1867 Kent was so badly hit that the War Office allowed men from the garrison at Chatham to help with clearance, the Great Eastern was briefly closed and in the North Riding of Yorkshire drifting was so bad that trains had been marooned and some passengers had had to spend a night in the snow.[36]

Labour troubles

Victorian railway managers were autocratic figures prepared to meet trouble head on and circumstances favoured them: railway jobs involved very long hours and quasi-military discipline but their security made them much sought-after and a grumbling driver or porter knew he could be easily replaced. An early example of a successful tough approach came in 1848 when the LNW was cutting wages in its southern area. The resultant strike was broken by sacking strikers and using a variety of hastily gathered substitutes, including drivers from the northern area and Thames steamboat men; where necessary, drivers ignorant of the route were accompanied on the footplate by guards who did know it. These strikers were later reinstated thanks to a director who was an M.P. but all were not so lucky later.[37]

However, the big stick did not always work. The East Lancashire was faced with various troubles in 1849: disputes about wages were settled but the locomotive men were so determined to receive their orders from 'their man', the Locomotive Superintendent, Beattie, not the overall Superintendent of the Line, Royale, whom they regarded as unfit for his post, that they struck. At first authority sought to keep trains working by bringing in replacements from the Enginemakers' Club (whatever that was). No train ran on time and there were various minor collisions; on occasion trains stalled and passengers preferred to walk rather than trust their lives to novices. After ten days, local shareholders' pressure forced Royale's dismissal and the return of the experienced men; those replacements judged competent enough were offered jobs as fitters, mechanics and porters.[38]

In 1850 trouble on the North British resulted in many men being replaced. According to *The Times* in April late trains were a daily occurrence and there was frequent damage to engines owing to the newcomers' ignorance. A mail train came to a stand and the fireman promoted to drive it did not know what to do; he became so alarmed that he jumped off, catching his foot in a wheel and severely injuring himself. One newcomer had driven straight through Dunbar station at full speed. The directors aimed to reduce wages to 4s a day when working in the sheds (the average overall daily wage was 6s).[39] On 11 May an inexperienced replacement brought an engine from the engine-house to put at the head of his train waiting in Edinburgh station, and put on additional steam instead of shutting it off, while the porter acting as his assistant turned the brake handle the wrong way. They collided with their train but an empty truck at its head absorbed most of the shock and injuries to passengers were only slight. Captain Laffan reported that of the 42 drivers then working, six were old hands who had returned, six old firemen who had returned and been promoted, nine had come from other companies and 21 were mechanics from the workshops, three of whom had some driving experience. The one who had caused the collision had been sent back to the workshops and the rest had been carefully selected and would soon be as efficient as the old. Would all passengers have agreed?

Later that year it was the Eastern Counties' turn. John Viret Gooch had recently been appointed and most of the company's drivers had resigned over what they saw as attempt to reduce earnings, get rid of longer-serving (thus higher paid) men and impose large fines for damage to engines for which drivers could not fairly be blamed. One consequence was a great reduction in trains, starting 19 August, including complete closure of the Maldon and Braintree branches.[40] On 20 August there were letters from 'Q' (season ticket holder), 'AB' and 'Norviensis' complaining about delays, business inconvenience and dangers of accidents; they seem to have blamed the company and taken the drivers' side. There were also letters about actual damage, minor accidents and general incompetence on the part of the replacements but much of this was hearsay with suspect technical detail. Next day the board put its side, saying Gooch had inherited a poorly run department and stern measures were needed to correct this, but John Hunter, the replaced locomotive superintendent, denied this and included a copy of his dismissal letter saying he had been a good servant but the board were determined to reorganise. Full service was resumed on the 26th, 'the staff of engine drivers now being completely reorganised': drivers had been given a week's notice and sacked.[41] However, an accident at Enfield on 8 September revealed a potentially dangerous state of affairs: the company had engaged Robinson, who claimed previous driving experience and for about a month had satisfactorily driven pilot engines and coal trains. On the day in question he was driving a passenger train on the Enfield branch, which he had only travelled once before, with a coal train; the guard was told to ride on the engine and tell him where to stop. He had reported a faulty brake but lacked the knowledge to describe the fault accurately and those responsible for repairs had not checked it properly so it was still nearly useless. He approached Enfield station too fast and his lack of experience meant that his first attempt at reversing the engine failed as the handle flew forward again; a second attempt was successful but they hit the buffers, without causing serious damage or injuries. The company's officers blamed the driver and his fireman and sacked them. This hampered Laffan's enquiries since they had reportedly gone overseas by the time he wanted to question them. Laffan's verdict was that Robinson was not the real villain but he was surprisingly lenient in his comments on the company. He put the accident down to 'the unforeseen difficulties into which [it] had been thrown by the sudden withdrawal of their old drivers [and] their being thereby compelled to accept the services, in some instances, of comparatively inexperienced men'. His moderation probably resulted from his belief that strikers were always wrong, whatever the circumstances; this view was then standard with officialdom and meant companies could behave in blatantly irresponsible ways, escaping the censure they sometimes deserved. At the start of 1851 this was shown to be a widely-held view when the LNW successfully faced down threats from their drivers. *The Times* fully supported the company and claimed the public felt the same: 'The past fortnight has proved that the public prefer submitting for a short time to the inconvenience of reduced trains and diminished speed on a particular line rather than yield to a combination amongst the drivers.' It also pointed out that drivers no longer possessed the bargaining power of ten years before since far more men now had their skill – the LNW had not experienced any problems when it had advertised for replacements. Indeed, it went on to say that the time had come to demand better qualified drivers since the existing ones were, 'in a vast majority of instances, illiterate and devoid of that mechanical knowledge which would seem to be absolutely a requisite in their position'.[42]

In 1867 there were strikes in many industries and the railways were no exception. In March the LBSC gave notice that its timetable had to be considered in abeyance; many trains would have to be taken off and the speed of the rest diminished. The strike was partly about reducing hours to 10 per day, 60 per week and how to calculate this; partly about the way in which men who had done their training were not promoted to their new rank because officials were pressing foremen to keep down costs. Some matters had already been agreed by negotiation. The strike soon ended, and normal traffic resumed, negotiation settling the other differences too.[43] At the same time there were threats on both the Midland and parts of the NE; that on the latter resulted in many losing their jobs but an LSW dispute was settled without this.[44]

Run-of-the-mill delays

Then, as now, late-running trains were a fertile source of complaint; until the telegraph was in full use delays could also lead to rumours of accidents as people at stations where a train was seriously overdue speculated, often wildly, on the reason. One such occasion was Sunday night 27 August 1837 when great crowds collected at Euston as trains failed to appear; a derailment at Harrow, in which there were no casualties, had blocked the line.[45] Complaints were usually mere factual recitals but occasionally a complainant adopted a more facetious tone. 'Punctuality' wrote in March 1846 about late running on the Barnes line which was supposed to have an express service: that morning he had only been 33 minutes late and had reached Waterloo at 9.43 thanks to a stopping train which pushed them for some distance, being itself afraid of the express from Putney due at 9.40.[46]

As an early line the London & Birmingham was particularly vulnerable. 'A Passenger' said there had been many delays but one on Tuesday 31 October 1837 had outdone the others. The 7 p.m. from Tring had stopped about two miles beyond Watford because there had been a derailment. The passengers at first whiled away the time by singing e.g. *Adam Bell, the Dustman*, but gradually lost patience. Initially all the company did was send an engine to try to move the blockage; eventually it sent an engine and carriages to rescue the passengers, but they had to walk past the blockage through mud, more time was wasted in transferring luggage and they finally arrived at 1 a.m. On Saturday 4 November 1837 shortly after 8, an engine was derailed just after Harrow, illustrating the difficulties sometimes faced in getting help to early incidents. A man made his way across the fields to Harrow and took a post-chaise to London to fetch a rescue train, which arrived between 1 and 2 a.m..[47]

Further north on 2 October 1837 the 11.30 trains from Liverpool and Manchester to Birmingham were delayed by nearly three hours. Usually they were joined at Warrington Junction and went on with both engines but this time one train arrived with a defective engine and all were taken on by one. There was no problem until nine miles from Whitmore, when the engine declined to go any further; a consultation of enginemen, conductors, firemen, guards and passengers was now held to inquire into the refractory conduct of the engine and they unanimously resolved that the load was too heavy. The Manchester train was unhooked and the engine, refreshed, took the Liverpool part on to Whitmore, left it, and went back for the Mancunians.[48]

Nearer London all was not going quite so smoothly either. In February 1838 'JS' described his experiences on the London & Greenwich. Since trains were timetabled for every quarter-hour, he was at their London entrance at about 4.35, hoping to leave at 4.45. He 'bivouaced' about five minutes over a coke fire, when the person who took the 'checks' said (alluding to the engine) 'here she comes', and he was directed to a carriage. It soon filled so he expected to go but 5 o'clock came, a quarter after passed and still there was no satisfactory explanation. Fares continued to be taken and more passengers were put in the overcrowded carriages. At half past five they moved about 200 or 300 yards, then returned to hook up the 5.30 and reached Deptford after a very slow passage a few minutes before 6. He understood that a breakdown had occurred.[49]

Particularly unlucky were the passengers on a Taff Vale train from Merthyr in April 1844. In a tunnel near Navigation House (Abercynon) the engine derailed and they waited two or three hours while it was put back; within about five miles of Cardiff it came off again and they had to walk the rest of the way in the dark.[50] Another unlucky group suffered on their way to Paddington late in February 1850. The train that should have left at 4 a.m. was delayed until 5 30 a.m. 'on account of the fracture of one of the cranks of the engine' so it was taken on by a goods engine which expired shortly before Shrivenham. A replacement from Swindon eventually got them to Paddington two and three-quarter hours late. One particular passenger was even unluckier than the rest: he was among a group who left the train to walk on to Shrivenham station and was caught so firmly in a poacher's snare that the others had to help release him. At least, once at Shrivenham, 'the landlady (Miss Coombs), very kindly and liberally afforded the guests the utmost attention' until the rescue engine arrived.[51]

Mr Blews of Birmingham complained about the LNW in October 1856 after goods accidents had blocked the line near Wolverton. He accepted these were inevitable but the company had continued to take money and issue tickets at Euston instead of giving passengers information that might have let them make alternative arrangements. Trains were still allowed to leave London and places north of Wolverton, then were stopped in mid-country. Passengers were held for six to 18 hours, the majority without food or fire. At length the wreckage was cleared and they went on, arriving at Birmingham 15 hours late. On the way they passed about 14 passenger and luggage trains 'at anchor' [presumably south-bound trains held north of Wolverton]. 'Orpheus', the husband of a lady 'in a condition where the consequences of such action might have been fatal' was also on one of the trains so held: she was kept for 14 hours without refreshment and for some time in anticipation of immediate death. The station-master at Wolverton had taken no steps to help.[52]

Some things do not seem to have improved by 1867, at least if an incident on the GN was any guide. 'A' left London on Tuesday 5 November by the 4.30 p.m. train; about 5 it stopped and they were shunted onto a side-rail, distant from any station. There they remained in darkness until 9.30 while several trains passed at full speed. At

9.45 they reached the scene of an accident and passengers from the injured train were moved into theirs, which took 1½ hours because of the difficulty of getting passengers and luggage off and on trains not in a station. About 11 they left Welwyn Junction and reached their destination at Huntingdon 12.30. At Welwyn the refreshment room was not open (he had had no food since 2), nor at Hitchin Junction. The people there said they had had no notice – but the accident was only a few miles away. 'G', his wife and another lady had left Kings Cross by the 5.5 p.m. At Hatfield, they were shunted to a side line and remained there until 12, shut up in the dark with no opportunity of even going to a refreshment room. They reached Biggleswade, their destination, at 3 a.m.[53]

Delays were sometimes caused when the status of a train was apparently changed in mid-journey. In 1851 there were accusations that the LNW was charging passengers extra for mail trains but providing an inferior service. 'EM' was engaged in a case at Carlisle Assizes and on 4 August joined the express mail advertised to leave Euston 8.45, arriving Carlisle 7.55 a.m, but it did not start until 10 minutes before 10 and reached Carlisle at 11 next morning. On the way they were told they were late because of the length of their train but at Carlisle the truth came out: the mail had arrived on time, made up of four or five carriages and a post-office van but theirs had been converted without warning into a 'train of ease' for Scottish excursionists. Next month 'One who has twice paid mail fare and each time had to travel by the excursion train' had in mid-August come from Scotland by the night-mail. At Carlisle the mail separated (according to the guards – he was not fully awake), at Crewe they were two hours late, at Atherston they were kept in a siding for 50 minutes to allow an express from Manchester (due London 4, theirs at 1) to pass and by then they had 27 carriages because a stopping train, variously described by porters as excursion or parliamentary, had been added at the rear. He arrived at Euston at 5.35; when he asked if he was in the second division of the mail he was told it was the third. Next day 'An Occasional Traveller' said he had taken a ticket at Euston for Aberdeen; a lengthy train, perhaps 27 carriages was at the platform and there was much confusion. A few minutes after the appointed departure time he saw an engine with two or three carriages and a Post Office van steal quietly out of the station on an outer line. Spencer Lyttleton (Guards' Club) wrote that he had tried to get a refund of the difference between mail and excursion fare in similar circumstances but the outcome had been a lengthy correspondence, many legal quibbles and a refusal to admit maladministration or to pay. The truth of these complaints was borne out in a report that followed an accident at Kirtlebridge on 11 September. The LNW's habit of letting excursionists use the Mail had resulted in lateness and complaints from the Post Office so they had adopted the practice of dividing the train. The first division was supposed to take mail and first-class passengers, who were given a slip of paper telling them to ask the foreman on the platform where to go for their train and, allegedly, this practice had recently been extended to second-class passengers; the complaints above suggested that this was not entirely true. The second division was supposed to run 15 minutes after the first but

Captain Wynne was told at Kirtlebridge that it was 'generally' between one and four hours late. He clearly regarded the company's conduct as dishonest, but, as in so many matters, the Commissioners were powerless to provide the passenger with redress.[54]

Inadequate engine power was regularly alleged. 'An Oxford Man' writing from Louth in 1847 complained about the worn-out character of Hudson's line between Nottingham and Lincoln. An engine stopped because the fire had burnt through the iron and cinders were falling on the line; happily there was a drain nearby and a pickaxe was used to get a large tile and break it in two so the hole was blocked and posts and rails were used to get the fire going; they crawled to Lincoln at the speed of an omnibus going up Ludgate Hill.[55] In 1850 Mortimer Adye, Captain Royal Artillery, complained about the North Kent line. Speed had slackened on entering a tunnel near Blackheath; they stopped, after a few minutes went on a little way, then slipped back. This continued for about 40 minutes and they arrived at Blackheath about 45 minutes late. Many passengers were terrified, especially as there was no information from the railwaymen.[56] In December 1857 a journey on the Eastern Counties was described by a passenger who had left London by the 2.30 on a Saturday afternoon. The engine could hardly draw its train to Lea Bridge station; it had managed to start again from there but had come to a dead stop before Tottenham. Three or four minutes later a chance engine was seen coming up behind; it pushed them on to Tottenham, where it got them going again and left them. It took 24 minutes to go from Ponders End to Waltham (3 miles) and then only with the help of a goods which pushed them from Ordnance Factory. They reached Waltham 43 minutes late on a journey of only 15 miles.[57]

William Tidmas wrote a lengthy letter in 1865 complaining about Midland delays connected with the four-year old station at Trent, giving statistics: in 1863 the average delay from Nottingham to Leicester and London was 33 minutes, in 1864 it was 27 minutes. In 16 journeys from 11 August to 11 September (inclusive) 1865 there were delays of 15 to 71 minutes, totalling 603 minutes. There were many local complaints, especially from doctors delayed in getting to critical illnesses and accidents, frequent in the mining and manufacturing district.[58] Later that year the LBSC was the target. OW had travelled 141 times on the Brighton line during the year: they were never on time – from 5 to 90 minutes late and the so called expresses were the worst. On 30 November it was reported that a memorial had been presented by a deputation of season-ticket holders complaining of late trains, defective engine power, insufficient porters, bad conditions of carriages and the habit of giving excursions precedence over regular trains, putting the latter into disarray.[59]

In 1867 there was a brief competition to see who could boast of the worst punctuality. 'A season-ticket holder' told readers that by the excellent arrangements of the LSW, Richmond to Waterloo was now being done in 50 minutes. 'A hardy annual' (Redhill) objected next day to the credit given to the LSW. They had an SE express to Dover which in the previous two days had performed the first 20 miles in 80 and 75 minutes, within about 30 minutes of time. The day after 'GPR' claimed a Sunday evening GE journey put all others into the shade: they had left Edmonton 9.20 p.m., and arrived at Bishopsgate 11.35, thus doing 9 miles in 2¼ hours.[60]

Some lost badly as a result of delays. H Butler, writing from the Clarence Hotel, Liverpool, on Christmas Day 1852, had intended to go to Ireland for Christmas and used a Parliamentary train supposed to leave Euston at 7 a.m., reaching Liverpool at 7.45 p.m. There was an unusual number of people buying tickets so it did not leave until 7.55 and more time was lost on the way. Eventually they arrived two hours late, it was past 10 before he cleared the station and the boat had gone.[61] Even the mighty could suffer similarly: in August 1853 a copy of a letter Lord Londonderry had written to the York & North Berwick was published, complaining about delays causing him to miss the fast train from Edinburgh to Glasgow and thus lose the last train to Gourock, where he had booked a steamboat passage.[62] Railway officials were not immune: when Captain Tyler inspected the line from Ladybank to Strathmiglo he was accompanied by various directors but the Chairman was missing since he had 'lost' his train from Edinburgh because one from Peebles was ten minutes late.[63]

There were some prepared to come to the defence of railway companies. After the letters criticising the LBSC in *The Times*, one signed by 17 regular users appeared on 8 January 1853, giving their testimony 'to the regularity and most satisfactory character' of its general arrangements. Two of the delays given special mention by the critics had resulted from failures on the SE; three of them claimed to have travelled more than 100,000 miles without injury or cause for alarm and they also considered that 'the fashion of indiscriminately censuring bodies of men – who in this instance deserve a high degree of praise for successful exertion instead – is calculated to dishearten them, discourage their efforts ... and is in every way mischievous'.

The credit side: keeping going

One theme that should already have been noticed was the variety of expedients used to keep things going, or at least to minimise delay. One factor in their favour was that large numbers could be rapidly mobilised to repair damage since there were many casual labourers earning their livings by the hour rather than the week. There were usually more of them than there was work available, especially in winter when bad weather often stopped some of what was available. The speed at which 'normal' service was resumed then was remarkable compared to the long delays often following road and rail accidents today as investigators search for clues about what caused them; then the primary concern was to get things moving again as fast as possible. The shortcomings of alternative forms of transport doubtless provided a spur to great efforts and there were no regulatory bodies to interfere. However, even today fast action is occasionally managed: a station was opened on 30 November 2009 at

Workington North to provide a connection between two parts of the town separated after floodwaters had destroyed road bridges across the Derwent a few days before.

After a collision between Hanwell and West Drayton on 28 July 1838 a guard obtained a post-chaise at Southall and went by road with the news; men were immediately sent to the spot to clear the wreckage.[64] Some interesting contrivances for getting defunct trains going again were suggested, and sometimes acted upon. In 1842 when 'No Railer' left Darlington at 3.50 a.m. about 27 miles further on a pipe in the engine was leaking, the train stopped, and the fire was taken out. No-one appeared authorised to do anything so he had suggested that since the train was very light they should detach the engine and get a pair of horses from a nearby farm to pull the train on to York but there was no response [did he explain how to get the engine out of the way?]. In the end the leak was filled with a wooden plug, the passengers broke down some neighbouring fences for fuel for a fresh fire and they went on to York, arriving an hour late. If this sort of thing happened very often it would help to explain why stray cows were a common cause of accidents.[65] Nothing further was seen about this incident but in 1850 a judge in the Lancashire County Court ordered the East Lancashire to pay £2 9s to a farmer for damage to his farm by trespassing passengers after a collision.[66]

Sometimes they were lucky to have someone qualified to attend to repairs. A train taking excursionists to see a Naval Review at Spithead in 1856 broke down. The driver, after tinkering and help from a passenger, Sir Charles Fox (a leading engineer of the period, knighted for his firm's part in building the Crystal Palace), was able to get the train going again and on to a siding; after another delay, a replacement engine took them on.[67]

The main companies had their preparations in place from a very early stage. In July 1839 the Grand Junction was interrupted when heavy rain brought loose gravel into a cutting near Bridgeford. A luggage train from Birmingham, pulled by two engines, ran into this between 3 and 4 a.m. and was derailed, blocking the lines. Soon after, up and down London mails approached the spot but both were stopped in time by signals; mail bags, passengers and luggage were then transferred across and spare engines were sent to take trains on, the carriages going back the way they had come – the rule then was that if a train was half an hour overdue at Warrington an engine was sent on the other line to find it They then sent another taking a gang of men and all the gear needed so the line was cleared by half an hour after midnight.[68] In the account of an accident at Colney Hatch on 30 August 1865 it was explained that it was the duty of those on the spot to telegraph at once to their superiors because there were always vans packed with cranes, screw-jacks and other necessary equipment ready to start at a moment's notice. In this case both lines were blocked and all traffic was stopped for fully two hours as gangs of men, totalling 200, were brought from London, Hatfield and Hitchin to clear 500 yards of track while others unloaded derailed coal trucks to make their removal easier.

Finally

Saturday 31 October 1846 was not a good day for travellers on the LNW. Northbound a train left London at 8.30 a.m. and found its way blocked because a goods train had run into a ballast one a few miles north of Stafford. That and a following passenger train reversed to Stafford; after a two-hour wait they set off again but were delayed, this time for two and a half hours, because a goods had been derailed. At Crewe the two passenger trains were combined and left nearly five hours late. They reached Chelford just after 9 p.m., and soon after were hit in rear by another wayward goods; it was now that Mr Greg's carriage was smashed and other casualties caused as their train was pushed 50 yards by the impact. The survivors reached Manchester about six hours late and many other trains were delayed. Meanwhile, it was not much better on the way south: 'A Passenger' related his experiences on the express which left Manchester at about 5 p.m. Near Crewe they were detained for 80 minutes because the line was blocked by spillage from one of those derailed going the other way and near Blisworth they were alarmed by the explosion of a detonator which warned them that a goods was just ahead; this cost them 15 minutes. Below Wolverton they were stopped by signals and whist they were waiting he smelled burning and saw that a wheel of his carriage was on fire; after 'considerable hollaing' he attracted a guard who had 'thought he had smelt something' but ignored it. 'The woodwork of the wheel was giving out a jet of sparks and smoke, a part of the iron work was red hot'. The fire was quenched and the damaged carriage detached, causing a further delay as passengers and luggage were moved. There were four more delays, two of which were caused by a cattle train in front and they finally reached Euston after 2 a.m., instead of at 11 p.m.[69]

It should be noted that trains could also be early: at one stage the guards and driver of a GW goods train (carrying third-class passengers) conspired to run their train early to Chippenham to give themselves a longer dinner break. Their employers were not amused when they found out about this little habit in 1847, though no complaints from passengers were mentioned.[70] William Tune, from near Barnsley, did complain after he had gone to Bramwith on 26 January 1857; when he went back to the station to return he found the train had already left, according to him, five minutes early. He successfully sued and received £1 10s damages and £1 5s 8d costs from the South Yorkshire Company. It had disputed his version but the judge could not have been impressed by the lack of a clock at Bramwith and conflicting evidence from various railway personnel.[71]

As his train approached Narborough on the LNW's South Leicestershire branch in February 1868, the driver saw something between the tracks but could not stop until he had gone 300 yards past. He, his guard and several passengers went back and discovered a drunken navvy asleep, and unharmed, between the rails. He did not like being woken and it needed the combined efforts of several men to overcome his resistance to being moved so they had to fetch a trolley to carry him to the train, which took him to Leicester to recover his senses in a police cell.[72]

The following year there was a cause of delays that would be a gift to the modern press. The LNW's top officials were anxious that their prestige trains should run to time and in 1869 they investigated regular delays on the Holyhead line. The cause was traced to 'fish droppings' from trucks of fish from Ireland. Their recommendation was that the truck bottoms should be sealed to prevent drips and a new design be considered for future trucks.[73]

Chapter 17: ACCIDENTS

Introduction

GREAT HUMSLEY RAILROAD

The directors of this undertaking, viewing with regret the frequent recurrence of inevitable accidents arising out of this else unparalleled mode of travelling, beg to submit to a liberal and discerning public a few regulations which have been adopted by them upon this popular line ... they have engaged an experienced surgeon to travel with each train, ... convenient hearses will also be attached to each, together with handsome coffins, suited to all sizes of persons, so that immediate accommodation may be afforded to the remains of the nobility and gentry ... and likewise light covered vans, furnished with clean dry straw, for the bodies of passengers by the third class carriages ...

From *John Bull*, copied by *The Times* 14 December 1840

The piece above was a caricature but fears might not have been allayed by an item in 1838 that the Manchester & Leeds had, 'in consideration of the probable occurrence of accidents on their line, ... given an annual subscription of five guineas to the Halifax Infirmary', though after reflection they might have felt this would hardly cover wholesale carnage.[1] An 1842 piece claimed feeling in Cheltenham was so great against railway travel that a lady had offered £5 for an inside place to London by one of the road coaches which was booked full and no-one felt inclined to relinquish his place for that sum.[2] The enthusiasm with which large numbers were taking to railway travel belies this contention, though, after a minor collision to a train almost immediately after leaving Paddington in 1846, many passengers 'from the fright they had experienced, returned to town, their money being given back by the clerks in the office'.[3]

The press regularly exaggerated. *The Times* began an item of 19 February 1839, 'During the last few days several accidents, some of them of a most serious and calamitous nature' had occurred on the London & Birmingham; the details showed that three of those listed were the results of individuals' own carelessness and only the fourth had caused injuries, mostly slight. An Act of 1840 ordered accidents attended with personal injury occurring in the course of public traffic to be reported to the Board of Trade; its returns frequently added phrases like 'none seriously' or 'mostly minor' in the injuries column.[4] The 1869 LBSC return even included one who had slightly injured his finger when a carriage strap (used for pulling the door closed and adjusting the window) broke and another whose thumb was pinched between a door and its frame owing to his carelessness.

However, there were many accidents and at times it seemed impossible to open a newspaper without finding a reference to at least one. Furthermore, during the period covered, they caused increasing numbers of casualties: trains were becoming more frequent, faster and heavier but safety measures were not being developed in proportion. It was far more dangerous to work on railways, whether on the footplate, on track maintenance or in goods yards, where wagons tended to be shunted about rather casually; even worse were the casualties suffered by navvies building the lines. In general the statistics show that Scottish lines had far fewer accidents than English ones, even taking population differences into account. An exceptional year was 1862, when more were killed there than in England, when a head-on collision near Winchburgh on 13 October, killed 15 and injured 33. Some statistics are given at the end of this chapter.

There were even instances of a company suffering more than one on the same day. The LY suffered two near Chorley on 18 January 1853. The first involved a goods train and the superintendent at Manchester was sent to organise clearance and while he was there he learnt that a passenger train had run into the back of a cattle train owing to slippery rails; however, the worst casualty in all this was a man who suffered a black eye and was able to continue his journey after the inevitable hour's delay for clearing up. On 7 June 1865 the GW suffered the Rednal accident, described later, and one near Keynsham in which 14 were injured when a mail special hit a passenger train which had stopped so its driver could examine his engine, which he believed was faulty; a train of empty carriages then hit the back of the second one.

Human beings have a strange fascination with disasters. As early as 1840 the site of an accident at Harrow was visited by 'hundreds of persons' and large numbers also turned up to the inquest.[5] The Sunday following an accident on the Hampstead Junction line in September 1861 many visited the scene, though little evidence was left. 'The Kentish-town fields presented the appearance of a fair green yesterday. During church hours thousands got up on the line and the embankments; but when the trains recommenced running the police drove them off. ... At half-past 3 o'clock the Rev Mr Fleming, of the Congregational Church, Kentish-town, mounted a portable pulpit in the fields, and preached a sermon to a very large auditory.'[6]

In the popular mind railways occupied a prominent position in the disaster league table, though in reality they provided a relatively safe means of travel. Perhaps the answer lies in their potential for large scale disaster; train crashes had the theoretical potential to kill hundreds, especially if one of those crowded excursions had come to grief. In order to put early Victorian casualty figures into perspective it should be remembered that there were many other sources of accidents, some far more horrific. Colliery explosions and textile factory fires received their due notice but there was not the same continuous interest shown as there was with railway safety, though there might very usefully have been. Presumably this was because many, particularly those who read *The Times*, did have frequent personal experience of rail travel and thus had a direct interest; a serious colliery accident might cause a temporary burst of outrage against those popularly believed to be responsible but this soon faded. Other forms of travel had their quota of casualties: people were crushed when coaches overturned, riders fell off horses, sometimes with fatal consequences, and pedestrians were trampled on, both as a result of their own carelessness and the failure of drivers to control their beasts. In December 1846, as a result of severe frost:

> On Monday the metropolitan streets and suburbs were to a great extent covered with ice, occasioning many serious and fatal accidents. In the Waterloo-bridge-road a horse attached to a cart heavily laden with hay, proceeding up the hill towards the bridge, ... fell down, and the cart being overturned, a boy named Farley, who was seated at the top, was dashed to the ground, and sustained a deep fracture on the head. On the same spot, shortly afterwards, a boy accidentally slipped down, and before he could recover himself the wheels of a cab had passed over his chest. Two other accidents of a nearly similar nature occurred during the day on London-bridge and in Fleet-street, opposite Fetter-lane, resulting in the serious maiming of two persons ... On Holborn-hill a powerful horse, attached to a brick cart, was thrown down opposite Shoe-Lane, and several persons who assisted in detaching the animal were severely kicked and injured by the horse, which the owner was compelled to kill. Very numerous accidents occurred on nearly every bridge, owing to the horses of omnibuses &c. being unable to ascend the slippery roadway.[7]

From 1856 to 1860 (inclusive) the average number of deaths in coal mines was over 1,000.[8] Then, as now, the home was a dangerous place: a recurring source of death and injury was the catching on fire of girls' and women's clothing resulting from carelessly held candles or letting voluminous skirts get too close to an open fire.

Victorians could also take a cavalier approach to their pleasures. In January 1861, when various notices and items testified to the intensity of the frost, skating on the Serpentine and in St James Park resulted in many casualties. On one day ten skaters were run down, had severely cut heads and were repaired at the Royal Humane Society's receiving house; one went through a hole in the ice but was none the worse once dried out. In the evening, quadrilles, skittles and races were all part of the entertainment; some skaters went around with lamps attached and fireworks were thrown and one woman was severely injured when her clothes caught fire.[9] Far more serious was an accident in Regents Park on 15 January 1867 when the ice on the pond gave way; by the 19th 41 were known to have died and some reported missing might still have been under the ice – bodies were still being recovered. This did briefly attract letters of the sort that followed railway accidents – reduce the level of water permanently, have more safety equipment, more park staff available, etc – but interest faded as the weather became warmer.[10] Indeed, skaters were happy to risk trouble: a piece four days later claimed there were 7,000 on the ice in St James's Park though it was dangerous in many places and as a result there were 15 'immersions' and 11 persons badly cut by falls.

Travel by sea was far riskier, though merchant ships would have been the major sufferers: in 1867 3,045 ships (including 145 steamers) were lost at sea, England losing 1,438 of the total and the United States 364.[11] American railways seem to have been far more dangerous. In 1859 'T.H.G.' copied figures given in the *New York Herald* of 4 July: since 1853 the total of casualties (including railwaymen?) on American railroads was 1,052 killed and 3,414 wounded, which he estimated as twelve times as many in relation to population as in the major countries of Europe, though he did not take the longer distances travelled into account.[12]

Descriptions

Even the index to *The Times* pulled no punches. That for 1853 included such items as 'Mr Whitcombe, by Stepping out of a Train in motion and Cut to Pieces' and 'to a Man at Dudley Station, whose Head was Severed from his Body', though nothing for Britain was seen comparable to one for 1868 – 'to the Overland Mail, Luggage Burnt and two Elephants'.

Journalists were able to give full vent to their descriptive powers. An accident at Nine Elms, then London terminus from Southampton, occurred on Saturday, 17 October 1840 when a passenger train, about 45 minutes late, stopped just outside the station to detach its engine and hook on the rope used to pull it into the platform; it was hit in rear by another that was 10 minutes early.

> [The second train ran with] the greatest force into the hindermost carriages of the first train, several of which, by the violence of the concussion, were literally smashed. Immediately the sound of the crash had subsided, the scene which ensued was beyond description. The screams of the females, joined with the crying of the children and the hallooing of the male passengers were most dreadful. Several of the passengers endeavoured to get over the doors of the carriages, but fortunately were prevented by their more collected companions, or the consequences might have been even more frightful. The train was immediately got up to the terminus, when persons of both sexes were to be seen running along with their faces cut and bleeding, and otherwise injured, several of whom, apparently half stunned by the concussion, instantly jumped into cabs, and were driven to their respective residences ... [Of those who remained, many] had received more severe injuries, among whom was an elegantly-dressed female, with a child, whose nose was literally smashed on her face, the haemorrhage from which had completely covered the child ... One female of decent appearance, was picked up quite insensible, but without any apparent mark of injury upon her. She was carried into a private room at the station, and placed on a table where surgeons attempted to bleed her, but to no avail, life being quite extinct, and on the body being moved blood flowed

profusely from her mouth and ears, from which it appeared that death had been caused from severe internal injuries ...

The report of the inquest included a description of the carriages, which had been available for public inspection. One first-class carriage, a coupé, had had its glass broken by the force of passengers' heads hitting it – thus the nature of their injuries. Two second-class ones had suffered 'a slight disturbance of their side panels' and a third had its back-boards driven in by the pole of a private carriage being carried on a truck behind; the private carriage had suffered no damage. However, in support, 'A Clergyman and a Sufferer' had claimed that the waiting-room was crowded with people streaming with blood. 'Your Constant Reader' arrived from Farnborough after the crash: there were no lights or policemen to warn arriving passengers of the wreckage, broken glass, etc, was strewn around so they had to pick their own way through or over this.[13]

There would be much more of the same. Near the end of the period, an excursion train drawn by two engines was derailed near Rednal. A Parliamentary reporter of *The Times* happened to be on the train and gave this account:

The engines got off the line and parted company, the one rushing to the right and the other to the left, and in a moment this work of destruction was complete. Not less than nine or ten souls were crushed out of their mortal tenements, and four or five more received such injuries that they survived but a short period. Numerous, however, as were the deaths, it was a matter of surprise to all who witnessed the wreck that many more were not killed. On the left there lay, first, the engine, which had run some distance down a siding, torn up the rails and twisted them, ploughed into the field adjoining, and then capsized. Further along lay the tender on its side. Further along still, towards the front of the train, but away from the main line, lay a first-class carriage, a complete wreck, with several persons underneath it, some evidently not dead. On the right of the train, the side on which the doors were locked (in the latter part of the train the doors were locked on both sides and the passengers were obliged to get out at the windows), the other engine lay embedded in a ditch, and immediately behind it were the splintered remains of a first-class carriage, the pieces piled upon each other as if broken up for firewood. Close besides this again, lying on the down line, was another first-class carriage, which had been thrown off its wheels and turned over on its side. However any of the passengers here escaped with their lives is a miracle. Several bodies were extricated with great difficulty from beneath the wreck of the first carriage. The other carriages were chiefly, if not all, second and third class and remained in line. The first was raised in front by the wheels of some other carriage, and it was left like a house without a front, with all the doors, windows and boarding torn away in the front and on the left side. The first seat was carried away but the others remained. Yet many escaped entirely unhurt out of this carriage. Beneath it, however, and under the one adjoining there was a heart-rending spectacle. A child, apparently three or four years old, lay on its face covered with the mud, with the exception of its legs and hips, which were naked; at its feet lay its mother, and at her side a man with his head completely severed from his body. Another woman and a little girl, about ten years old, lay dead on the left of the line terribly blackened and disfigured, and all around were faces streaming with blood; some had broken arms, others broken legs, and many more severely injured were gathered up and conveyed on stretchers made of the doors of the broken carriages to a shady spot in a field adjoining.[14]

The Board of Trade summary version said that 11 passengers were killed, 30 injured; both engine drivers were killed and a fireman injured.

Very full details of the dead were often given, sometimes to help identify them, but not always in ways that would have pleased their relatives. After an accident at Warrington in 1867 the listed included:

A woman unknown, supposed to be from 45 to 50 years of age. On her person were 2s 6d in money and a copper cent piece of United States coinage. She wore a gold keeper ring on her finger, and had in her pocket a snuff-box, box key, and a pawn ticket for a Geneva watch pledged with Joseph Ion Whiston, 113, Birkenhead-road Liverpool, in the name of Frederick Bell, of Orient-street, for 15s; a newspaper cutting relating to the sailing of the vessels Farnam and John and Henry; a ticket from Lime-street Liverpool to Birmingham, and a pair of spectacles in case. She wore a black lustre gown, black barege shawl, black ribbed silk bonnet, trimmed with black lace and bugles, black kid gloves and elastic-sided boots. ...

A young lady, supposed to be Miss Allcock, of Liverpool, aged from 21 to 24 years. She was dressed in a dark linsey or stuff frock and a black cloth jacket; her bonnet was entirely crushed. It had pure silk strings. She wore elastic boots and kid gloves. She had in her possession a gold watch (going), a bunch of keys with perforated token attached, 20s 6d in silver, four postage stamps and a lock of hair in a portemonnaie. She also had a small pocket diary containing daily entries from the 1st of January of the present year to yesterday. The last two of these entries were:-

June 27 – Went to see mamma; Jones came for me.

June 28 – Oh! What a miserable day! Letter from Ayr (?); disappointed; very unhappy.

In the book were an envelope addressed 'Miss Hirsch, Breck-road, Everton, Liverpool'; a bill from Jane Owen, obviously a dressmaker; a card 'Mr Jonas Hirsch'; a pencil case; a number of addresses of houses in

Liverpool, on a separate piece of paper; and a letter addressed to 'My dearest Lettie' from A S Fay, 227 East-India Road. She also had in her possession a number of articles of female adornment, among others, a jet cross; and a ticket from Edge-hill station to Wolverhampton.

The confusion that could arise as a result of fear of an accident was illustrated by the details given in a claim for damages against the GN by Mrs Carstairs, a widow trading as a wine merchant in Mill Street, Hanover Square. She was travelling with her 10 year old daughter on 16 September 1854. Their train was about 1½ hours late at Hatfield, at 8 p.m. and about a quarter of a mile further on a coupling broke ahead of her part of the train. A porter told her to get out because an express was due; she and her daughter alighted and waited on an embankment for about half an hour. The carriages were 'adjusted' and she was told to get back in; at first she refused when she was told the express was 35 minutes overdue, but, threatened with being left there all night did so. They moved on but about five minutes later a guard shouted, 'For God's sake get out or the train will be upon you'. She and the girl followed other passengers out, the door swung against her and she was thrown onto the bank; the other passengers at first thought she had been killed. The company argued that it was her own fault for alighting when the company's servants had told her to stay put; a goods train had hit them in rear but so gently that no damage had been done to the carriages. The jury clearly believed her version and awarded her £620.[15] The Board of Trade summary version of this (published earlier) was that seven passengers were slightly injured when a goods train collided slightly near Hatfield with a passenger train which had stopped because the engine of a cattle train in front had broken down.

Early approaches

A completely new form of transport was bound to face problems with no ready solution available. In some respects the very fears aroused contributed to safety because all realised the potential for disaster if steam engines were let loose without restraint. Acts of Parliament authorising lines normally contained some clauses dealing with safety matters and the Board of Trade (at one stage briefly replaced by the Railway Commissioners) was soon given a degree of oversight. From the autumn of 1840 new lines had to be submitted for inspection by one of its men, then invariably a Royal Engineers officer. At first their reports were only advisory, but this was soon amended so it could order opening to be deferred until faults had been remedied. Companies also had to report accidents involving danger to the public and the Board's inspectors would then investigate if necessary and issue a report including recommendations for preventing repetitions. Unfortunately, suggestions were only advisory; the same criticisms were repeated *ad nauseam* until well after 1870.

In January 1841 the leading officials of at least 20 companies met in Birmingham under the chairmanship of George Carr Glyn, chairman of the London & Birmingham and adopted a number of resolutions unanimously:

1 – That in consequence of the public anxiety occasioned by the accidents which have taken place on various railways, the companies here represented, in order to profit by the combined experience of the principal lines, have deemed it expedient that a general conference should be held for the purpose of taking into consideration the causes and circumstances of such accidents, and the means that may be available of more effectually guarding against their occurrence for the future.

2 – That this meeting acknowledges the grave responsibility which attaches to railway directors ... for ensuring the general accommodation, comfort and safety of the passengers entrusted to their charge. ...

3 – That this meeting, while it deeply regrets the accidents which have occurred, looks forward with confidence to the beneficial result of unremitting vigilance and habitual caution steadily enforced and established, as the great means of safety to railway conveyance, and accordingly would deprecate any sudden or hasty legislation on the subject; being convinced that the means referred to, aided by such improved arrangements and mechanical adaptations as a more mature experience may suggest, will, amply accomplish the desired object.

4 – That the moral character and general fitness of enginemen and firemen, as well as of policemen and other servants, in the correct performance of whose duties public safety is involved, are so essential to the security of railway travelling, that this meeting recommends to all railway companies the strictest examination into these points; and that it should be a rule more generally adopted amongst different managements, not to employ servants having worked on other lines, without authentic and satisfactory testimonials from their former employers.

5 – That in case of serious neglect of duty on the part of railway servants, it is desirable more frequently to put in force the penal provisions of Lord Seymour's Act [which allowed criminal prosecution of negligent men], in order that the strictest discipline may be maintained; at the same time this meeting considers it is due to men whose services are arduous, to encourage the requisite discipline and obedience of orders, by adequate remuneration, and by suitable rewards for extraordinary exertions, or long sustained good conduct.

6 – [Have considered putting a third man as captain on the footplate; decided would cause extra danger by dividing responsibility and providing distraction.]

7 – That this meeting considers it desirable that there should be a uniform system of regulations and signals recognised as applicable to all railways ... .[16]

In short: we know best; if anything goes wrong it is the driver's fault, not ours; we will work together. The following years showed great consistency on the first two parts but the third was woefully neglected. This looks suspiciously like a piece of window-dressing: the Board of Trade's annual report, mentioned later, was nearly due and they must have been acutely aware that criticism was coming their way.

Level crossings

The most obvious immediate danger came from the need of many lines to cross roads on the level, though road traffic then was only a tiny fraction of what it is today. From very early on gates had to be provided and there was much debate about whether these should normally be open for trains and closed to road traffic or vice versa; the railways wanted priority and at first were usually supported by law. However, road users were not keen to wait for gates to be opened. On the North Union an accident occurred near Euxton on 7 September 1841 when a train hit a stage-coach whose driver thought the way was clear because the gates were open. The rule on that line was that gates should normally be kept closed across the road; the gate-keeper's excuse was based on the impatience of road users, which, on one occasion, led to some of them pulling the gates open by main force, resulting in his leaving it too late this time. An Act of 1842 allowed the Board of Trade to authorise exceptions and gradually it became usual for gates to be closed across the railway except when a train needed to pass. Men (and occasionally women) were provided with cottages beside these, with the duty of opening and closing them when necessary. This looks an easy enough task but on lines with only a few trains per day it must have been difficult to keep alert. Furthermore, companies sometimes used gatekeepers' jobs as a sort of pension fund, giving them to ageing or injured servants after faithful service. There were also 'occupation crossings' where lines crossed private lanes or farmland and it was up to the occupants to ensure that gates were closed after they had used the crossing – in this case they were normally open for trains. The House of Commons defeated a proposal for keeping these locked on the grounds that it would be a burden on the occupants, though some did do this on their own initiative.

In this respect the public caused far more accidents than railway companies. Most did not cause death or injury to railway passengers but the potential was there. There was a steady stream of deaths of people being careless at level crossings despite the efforts of railway companies to enforce the rules. The Grand Junction took Thomas Linley to court for leaving gates open near Newton and had him fined 20/-, including costs on 7 August 1842. Thomas Rider crossed the line between Derby and Nottingham with two cows on 9 November of that year, so close to the train that the driver believed he had hit him with the buffer; he could not pay his 40 shilling fine and went to prison for a month. A third culprit that year was George Elmore the younger of Uxendon who clearly regarded crossing gates as an unjustified impediment to his hunting so he broke off the locks and forced open two gates near Harrow, creating the risk of cattle straying onto the line. The novelty of railways meant that this one puzzled lawyers too. The directors were very anxious to secure a conviction since the offence was likely 'to Compromise the Public safety if passed over with impunity' so after various courts had struggled to define his offence exactly all resorted to a little chicanery. The prosecution put its case, the defendant pleaded guilty and was fined one shilling and the company had its precedent.[17]

Brakes and communication cords

Another obvious problem was how to stop a steam-engine. One of its advantages over road vehicles lay in the greatly reduced friction as metal wheels ran on metal rails, but this meant it needed lengthy stopping distances – and there was no way of steering round obstacles. In December 1849 Captain Laffan made various calculations: an ordinary goods train going at 25 m.p.h. needed 564¾ yards to stop completely on a level line and 837 yards (nearly half-a-mile) downhill while a passenger train of average normal weight, going at 45 m.p.h. took 779 and 889¾ yards respectively – all assuming dry rails.

Inadequate brake power was one of the most recurrent themes in accident reports. There was a long-running battle between Board of Trade inspectors and companies over what was adequate; the former's accident reports repetitively condemned the latter for not providing adequate numbers of brake-vans on their heavier trains, especially excursions. Colonel Yolland reported in 1860: 'I am almost tired of making the remark, – a train furnished with a sufficient amount of break power for the speed at which it is intended to travel is the exception and not the rule'.[18]

When a train ran into a stone building at the end of the Carliol Square station in Newcastle, terminus of the line from North Shields in 1846, the reason given was that it was fine weather and holiday time so larger numbers than usual had travelled so the weight was too much for the brake to hold when the crew turned off steam and applied the brakes where they normally did.[19] Greenhill Junction, where the Scottish Central company exchanged traffic with the Edinburgh & Glasgow and the Caledonian, was the scene of an accident in 1852. On 22 April the engine of a train from Glasgow was uncoupled just before the junction and ran on along the main line towards Edinburgh and the carriages were left to go on under their own momentum onto the Scottish Central line, to run up behind the engine waiting to take it on. On this occasion, though there were three brake-vans, there was only one guard and he was in the front one, not the rear, as the rules stipulated; after screwing down his brake, he started climbing over the roofs on the intervening carriages to reach one in the middle, but he was too late to prevent a collision. One point that emerged was that the two companies' brake-vans worked indiscriminately on both lines; on the Edinburgh & Glasgow the handles had to be turned from left to right, but on the Scottish Central from right to left. Needless to say, the circumstances gave both companies a chance to blame the other.

It was not enough just to improve brakes: they needed to ensure that they worked evenly so that engine and carriages stopped together, without throwing passengers about. The risks of damage to the engine's wheels, by causing the tyres to overheat and break off, were considered so high that braking was confined to the tender and some carriages included at intervals along the train. In the last resort a driver faced with an emergency could put his engine into reverse. Too violent a brake on the tender would send the relatively flimsy carriages of that day against it, causing a potentially disastrous pile-up; too fierce a brake on carriages could cause couplings to snap, leaving stranded carriages at the mercy of a following train. Clumsy use of brakes could also result in trains stopping before or beyond platforms at stations. All depended on the driver and guards situated at strategic intervals along the train working together according to a code of whistles. The guards at first were perched on outside seats so that they could see over the tops of carriages, stage-coach fashion, and had to do their job with smoke flying in their faces, taking care not to be smashed against the bridges they passed under; gradually separate, and safer, compartments were devised for them. Various systems of continuous braking that could be applied by the driver were experimented with but there were real problems involved in devising something that was reliable and effective; for instance, the device needed to work so that if part of a train broke off, the brakes would automatically stop both sections, but one early version actually became completely ineffective in such circumstances.

Various 'helpful' ideas were put forward: one writer to *The Times* in 1840 suggested issuing boatswains' whistles to guards.[20] Some form of communication cord was a standard request; this would also enable passengers to attract attention in case of fire and be of benefit to harassed ladies or anyone shut in with madmen. Then nearly all carriages were divided into compartments by partitions from floor to roof so anyone needing help was reliant on those in the same little box – and at their mercy. For a while after the only known murder committed in a train during this period some companies removed the upper portions of the partitions but complaints about lack of privacy meant that they soon reverted to full division. As early as November 1840 the relevant LNW committee sanctioned trials of Mr Pettit's device for communicating between guards and drivers, an effective means of which was 'much needed'; presumably it failed its test.[21]

In January 1841 *The Times* included an item that looks suspiciously like a leg-pull but the name of the inventor was given and no subsequent denial was seen – and neither was any evidence for the use of the device, which seems to have been based on marine flares. Manager Mr Hall of the Eastern Counties had apparently invented a 'Railway Night Light'. A reflector was placed on the back of the engine's chimney, inclined to reflect its light on the driver. The guards were provided with red and blue lights as well as plain and on the removal of a piece of tin, a screw pressed on fulminating powder which ignited a light and sent an intense beam onto the reflector, so that the driver was immediately warned: blue = caution; red = danger.[22]

A Board of Trade survey in 1857 showed great diversity in the way guards and drivers were supposed to communicate. Most used codes of whistles or brake applications but some were experimenting with various devices. The GN used Mr Tattershall's Patent on its long distance trains; this consisted of a rope extended through loops under the locked doors on the off-side of carriages to link a bell on the tender with a wheel in the rear brake-van. The Morayshire's answer was that the guard and driver were within shouting distance of each other so nothing was needed. Many piously said they would adopt anything that could be shown to be effective but inevitably mentioned the difficulty involved in providing something compatible with all companies' carriages, needed because there was so much interchange of these to provide passengers with through services; the blindingly obvious solution of working together was not considered by any, despite the promise made in 1841. Too many railway officials valued their own egos more highly than public safety and would only treat the Board of Trade's inspectors as enemies rather than allies, so a satisfactory answer waited until after 1870.

One fear was that a cord would be an invitation to the prankster and the vandal. In August 1867 Mr Scott, manager of the LSW said he would not trust his passengers with one; there was scarcely a day without some of their carriages being damaged – cut linings and fittings, broken glass and destroyed lamps all being common. Seymour Clarke (GN) said local passengers in London and Yorkshire were very 'mischievous'.[23] It was not long before the fear was borne out. At Hertford County Sessions Mr Joseph Hayes, a gentleman residing at Hertingfordbury, was accused of stopping a train without cause. On 12 August he had travelled by the GN Kings Cross to Manchester express and should have joined the coach slipped for Hatfield but entered one in the middle of the train labelled 'Bradford'. Soon after Hatfield, he pulled the cord, he and the guard put their heads out, he signalled that he wanted it to stop, and the guard that it could not. Soon after Hitchin the gong sounded again; the train stopped and he got out. His defence was that could he not find the slip carriage at Kings Cross and believed from the timetable that it stopped at Hitchin. One Bench imposed a 5/- fine and costs, though this only concerned the first use of the cord since the item added that he would be prosecuted again at Hitchin; nothing about that was seen.[24]

Fire from cinders blown back from the engine and lodged amongst luggage loaded on roofs was one potential danger that highlighted the need for a communication device, especially since passengers might be panicked into jumping out. In 1840 some magazines were put on top of a North Union first-class carriage, with passengers' luggage, on the London & Birmingham mail which left London at 8.30, on Thursday, magazine night. Between Leighton Buzzard and Wolverton fire was seen; the train stopped and all ten passengers alighted unhurt.[25] Later that month the GW suffered one with added comic touches. A fire on the roof of a mail train from Paddington was seen when it was just beyond West Drayton; this was put out in about a quarter of an hour, 'the passengers rendering great assistance by conveying water in their hats' but just before Slough it was realised that they had 'lost the mail'. They went on to Slough where they dropped passengers for there and took on fresh water; the engine and tender went back in search of the 'whole of the long line of trucks, with several mail carriages' it had lost. After about a mile the fire had restarted so a guard had scrambled over and unhooked them and the fire had been finally quenched.[26]

Such episodes were described at fairly regular intervals. In October 1847 a fire on a North Midland train which had left London at 6 15 a.m. was discovered when it left the tunnel between Ambergate and Wingfield; the guard had difficulty in getting people to keep their seats and by the time they were able to stop, the luggage on top of a second class carriage was all in flames.[27] About a year later there was a fire on the roof of a first-class carriage on an express from London, about 15 miles south of Berwick; the driver was stopped by passengers shouting and waving their hats out of windows and the fire was put out with water from the tender – the guard was on a carriage in front of the fire.[28] In 1863 'H.H' wrote that between Euston and Crewe the 'tarpauling' covering the luggage on one carriage had caught fire; a guard had seen it and was able to stop the train and cut away the burning material.[29] An incident in 1868 illustrated another way in which fire could be caused: two miles north of Huntingdon, luggage on a carriage in the middle of a Scotch express caught fire because the edges of the tarpaulin covering it had come into contact with the carriage lamp, which was fitted through a hole in the roof.

This could also affect stage and private coaches being carried by train. The luggage on a stage-coach being carried to Paddington caught fire in 1839; the coachman, who had stayed with his coach, climbed up and pushed the luggage off, so much of it was saved [from fire, anyway] but the coach roof caught fire and he and a guard were only able to put out the fire once the roof had collapsed. The train continued on the move through all this.[30] The Bristol mail suffered in similar fashion the following year; cinders from the engine were blown onto its front boot, the mail guards were unable to alert the engine-driver by shouting and blowing horns so by Twyford nearly everything in that boot had been burnt though the fire did not reach the letter and newspaper bags.[31] As the 1 pm from Leeds was approaching Rugby in December 1847, an umbrella behind Lord Zetland's private carriage caught fire and spread to the upper part of carriage so the Countess and her maid descended onto the truck carrying it. Despite a warning from a man leaning out of a carriage window, the maid jumped off and was badly hurt. A pilot engine and carriage were sent to pick her up. The government inspector blamed the maid's injuries in part on the carelessness of those on the rescuing engine, which ran over her – she lost three fingers and had severe, perhaps fatal, head injuries.[32]

Two fires in carriages occurred in October 1857, one between Carlisle and Lancaster and the other on the approach to Paddington. In the first case a passenger climbed along the outside and back to the guard, only to find that the latter had no means of contacting the driver; he then went on his way to the driver but just before he reached him men working on the line used detonators to alert the driver. In the other case a passenger tried to give the alert by tying a handkerchief to his umbrella and waving it out of the window but the driver did not see it and men on the line, who were on the opposite side to the part of the carriage that was alight, thought that he was merely fooling around.[33]

Argument about the device was still going strongly in 1868. The engine and tender of the Edinburgh to London Mail parted from its train in the dark near Oxenholme on 7 January 1868 and it was several miles before the driver realised this. He went on to Carnforth, switched to the other line and returned in search of his train. W Fletcher, a passenger, complained that human ingenuity had 'fallen to so low an ebb that no better means of communication between guard and driver can be devised than a piece of string', which had managed to break without alerting the latter.[34] Later, in July and August there was a rash of letters giving instances where such a system would have helped. 'A passenger', writing from the Edinburgh New Club, described a fire in the luggage on the roof before Retford, on 22 July, 'WD' was on a South Wales express when a carriage wheel caught fire and shortly after a tyre on a GW train broke and bits smashed a window.

In that year Parliament passed a half-hearted Act, to come into force the following April. Any train that travelled more than twenty miles without stopping on any stage of its journey would have to have some device to let guards warn drivers of danger. Colonel Yolland pointed out the limited usefulness of this: very many services would not be affected, including one he had just investigated on the Cornwall Railway, where a derailed carriage was hauled for more than 1¼ miles on 25 November 1868 before the passengers and guard were able to attract the driver's attention.

Signals

Given the distance needed to stop a train, it was vital that there should be some means of telling drivers if there was likely to be anything on the line in front. As early as the 1830s companies took powers under their Acts to require JPs to give their formal sanction to police nominated by directors. Originally their powers were confined to their own premises but they were soon widened to 'within a mile of railway property' or something similar. Gradually specialisms developed: some became signalmen, others became responsible for law and order on the railways.[35] For the first task 'policemen' were stationed at strategic points to tell drivers whether or not it was safe to proceed; inevitably means differed and at first varieties of hand signals, coloured lamps and flag wagging were used. Arrangements could be complex. After an accident at Wolverton in 1847 the Board of Trade investigation showed that at night passenger trains carried a white light at the front; on seeing this the policeman signalled to the station with a green one and was answered from there with green if it was all clear and he then showed the driver white to go on. A red from the station was relayed in red to the driver. Goods trains did not need any light to be shown to the station but received a green from the signalman who then had to go to the points to send it into the goods yard.

Soon mechanical devices were substituted, worked from a distance by wires and the signalman was given protection from the weather in his own box – again not to a standard pattern. Some oddities were used: that at Stratford, on Halle's principle, features in the final chapter for its contribution to an accident in 1845. Various combinations of posts and arms, with coloured lamps at night, gradually became the norm. Safety was further improved as increasingly points and signals were designed so that a signalman could not not signal a train one way and set the points for another.

A serious weakness was that once a train was out of sight, it might have broken down before the next signalling point. They relied on time intervals, depending on the nature of the train which had last passed the signalman; clearly a passenger express following a slow goods needed to be held back much longer than the other way round and there was fierce argument about what constituted a 'safe' gap. If a train broke down, a guard was supposed to go back and signal following trains to stop but the latter might be too close already and his signals not be seen if the driver and fireman were occupied with working their engine. The placing of detonators on the line gave an audible warning; a letter of 18 April 1844 from General Pasley, supporting their use, stated they were already in use on the London & Birmingham.

Inadequate time intervals between trains caused much unfavourable comment. Matters could become particularly fraught where more than one company was involved, such as the line out of London Bridge, used by London & Greenwich, London & Croydon and London & Brighton trains. After enquiries in May 1842 the Board of Trade received the following reassurance from the Secretary of the Greenwich company:

> On ordinary occasions the Croydon trains have been despatched from the London Station five minutes after the Greenwich trains.
>
> The same regulation has been observed in regard to the departure of the Brighton trains.
>
> To prevent collision between [the various] trains as they come onto the Greenwich line at Corbett's Lane, the following arrangements have been found effectual:
>
> A post is fixed on each railway, half a mile from the junction, on passing which the engine-men whistle to notify the switchman on duty at the junction, which train is in advance, and to be allowed first into London. The succeeding train is informed thereof by the switchman showing a flag, which stops the latter, until the former shall be 400 yards in advance, which distance is maintained all the way to London.
>
> In foggy weather the Croydon trains are distinguished by a double whistle.

At holiday times extra trains are occasionally run to and from Greenwich every four minutes; and the only precaution found necessary is to keep the trains 400 yards apart.

With these precautions accidents have been avoided, even on the busiest days at Easter and Whitsuntide, when upwards of 30,000 passengers have been carried on the day.

However, reassuring noises were not always the same as ensuring consistent regard to safe practice. A regular traveller on the London & Greenwich, on which at quarter-to and quarter-past every hour trains to Greenwich and North Kent started at nearly the same time, claimed in December 1845 that the rule that North Kent trains (a later addition to the party at London Bridge) went first since they did not stop at Spa Road was frequently infringed.[36] 'Verax' complained in June 1847 about inadequate time intervals on the GW and cited a case where there were 45 minutes between a stopping train to Reading and an express. He had recently travelled to Twyford at a crawl on the former so that they were 30 minutes late. The passengers were hurried out and there was no time for luggage to be unloaded as the train rapidly backed onto the other line and an express rushed through.[37] As a result of his experiments in 1849 Captain Laffan had argued that the intervals allowed were not enough: the LNW's rules then said a stop signal had to be shown for three minutes and a 'go slowly' one for a further five minutes after a train had passed – worse, the rule was not properly enforced. As usual, Huish returned defiant answers to official criticisms.

The Board of Trade advocated absolute block working, which meant that a line was broken into sections for operating purposes and no train was allowed into a section before the one in front had left. This was adopted in some places but suggestions for universal adoption met the usual resistance. Its safe operation needed reliable telegraphic instruments to be available for information to be passed from one signal box to another. These were in some use from 1841 but were not always fully reliable and those using them not well-enough trained. At the end of 1843 the telegraph had only been brought into use on the Blackwall and on the GW as far as Slough. Within the next two years the whole of the Southampton and Dover lines were covered. In the 1850s *The Times* frequently included items on its extension: for example, on 26 July 1852 it announced that the day before it had been completed from Bridgwater to Taunton and in 10 days' time would be extended to Exeter. However, it was not initially always fully integrated into the system, as was shown by various complaints. 'A Passenger' claimed that after an accident at Paddock Wood in 1846 he had been told by the station clerk that the man who could read the telegraph had gone to bed, he himself could not understand it, anyway, the wet weather had probably affected it.[38] 'DP' wrote in February 1850 about a lengthy delay when his train's engine had failed at Basingstoke; he had seen a telegraph line alongside the railway and suggested using it to get help but was told it only provided a link between the termini so they waited nearly 2½ hours until found by the engine sent to look for them.[39] There was reliable confirmation of at least one deficiency: the report on an accident at Stormy, on the

South Wales line said it happened because 'the transmission and reception of messages involving life and death were intrusted to men, who from their position [porter and clerk] could hardly be expected to appreciate the responsibility involved in their acts, and who were, moreover, imperfectly educated to the use of the instrument intrusted to them.'

A regular theme of letter-writers was that trains were allowed to run too close together; some even claimed to be able to see following trains. The following are a small sample of the many; in 1853, 1854 and 1862 there were sustained campaigns not treated here. Even horse-drawn passengers were at risk: in 1845 there was an accident on the Edinburgh & Dalkeith when a carriage from Dalhousie Mains came into contact with one from Dalkeith near Sheriffhall, where the lines met. Apparently the driver from Dalkeith was several times called upon to pull up but either he did not hear or was unable to stop his horse in time.

On 9 September 1837 a train from Manchester that was one hour late had stopped at Kenyon Junction to detach carriages for Bolton when it was hit by a Grand Junction train whose driver did not expect it to be there and at least one passenger was killed.[41] In 1840 there was a collision between two Grand Junction trains on the Liverpool & Manchester when the 5 p.m. from Birmingham had made fast progress and caught up a second-class train which had left at 3.30; at first it followed at a safe distance, but on rounding a curve near Ordsall Lane the driver suddenly saw the other just in front and was not able to stop. The passengers were thrown about and some severely but not dangerously hurt. [42]

The lines from Shoreditch, then the terminus for the Eastern Counties and the Northern & Eastern, were the scene of two such accidents in 1840. On 15 September there was one in which four passengers were injured. A train left Shoreditch about 4, stopped at Devonshire Street Mile End to collect passengers and went off again. Five or six minutes later a Stratford train also started from Shoreditch; it was behind time so the driver put on speed and on reaching Old Ford, near Bow, he caught up the first, was unable to stop and collided with its rear. In November there was another one at a short-lived station at Bow when the 10 a.m. Eastern Counties train was hit in the rear by an engine and train of the Northern & Eastern; three carriages were smashed, several passengers thrown about and injured.[43] Five years later this line provided a variation: it was the custom to help trains up the incline at Brentwood by running a 'pilot' engine up behind it but on an occasion in July 1845 the latter came up too fast, hitting the rear carriage hard enough to injure two passengers.

In 1850 there was an accident at Cowlairs on the Edinburgh & Glasgow, where a special from Perth on the Scottish Central had been split in two at Greenhill because there were large numbers going to see the Highland Society's Exhibition. The first section, whose last two 'carriages' were cattle trucks with 25 to 30 in each, stopped at Cowlairs for ticket collection. The second part came up at full speed; the guard and some of the passengers jumped clear in time but much damage was done – three dead, two probably dying.

On Sunday 25 August 1861 the worst accident so far occurred when 23 were killed and 176 seriously injured in a collision in Clayton Tunnel. Three trains, two of them excursions, left Brighton within seven minutes, though the regulations demanded minimum five-minute intervals. This was compounded by a signalling failure on the approach to the tunnel and working practices that involved signalmen being on duty for twenty-four hours continuously in order to earn one day of rest per week.[44]

A standard variant on this was collisions with goods trains that were being shunted out of the way. The theory was that if a passenger train was expected a goods train should be shunted into sidings in time to give the faster train a clear run through but railwaymen, often under pressure to move goods through as fast as possible, sometimes left it too late. One such episode was on the Great North of England near Hessay in 1846. A coal train was being shunted; when its driver realised that a passenger train was coming up behind and he could not be got out of the way in time, he put on steam to try and get far enough ahead to give the other more room to brake. Despite this a collision resulted and several were injured. There were many more of these. The 5.15 p.m. passenger train to Hereford left Newport about 20 minutes after a goods on 11 July 1854; the goods ran short of steam and was backing into a siding when hit by the passenger train, resulting in injuries to two passengers. At Lea station an excursion train from Oldham to Blackpool ran into a goods train which had been shunted onto the 'wrong' line to get it out of the way of a passenger train going towards Preston on 27 September 1865.

Potentially the most serious accidents were head-on collisions, which would receive the full force of the combined speed of the two trains involved – at least when an engine ran into the rear of a train going the same way the brakes were usually already applied, thus diminishing the impact. Particular problems were faced on single lines. The Taff Vale had an interesting answer to this when it opened fully in 1841. The line was effectively in two sections, with a double-line incline in between and trains were timed to leave Cardiff and Merthyr so that the carriages could pass on the incline. They had two engines, each of which worked traffic on one side of the incline and swapped trains after the carriages had been taken over it; mineral traffic was confined to the hours after passenger traffic had ceased – there were only three each way per day.[45] On the first section of the Somerset Central from Highbridge to Glastonbury, opened in 1854, a guard had to be designated each day for the job of accompanying all trains; a variant on this was the use of 'travelling porters' on the South Yorkshire, each of whom was allocated a stretch of line between passing places. In both cases no train could run without the relevant man on board.[46] Increasingly the staff and ticket system was introduced, the staff replacing the man. Each section had its own token and no train could be sent from one end of it unless the token was present at that end; at its simplest trains alternated in direction, taking the token with them, but if two or more trains had to go the same way, the first was shown the token and given a written permit to go and the last took the token. Another favourite, on short lines, was to make Board of Trade permission to open conditional on an undertaking that only one engine would be at work at a time. Perhaps because of the very obvious dangers inherent in single line working, accidents were relatively rare but there were at least two head-on collisions in 1855. Two passengers were killed and two injured between Barton and New Holland, on the MS&L, when an engine was sent to look for a train that was wrongly assumed to have become stuck in the snow on 14 February. Two passenger trains met head on at Dudley, on the South Staffordshire, on 21 May, injuring 45. When they did occur it was usually where a normally double line was reduced to single for some reason; examples of this were at Ramsgate on 13 February 1860 when snow blocked one line and near Donington on the Shrewsbury & Hereford line on 27 July 1864 when engineering works occupied one line.

Mechanical failures

Mechanical failure of one sort or another contributed directly by disabling one train and indirectly by stranding the casualty as a target for following trains. Poor maintenance and training of staff played a part but companies were also at the mercy of their suppliers. There was no effective way of testing the quality of an iron, and later steel, product effectively so something that looked right on the outside might possess internal flaws only revealed by a breakage. Railways did build up records showing how long vital components had been in use and when they should be replaced but this required time and experience. In much more recent times the aviation industry had to learn the realities of 'metal fatigue' the hard way so inevitably equivalent railway problems were solved in a rather hit and miss fashion by those who had far less scientific knowledge at their disposal.

The track was sometimes deficient. It was accepted that trains should go slowly over a newly-built line until the earthworks and ballast had become fully settled but a number of accidents, some of which are detailed elsewhere, resulted from ignoring this. Even after enough time had elapsed for consolidation, there could be problems. The last carriage of a LY train was derailed in 1847 (16 September), killing two people, the accident was simply put down to 'the bad state of the road.' Late in 1860 nine people were injured near Templecombe on the LSW when a train went too fast over a stretch in poor condition. Even apparently trivial defects could have serious consequences: Captain Tyler, one of the Board's inspectors, pointed out that in the period 1860 to 1868 sixteen accidents had at least partly been caused by the failure of wooden trenails, which fixed the chairs holding the rails onto the sleepers; the rails then went out of true and trains were derailed.

An accident in 1851 illustrated one company's apparent indifference to safety matters – and the limited powers available to the Board of Trade. 'EJ' was on the 5 p.m. Carlisle to Newcastle train on 3 August which stopped when three carriages had become detached and slid down a steep slope towards the river. He had walked along the line towards Newcastle and in a half-mile he had seen several gaps of half-inch to upwards of two inches between the ends of sections of rail; in some cases pegs of rotten wood had been driven into a chair to close a gap. Captain Laffan later found the rails defective: they had been laid in patches, using rails of six different weights to the yard, from 42 lbs to 82 lbs, though nothing under 60 lbs was considered safe for 'modern' heavy engines. The Railway Commissioners had ordered the railway to alter its timetable, reducing speed until the weak rails had been replaced but it paid so little attention that on 6 September they had to remind it, saying that until they complied they would withdraw their sanction for Parliamentary trains, so that all would be liable to passenger duty.[47]

The Eastern Counties was the subject of concern in 1855: in December Norwich Corporation went so far as to petition the Board of Trade:

> Your Memorialists ... represent ... that such apprehension of danger is general, and that the said lines of railway are not believed to be in a secure and proper state by very large bodies of the citizens of Norwich ...
>
> ... the permanent way of the said lines is in *very bad condition*, that the timber and sleepers on the road are greatly decayed, that many of the bridges are defective and in want of repair, and that travelling upon the said lines is disagreeable and *hazardous*.
>
> That from fear of personal danger, numbers avoid travelling on the said lines, whilst persons, not in robust health, and females, cannot bear the shaking and jolting which the uneven state of the rails causes ...
>
> That Mr. Simpson, one of the Directors of the Eastern Counties Railway Company, to whom, with others, it was referred to examine into and report on the state of the permanent way at the meeting of the shareholders ..., held on Friday last, declared that 'things are in such a state, that not an hour must be lost, for the sake of public safety, in supplying some defects, the nature of which it would be inconvenient at a public meeting like this to explain.'

Lt Col Wynne found many of the bridges in an advanced state of decay, particularly those which had been patched at some point in the past: 'the piles were deeply rotted between wind and water, or where they enter the ground, their heads decayed, and the parts exposed to the weather more or less gone'. At various points he had seen old sleepers, badly decayed, thrown by the side of the line; while this was evidence that some work was being done, many in equally bad condition remained in use. A further plea from Norwich led to a survey of the lines to Yarmouth and Lowestoft, which were found to be in an equally bad state. Others, including Cambridge Council, joined in. The Board refused to act on many complaints on the grounds that they were not specific enough but it did emerge that the Company had reduced the line to St Ives from double to single track with a lack of safety provision that would have caused the Board to refuse permission for opening if it had been submitted as a new line. It said it had no power to enforce improvement but hoped the directors would take action. Three weeks later it was reported that repairs between Cambridge and Norwich were vigorously in hand and substantial brickwork was being built at some bridges; Peter Bruff, the Engineer, told his Board of Directors on 8 March that large numbers of men were being employed and no expense was being spared, meanwhile, the weight and speed of trains had been reduced. CP Bidder wrote a lengthy and unconvincing letter rebutting criticisms and denying that the line was dangerous. He asserted that the inspectors (Captain Galton and Lt Col Wynne were both involved) were men who had never actually built railways so were not competent judges. If there were improvements, not all were convinced: 'MW' complained about a journey in August 1857 between Cambridge and Ely in a second-class carriage, when on crawling out at his journey's end he was so battered and bruised he felt as if had been pounded in a mortar; he blamed this on the poor state of the track.[48]

Repairs to existing lines could cause trouble; in theory drivers were supposed to be warned to go slowly but this was not always done effectively. The accident at Rednal, described above, resulted when a flag was waved in warning but was only seen by the driver of one of the engines; the Board's inspector's view was that detonators should have been put down as well. Even worse was the failure, only two days later, of the foreman in charge of repairing a bridge near Staplehurst to read his timetable properly: a boat train, which ran at different times, according to the tide, arrived when part of the track was completely missing and derailed killing 10 passengers and injuring 49, though its most famous passenger, Charles Dickens, escaped with a shaking.

Another potential weakness was at sets of points. The second carriage of a horse-drawn train on the Edinburgh & Dalkeith was derailed when the front wheels went one way at a set of points and the rear another and 'The alarm of the passengers caused them to make a great noise, which frightened the horse, so that he drew the coach down the slope'. The best suggestion the company's manager could offer was that the horse had kicked back a loose stone, thus altering the points. Seven were killed and four injured when a train was diverted into a siding and smashed into a waiting coal train at Wolverton on 5 June 1846. A points failure as a train was being backed out of Leeds Central onto the main line on 3 January 1853 caused a composite coach to be thrown off the line and over a 26 foot high viaduct. In theory points were supposed to be fitted with safety devices to prevent their misuse, but near Gateshead a signalman managed to move a set before a train was fully clear on 2 August 1869. The last carriage was derailed and fell on top of a passenger who had jumped out, killing him.

A regular problem was that of engines running out of steam due to the short-comings of the driver and his fireman or to a poorly-maintained engine. In 1847 eight passengers were injured on 4 July when an excursion train ran into the back of a passenger train at Croydon; the victim was stationary because it had been stopped 'by a luggage train in advance, the engine of which [was unable] to proceed from want of steam'. Nearly two months later, on 3 September, three people were injured when their train suffered the indignity of being hit in the rear by a third-class Parliamentary train within 100 yards of Sheffield station because the steam in their engine had 'failed'. Sometimes inadequate provision was to blame, an example occurring on 28 May 1849 on the East Lancashire. It was Whitsun and an excursion train of 32 carriages was so heavy that it set out from Liverpool with one engine pulling and another pushing from the rear. After various stops and starts another incline, just before Burnley, proved too much and their train came to a stand. A following passenger train now hit them, and was in turn hit by a 21 carriage special from Preston. Fortunately, both following drivers saw the obstacles in front of them in time to reduce speed to such an extent that there were no serious injuries.

The most spectacular effects were produced by burst boilers; worn metal, allowing the water level to get too low and tampering with safety valves could both have this result. This was a journalists' favourite explanation for accidents but in many cases some more mundane defect was responsible. Fortunately for passengers (but not for railwaymen) these tended to occur on goods trains or in engine sheds. One burst did occur on a passenger train at Halshaw Moor on 31 January 1868; no passengers were hurt and, although badly injured, the driver was expected to recover. Similarly surprisingly little harm came to humans when a locomotive's boiler exploded in Northallerton station on 30 December 1870; some fragments were allegedly blown more than a quarter of a mile and one of the large driving wheels went through a roof 20 yards away but the only casualty was a telegraph clerk whose leg was broken.

Wheel and axle failures were a regular cause of accidents. In April 1835 the 'axis' of the first carriage broke and derailed the train on the Liverpool & Manchester; there was only one serious injury.[49] On 19 August 1840 on the Newcastle & Carlisle there was much jolting, eventually a carriage was thrown over and landed in a potato field because the axle of an overloaded luggage coach had broken. A carriage was derailed on the London & Birmingham in December 1842 when an axle on the engine broke owing, it was said, to the bad quality of the iron; one passenger was killed and two injured. Three days later an LSW engine suffered the same fault when about a mile and a half out from Nine Elms but it and the carriages stayed on the line and a relief engine was able to tow the failed train back to Nine Elms and then take it on its way, with a total delay of only 35 minutes. A particularly spectacular example occurred in March 1851 to a train from Birmingham to Bristol. A wheel on a second-class carriage had disintegrated allowing the axle to bump along the ground, giving the passengers a very uncomfortable ride and starting a small fire. Shouts from the passengers were not heard by the driver and 'a working man, who was in one of the last carriages, ... got out onto the steps, and, at the peril of his life, passed along the whole length of the train, then going at top speed – having to stride from one set of carriages to another – until at length he reached the engine'. A note of anti-climax then intervened – the brakes were already being applied.[50] Two female passengers were drowned in a ditch alongside the line when the tyre of a second-class carriage broke near Dinmore, on the Shrewsbury & Hereford, on 4 January 1861. Two were described on the same day in October 1863, one on the LNW between Colwich and Rugeley, the other on the North London near

Bow Common; in both cases passengers escaped with nothing worse than bruises.[51] *The Times* of 4 November 1868 reported two such breakages: the previous Saturday a train from Llandovery to Swansea on the Vale of Towy had been derailed and the following Monday a NE Leeds to Scarborough express suffered a broken tyre soon after leaving Leeds but the driver was able to bring the train to a stop without any injuries and only a screw jack was needed to put the engine back on the rails.

Another common failing was broken couplings; the rough and ready braking system of the day meant that these were subject to much jolting and stretching. An engine and tender became separated from their carriages on the GW near Faringdon on 21 September 1846 and when the driver realised what had happened he ordered his fireman to apply the brakes; unfortunately the carriages ran on under their own momentum and two passengers were killed when they hit the tender. In August 1851 a train was being hauled up the steep incline from Folkestone Harbour to the main line when the coupling next to the tender broke, leaving the carriages to run back with 'fearful velocity' and demolish the station. Fortunately luggage waggons at the rear of the train absorbed most of the shock and the passengers escaped with 'a few slight contusions'; less lucky was a painter working in the station who was thrown about thirty feet by the shock. A large number of people travelled to a fete at Belle Vue Gardens near Manchester on 3 September 1860 and late that evening three trains, carrying about 2,500 excursionists set out for various places along the East Lancashire line; the first reached its destination safely, but the second stopped at Helmshore and when the guards released their brakes as they left there was a rebound which broke a coupling, leaving 14 carriages behind. Since the station was on a gradient, these rolled back down the line, the one guard and brake on this part not being enough to hold it, and ran against the third train about 400 yards from Helmshore. Two carriages broke into pieces against the engine and several others were badly damaged: 10 were killed and about 38 injured.[52]

On the GW the wheels extended into the floors of the carriages, screened by sheet iron, wood and carpet. Near Ealing on 9 October 1857 the iron came down into contact with a wheel and the friction started a fire. 'Salamander' wrote that he was in the affected carriage and they had kept the fire under some sort of control by piling coats on the flames but they had to endure suffocating smoke for some time because they were not able to attract attention.[53]

Various other mechanical defects contributed occasionally. Accidents could be made a lot worse if a train was made up of carriages with their buffers at different heights since a slight collision, which would otherwise be absorbed, might cause one carriage to ride over another. The LY received severe criticism over this following the Bolton accident in 1852; its habit of running heavy excursions with the inadequate rolling stock at its disposal meant unsuitable combinations were made up with anything available. A broken spring caused a third-class carriage to be thrown off the rails and over a bridge into the yard below near Bridge Street station in Glasgow on 14 June 1867; 18 people were injured, some seriously.

Rope and cable haulage lines were prone to accidents. Allegedly the Blackwall suffered two breakages of its cable within ten days in September 1840 and a related mishap occurred soon after on the Canterbury & Whitstable; on the latter the trains ran down an inclined plane from Tyler's Hill to the Canterbury terminus and were normally slowed by a rope but it was not fixed this time and six carriages heavily laden with corn and fish ran away since the rain had made the 'skids' inadequate so one man in the passenger carriage was crushed at the bottom and three or four injured.[54] The wire rope of the Goathland incline on the Whitby line broke on 10 February 1864; the train ran down at great speed, killing two passengers and injuring thirteen.

A special case was an accident on the Dowlais Railway, a two-mile long line, much on a steep incline, connecting the ironworks with the Taff Vale line below. A locomotive drew the carriage from the ironworks on the upper stretch, was unhooked 467 yards from the top of the incline and run into a siding, allowing the carriage to go on to the top of the incline – if it stopped short two horses pulled it the rest of the way – where it was attached to a rope to control its descent. On 27 December 1853, a high wind took the carriage over the brow before the rope could be attached; the brakes, which had been reported as defective, failed to hold it, the brakesman bailed out part way down and the carriage smashed to pieces at the bottom, killing the one passenger who had failed to jump out. The matter was complicated because originally the Taff Vale had been responsible for operating the line, but responsibility had, not very clearly, passed to the Dowlais Company just before the accident and no-one seemed to be sure who should have seen that the brakes were in order. In this case, the passenger service was never resumed.[55]

Operational failings at termini

A particular danger existed where engines were detached short of a terminus and carriages allowed to run on under their own impetus; this was sometimes made necessary by the shortness of the platforms and in any case saved moving the engine out from the front of its train. On 13 July 1837 the directors of the London & Birmingham managed to suffer even before their line had been opened to the public when they gave an excursion to a select party of their friends, using two trains of eleven and twelve carriages. As the first returned to Euston the engine was 'disengaged' and the carriages ran on but the brakesman was either not sufficiently expert or miscalculated and the carriages smashed into a barrier wall, demolishing it; there were some serious injuries – broken noses, lost teeth – including an MP and a peer.[56]

A train dashed through the station at Gravesend (then a terminus) on 15 February 1845 after the engine had been detached from its carriages though fortunately the latter were prevented from running into the canal basin a short distance on; the wording referred to 'another accident', so presumably this was not the first but this line had only opened on 10 February.[57] One occurred when a train from Chester to Monk's Ferry (Birkenhead) had its engine cast off before entering the downhill tunnel leading to the station; the guard put his brake on 'but the carriage having only five passengers, instead of the usual about twenty passengers, and the rails being very slippery from the sudden change in the weather, there was not weight enough to create friction sufficient to check the velocity of the train, and it ran into the station-yard against very strong buffers'.

At Ramsgate the SE stopped trains at the ticket platform just outside the station, unhooked the engine and added a tow rope between it and its train. The engine then took the carriages forward, the idea being that it would be unhooked again once they were moving and the rope's length would give enough room for the engine to go one way and the points to be changed for the carriages to run into the platform. On 9 August 1858 the guard misjudged the carriages' speed (he blamed a following wind) and they ran against the buffers, causing minor injuries to 13 passengers. As a result they stopped towing and adopted shunting from the rear but elsewhere the practice continued. A couple of passengers were slightly injured when their carriages hit the buffers at Ormskirk on 30 June 1859. At the LSW station at Windsor two or three were injured when a train hauled in by rope from the ticket platform came in too fast on 7 June 1868. On 14 September of the same year a train being run into Windermere station under gravity had a slight collision with the buffers.

Even when the engine was still in front, there could be trouble. 75 passengers complained of being more or less hurt when their Caledonian train came into violent contact with fixed buffers at Wemyss Bay on 16 September 1865; the inspector recommended the use of spring buffers to reduce the effect of any repetition. 20 were injured on 7 May 1868 when a train ran into the buffers at Waterloo.

Dangerous loads

Dangerous loads were not always treated with respect. Mostly these were carried in goods trains but there was always a chance that passing passengers might be affected. 'On Sunday morning [17 December 1848] between 2 and 3 o'clock, the inhabitants of the town of Witham on the Eastern Counties line, were aroused from their slumbers and alarmed by a violent explosion'. A goods train had brought two barrels of gunpowder, for Maldon and Braintree, whose branches ran from Witham. The explosives were carried, as usual, in the last van which was 'several hundred yards' back from the station itself because the train was an unusually long one. The porters sent back to unload them left them on the ground, to wait for the goods train to move on out of the way but the mail train then arrived and they went off to deal with that. After the mail had unloaded its bags it left and somehow ignited the gunpowder; miraculously no passengers (there were only 'six or eight') or railwaymen were injured beyond the odd bruise. The nearby Albert Hotel had 46 panes of glass shattered and allegedly the explosion was heard in Colchester, 14 miles away. A collision on the Eastern Counties on 6 March 1858 involved a passenger train running into some goods wagons, one of which was carrying gunpowder, packed in wooden crates, which were scattered all over the line but fortunately there was no explosion. Not so lucky were two railwaymen killed at Clifton, near Penrith on the LNW on 26 February 1867, when their goods engine ran into a wagon which had spilled across their line after being derailed going the other way. This contained 4,000 lbs of gunpowder which ignited, causing a 'terrific explosion'.[58]

The following year, on 20 August, clumsy shunting caused wagons containing 50 casks of paraffin oil to run away from Llandulas, towards Abergele. They were hit by the Irish Mail and immediately burst into flames which engulfed the latter's front carriages. 31 passengers and two railwaymen were killed; probably all had been knocked out in the collision before they were burnt. Following this the goods managers of the leading companies met in October and agreed a new set of regulations, which were issued via the Clearing House. In the course of their discussions they had discovered that whiskey, 25% over proof 'as carried from Ireland' was the most easily ignited cargo, catching fire at 67 degrees Fahrenheit; naphtha was not far behind and both refined petroleum and spirits of turpentine were more inflammable than paraffin. The new rules included extra paperwork and labelling of waggons to warn railwaymen that such products should only be handled in daylight.[58a] Despite this, on 13 December men at Three Bridges heard an unmarked wagon leaking in the dark and took a lamp to investigate; both were killed when the naphtha burst into flames. Thomas Kay, goods manager of the LNW, where the cargo had originated, blithely told the inquest that they had always been used to moving such cargoes without special precautions.[59]

Fitness of employees

In the last resort much depended on the fitness of employees; some very pertinent remarks about this appeared in various accident reports. One often-repeated complaint was the youthfulness of many employed in jobs affecting others' wellbeing: when a train from West India Docks, on the Blackwall, had come into such violent collision with the previous one in 1840 that many passengers had been hurt, especially in the second-class where there were no seats, a policeman had said it was the fault of the 'conductors', one of whom was 'quite a lad'.[60] In the 1840s companies' replies often took refuge in saying how difficult it was to find suitable men; many of those they took on proved unsatisfactory and had rapidly to be dismissed or transferred to jobs carrying less responsibility. Looking back one might equally wonder how they managed to train so many for a new industry since few at the start of 1830 can have even seen a railway, yet a Board of Trade return showed that on 31 May 1848 52,668 were employed on the 4,252 miles of line then open. Mining and associated industries provided a source of basic engineering skills, the armed forces many of the officials at what might be termed NCO and Officer levels and the growing population, which included many underemployed casual workers, the rest. Even so, they all had to learn at least new adaptations of their skills, and safe railway working required many written rules and day-by-day instructions so the pool of men available for some jobs was restricted; only in 1870 did Parliament pass an Education Act intended to make education available to all. Once a base had been laid ladders of opportunity were developed: for example, a man could progress from engine cleaner to repairer, to fireman, to driver of local goods, and so on to passenger expresses and clerical workers could progress from routine to more responsible jobs. However, there remained a barrier similar to that in the armed forces, where very few from the ranks were then commissioned.

Companies seem to have tried to be selective, many calling men seeking even porters' jobs for interviews before the Board of Directors. However, quite a lot of appointments were gained through the patronage of directors who claimed the right to nominate for some appointments and it may well be that some of those found later to be unfit owed their jobs to a director's desire to rid himself of the importunities of those seeking to find posts for friends and relatives – some of the defects of the Civil Service of that time were put down to such causes. They did demand high standards from their staff and those believed to have broken them were called before the Board to answer for their conduct, though they do seem to have been reasonably fair. When in 1848 the Rev. B. Pope complained about the incivility of Mr. Swann, the station clerk at Highbridge, when he was refused a ticket, the booking-clerk was also called in and he gave evidence that Pope had arrived when the train was already late and could not be detained so Swann was merely admonished to be polite. However, one wonders what a modern tribunal would make of the sacking in October 1849 of policeman Hughes at Box for having had an improper relationship with his wife's sister, conduct regarded as too disgraceful for him to be allowed to remain in their service.

Drivers inevitably came in for the closest scrutiny. On 12 November 1840 there was a collision 1¾ miles the London side of Harrow: a goods train due London at 3 p.m. had been derailed and immediately notices were sent to Watford, Harrow and Camden to stop other trains. A luggage train, hauled by two engines was signalled to stop, the driver of the first engine shut off steam but the second driver ignored the signal and they collided with an engine which had been sent to help clear the blockage. The driver (Simpson) and fireman of the second engine were killed. The inquest verdict was wilful murder of the fireman by Simpson and suicide by the latter; it was very critical of the directors for continuing to employ a man known for reckless driving and for doing nothing about acts of disobedience and carelessness previously reported to them.[61]

However, companies sometimes encountered difficulties as they sought to enforce rules. A careless 'Engine man' who had run his engine against the 'assistant Engine' stationed at Wigan in 1841 was prosecuted for breaking a North Union bye-law prohibiting engines running through Wigan station at faster than six miles per hour; he was acquitted because no means of accurately measuring speeds then existed. Companies also had to cope with much unsatisfactory behaviour. Drunkenness was a perennial problem: the minute books of the Traffic and Coaching Committee of the

LNW frequently recorded dismissals for this and there were many instances of fines or reprimands resulting from other offences. Following an accident at Nine Elms on 17 October 1840 there was an exchange of letters between the Board of Trade and the LSW concerning the latter's failure to prosecute the two men whose breach of rules had caused it and amongst the reasons given was that they had shortly afterwards had to dismiss their supervisor, who would have been the key witness, for drunkenness. Even horse-drawn vehicles were at risk: John Bell was fined 1s with 11s 6d costs for being in charge of a horse coach on the Stockton & Darlington while intoxicated. A particularly spectacular example was reported at the beginning of 1848 when William Hatfield and Mark Clegg, driver and fireman of the night mail, Liverpool to London were accused of drunkenness and neglect of duty. They had approached the points at Warrington Junction so fast (about 40 mph) that the pointsman decided not to turn the points for the south and let them go straight on, thus saving a derailment on a sharp curve. Seeing that they were heading towards Manchester, the guard signalled them to stop, but without effect. He passed from carriage to carriage along outside of the train to the engine where he found both drunk and insensible; he could not wake them but managed to stop the train on his own, just before Patricroft, 14 miles on. They received two months with hard labour from the magistrates, who did not send them for trial because a porter at Liverpool was partly to blame for letting them go with the train. Another was provided in 1867 when a long and heavy cattle train, with several drovers on board, went from Welshpool without a driver, though a crew sent in pursuit were able to bring it under control safely. The driver, Buchanan, was drunk, had pushed his fireman off the engine and then fallen off. The magistrates initially sentenced him to two months with hard labour but then agreed to fine him £5 – it was nearly Christmas.[62] However, this problem was not confined to railways. Many a career in the Metropolitan Police ended abruptly as a result of drunkenness or unauthorised visits to public houses: in 1834 a Parliamentary Committee was told that four-fifths of dismissals during the previous four years had been for this.[63] It might also be added that officialdom hardly set a good example when the celebrations accompanying the opening of new lines included a seemingly endless succession of toasts.

There were particular worries about men taken on to replace those lost during disputes and it was frequently alleged that in their eagerness to defeat their workers companies were prepared to take others' rejects. The Board of Trade expressed worries about the actions of the directors of the North Midland in 1842, whose economies had caused the affected men to resign, after giving a week's notice. The company immediately replaced them with others 'represented in various quarters as incompetent'; it replied to the letter of concern by assuring that the new men were competent and the Board had to content itself with a letter advising the company to act cautiously. The next day a luggage train ran into the back of a passenger train standing in Barnsley (later Cudworth) station; the inspector sent to investigate found that there had been another collision, between Derby and Belper, and that only the rapid reaction of a pointsman had averted a third. Further enquiries revealed that 10 out of 18 new men engaged had been dismissed after a few days' trial and at least six of these had been previously sacked by other companies (two of them twice) for such offences as running an engine through a gate, intoxication, running an engine on the wrong line and disobedience leading to an accident. The man who had caused the first accident had been described by the company as having a good character but the reality was that during a break in his service with the North Midland he had in less than a year been sacked as an engine cleaner by the LSW for neglect of duty and by the GW for being drunk and quarrelling with other men. In a letter of 10 February 1843 the company asserted that now all were competent and it blamed its troubles on men who 'refused to submit to a reasonable and proper reduction' in wages and the Board had to leave it at that.

The long hours worked by railwaymen were another source of worry, and one where it is difficult to believe officialdom's regular denials. In 1851 Priswell, in charge of a luggage train near Bishopstoke, and his fireman fell asleep and the train slowed as the fire ran down; when the guard saw Priswell fall off he realised something was wrong and stopped the train easily. The men said they had been up for two days and two nights.[64] Two years later 'A voice from the luggage train' reported a conversation he had had with a couple of guards on a recent journey who looked tired and haggard, claiming they had been out since 6 p.m. the previous day (it was then 1 p.m.); they said the driver would not finish for another hour and would have to be out again at 5.50 p.m. without rest or break for food. The officer responsible for working goods replied, including the statement that the writer had been taken up at Whittlesea as a favour, contrary to the rules – a standard management counter-attack gambit when criticised. His lengthy answer included claims that they had been able to spend 4¾ hours rest in a room provided for purpose on the way out and 2½ hours on the return trip. 'A lover of justice' ['voice' again?] stood by the earlier letter: both engine drivers and firemen claimed there had been occasions when they were 48 hours on duty; all had to do 15 hours. Porters at Bishopsgate were in three groups: 3 a.m. to 6.30 p.m., 6 a.m. to 9.30 p.m., 9 a.m. to midnight; often the first lot were made to stay until the last train arrived at midnight without extra pay. He had found by enquiry at the station that drivers on the (North) Woolwich line had been out from 7 a.m. to 2 or 3 a.m. every day, including Sunday.[65]

After an accident ay Hyde on 28 May 1858, which had been caused by a signalman sending a goods train into (and through the end of) the station, then a terminus, Lt Col Yolland commented on the hours worked. The man had to work from 7 a.m. to 10 p.m. without intermission (and on the day in question had stayed on an hour longer). He received 1 shilling per week more than when a porter at Guide Bridge, and no more than porters at Manchester. He felt that higher wages would attract the best men and that such hours were inconsistent with safety. The company's secretary answered in a way that was all too common: 'Your ... recommendations will have the best consideration of the directors'.

The Peebles Railway clearly thought it had found a novel way of keeping its servants awake when they were on duty for long hours but spent much of their time waiting for something to happen. It only ran five trains each way most days, with one extra on Mondays and Saturdays, and as a result its signalmen were alleged occasionally to have fallen asleep. They employed a shoemaker at 10 shillings per week, allowing him to carry on his trade in his box. Yolland decided that the likeliest cause of a derailment on 31 July 1857 was that he was too busy with shoes at the vital time.

Some points do need to be made in the companies' defence. In November 1841 the LNW reduced policemen's hours from 12 to 8 – and, at the same time, ordered that things should be arranged that every clerk and servant should be able to attend church or chapel on Sundays.[66] Some did keep their promise to reward good service; the Board of Trade report of 1841 listed several companies that did this. The LNW was one: in 1842 its top officials recommended various gratuities of up to £5 for switchmen and a week's pay for porters who had shown good conduct.[67] An occasional exceptional deed reached the press, one such concerning an engine that had somehow lost its own driver and was heading for Newcastle station in 1870. A driver, Steel, his fireman and guard set off in pursuit, on their own engine and when he was close enough Steel jumped on board and stopped it; the guard also tried and missed. Steel was called before the NE Board at York and praised for his action; the directors said they would put £50 into a savings bank for him, £20 for the guard and £10 for the fireman and all three would receive an appropriately engraved silver watch.[68]

Causes outside companies' control

Destruction, or attempted destruction, of property was not new. Those with a grievance had often destroyed anything new that threatened their interests, whether it was looms in factories, threshing machines on farms or toll-gates on roads. On a Sunday in 1844 the passengers in the Norwich road mail were alarmed by sudden jolting at about 3 a.m.; for about three miles the road was littered at intervals of 50 or 100 yards with gates taken from fields and parts of ploughs and other farm machinery. Fortunately the horses were not thrown by the first contact and it was a moonlit night so that the rest could be seen and the guard was able to descend from time to time to remove them.[69]

Inevitably acts of sabotage spread to railways and all areas seem to have been vulnerable. In November 1834 a large piece of wood was deliberately left across the rails of the Stockton & Darlington; the engine was overturned and the 'engineer' killed.[70] Various potentially dangerous acts were reported in the Wigan area in November 1839, when the blame was put on ruffians frequenting pubs and the implication was that these things were happening because the richer sort were using the trains. On a Monday a gate was put across the line between Wigan and Parkside but the engine cut through it; soon after a sleeper had been laid across line, but was fortunately seen in time and the next evening a heavy stone was thrown down onto a train without hurting anyone.[71]

In August 1840 a railway bar and a large piece of iron had been placed across the Birmingham & Gloucester about 1½ miles below Bromsgrove, at dusk, ¼ hour before the last train due, but was removed in time; the culprit, Williams, was found and given the 'full fine' of £10 and costs by magistrates. 'Old Subscriber' wrote that the penalty had been insufficient; a crime that could have killed many people was more atrocious than many punished by transportation or imprisonment with hard labour. He had a point because following Williams's appearance in court stones were placed that night on the line between Spetchley and Norton; the company offered a reward of £5 for information.[72]

Every year there were similar incidents: 1843, for example, saw a crop, well-spread across the country. At the start of the year, on a Sunday evening, the 5 o'clock Glasgow to Edinburgh train hit an empty truck which some malicious individuals had drawn right across the line near Polmont.[73] In late February the Brandling Junction train from Newcastle to Sunderland, which had left Gateshead at 8.30 with 40 passengers on board, hit two gates laid across the lines.[74] In October it was the GW's turn when on a Sunday a plank was laid across the line at Twyford to upset a mail train; the attempt was thwarted by a policeman who found and removed the plank and 'a fellow' employed as a shepherd by Mr Cotterell of Ruscombe was reported to be in custody.[75]

There were no casualties in the incidents described in the previous paragraph but luck could not hold for ever. The driver and fireman of a Midland train were injured when their train was upset in September 1845 after an iron chain and piece of stone had been wedged into points; the company offered 100 guineas reward but seems to have no success in catching the culprits. Next year the sufferer was again not a passenger though in this case there was not complete certainty that sabotage was the cause. The 10 a.m. from Gateshead was going fast between Brockley Whins and Shields, on the Brandling Junction when it was derailed on a curve near Jarrow Alkali Works, came off the embankment and went through the roofs of a row of dwelling-houses. One elderly woman was badly scalded, and later died, another woman and a child injured. The report said no defects had been found in any equipment and the likeliest cause was an obstruction placed on the line: there had been one some time before which had not been publicised and they had kept observation for a while but not been able to catch anyone.[76]

There was no doubt that the derailment of an LBSC train near Falmer in 1851 was caused by the placing of a sleeper left behind after repair works across the line; both men on the engine and three passengers were killed. Suspicion fell on James Boakes, a ten-year old farm labourer's son living nearby who had often been seen watching trains pass. He broke down in tears at the first inquest (on the dead passengers) and the jury interfered to stop him from being fully examined and the inquest was adjourned so the police could make further enquiries. It was then rumoured that Boakes had confessed but at the later sessions of this inquest and the one on the driver he denied it, after explaining to the coroner that he had been seen by the local curate and believed he would go to hell if he lied on oath. They established that he was physically capable of moving the sleeper but there was no evidence that he had been seen on the line and the jury's verdict now was that it had been put there by some person unknown. Exactly a year later he was killed by lightning at that spot.[77]

A sprinkling of later incidents illustrates the continuance of the problem. Professor Rogers had his jaw broken by a stone thrown at his train near Wymondham in October 1857; the Chairman of the Eastern Counties offered a reward of £10 and sent a special policeman to watch the spot but to no avail.[78] In 1863 the GN offered a reward of £50 to catch whoever had put several items on the lines between Seven Sisters and Holloway Road.[79] Only one person was injured, and that only slightly, later that year when 'some mischievous person' caused a passenger and a coal train to collide near Hull by interfering with the signals.[80] The difficulties involved in catching vandals were highlighted by 'GEH': in October 1867 he was near Chesterford on a train from Cambridge when a stone broke a window, showering the occupants with glass. One of the occupants saw two boys of about 12 on an embankment. At Bishops Stortford the station-master said a reward would be offered to catch the culprits but he doubted whether much would be done since the companies had no incentive to act. On the same day he had read that at Worship Street two 'respectable' boys had only been fined 2/6 each and warned about their future behaviour though an inspector had testified that during the previous few months three passengers and two engine-drivers had been severely injured by the throwing of stones.[81]

A variant was the inconvenience caused to early morning travellers from Twickenham when someone used sand to fill the axle-boxes of carriages left there overnight ready for the next day's service in August 1865, making them unusable.[82]

Stray animals were a regular hazard. In 1840 a train on the Eastern Counties met oxen about a mile from Brentwood because dilapidated fencing had allowed them to stray. The driver saw them in time to reduce speed but the engine and tender were derailed; there was no injury to passengers but some 'remarkably fine fat beasts' were killed.[83]

A miscellany of animals contributed to accidents in 1842, though only in one case was a passenger hurt. A letter to the Board of Trade from the Midland Counties, dated Leicester, 23 June, 1842, read:

> On Saturday afternoon [18th] a cow jumped over a fence, within a few yards of the engine of a passenger train. The driver, the instant he saw her, reversed his engine, but she got on the rails, was knocked down by the engine, which, after dragging her nearly 100 yards, passed over her, and six passenger carriages were thrown off the rails, one guard was thrown off the carriage, and a good deal bruised, and a lady had a blow over the foot, but no one else was hurt. The fence was in perfect order,

and three feet seven inches high – our usual height. Ten cows had only that morning, for the first time, been turned into the field.

Three months later a herd of the beasts escaped onto the North Union, derailing the train. In October a bull which had been 'overdriven' jumped a fence on the London & Birmingham near Leighton Buzzard and was run over, claims being made that this was the fourth incident of its kind on this line. Later that month a pig escaped from its wagon on the Grand Junction while the train was in a tunnel; it was hit by the following Mail train and a carriage was derailed but none of its 13 occupants were hurt. In November it was the turn of horses; at the start of the month one ran loose on the Brandling Junction and less than a week later several strayed from marshes near Wigan onto the North Union. As in many other instances, the blame for the last was put on the farmer for not keeping fences in repair.

A bullock being driven one night across the line between Headcorn and Pluckley in January 1851 strayed from the crossing; the drover had nearly turned it back to the gate when the mail approached. It then made straight for the lights, tail in the air; it was dashed to pieces, parts of its body being picked up 60 yards away, but the train stopped without harm to the passengers, thus, this time at least, vindicating Stephenson's views quoted in the next paragraph.[84]

When a train came off the rails after hitting a heifer between Lynn and Hunstanton, killing 7 and injuring 30 passengers, the editor of *The Times* used it to justify an assault on several malpractices but only the relevant part is quoted below:

> On Monday evening [3 August 1863] five persons were killed and some five-and-twenty others were more or less injured, on the Lynn and Hunstanton Railway .... The immediate cause of the accident was an unhappy bullock, which had strayed on the line. ... Strangely enough, the danger of cattle straying on the line had been thought of by one of the opponents of the railways before these means of communication were yet in being. GEORGE STEPHENSON was asked by an adverse committeeman, 'Suppose a cow gets in the way?' 'So much the worse for the cow', he replied. The greatest men are sometimes wrong ... [85]

Here there was clearly neglect; the fences were too low, the dikes dry and no action had been taken following earlier reports of stray cattle and horses.

Various weather problems regularly caused accidents; since these were beyond the control of railwaymen only a few examples are given here. Several instances of floods causing trouble have already been given elsewhere. Fog was regularly mentioned in accident reports: the Mail ran into a coal train at Hitchin on 3 January 1859 and 22 were injured when the 8 a.m. express to Brighton ran into the back of the SE's down tidal train between New Cross and Forest Hill on 6 November 1862, 20 were injured in a collision near Surrey Canal Junction on the SE on 19 December 1864 and 47 were hurt (most slightly) when a North London train hit a goods near Bow on 27 December

1866. Two passengers were killed when a passenger train collided with one carrying labourers to clear snow from the line between Thetford and Harling; on the same day, 5 January 1854, slippery rails were blamed when a passenger train ran into a ballast train on the LNW. The unluckiest casualty of the weather must surely have been an East Lancashire train which was derailed near Clifton Junction when it hit the roof of a passing goods wagon blown off by the high wind.

Passengers' own ignorance and stupidity

Passengers took time to adjust to the particular 'road sense' demanded by railways. Every annual report to Parliament included many instances of passengers killed and injured as a result of their own lack of caution. This was not entirely surprising since even those who should have known better did stupid things. On 13 June 1839 Brunel took an experimental train part way along the line and came back on the same track, colliding with another engine, not yet on its train, near Paddington.[86] Many ordinary railwaymen featured frequently in the lists of those killed as a result of their own carelessness: in 1868 one guard even climbed onto the roof of a carriage on its way to King's Cross in order to see a band playing nearby, hit his head against a bridge and was killed.[87]

The first (and most famous) passenger casualty, William Huskisson, alighted on the wrong side and was run down by a train coming the other way on the ceremonial opening of the Liverpool & Manchester in 1830. In July 1836 Mrs Fletcher of the Navigation Inn, St Helens, was killed on the Warrington Junction line when she alighted on the wrong side as a Manchester train was passing.[88] At Keynsham on a Sunday in March 1842 a passenger, upwards of eighty, was knocked down and killed when he persisted, despite warning from an official, in staying on the wrong side of the line until the train was nearly there; he had been planning to go to the Counterslip Chapel in Bristol. This type of accident was a recurrent one, especially in cases of panic. At 'Lea Gate' station near Preston when a passenger was about to alight on the wrong side in 1853 as an express came past on the other line officials shouted at him not to get out but many of the passengers in the train heard the whistle of the approaching train and interpreted the shout as 'Get out!' About twenty jumped out; most chose the right side, some in their haste clearing an adjoining fence at a bound but two chose wrongly so 'the whole train passed over them, and they were literally cut to pieces'.[89] Doubtless some regarded John Cheetham's fate as rough justice when he alighted from his train on the wrong side at Middleton on the Manchester & Leeds in January 1845 to avoid paying his fare and was hit by a train going 'the contrary way'; he suffered cuts and bruises.

At first some would-be passengers thought they should follow the procedure used for catching a stage-coach and did not appreciate that railway engines lacked comparable steering and brakes. In August 1839 a deaf old cooper called Wright, who had been standing on the line waiting for the train, was killed at Holmes near Rotherham; a policeman got two females clear but Wright did not hear.[90]

A common idiocy was that of men jumping out of trains either when drunk or when trying to retrieve their hats, particularly when they were travelling in open carriages; surprisingly, many survived, often with little injury. In February 1839 a servant of Lady Baring lost his hat on the London & Birmingham and jumped out after it. Luckily he landed in a pond, though whether he felt so lucky when her Ladyship caught up with him was not recorded: he had the tickets and she had had to pay again at Euston. At about the same time on the same line, a drunk jumped out and was later found sitting on a piece of timber by the line, severely bruised.[91] Much depended on whether or not the person involved landed clear of the train; the worst consequences usually resulted from being caught up between carriages and run over by following ones.

Not all were so lucky. The following year when a Sunday evening train was on its way back to Romford, Henry Jay's hat blew off before Brentwood and despite his brother-in-law's warning, he jumped off to retrieve it. The train stopped; he was found senseless and the damage to his skull was such that there was no hope of his recovery.[92] Only a few days later, on the Wednesday evening, a man named Dean, fell from a train of the Preston & Wyre near Fleetwood while in a state of intoxication, was run over and beheaded.[93]

The *Reports* for 1842 included a crop of such actions. John Anderton had an altercation in a second-class carriage between Paisley and Glasgow in April and his hat blew off; he escaped with a broken thigh. Less lucky was a soldier who had to have his leg amputated after going over the side of a similar carriage between Roby and Broad Green in July; in this case the carriage was described as having sides 'forming arms or elbows to passengers'. On 20 May Mrs Bennet died of her injuries when she leapt out of a horse-drawn carriage in motion on the Edinburgh & Dalkeith after failing to warn the driver where she wanted him to stop. A sailor escaped with severe concussion when he went after his hat in August – again between Glasgow and Paisley. There were four similar episodes in October. A varied crop in 1844 included a young man who fell out of an open Edinburgh & Glasgow carriage near Linlithgow when he was standing on his seat to view the scenery.

There were still those whose luck did hold. On 24 January 1845 a drunken female passenger who lived in Jarrow leaped from the top of a carriage of the 5 o'clock from Brockley Whins to South Shields while it was going at full speed. On the return journey they found that she had, with help, scrambled back to Brockley Whins and only hurt her knee.[94] However, within a week a passenger on the Sheffield and Manchester line failed to get out at his station and jumped out while the train was at full speed; he was killed.[95] Another fatal casualty was one who tried later that year to retrieve his hat from the roof of his carriage between Chester and Crewe and collided with a bridge.

. Cases seem to have become fewer as time went on: were passengers learning or did improvements to carriages make it more difficult to jump out? Some still managed, though. The Glasgow & Paisley again provided the setting for a severe injury to a second-class passenger who lost his hat while looking out of the window on 7 July 1855 and jumped out to retrieve it. Mr Jolly lost his when was looking out of the window in 1859 to see why they had stopped (it was a mechanical failure); despite warnings from other passengers he jumped out and was run over by a train coming the other way.

Members of the armed and merchant services showed remarkable resilience in some incidents in the 1860s. In 1864 Edward Apter, a seaman of about 21, was drunk on the 5 p.m. from London to Liverpool and in mid-journey he got up and said he wanted to alight since he was at Euston-square. Murphy, another seaman, seized him by collar and pushed him back into his seat; he rose again, staggered against the door and it flew open. Immediately this was known, the others in the compartment were detained (four merchant seamen and a sergeant on leave from Royal Artillery). The line from Rugby was searched for his body but nothing was found, so the others were kept in custody. However, the missing man presented himself by the train which arrived in Liverpool at 11 a.m. with hardly a scratch. He remembered being in a railway carriage but then all was blank; he found himself waking up from a damp sleep in a ditch at the bottom of a high embankment, managed to find his way to the next station and went on to Liverpool at the first opportunity.[96] A sailor, William White, travelling from Liverpool to Garston in January 1866, needless to say also drunk, jumped out of a carriage window and was later found in a ditch at the foot of an embankment, dirty but unhurt.[97] In December 1867 it was the turn of a soldier of the Rifle Brigade, recently returned from India who jumped out of a Falmouth to London express near Slough and was found beside the line by a porter; he had only suffered a wound to the head and was able to continue his journey.[98]

Some had more pressing reasons for jumping out. In March 1841, John Brazin, a prisoner on his way to Wakefield jumped out of a carriage on the Manchester & Leeds in an attempt to escape the constable escorting him; his broken leg did not help him in this. One in police custody jumped out, with fatal results, near Woolwich Arsenal on 26 March 1867. 'Intending passengers' who had overlooked the formality of buying a ticket seem to fit in here also. 'A young woman' was severely bruised when she jumped out of a Brighton train on 29 September 1849; her explanation was that she had no money to pay her fare. A man was killed trying to board a moving Midland train at Holbeck on 12 June 1860 and another at Farringdon, near Preston on 16 March 1867.

Passengers took liberties with moving trains. William Taylor fractured his skull when he fell off the step when he had 'imprudently left the carriage in which he had been seated' and tried to go to another carriage. Near the end of the same year, 1841, John Edwards was severely injured: apparently he had been jumping up and down on his third-class seat at Shrivenham station in order to warm his feet and was thrown out by the jerk as the train started and a passenger on a MS&L goods train persisted in sitting on the side of a wagon, despite being warned and was killed when he fell off. John Ward was leaning out of a third-class carriage and died when his head came into contact with the Bishopton tunnel on 21 October 1853. The inquest verdict on a South

Staffordshire third-class passenger four days later was accidental death caused by his meddling with the door handle. Mr Blaylock, late registrar of births, deaths and marriages for Birkenhead, was killed in 1855 when he tried to jump on a train at Tranmere though it was not booked to stop there.[99] Near the end of 1863 another who should have known better, Mr Arthur Jones, Clerk to the House of Commons for 30 years, tried to join one of the carriages of the Oystermouth Railway when it was already slowly in motion; he had to have one of his toes amputated and died 'unexpectedly' a few days later.[100]

Inquisitiveness could lead to injury. In an accident near Castle Howard in 1869 the majority of the casualties were people who had been looking out of the window as their train was hit in rear by a goods; they were trying to find out the cause of the frantic whistling that was coming from the rear as the driver of the oncoming train sought to warn those ahead and were hit about their heads by the window frames.[101]

Some helpful suggestions

Since accidents were so common many ways of minimising their effects, including some peculiar ones, were suggested. In 1838 several advocated cowcatchers, though the consensus seems to have been that British conditions allowed the safer alternative of fencing. In 1850 'Humanitas' revived this one, advocating a scoop in front of the engine to deflect people, animals etc; people would get broken legs but that was better than death.[102] In between a West-Country 'Viator' suggested that every train should have a 'damper truck' carrying a 15 to 20 foot length of wool packs at front and rear to absorb the shock when collisions did occur.[103]

A protracted debate concerned the use of luggage vans as safety buffers. In June 1841 'W' pointed out that railway directors claimed it was safe to put passenger carriages next to the tender but then asked why if that was so, had two carriages been put between Queen Victoria and the tender on her recent journey? This, incidentally, was not the only occasion that the Queen was brought into the safety debate. A series of accidents was caused by faulty wheels in 1861; at about the same time it was reported that the tyres of special coaches provided for her were put on cold and then hardened. If this was a 'more secure' way why was it not in general use?[104]

After an accident at Haywards Heath in 1841 the jury recommended, amongst other things, that luggage vans should be placed between engines' tenders and the leading passenger coach, to act as shock-absorbers and on 9 November the London & Brighton issued a notice that it would be complying with the recommendations. 'Homo' continued a well-worn theme with a slight variation; he suggested it was deliberate policy to put second-class carriages between the tender and luggage to encourage travellers to pay higher first-class fares. HC (December 1841) claimed that after their most recent fatal accident the GW directors had promised an empty carriage between the engine and the first passenger carriage but he had recently made three journeys and not found any such provision; according to 'Chemin de Fer' in August

1845 the GW were still refusing to do this.[105] The GW was not the only culprit. In January 1843 'TA' complained about the lack of protection between tender and carriages on the previous Monday night on the Birmingham & Gloucester. On the same line 'A Barrister' complained in November that despite promises he had obtained to the contrary, his carriage was put on truck immediately behind the tender at Gloucester. Whilst he was still complaining and trying to get it changed the train started and he had to jump on the truck and travel in his carriage, exposed to red-hot cinders which burnt leather and cushions.[106]

However, there seems to have been no certain 'right' answer to this. The Leicester & Swannington was a mineral line which added couple of passenger carriages for the convenience of people in that rural area. They were put in the middle so coal waggons could be attached and detached on the way with the minimum of shunting. On 28 August 1844 an axle of a wagon in front of the passenger carriages broke and the rear wagons piled up against the rear passenger carriage, killing one of the only two passengers on the train; the local jury followed the views given above, recommending that passenger carriages should be put at the rear. Major-General Pasley's view was that points could be put in favour of any place: if a train was hit from the rear, the safest place was at the front but if the engine hit an obstacle they were safest at the rear; the middle was a compromise with something to be said for it.

Finally

Occasionally deaths were attributed indirectly to railway accidents. At first it was thought that John Jones had died as a delayed result of an accident at Colney Hatch in 1865 and various representatives of railway companies attended his inquest but there it emerged that he had seen it from another train standing in the station. He had been in ill health and it was assumed that the shock had caused a fatal collapse; the verdict was 'natural causes'. It is also frequently asserted that Charles Dickens never recovered from the shock of the accident at Staplehurst and that this hastened his death.

Some accidents defy easy classification.

In April 1842 John Sayer took his bullock on a Northern & Eastern train and bought a second-class ticket for himself but, instead of getting into the appropriate carriage, he joined his bullock in its wagon. Near Stratford it became restive and kicked him out; he was severely bruised but his 'truck being the last in the train, no impediment or other inconvenience was sustained'.

On 2 November 1847 a first-class passenger on the GW was severely injured in the face when an iron bar became dislodged from a goods train going the opposite way and went through the window. Joseph Stobart, a passenger in an open third-class carriage was killed on 7 October 1854 when he was hit 'it is supposed, by something which had been thrown up from the line, or by the handle of a door which was knocked off a passing train, the door, it is supposed, being open at the time'. An iron girder being placed over the line near Aldersgate, on the Metropolitan, fell on a passing train, killing three passengers on 19 December 1866.

The description of the formal opening of the Sheerness branch in 1860 included:

> As the train approached Sheerness terminus the 13th Kent Artillery Volunteers were in readiness to fire a salute but we regret to say that one of the "gunners" fired "point blank" into the carriages. One gentleman was thrown from his seat; and a second injured in the face; a third was "twisted around"; a fourth suffered a severe cut in the forehead and many were exceedingly annoyed. An excellent dinner was provided …

Perhaps they might have given the excellent dinner a new paragraph?[107]

Statistical summary

At first companies were not obliged to report accidents so no reliable statistics are available. They were clearly common. In his book on the Liverpool & Manchester RHG Thomas listed more than 30 involving passenger trains 1830 – 1840; however only a few passengers were killed and in many cases there were no injuries. From August 1840 companies had to inform the Board of Trade (briefly later, the Railway Commissioners) of accidents involving injury to passengers; this was soon widened to include all accidents involving danger to the public, even if no casualties occurred. Below, Irish casualties are included with the rest until 1852; thereafter, except for 1868, the figures relate to England, Wales, and Scotland. The figures for injuries were not in reality always quite as accurate as they look; in addition they do not seem always to have added in deaths resulting from an accident that occurred some time afterwards. The figures below refer, with few exceptions, to passengers actually in trains. Casualties were divided into two categories: those killed or injured through circumstances beyond their own control and those suffering through their own careless or stupidity.

	Not own fault		Own negligence	
	killed	injured	killed	injured
1840 (a)	22	131 upwards	6	10
1841	24	72 upwards	17	20
1842	5	14	26	22
1843	3	3	24	17
1844	7	65	7	9
1845	4	83	9	10
1846	3	106	19	9
1847	19	87	11	6
1848	9	128	12	7
1849	5	84	18	21
1850	12	171	20	12
1851	19	355	17	20
1852	10	372	22	8
1853	16	269	25	20
1854	11	327	17	15
1855	9	304	17	16
1856	8	280	18	14
1857	25	631	20	14
1858	26	409	23	14
1859	4	268 (b)	21	8
1860	29	471	13	12
1861	46	780 (c)	29	8
1862	24	522	6	-
1863	14	382	19	1
1864	13	656	21	6
1865	22	1,026 (d)	25	3
1866	15	540	14	6
1867	16	659	17	8
1868	40	519 (e)	22	6
1869	17	995 (f)	21	16
1870	65	1,050 (g)	21	9

(a) – last five months only.

(b) – includes six injured by collapse of platform they were on.

(c) – of these 23 killed, 176 injured in collision in Clayton Tunnel and 15 killed, 317 injured in Kentish Town collision.

(d) – includes an accident to a GN excursion at Colney Hatch in which 250 were injured, the greater number very slightly and 75 hurt when a Caledonian train ran into Wemyss Bay station too fast.

(e) – includes 31 killed in Abergele crash; also includes Ireland.

(f) – includes 357 hurt in New Cross excursion accident; at least one died later, but not listed as death in the yearly return.

(g) – includes 110 hurt in collision at Penruddock; 16 killed and 40 injured when an MS&L goods wagon broke an axle and a GN excursion hit the wreckage near Newark; 15 killed and 59 injured when an MS&L passenger train ran into wagons that had broken from their goods train.

Chapter 18: WHO WAS TO BLAME?

Failings of the sort considered in this chapter were not confined to railways. The Crimean War provided a multitude of examples of negligence while at home Parliament and local authorities were reluctant to spend on such basics as public health – an epidemic of cholera might provoke a call of 'something must be done' but often once the panic had faded and the costs calculated little was done. The approach to fire fighting was example of this attitude. Many towns and cities still contained wooden buildings and serious fires were frequent but most local authorities recoiled from the costs of setting up public brigades and relied on those run by various insurance companies, which, despite much in print, did attend all fires, not just those in insured premises. A spectacular example of the consequences of this short-sighted attitude was provided by events in Gateshead and Newcastle. In Newcastle suggestions of setting up a public body had been made in 1837 and 1845, when a public petition provided support, but failure to agree on details meant insurance brigades were left to do the job; Gateshead had no cover and some of its merchants had quaint ideas of safe storage. In October 1854 a fire in a warehouse containing large quantities of sulphur and sodium nitrate caused an explosion which scattered warehouse debris over a big area, some landing on houses whose sleeping occupants stood no chance. 53 were killed (6 of them on the Newcastle side of the Tyne) and hundreds injured. Even after that, it was only in 1866 that the Newcastle authorities set up a public brigade after one insurance company had given notice of disbanding its brigade.[1]

Railway companies could inflict fines and dismissal and they had powers under their own Acts and various General Acts of Parliament (including Lord Seymour's) to take servants who had broken their bye-laws before magistrates for summary punishment; where an accident involved death the ordinary criminal law could be invoked and the alleged culprit charged with manslaughter. English Common Law normally required proof of deliberate criminal intention but in the case of railways Parliament made negligence an absolute offence. The tendency at first was to blame ordinary railwaymen, whose failings covered the spectrum from momentary lapses of concentration while under great pressure to outright foolhardiness, but over time critics increasingly made companies' senior officials their targets though no law then allowed action against management collectively.

In November 1840 an embankment between Leicester and Syston on the Midland Counties gave way after heavy rain and let the rails down several inches. The drivers were cautioned to go slow, but one went on at the usual pace and his train was derailed, though there were no serious injuries; he was suspended for some weeks and fined £5.[2] That same month Cornelius Revis, a gatekeeper on the Northern & Eastern was charged at Cheshunt petty sessions with neglect of duty: he had failed to open the crossing gates at the bottom of Cadmore's Lane so a train crashed through, damaging the carriages but not injuring any passengers. The directors said that owing to his excellent character they did not wish to proceed further than his dismissal and he was sent from the court with a reprimand.[3]

The Board of Trade's report issued in January 1841 complained:

> A great defect of the present system is, that owing to the facility with which engine-drivers discharged from one company get employment upon others, it is exceedingly difficult for the companies to enforce the strict system of discipline which the nature of their duties require. ... Railway Companies generally have shown reluctance to exert the powers placed in their hands by Lord Seymour's Act for the punishment of misconduct on the part of their servants. In several [cases] the offenders have escaped with a degree of impunity which cannot be fail to be productive of the worst consequences.

Despite this punishments often continued to be minor. Slippery rails plus carelessness of driver and guard were given as the reasons for one train running into the back of another in Nottingham station in December 1842; the driver was sacked and the guard fined a week's pay (25/-). A collision on the SE, 26 August 1844, occurred when a train laden with lime ran into a passenger train as the latter was entering Tonbridge station, causing some minor injuries. At first they thought faulty brakes were probably to blame but after an enquiry Cubitt, the company's Chief Engineer, told its directors that the driver was responsible; although he could not have expected the passenger train to be there, he should have been alert enough to stop sooner so he was suspended, brought before the directors, reprimanded and fined one week's pay. On 5 July a collision on the Manchester & Bolton resulted from a 'misunderstanding' by a driver failing to obey his orders when single line working was in operation during repairs. An enquiry received the answer that the man at fault had been suspended; the Board of Trade considered the punishment 'quite inadequate to the gravity of the fault ... committed' but had to leave it at that. On the other hand it was content with the dismissal of a driver who carelessly ran into the back of a passenger train being shunted from ticket to arrival platform at Shoreditch in October; the Eastern Counties had said they would not take criminal action unless ordered by the Board owing to his 'long service and excellent conduct'. He had been with them only for four years, but that was 'long service' given that the company's first line had opened in June 1839.

There were, however, many instances of men being prosecuted both for carelessness that caused accidents and for conduct that might lead to them. A policeman at Rugby received 14 days with hard labour in 1840 for giving an incorrect signal.[4] Near the end of 1840 William Davidson, a guard on the Liverpool & Manchester failed to apply his brake on coming into Lime Street on Christmas Day and his train had crashed into coaches waiting in the station. Though he was previously of good conduct, the magistrate felt it necessary to make an example and gave him the maximum sentence, two months in prison with hard labour.[5] In January 1841 a GW policeman was sent to gaol for one month with hard labour by magistrates at Keynsham after an inspector had seen him asleep by a fire he had lit, leaving his lantern on so it could be seen by trains.

In April 1845 the Manchester & Leeds told the Board of two successful prosecutions: a man who had failed to work his points properly was given the option of a £1 fine or a month in prison and a driver who negligently left his engine on a sharp curve where it was hit by a passenger train was given a similar fine. Also that year Edward Laws, a Brandling Junction engine-driver was charged at Sunderland police court with having by his negligence endangered the lives and limbs of passengers on 15 August; found guilty he paid a fine of £5 rather than spend two months in prison.[6] In February 1846 a driver of a coal train hit at Sessay, paid a £5 fine rather than serve a month with hard labour for leaving his train without proper safety precautions where others would run into it.[7] A few months later Beech received two months for neglecting his points, thus causing the derailment of a goods; he had been too busy making a mousetrap to notice the train.[8] Later that year two SE drivers were sentenced to 2 months and 1 month in prison for inattention to signals at Reigate, following a collision on 28 August; their two engines were on the same train, the 2 months going to the driver of the leading engine.[9]

Examples from 1852 showed how treatment of offenders could be light, even when taken to court, given the potentially serious consequences of their lapses. A driver and fireman, both drunk, ran their engine out of steam near Brockley Whins on the York, Newcastle & Berwick and were then hit in the rear by the mail train on 22 May 1852. They were dismissed and fined £5 by the magistrates, refusing the option of 14 days in prison but Captain Galton felt that they should have been sent to Quarter Sessions for more severe punishment. The press dealt with this one under the heading 'Railway crimes licensed' since they could have been charged with a misdemeanour (punishable with up to two years in prison). It assumed officials acted thus because they were partly to blame; the men had clearly been drunk when let loose with an engine.[10] The station-master at Kings Norton on the Midland was fined 50 shillings by the magistrates for the improper shunting of a train and failing to make sure his signals were lit.[11] One did not wait after he had driven his engine into the booking office at Barton-on-Humber: 'The driver ran away immediately, and has not been heard of since, though the Company have offered a reward for his apprehension. The man had been observed to be in dejection of spirits the whole of the day.'[12] Later examples of punishments included a driver and fireman being fined £5 each and dismissed for going past three danger signals and running into a stationary mail train on the Bristol & Exeter on 19 October 1858 and twelve months for a drunken driver who took his engine for a solo trip along the Caledonian in 1863.

Some serious penalties were imposed even where juries took a sympathetic view of momentary errors; since most jurymen would also have been passengers from time to time they would hardly have shown sympathy unless really deserved. Fossey, a signalman who sent a passenger train into a siding at Wolverton on 5 June 1847, killing seven passengers, was sentenced to two years with hard labour for manslaughter despite the jury saying that although he was guilty the fault really lay with the company for not employing separate men to attend to points and signals: one who should have been involved in the passage of the relevant train was engaged in moving an engine, leaving the full responsibility to Fossey. The judge said it was necessary to protect the public against the carelessness of people who had accepted positions of responsibility. During the trial his superior had stated that Fossey had joined on 13 December 1846 and after two weeks' probation under an experienced man he had been left on his own; this seems hardly sufficient training for a job where others' lives might be imperilled.[13] Oddly, the following year another signalman, George Pargetter, found guilty of manslaughter after an accident at Shrivenham when he had given the all clear before empty wagons had been shunted out of the way received three months, the judge recommending that he should then have his job back because the experience of prison would make him more careful in future.[14]

In 1848 the LNW faced labour problems and took on new men to replaced drivers who had left. A driver of excursion empties, who, according to Captain Laffan, was unfit to be in charge of a train ran into the back of a troop train at Rugby. He was sentenced to six weeks with hard labour but Laffan wrote that the fault lay with the foreman who had sent out an inexperienced driver with a fireman little-more experienced and a guard who was normally a porter. After a lengthy delay, including a reminder requiring an answer, Huish replied that his directors could not agree; he was equally unrepentant after an accident at Roade on 17 August where the competence of the driver was again questioned.

The SE driver of a boat-train which hit a goods train that was shunting at Headcorn on 26 July 1852 was sentenced to six months in prison although the jury who had found him guilty recommended him to mercy. They might well have been influenced by evidence that the company was wrong to allow shunting on its main lines and that the guard's and station-master's watches differed by nine minutes but Captain Wynne's report had said that the vital contribution was the driver's failure to obey a signal and that exemplary punishment was required.[15] A leading Scottish engineer, Thomas Grainger, was killed near Stockton on 23 July 1852 when a goods train ran through a signal and hit the passenger train in which he was travelling. George Wellborn, the guilty driver, received six months; the jury had recommended mercy and the judge seems to have taken that into account but stressed that public safety demanded the punishment of negligence.[16] A report of the trial of an engine driver for an accident at Heriot on 20 October 1858 said the driver got six months for the Scottish version of manslaughter although the jury had appealed for leniency because it had happened in fog.[17]

Sometimes juries went the whole way and produced what can only be described as perverse verdicts. Samuel Healey, 22, and William Watkins, 20, driver and 'labourer' of an engine involved in a collision at Richmond, were charged that:

> they being employed on a certain railway called the South-Western Railway, and having the care and management of a steam engine called the Vulture upon that railway, and being with such engine on a side-line of the railway unlawfully and contrary to their duty, came out upon the main line at a time when they knew another engine, carrying passengers upon the railway was about to arrive, and they drove and forced Vulture against the engine, and by the concussion cast and threw one Richard Perry to the ground, and thereby gave him various mortal injuries of which he died, and that the prisoners by the means specified did feloniously kill and slay him.

The jury found them not guilty of manslaughter but added that they had 'shown great neglect'; was this a way of saying a lesser charge should have been brought? During the case one of the prosecuting counsel drew the court's attention to the company's rule 85 which directed the fireman to obey all the driver's directions provided they were not inconsistent with other rules. The judge commented: 'That is something like the interpretation clauses in an Act of Parliament which nobody can understand'.[18]

There were instances of 'applause' greeting juries' acquittals; one such concerned the Eastern Counties and the Stratford accident in July 1846, to be mentioned in the last chapter. An 'attempt at manifestation of applause' was promptly suppressed when William Jones was acquitted following an accident near Brookwood in 1848. The passenger train in front had broken down and the driver was underneath it, attempting repairs, when Jones's goods ran into the back of it, killing the driver. There was conflicting evidence about the weather (there had been patchy fog) and the guard of the broken-down train had failed to put down detonators; he had gone back with his lamp but this had not been seen.[19] 'Considerable applause' greeted the acquittal of John Thompson, a Midland guard, at Derby Quarter Sessions who had been accused of negligence in not going back with his lamp to warn following trains when his had broken down near Clay Cross, but stayed beside it so his signal was too late. Counsel for the defence commented on 'the abominable management of the railway' and said that any example should be made of 'those who were in high places' for allowing a goods train, at times running at 40 m.p.h. to leave only five minutes after a passenger train which had to stop at all stations.[20]

Earlier that year there had been an acquittal by the trial jury after an accident at Ponders End. The inquest jury had previously found Ronald Baxter, driver of the special which had killed a railway worker guilty of manslaughter, but added:

> The jury cannot separate without expressing their unanimous opinion that the duties assigned to the deceased ... were more multifarious than a person in his station in life and with his emoluments [22 shillings per week] could reasonably be expected to perform, and that

> greater precautionary measures, by means of the electric telegraph, might
> have been adopted ... the regulations of the Eastern Counties appear to
> need modification, and that punctuality should be more strictly enforced.

It had been established that the deceased, 'a night inspector', was alone at the station and had to attend to the telegraph, gates of the level crossing, signals, trains, and shunting. He had been attending the shunting of a truck from a goods train when the special hit him and crushed him against a wall. Mr Richardson, the traffic superintendent, in the hand-washing style so frequently then adopted by senior railway officials, said that if he had obeyed the rules and put down detonators 600 yards before the obstruction, the accident would have been avoided. He also said telegraph messages had been sent along the line to warn of the special; several of the jury reasonably asked if the victim would have received the messages, given what he had to do. At the inquest evidence had been given by Alexander Kirkland, 22, an engine-driver who had been taken on at seven shillings per day after the recent strike: 'his singular and vacant manner on the oath being administered to him, created some remark, and it was two or three minutes before he could be made to understand, apparently, the meaning of it'.[21] Captain Laffan's report would suggest the jury was right; it had showed up much laxity and confusion by the managers. Worse, it said that Mr Haviland, who had hired the train, had wanted to give evidence on behalf of his driver, who had been told to use the utmost speed, but he was not given adequate notice of the inquest. When he arrived at Ponder's End, he was met by Richardson, who told him that 'the jury had dispensed with his evidence' and shooed him on his way back to London as fast as possible. The reality was that Richardson had told the jury that 'the company would forgo' his evidence and the jury 'not understanding much of railway management' had brought in a verdict of manslaughter against the unfortunate driver.

After an accident at Bolton in 1852, Bancroft, the man to blame killed himself before anyone could question him. The inquest jury found him guilty of the manslaughter of those killed and suicide resulting from temporary insanity in his own case. They added:

> [We] cannot separate without expressing [our] opinion that the servants
> employed on the LY Railway, from Liverpool to Bolton on Monday 23rd of
> August, were totally inadequate to meet the extraordinary demands upon them
> consequent on the running several excursion trains, and permitting excursionists
> to travel on ordinary trains.[22]

In 1853 successive weeks' papers covered two instances of inquest juries giving verdicts (though neither take unanimously) of manslaughter against the directors of the companies concerned. The first involved a derailment on the York & North Midland at Hambleton where the jury presumably believed that inadequate track maintenance was to blame. The second concerned an accident where a Charles Canning had been killed at Farnham by a special survey train; the staff had not been warned it was running and, assuming it was an ordinary one which would stop at Farnham, had not taken action to prevent him crossing, though the coroner had said the victim's carelessness was at least partly to blame. The same verdict was given the following year after an accident on the Eastern Counties. Nothing came of any this.

Increasingly this became a much more general view. *The Times* made some scathing comments about the general run of accidents covered by the return for the second half of 1853:

> Many of the disasters must be attributed to the fault of management. ... it is manifest that most of them would have been prevented by due care and attention. The following are causes assigned in this return: – 'Ran into a station at too great a speed'. 'Break not applied in time'. 'Trucks were being shunted'. 'A train of trucks was standing in the station (after time)'. 'The points left open'. 'The train ahead, disabled'. The space between the carriages and the platform is mentioned frequently as the cause of injury or death. Where passengers get out of or into a train in motion, it is here that they fall and get caught. It may be said that foolhardy people must be left to their fate; but it is not always easy to avoid this risk. You stop at a refreshment station, and there is no known regulation of the time you are really to have, and when you return to the train there is no large or prominent letter or number over your carriage to guide you to it at once. Many, too, among the occasional railway travellers, arriving at a strange and bustling station after a considerable journey, are apt to feel hurried and unsteady, and ought not to be exposed to preventable risk.

A serious accident (with a dozen or so killed) occurred on the Hampstead Junction on Monday, 2 September 1861. The train involved was one of a batch of excursions arranged by men working for the North London Railway to take themselves, their families and friends, and anyone else interested from Bow to Kew for the day, partly as a day out, partly to raise funds to help men suffering as a result of railway accidents. On its return journey it ran into a ballast train that was being shunted just before Kentish Town station, where a new siding was under construction. At first blame was thrown in several directions. The returning excursion concerned had left Kew considerably earlier than planned because some were anxious to get home and this would ease pressure at Kew. The North London (providing rolling stock) and LNW (station staff) tried to blame each other – the Hampstead Junction had no staff its of own. Eventually blame fell on Rayner, a porter at Kentish Town for failing to operate the signals correctly. He was only 19 and had been employed less than a year, yet he seems to have been left in complete control of signals, telegraph etc and to have had only a vague idea of his duties. At the inquest 'The jury regret that there is no alternative, from the weight of evidence, but to return a verdict of *Guilty* against Rayner. At the same time they cannot separate without expressing a strong opinion that the directors and managers are much to be censured in not employing more experienced persons to fill such important positions as those of signalmen'. When Rayner went on trial two Grand Juries 'ignored' bills against him; the prosecution wanted to go ahead anyway but the judge said there was no precedent known to him so no evidence was offered and he was acquitted.[23]

The Board of Trade was the official dispenser of blame. The onus was on companies to report accidents, though the Board clearly had other sources such as newspaper reports and letters from interested members of the public. In 1842 the Chester & Birkenhead failed to report the accident to the smoker knocked off the outside of one of its carriages on 3 May and on 27 June the Board wrote to enquire 'whether an accident did not take place' on the relevant date. After the company had sent a report, the Board asked what reason it could give for not suffering the £20 per day fine liable for their failure. The company pleaded 'inadvertence'; it was the first accident on its line and it was ignorant of its responsibility. The Board relented and said it would not this time impose the penalty provided the further information they requested was forthcoming; it was. The Board first learnt of an accident at Brockley Whins, a particularly bad black spot at that time, in August 1845 from *The Times*; again, no action seems to have been taken against the company.

The Board was able to report to Parliament on the relevant accidents which had occurred between 7 August 1840 and 25 January 1841. It said that out of 35 accidents (some of which had more than one cause), 21 were attributable to 'defective arrangements', 18 to 'misconduct of servants' and six to mechanical causes, particularly the breaking of axles. The conclusion was that 'the inherent danger of railway travelling is very small, and even under the present system less than that of other modes of conveyance'; however, they needed to consider absolute not comparative safety and a high proportion of accidents could have been avoided. It asked for more power to enforce its will: particular points they wanted included provision of proper timetables for drivers and other staff, a fifteen-minute interval between trains, with non-passenger ones moved out of the way thirty minutes before others were due, brakes on every fourth carriage and the rear one and a more uniform approach to signalling, using green for caution and red for danger. The strongest recommendations concerned discipline and the fitness of engine-drivers; they favoured some system of licensing of the latter, ensuring that they were literate, sober and knew how to act in emergencies.[24]

In 1843 a great improvement was reported; there were far fewer collisions and it claimed much of the credit, saying it resulted from a more general adoption of the measures it had advised. A 'wait and see' approach to the idea of licensing drivers resulted; it seems to have been forgotten for all time and, given the attitudes of the directors of the day there was little chance of its adoption. Unfortunately the trend did not last; during the last eight months of 1845 there were more accidents due to the carelessness of drivers than at any other period – the Eastern Counties contributed three in 22 days. They blamed the rapid expansion of the system, causing the demand for experienced enginemen to exceed supply so companies were taking on 'persons of whose merit they are not perfectly assured'.

The 1850 report said that several accidents had been caused by the failure of senior officials to enforce their rules and regulations; in some cases they clearly had known what was happening but had turned a blind eye to regular breaches, especially when they allowed lost time to be made up. 'Want of punctuality' was singled out as the main contributory factor in accidents. A detailed example of the former was a minor collision in fog at Woodlesford, on the Midland on 18 September, when a regular passenger train ran into an excursion. On his own initiative, 'in the longer days' the station-master there had stopped putting oil in the lamp that was supposed to light up a signal. Captain Wynne's verdict was that he was to blame but 'it is evident that there must be a want of vigilance in some department of a railway when an important signal can be discontinued for six months, and the negligence only discovered by the accident'.

The uphill battle the inspectors had is indicated by the presence of essentially the same complaint in 1851. A series of reports concentrated on this theme of casual ways in the giving verbal instructions where written ones were essential, lack of system and inadequate staff; the companies' responses consistently denied that Directors and other higher beings could be at fault. A sorry tale was revealed on the Birkenhead, Lancashire & Cheshire Junction when a train returning from Chester Races stalled in Sutton Tunnel on 30 April. A second train drew up carefully behind it and tried to push it on but the task was too much for it. The guard of the second started to go back to warn following traffic but when he heard a third one coming, he lost his presence of mind and fell onto the ballast to save himself and a collision resulted; in fairness, it is unlikely that he would have been seen in a notoriously smoky tunnel. Captain Laffan's enquiry showed that a company with 'crippled means' had attempted to carry far more passengers than it was capable of doing. The normal traffic through Chester was about 1,000 passengers each way per day. On this occasion about 18,000 wanted to leave through the station after the races; trains were sent off as soon as they were filled, some of them from sidings since as soon as would-be passengers saw a train of carriages, they rushed onto it without waiting for it to be moved to a platform. The only safety provision was a seven-minute interval between departures, which was of limited use because the company did not require its servants to carry watches and the only clocks were inside stations. Far worse was the lack of engine-power available, despite the warnings of the locomotive superintendent that more engines were wanted. In addition, extra carriages, mostly open, had been hurriedly borrowed from other companies and there had been no time to check them; afterwards it was found that the weight of the passengers packed in one had compressed the spring so it acted as an extra brake. There should also have been 'stations' at either end of the tunnel, with signals to warn trains of what was ahead; they had yet to be provided. In this case the Commissioners were able to apply one sanction, that of refusing to license any more excursions when the company would not give assurances about providing itself with extra engines; its licence was required to confirm a company's exemption from passenger duty on fares of less than a penny a mile.

An excursion returning from the Great Exhibition was derailed on 6 September 1851 at Bicester on the LNW following a muddle over whether it should stop there; the driver believed that he would go through non-stop onto the Oxford line, and that the points would be set accordingly, but the station-master decided to stop it because he believed there were passengers on it for his station. Whilst the driver was clearly at fault, Captain Laffan listed several other failings: amongst others, the station-master had failed to inform his superiors that drivers had been habitually taking the junction too fast and no-one had given the engine-driver clear orders. Behind this was pressure from management to maintain high speeds and be competitive with the GW for the lucrative Exhibition traffic which had resulted in staff habitually ignoring regulations. Captain Huish counter-attacked and sought to put the whole blame on the engine-driver. Part of his defence was that Laffan had based much of his report on what the station-master had told him and that this had been a misunderstanding cleared up by a letter sent to him by the station-master. Laffan told the Commissioners that he had disregarded this letter because the writer had been pressed into sending it at the 'recommendation' of a superior; when he had been making his enquiries on the spot the station-master had repeatedly insisted on his version when Laffan had asked him about discrepancies between his and his superiors' versions. Needless to say, neither Huish nor his associates shifted their position.

Captain Wynne referred to a 'laxity of discipline' following a collision at Eckington on 1 October, which was the sixth collision on the Midland since 17 March. No-one at the station had sought to enforce the rule that the driver of a goods train should have shunted it out of the way when a passenger train was due, the driver of a passenger train had run past a signal because he and his fireman were occupied with routine tasks on the engine instead of watching for signals, the whistle on the engine was broken and had not been repaired though reported three days before and the guard had failed to use his brake. His conclusion was:

> I do not think this combination of disobedience or indifference to orders and carelessness ... could have occurred had a proper supervision and strict enforcement of duty been maintained over the servants of the Company; and unless a speedy change in this part of the Company's economy is introduced, I fear that still more serious accidents will occur.

The company counter-attacked, claiming that its directors did their best to select good men and punish infringements of rules and that in the last resort safety would always depend 'on the individual conduct, at the moment, of subordinate servants'. They also claimed lack of support from the legal system. In one case Quarter Sessions had acquitted men whose guilt was obvious (at least to the company) and a County Court Judge had even ordered it to pay wages, back-dated to the time of his committal, to one they had prosecuted. However, it was able to report that the driver responsible for the Eckington accident had been sentenced to two months with hard labour by the Chesterfield magistrates. Despite the evidence of the recent crop of accidents, they also disagreed with a number of the recommendations made by inspectors, claiming that they knew better how to run a railway. Clearly there was no immediate cure because on 13 October a passenger was killed when he got out on wrong side at Countesthorpe after the guard could not unlock the 'safe' side and had told passengers to get out the other and the station-master was at the exit collecting tickets instead of supervising on the platform.

Another example of passing the buck occurred on the LY's Blackburn line when a passenger train ran into the back of a goods train in Cranberry Moss Tunnel on 21 October, an accident that only reached the attention of the Commissioners about a month later because an injured passenger wrote to them. Captain Wynne found that the company had dismissed the station-master at Entwistle for breaking their printed rule that trains should be held at stations until five minutes after the departure of the previous one. Wynne commented: 'Unprovided as he was with a time-piece, I do not see how he could be held responsible for obedience to an order of this kind' .

This company received further scathing criticism the following year. The way inexperienced men could be given great responsibility was shown by an accident to the second of a pair of Sunday school outings on its return to Burnley on 12 July 1852, in which a man and three girls were killed and many injured. The carriages were released from the engine some distance short of the station and were supposed to run under gravity into a siding because the station could only hold about six carriages and the train was made up of thirty-five (on the outward journey they had boarded directly from beside the main line). The points were wrongly set and it ran into the buffers of the station platform, causing two carriages, whose buffers were misaligned, to rear up. The investigation showed that the station-master had already gone home and the running of the station was left to a porter assisted by a calico printer and a blacksmith, commonly employed in the evenings by local arrangement. More criticism came after the Bolton accident on 23 August, where the inquest jury's views after the suicide of the pointsman have already been given. Amongst other failings, they had continued to run excursion trains after their own superintendent had recommended their discontinuance.

Defiance had also been the reaction of the Glasgow & South Western after an ordinary passenger train had run into the back of an excursion near Cumnock on 5 July 1851, fortunately without injuring anyone. Captain Laffan felt that the basic reason was that a goods engine had been used to pull a train that was too heavy for it. The company denied this and ignored the recommendation that they should buy extra engines. The Commissioners' threat to with-hold permission for extra excursion trains was answered with a letter that could be summarised: 'So what? The excursion season is nearly over anyway.'

In 1853 a Commons Select Committee had recommended placing more responsibility on senior management and advocated that some sort of enquiry, akin to that required under the Merchant Shipping Act, should follow serious railway accidents. It had emphasised that only a small proportion of accidents resulted solely from the negligence of inferior servants but they were liable to heavy penalties while 'the chief officers and directors of a Company, whose parsimony, insufficient regulations, or lax discipline have in reality led to the accidents are not punishable'. However, there was no likelihood of the law being altered.

One of the accidents illustrating this problem occurred at Lewisham on 28 June that year. Lt Col Yolland found that drivers were in the habit of stopping just beyond red distant signals, despite a rule against this and he criticised the SE's management for turning a blind eye. He was not impressed by Mr Eborall's attempts at denying his own and his fellow officers' guilt. Yolland agreed that the driver should have been more alert but argued that he was working within a defective system. As usual the company tried to blame the driver:

> Subsequent to my report ... the engine-driver and fireman have been brought to trial on a charge of 'manslaughter' at the Central Criminal Court; all the evidence which the legal advisers of the South-eastern Railway Company (the prosecutors) thought necessary to bring against them was heard, not a witness was heard for the defence, neither did the counsel for these men address the jury, and yet this prosecution resulted in the acquittal of both men; the jury expressing their 'extreme dissatisfaction' (I quote from a newspaper report of the trial) 'at the extremely defective state of the signals and the bad time kept by the North Kent line'. ... It is a very easy matter for the managers of a powerful company to give one of these [ordinary railwaymen] into custody for culpable neglect, and to offer such evidence as will keep him confined in a common gaol on charges which are eventually not proven ... but it is no easy thing to induce these managers to look into their own acts of omission or commission, or to induce them to ascertain whether their system of working may not require some alteration.

The introduction to the 1857 report repeated much of this and stressed the difference between English and Scottish law. In Scotland any serious accident could lead to an enquiry by the Procurator Fiscal and he could authorise any necessary prosecution. As a result a locomotive superintendent had been sent to prison for two years for sending out a defective engine. In England coroners' juries had returned verdicts of manslaughter against directors and higher officials but the judges had held that English law did not provide for their prosecution although in two cases it was clear that they had violated the regulations and in one case had even broken the conditions under which they had been given permission to open. It was noteworthy that the casualty rate, per mile travelled, on English lines was about double that in Scotland. The only restraint on English companies was provided by Lord Campbell's Act which made them pay compensation to casualties and their families but the burden of this fell on the shareholders rather than directors.

There would be much more of the same over the following years. Careless habits were criticised for an accident at Horbury Junction on 5 February 1868 during single-line working. The inspectors wanted clear written orders to be given instead of vague spoken ones which could easily lead to misunderstandings. Lt Col Hutchinson wrote in a report dated 8 August of that year that on returning from reporting on an accident at

Grayrigg he had travelled on the engine, along with a senior LNW official. They had passed three signals at danger. In two cases they were thus because the heat had made the wires slack, though the crew did not know this at the time. When they passed the third one, just north of Preston, the driver told him it was always at danger and thus nobody ever took any notice of it.

This was also the year of the Abergele accident. Lt Col Rich said that three local railwaymen were seriously at fault but 'men of that class cannot be expected to do their duties well if the railway companies do not give them the most convenient and best appliances and do not look after them strictly and enforce their own regulations'. Amongst other failings of management were the failure to provide chains costing about 3d to fasten brake levers securely when guards had to leave their vans, timetabling goods trains too close together and the provision of inadequate sidings at Llandulas, which led to dangerous shunting. 'I fear it is only too true that the rules printed and issued by railway companies to their servants, and which are generally very good, are made principally with the object of being produced when accidents happen from the breach of them, and that the companies systematically allow them to be broken daily, without taking the slightest notice of the disobedience'.

Although one might have expected the awards of damages to victims of accidents, covered more fully in a later chapter, to make companies more careful, Colonel Yolland's report on the New Cross accident in 1869 was characteristic of many of this time. His conclusion was that:

> The collision resulted from gross neglect on the part of the company's servants in charge of the goods train, more particularly the driver, and I am not assured, by any means, that the guards were attending to their breaks. The collision would not have occurred if the traffic had been worked on the absolute block system.

The reaction of the Brighton's Chairman was typical. He clearly felt they were doing their best to provide safe travelling conditions and it was unfair to punish companies and their shareholders for avoidable accidents resulting from the carelessness of their employees. They continued to say that professional railwaymen knew better than the Board of Trade's inspectors and generally behave as if their particular company could not possibly learn anything useful from any other one. Many accidents would occur in the 1870s and 1880s before Parliament forced the issue with its legislation on braking and signalling. In the many, admittedly summarised, press reports of company half-yearly meetings seen, there were instances of shareholders' fury at low or non-existent dividends but very few complaints about their companies' safety records.

That brings us to the ultimate responsibility: Parliament had power to order better safety measures but failed to use it. It is unlikely that legislation would have provided an overnight magic wand – there were genuine technical obstacles to be overcome, and its legislation has rarely worked first (or even second?) time, as the lengthy list of laws on such matters as child labour, public health and safety at sea shows. Its offence was that it did not try; one obvious tactic would have been to force companies to act together and in concert with the Board of Trade. This failure was in part owing to the large railway interest in both Houses, which could normally be relied upon to block unwelcome bills. *Bradshaw's Shareholders' Manual* for 1861 listed 44 members of the Lords and 112 of the Commons who were directors; many of these were only on the boards of minor companies but they would have seen their interests as identical, and there would almost certainly have been others in the two Houses with substantial shareholdings, even if they were not directors. Many others would have felt that if the law was allowed to interfere with railways' conduct of their Property, landowners' Property would be next to suffer.

Bradshaw's Railway Manual,
Shareholder's Guide, and Official
Directory.

1861 -> ~~SGM'/12~~. NAT. ARCHIVE

RAIL 1140/14

Chapter 19: TREATMENT OF CASUALTIES

No nationwide arrangements existed for dealing with accident victims. There were hospitals in some places and the number was increasing but most were associated with 'charity'; the better-off were treated at home. Thus railway (and other) casualties depended on improvised help. This was often forthcoming from medical men, usually described as 'surgeons' who happened to be on the affected train. Many press reports stressed the zeal with which these acted, which was just as well: in 1857 Ralph Bernard, Surgeon to the Bristol Royal Infirmary wrote indignantly about the failure to mention three of his senior pupils and dressers in a train involved in an accident on the South Wales Railway who had worked hard, improvising rough dressings and splints for the injured.[1] Otherwise, they had to send for the nearest doctor, which might take some time if the accident had occurred at a spot difficult to reach by road.

The Nine Elms collision of 1840 illustrated the earliest approach. About 20 of the most-seriously injured were taken to the company's offices, where they were attended by two local surgeons and their assistants. A report following a collision in fog at Rugby on 13 January 1841 said that five or six passengers were 'more or less hurt'; all but three continued their journey. Those three were taken to the Eagle Hotel at Rugby, and Mr Bucknell, 'the principal medical man of the place', was called; he found no bones broken and they well enough to continue their journey next day.

RS Young, Secretary of the London & Croydon, wrote a report about a collision on 5 October 1844 at Anerley; part of the front train was derailed but as soon as they could get the carriages back onto the line it was sent on, with passengers from both trains apart from eight or ten who refused. One female, severely shaken and insensible was taken to the Anerley Tavern, where she was attended by a surgeon. All who arrived in London were attended by Mr Cock of Guy's Hospital; those who were unable to walk were sent home in cabs. When the inspector went down next day he found two passengers had stayed overnight at the inn; one had already been sent home, the other was said to be progressing favourably and 'in a few days' could be taken home safely.

Soon after, on 21 November, there was a collision about ¾ mile from Nottingham. A couple of unhurt passengers did their best to release the injured, then one of them ran across the fields for help. About an hour after the collision several vehicles, including two carts containing straw arrived. Some were taken to Beeston and Lenton; others went to Nottingham by a special train, some going home, others to the infirmary. The local press praised a couple of local innkeepers for their help but was very critical of others: one had refused to take in a dying man, who found shelter with a local florist for his last few minutes. The Misses Lewis, whose dresses had been badly torn in the impact and had been otherwise injured, were left in a nearby field without care for nearly an hour before being taken off in a baker's cart to the home of the person they were visiting.[2]

After an accident near Wenden in August 1845 the injured passengers were carried to adjacent meadows where they were laid down until help arrived from surrounding towns. They received every attention from 'a large muster of medical gentlemen' and 'late in the day posted to their respective homes'.[3] At Stratford on 18 July 1846 the stationmaster helped the injured into the waiting-room and local medical men were fetched within a few minutes; after preliminary attention some were taken by omnibus to the London Hospital, others, at their own request, to their homes. Mr Hind was taken by cab to his home in Dalston by three men; his injuries were so severe and his clothes so tattered that at first his family, who had not known he was going to take a train ride, thought some stranger had been brought to them. He had suffered severe internal injuries and nothing could be done to save him or alleviate his pain.[4] A special train was provided by the York & Newcastle to carry Mrs Whitehead to her home in Saddleworth some months after she had been injured in a derailment in October.[5]

One of the LNW's crop of collisions in November illustrated the nature of the personal details often given:

> Mr Cooke, of Oldham, received a severe fracture of the ribs, but is doing well and has been enabled to proceed to his home. Mr Lawrie, a commission agent from London, was most severely injured, having three of his ribs on the left side fractured, besides numerous contusions and other wounds. He is now lying at the Queen's Hotel, Alderley, and although much hurt, is better than might have been anticipated, and is daily attended by Dr. J.G. Harrison, the medical officer of the company for this immediate district. Mr Hill, a teacher of music from London, who came down for the purpose of being married on the following day, is suffering from severe contusions of the right arm and wrist, which he is scarcely able to move. He remains at the Queen's Hotel ... where he is also visited by Dr Harrison.[6]

On 11 May 1848 a GW express hit a horse-box and cattle truck on the main line during shunting operations at Shrivenham. Several passengers were killed and injured; some were thrown out at the station by the shock, others carried along in wrecked carriages – it took the driver nearly half-a-mile to stop since the engine had been little damaged as it reduced the obstacles to shattered remnants, some of which were thrown back on to following carriages.

> Mr Hudson, the station clerk, who, although a young man, has been several years in the situation, displayed great presence of mind under the terrible circumstances in which he was placed. His first act was to despatch a messenger for the nearest medical man; he next obtained some water, and went around the sufferers to assuage the parching thirst of which they all complained. In a short time the villagers from Shrivenham, about a mile distant, began to arrive, and as soon as possible the dead and wounded were removed from the line and carried to the nearest habitations.

Local doctors were soon there and Mr Seymour Clarke, the superintendent of the line, came from London as soon as he heard, bringing Mr Caesar Hawkins, 'the eminent surgeon' with him.[7]

The mail train that left Carlisle for the north at 9.16 p.m. on 10 February 1849 was derailed shortly after, leaving the carriages in a confused mess. The railwaymen present mostly escaped injury and were able to work, but only by moonlight; a rescue party arrived after a messenger had been sent on foot to Carlisle, about four miles away.[8] Self-help was much to the fore on 14 October 1850 when a North British train was derailed on the Haddington branch. There were only twelve passengers on the train, six of whom were in the third-class carriages that received the most serious damage, ending on its roof and injuring all within. The others were unhurt and helped the railwaymen to free all the casualties from the wreckage except one old woman who could not be extricated until the 'dumbcraft' had been applied to raise the carriage. A servant on a nearby farm heard the crash and rode to Haddington for assistance. A special train, with a doctor on board, was sent; four were immediately taken back to Haddington for treatment and the others were able to go on to Edinburgh after being patched up.[9]

A trio of incidents in 1851, two in August and one in November further illustrated the problems involved and the ways they were 'solved'. A collision at Beighton left about 17 injured though little damage was done to the train. 'The passengers were induced to re-enter the train, which then proceeded on to Sheffield, where medical aid was procured for the numerous sufferers'.[10] Shortly after a train bound for Richmond was hit from behind whilst waiting at Vauxhall. *The Times* indignantly reported

> What a sight was presented in the waiting rooms! – wounded and bleeding ladies and gentlemen in every direction. With the exception of the station master, who seemed half bewildered, no aid from other railway officials. Although the porters and policemen in such an emergency, might have greatly assisted in procuring hot water, &c., which was much wanted, scarcely even was there any cold water, and not a single glass to put it in. Not a female attendant for the ladies. Medical aid was brought after a lengthened interval only. In fact, there was such an absence of all that was required under the circumstances that it is highly disgraceful to the South-Western Railway Company.[11]

More creditable was the great help was given by soldiers from the nearby barracks, especially the 'veteran' surgeon and his assistants, after the accident at Weedon.[12]

The four passengers most seriously injured following a collision with rubbish in the Bramhope Tunnel in September 1854 were reported as being looked after in the Wharfedale Hotel, near Arthington station, under the care of two surgeons from Leeds and two from Otley. Those less injured were taken by road to Leeds and then sent on to their destinations.[13] Mrs Carstairs, injured in an incident at Hatfield that same month, was attended by the GN's company surgeon, who was sent to Hatfield, attended her there, accompanied her back to her home and continued to treat her until 29 October when he 'surrendered' her to the care of her own doctor. When a train derailed spectacularly near Tuxford in 1857 the wreckage fell from a viaduct and the carriages were smashed to pieces. 'Such assistance as was at hand was rendered as promptly as possible and messengers were dispatched to the nearest stations and the nearest medical men'. The bodies of the dead and one or two of the most seriously injured were taken to the Newcastle Arms at Tuxford, the rest taken on to Retford.[14]

Particularly unfortunate were those in an overnight train to Edinburgh whose carriages plunged into a ditch after heavy rain had washed the low embankment from under the rails on 14 August 1857. They had to wade about in muddy water to help each other to safety, using their hands to tear away broken pieces of carriage in order to free some of their fellow travellers. Help was inevitably slow in coming because some of them had to wade through the floods to the next station, Carlton-on-Trent, where they found a train which, after the 'very protracted decision' of the station-master they were able to take back to rescue those too injured to move on their own and they were left shivering in their wet clothes from midnight. There were conflicting claims about the time taken to get help. James Withers said it was four hours but AGH Buckby, the nearest surgeon, claimed that he had been woken at 1.15, had ridden to Carlton to treat the wounded who had reached there and then went to the scene of the accident, often up to his knees in water; he reached there at about 2.30 but the dark and the limited help available meant that it was about an hour before he could do much. He also said that the station-master had acted 'not only with prudence but much promptness'.[15]

Sometimes they did not wait for help but took the patient to the place where it was most likely to be available. A 'slightly intoxicated' seaman persisted in leaning out of a window on the NE, despite warnings from a fellow passenger, and was badly injured. They told the guard at Felling but no medical help was available there so he was taken on to Newcastle and sent to the infirmary, where he died a couple of days later.[16]

After the accident in sight of many houses on the Hampstead Junction line in September 1861 the locals promptly sent for doctors and ambulances. Within about 20 minutes a strong body of policemen arrived from Kentish Town and Camden Town stations. Many injured were taken straight to the homes of medical men but some asked to be let lie in the adjoining fields and just asked for water; later the more-seriously injured were spread between several hospitals. Groups of locals gave such help as they could and since it was getting dark, light was provided by setting fire to the remains of the guard's van, which had already been broken into small-enough pieces by the collision.[17]

A train was derailed and struck trucks in a siding near Little Bytham in 1863. The carriages were so shattered that it was 'apparently hopeless to expect that any of the passengers could be found alive' but in fact none were killed. Since they were near the station help was immediate and the terrified were helped out, some through the windows; the standard help followed.

This frightful occurrence was not without its ludicrous incident. One
of the passengers was extricated from a shattered carriage without having

sustained the slightest personal injury; but, although he had just escaped from the very jaws of death, he could not be pacified because the railway officials could not find his pipe among the ruins.[18]

Shortly after there was a collision between Dinton and Wilton on the LSW. A portion of one train ran back to Dinton to give the news, which was telegraphed to Sailsbury. A special train was sent to collect the injured who were immediately despatched to the infirmary on its return to Salisbury.[19]

Various expedients was used in 1865. When an excursion train was derailed in June between Rednal and Whittington. Mr Leather, a Liverpool surgeon who was on the train did his best but there was no village nearby and there were two hours of pain and suffering before help arrived from Shrewsbury, 12 miles away. The worst injured were put on stretchers improvised from bits of broken carriage and placed in a nearby field until a train arrived, when they were lifted into luggage vans and taken to Shrewsbury Infirmary but there was not enough room there so some were taken to hotels and private houses. Mr Leather went with them to the Infirmary and remained in attendance all night. The dead were taken to the goods shed at Rednal station, to await the coroner. Shortly after TY Jones wrote to *The Times* to express his thanks to a lady and two young gentlemen who had risked their lives by helping several of his relatives through the window of their carriage which had turned over on its side with the door locked.[20] Following the collision at Lea, between Preston and Blackpool, in September,

> A scene of indescribable confusion and alarm succeeded. Passengers were shouting and screaming out of the windows, and numbers were thrown about in the carriages in all directions. Some were upon the floors, others were thrown against and upon each other ... Those who could get out did so, while others had to be removed to the station, a very small and most inconvenient place. It was soon found that a large number had been injured, but for a time nobody seemed to know what to do, and as there is no telegraphic communication between Lea-road and the other stations, full assistance could not for a considerable time be obtained.

However, the stationmaster gave what help he could, especially in procuring 'stimulants' from nearby gentlemen's houses and Dr Monks of Wigan, who happened to be on the train and was uninjured, 'at once attended to the injured in a most energetic manner'. In fact, about 20 had been injured, though all of the 700 passengers had been severely shaken. Most went on to Blackpool but the worst-injured were removed to their homes.[21]

When a coal train was being shunted out of the way near Warrington in 1867, the driver of a passenger train thought that line would be clear in time but the points had not been changed and he ran into the back of it. Immediately messages were sent to all the medical men in the area to come and help. Some of the dead were taken to the waiting-rooms at the Bank Quay station, Warrington and later removed to the Norton Arms at Latchford. A special first-class train took the wounded on to Warrington.

There, Mrs Trumble, the workhouse matron was in attendance with efficient nurses; 'the only lady volunteer present was Miss Tunstall'. A clergyman and lawyers were also present, the latter because some of the badly-hurt wanted to make their wills – and at least one died after doing so. 33 were officially said to be injured. Of these one was sent at his own request to Bury Lane, five to Liverpool, and four to the Patten Arms Hotel in Warrington (where one later died); the remainder were taken to the convalescent hospital, a wooden building put up about a year before when the area was threatened with a cholera epidemic.[22]

An excursion returning from London to the Leeds area in June 1870 was badly damaged near Newark on the GN when it hit the debris of a derailed goods train. As soon as news was received at Newark (after 1.0 a.m.) messengers were sent to all the inns in the town to send conveyances and prepare beds. The local hospital was empty, having been 'dismantled' for whitewashing, but beds were rapidly put up and all the medical men of the town rushed along. This clearly did not provide enough room; a week later a progress report stated that several injured were still recovering at various inns and private houses. In this case they were comparatively lucky because the accident had occurred near a main road. There was a very unpleasant sequel: on the Saturday *The Leeds Mercury* claimed the bodies of the dead had been plundered, accusing the police in particular. This was rebutted by the coroner at the inquest on some of the dead and the Chief Constable said nearly a vanload of property had been collected and taken to the station where nearly all had been identified. Items allegedly stolen had been accounted for: an insurance ticket had actually been left with a friend in London, as had a 'stolen' watch and the owner of the latter wrote to the Leeds paper explaining this. The Mayor of Newark, Thomas Earp, wrote to *The Times* to assure people that there was no truth in the 'odious accusations' brought against the Newark police who had acted correctly in collecting and listing the scattered possessions; far from 'no further information' having been received about a purse of which a victim 'had been despoiled' it had been handed to a solicitor representing the deceased's friends at the inquest on the Friday (i.e. the day before the article was published). Several days later it was reported that 13 of the wounded still lay at Newark: seven were at the hospital and not expected to be able to 'bear removal' for some time. Most of the others were at inns and expected to be able to go home within a week but Mr. Hellon, of Leeds, whose wife had been killed in the crash, was at 23 Wilton Street – an act of local kindness?[23]

Spiritual help for the wounded also gained the odd mention. Following the accident in the floods near Newark in 1857 it was reported that the vicar of East Retford, had visited the injured left at the Queen Inn.[24] Later in the year a higher dignitary received a far less favourable press. On 24 August a train from Brighton had gone through a warning signal and hit goods trucks being shunted near Redhill. One passenger was the Bishop of Oxford, Samuel Wilberforce, sometimes called 'Soapy Sam' because of his talent for ingratiating himself with those in the highest reaches of society; on this occasion he was sharing a carriage with a duchess as he travelled to speak in the House of Lords. The first account said he had been 'very active' in helping his fellow passengers, though it also pointed out that later he had 'rather forcibly demanded to know from whom he was to obtain compensation for the inconvenience he had suffered'. Two days later *The Times* published a very different version, sent by a correspondent of *The Globe*. The latter wished to correct the idea that the bishop had gone among the wounded and alarmed 'as a mere ordinary clergyman' might have done.

> [He] did no such thing – not for a moment did he lose sight of the far higher importance to society and the church of his own safety, and, I may add, the recovery of his portmanteau ... by the aid of one guard and two porters the second object of pastoral care was secured and [he] arrived on foot at the Reigate station, bag and baggage, sound in wind and limb, and ready for the legislatorial labours of the evening.[25]

Chapter 20: COMPENSATION

Early railway accidents in England were covered by established law, which enabled a jury to impose a fine or 'deodand' on whoever or whatever (usually the engine, its tender or a wagon in the case of railways) caused a death by carelessness. The deodand was received by the owner of the land nearest the accident, not the victim. A couple of accidents in 1840 illustrated the erratic operation of this. In August there was one on the Eastern Counties, near Brentwood, in which one passenger died and ten were severely injured; the directors who inspected the spot found a considerable length of track deformed and said this was due to the reckless speed set by the driver despite repeated cautions. At the inquest a deodand of £500 was awarded against the engine; in its half-yearly report the company protested against this since the verdict had been accidental death.[1] An accident on the Canterbury & Whitstable resulted in a verdict of accidental death and a deodand of only 20/-.

The question could lead to heated arguments. In November 1840 a coal train from Leeds was hit by a passenger train from Hull on the Leeds & Selby at Milford Junction and two were killed. One inquest's verdict was accidental death with a deodand of £500. That on the other victim did not go smoothly: the jury were locked up until midnight, 'when becoming very violent with one another', some for £10 deodand, others £1,000, they were dismissed by the Coroner, who bound them over to appear before the judges at the next assizes.[2] The accident in the Sonning cutting late in 1841, mentioned earlier, led to a £1,000 deodand which went by right to R Palmer Esquire, MP for Berkshire, Lord of the Manor. *The Times* said he intended to give the friends of the deceased and the injured all of it. However, the Board of Trade enquiry found that the slip could not have been foreseen and the deodand was reduced to a nominal amount on appeal.[3]

Lord Campbell's Act of 1846 enabled passengers and their immediate dependants to recover damages for injury or death in accidents provided they could prove negligence by the railway. Juries determined whether or not there had been negligence and assessed the amount of damages, though the judge gave guidance on what constituted negligence. The amount paid was supposed to be related to the severity of the injuries and standard of living of the injured prior to the accident. This was explained in the case of Mrs Thorne, a widow with two small children, one of whom had been born six months after her husband's death. She was expected to take six to twelve months to recover from her injuries in a collision between arriving and departing trains at Victoria. The Under-sheriff acting as judge warned the jury that while it was not his job to advise on the amount, he would say that it was not its job to punish companies, nor was it right to award amounts allowing people to set themselves up in higher positions than those to which they were accustomed. She received £250.[4] Many claims were settled by agreement without court action and thus did not make the news;

254

this would seem to have been so with some cases resulting in higher amounts than any quoted here since the Board of Trade report for 1857-8 referred to one where nearly £9,000 had been paid. If a company or claimant was dissatisfied with the original result the matter was put before judges who would order a retrial before another jury if they felt there were sufficient grounds.

The commonest source of claims was the throwing-about of passengers in minor collisions. There was a repetitive element to these, summed up by a reporter who had heard it all before:

> Circumstances of the most ordinary character. A blow and rebound, a nervous shock, pain, loss of flesh and profits of business.

In this case the company had paid £100 into court and the jury added another £100.[5] Another regular type of claim was made by passengers injured when alighting. There was a monotonous thread to these: the passengers said the train had stopped, he or she started to alight, and the carriage then moved on again, causing a fall and injury, but the companies, invariably supported by their staff, that it had not fully stopped.

There was some variety. Mrs Blackman received £30 when she fell over a weighing machine at Horsham, though the company claimed it was in its proper place.[6] There were also claims from falling down unlit or slippery steps. A case which attracted much attention was that of Miss Warren, a dancing teacher, injured when she attempted to save herself from falling after tripping against a hole in the carpet at Spalding station. It was claimed that she would probably not be able to resume her occupation and part way through the case damages of £1,500 were agreed.[7] Two cases concerned incidents when girls fell out of moving trains. Needless to say, their parents blamed the mishaps on failure to close doors properly while the companies blamed the girls. Miss Ody (aged seven) fell out just after Purton, was insensible for three days, and ill for seven weeks; she received £50.[8] Miss Bratt (eleven) was ill for eight weeks after falling out of excursion train returning to Liverpool; she received £91 11 6d.[9]

The highest award seen in a survey that concentrated on cases reported in 1869 went to Mr Farr, a young clergyman (27) with great prospects, already receiving £250 per year as Travelling Secretary to the Irish Church Mission, who was crippled for life in a collision and unable to attend court; he claimed £8,000, to provide himself with an annuity of £250 for life, and received £5,000 plus £250 expenses.[10] Mr Sagar, an engineer from Burnley, in receipt of 'a large income' originally received £4,000 for delayed paralysis in his arms resulting from an accident between Manchester and Bury in 1865; when the company appealed he agreed on £2,000 to save the 'peril' of the retrial that was ordered.[11] Mr Chadwick, a patent safe and lock inventor who claimed his earnings had risen to £866 per year before the accident received £2,000 for head injuries.[12] Another recipient of £2,000 was Mr Milne, an Independent Minister officiating at Tintwistle, injured in an accident at Copley Hill in October 1867; initially he thought it only a slight matter and was able to go on to Leeds and address a meeting, though not for as long as usual. Serious symptoms appeared later so that he was now having to re-use sermons instead of composing two new ones per week.[13] However, Mr Foster, an accountant earning £300 prior to the accident, who had received back injuries and claimed it would take a year or more to recover fully, only received £400.[14]

The lowest sum seen went to Mrs Colmer, who received £2 for injuries to her thumb when a porter slammed the door on her, while Mrs (or Miss?) Long, a domestic servant received £20 for a similar incident on the Metropolitan.[15] *The Times* understood that most cases of compensation for personal injury in the excursion accident on the North London line were settled for sums ranging under £50; the company had been very prompt, helped by the fact that many were its own servants – it did not say whether any arm twisting had been involved. Mrs Everett, a gardener's wife, received £75 from the LSW after her advocate had 'broken down' the railwaymen's evidence in an alighting case.[16] Mr Beck, a master-plasterer, received £150 for injuries in a collision at Bishops Road.[17] Mrs Onions received £200 for injuries received in alighting at Birmingham while she was taking a bundle of her husband's hinges for sale, as did Mrs Bennett of Liverpool for being temporarily unable to help her husband in his jewellery business when she suffered a severe jolt on the way back from Southport, and Mrs/Miss Cooper, a cook, for an arm broken in a fall when an accident to another train had caused passengers to alight and walk the last 100 yards to Loughborough Park.[18]

Examples of damages received by relatives included £300 (£75 of which was for possessions destroyed in the fire) by Mrs Outen, mother of Lord Farnham's valet, killed at Abergele; she had been provided with £25 per year by her son.[19] In 1847, Mr Whitehead, a woollen manufacturer from Saddleworth, received £525 for medical and nursing expenses incurred after his wife had received severe injuries, from which she later died, in a derailment between Darlington and York; they had been travelling in their own chaise, carried on a truck near the rear of the train.[20] Mrs Cargill received a £75 annuity for life in January 1849 for loss of husband (a farmer) in an accident on the Dundee & Perth.[21] Mrs Maycock, widow of a farmer killed in an alighting incident at Ongar, was originally awarded £1,500 – £400 for herself, the rest divided between her six children; this was reduced in a retrial to £1,000, of which she received £300.[22] As for the New Cross victims, Mrs Bradley, the widow of the publican who died of his injuries, received £500 as a widow plus £224 for her own injuries. Amounts from £50 up to £350 went to her nine children, aged 21 to 8, the eldest receiving the smallest amount, presumably because he was regarded as capable of earning his own living. In total this family cost the railway £2,724.[23] Mrs Way, widow of the publican whose death was hastened by the accident, agreed £500 for herself and her one daughter.[24]

One such case showed compassion by a company not normally associated with this: Mrs Hampshire received a 'considerable sum' in agreed compensation for a leg broken on the Eastern Counties in 1846 and the following year her husband sued for extra damages for loss of her services and society while she was recovering. In the event it was agreed between counsel that he was unlikely to win so the matter was settled without hearing the evidence; the verdict went to the company, but since the plaintiff was a poor man the company would pay the costs.

As the numbers of accidents increased and individual ones tended to involve more people, the costs to companies mounted. The LY had to pay more than £7,000 following an accident when a train was derailed near Dixon Fold on 4 March 1853, £3,000 of this going to the widow and children of the one man killed. An engineer who inspected the line afterwards said he found loose bolts and other deficiencies and gave his opinion that the line was not safe for speeds of 40 m.p.h., especially for four-wheeled engines like the one concerned. The company involved, notorious at the time for its poor record, seems to have been unrepentant: an item copied from *The Bristol Mirror* said it had added a clause to season tickets and to be stamped on ordinary tickets, that they should not be held answerable for the results of any accident, however caused, though the paper added that there was little fear that the law would allow them to get away with this.[25] By the 1860s this had become a serious matter for railway companies: over the seven years 1860-66 they paid £1,372,624 in compensation, an average of nearly £200,000 per year, for 169 passengers killed and 4,468 injured.[26]

One apparently simple collision proved very expensive. On Wednesday 23 June 1869 the LBSC ran an excursion to Crystal Palace and back for the Licensed Victuallers. The return stop at New Cross was longer than at previous stations so tickets could be collected. A large staff were doing this as fast as they could, given the passengers' 'drowsy' state, when a goods train ran into the back of it. Those on the platform realised what was about to happen and managed to get the excursion under way but not sufficiently to avoid a collision. Only an estimated £40 of damage was done to the carriages but passengers were thrown about and injuries were worse than they might been because many were out of their seats. One died later of his injuries and another, known to have been suffering already from tuberculosis, was held to have had his life shortened when a post-mortem showed that serious bleeding had been caused to his non-tubercular lung. Out of the 568 passengers which the train 'was supposed to contain' one had an ankle-bone broken, two were returned as very seriously injured, 36 as seriously and 49 as slightly but 350 lodged claims for compensation.[27] The company wanted to settle all claims by agreement but 126 resulted in litigation; originally it set aside £45,000 for claims but eventually paid out more than £70,000. The Chairman claimed that it had only received £17 in receipts. The highest award seen was £3,500 to Mr Squires, a second-class traveller who had claimed £7,000; he was a 29 year-old publican with a wife and two children and had had to sell his inn at a loss after receiving injuries which had paralysed him with little chance of recovery.[28]

Railway directors had long felt that they were subject to unfair treatment and their complaints were a regular feature of company half-yearly reports and meetings. A particularly vigorous attack was made by Mr G Wilson vice-Chairman of the LY in 1860:

Taking the number of people travelling down Market-street, Manchester, and the accidents occurring to them from vehicles, signboards, or chimney-pots, he maintained that there were fewer people injured on this line in proportion to the number of passengers than there were pedestrians in Market-street. (Cheers.) Very little was heard of these; a stretcher carried them to the Infirmary, and a paragraph in the newspapers disposed of them for the future; while, if a railway company had the misfortune to injure any one, of course large claims were made against them, though ships might sink with 500 passengers on board, for which not the smallest shadow of a claim was made against the owners. Many complaints had been made to this company for defending their interests in law courts against extraordinary claims believed to be false ones. No claim for compensation was ever made to this board that was not referred to a committee composed of men as humane in their judgement on these subjects as any in the kingdom, and, if a choice had to be made in the interests of the claimants, he believed no tribunal could be found more actuated by a desire to meet all the exigencies of the cases. But claims were made which by no means represented the injuries sustained, and which put it entirely beyond their power to deal with them, except through an English jury. If he were to mention the singular instances of recovery after a verdict for large damages, the shareholders would be very much surprised. He confessed he had never seen yet a remedy proposed so successful in restoring an injured person to health as a good heavy compensation paid by a railway company. (Cheers.)[29]

In 1869 the Chairman of the North Staffordshire complained about damages awarded to a passenger who had stayed in a waiting-room long after a train had left and then stepped out into a hole in the platform where some boards had been lifted to enable pipes below to be repaired in the interval between trains. Although the passenger had been warned, the judge's summing-up had left the jury little to do other than fix the amount of damages. The most recent Board of Trade Report had shown that in 1868 only 40 passengers, out of 288,000,000 carried, had been killed on the railways through no fault of their own (31 of these at Abergele) but on the previous day there had been eight fatal accidents on London streets through people being run over.[30]

Comparisons between the liabilities faced by railways and the freedom enjoyed by other companies were frequently made. Some of these overlooked the fact that passengers had paid fares and therefore entered into a contract for safe carriage whilst many of the examples they quoted, such as factory and colliery accidents, were of a different type; it was also much easier to show negligence after a railway accident than it was in the case of a steamer that went down with all on board. People rarely, if ever, sued cab drivers who caused death or injury to their fares by careless driving since it was not worthwhile; an item in the paper of 16 October 1867 stated that in 1866 205 people had been killed in the streets of London in accidents involving falling off vehicles or horses, collisions and being run over; 29 per cent of these involved cabs and omnibuses.

A piece in *The Examiner* immediately after Miss Warren's case said journalists rarely felt called upon to defend railway companies since their interest was powerful and their boards' conduct so arbitrary and tyrannical but even they had rights and her award was absurd. Accidents of the sort that befell her happened every day in many places – would she have sued the Royal Academy if she had tripped over matting at one of its exhibitions? It also pointed out that the law rewarded the rich at the expense of those less well-off since damages depended on status and the money would have to come out of fares paid by all. Rich widows came in for particular comment (was it felt that they had already received their reward?); would they sue the maker of a defective gun which burst, killing a man out shooting? 'Rob Roy's rude efforts at practical socialism had a certain poetic picturesqueness about them which these raids against railway companies lack.'[31] It might have added that pain was likely to be the same, regardless of the sufferer's wealth.

Companies had a further sense of grievance in that they felt they took great care to look after casualties. According to the paper's description of the New Cross accident, Mr Cornish, 'a resident medical man' was sent for and gave all needful assistance. One of the worst cases was that of Mrs Hay (fractured ankle) whom Mr Cornish accompanied to her home in Stratford. A special train was sent to bring the survivors back to London Bridge, where it arrived at 12.15 a.m. though counsel in one case complained that their insistence on taking the injured to London Bridge for treatment had aggravated some injuries. Preparations had been made at the Terminus Hotel to receive any who wanted to stay there but all preferred to go to their own homes and three surgeons had been engaged as soon as possible to attend to the injured. Mr Dunford, a barman at Bromley, was even given a free pass to go to the Isle of Wight to recover; he later claimed £25 for doctors' fees and £1 per day expenses for his holiday (of unspecified length) and was awarded £35, of which £5 was for medical treatment.[32]

There seems to have been a random element to jury awards, hardly surprising given that they were laymen called upon to decide the extent of victims' injuries in the face of often wildly conflicting 'expert' evidence: claimants would produce evidence that they had received injuries that would impair their activities for a long time, if not for life, while the company's witnesses argued that they would recover soon or that much of their trouble resulted from earlier conditions. Even more potentially perplexing was that many claimed some sort of nervous impairment as a result of the shocks they had received, often as an effect delayed by two or even more years. There were so many references to 'fits', 'hysteria' and the like (among men as well as women) that this writer was given cause to wonder whether Victorian upper lips were quite as stiff as is sometimes assumed.

There was also the question of alleged malice by juries; some felt that they used compensation cases as a way of gaining revenge against unresponsive railway boards.

'Pennyweight' of Great Malvern complained that he had suffered because of the behaviour of rival companies at Worcester. He had a Midland ticket so the GW made him wait for the next Midland train and then delayed the latter by their shunting operations near the time of its departure: the GW might have had 'a crow to pluck' with the Midland but railway directors needed to remember that passengers were sometimes jurymen.[33] 'Viator' of Preston said it was no wonder that Lancashire juries hit companies hard when nothing had been done for three years to Preston station which had been condemned as inadequate and dangerous by the Board of Trade and was owned by two of the richest companies, the LNW and the LY.[34] *The Pall Mall Gazette* joined the fray saying that each excessive jury award was a blow against a vicious system in which regular protests failed to stop practices such as providing sufficient carriages so that second and sometimes even first-class passengers found 'half-a-dozen navvies fresh from their work, unwashed, half-drunk, obstreperous and perhaps obscene, bundled in among a number of other passengers who have paid their money expressly to avoid such company'.[35]

The only way to attempt even a rough assessment of juries' fairness is to look at the cases they decided. They did not always favour the passenger. Out of 'alighting' cases (including those where passengers had alighted off the platform) only 7 out of 18 seen were initially settled in favour of passengers. One case that might have been expected to arouse sympathy but failed was that of an infant which fell from its mother's arms whilst she was alighting.[36] In nearly every other type of case negligence was admitted (only some unforeseen Act of God could otherwise have caused an accident) and the jury's task was to fix damages.

The evidence of appeals is conflicting. Companies 'won' eight out of ten appeals seen, in the sense that the verdict was overturned or the amount reduced, suggesting that juries were inclined to be over generous. However, it is possible that companies used their legal muscle hoping that the random nature of jury awards would favour them in a retrial. Mrs Sims lost her £300 awarded for injuries sustained when she jumped out of a carriage stopped beyond the platform because it was held that her own negligence was to blame and Mr Praeger, a dancing-master, who had alighted onto the inclined part of a platform lost his £1,500.[37] Mrs Trowbridge, a widowed cheese-monger travelling third-class on the Metropolitan had her damages reduced from £3,000 to £1,250.[38] On the other hand, Mr Farr and Mrs/Miss Long kept their original sums after retrials.[39] In a number of New Cross cases the original juries savagely reduced absurd claims. In proportionate terms the worst cases included Mr Scott, who claimed £5,000 and received £125; Arthur and Elizabeth Johnson who helped their father with his six public houses and claimed £15,000, received £800; and Mr and Mrs Fenton who claimed £600 but only received £15.[40] Mr Wilson, for twenty years a drayman with Barclay & Perkins claimed £1,500 for concussion to the brain and spine and for having 'fallen away in flesh' and was originally awarded of £800; on appeal another court decided that this was excessive and said it would order a retrial unless he agreed to accept £600.[41] Mr Plank saw his damages reduced from £1,150 to £650.[42]

There were also complete failures. A woman called Farrell sued the Eastern Counties *in forma pauperis* after she had been injured while alighting at Shoreditch and was no longer able to continue her occupation of selling fruit in the streets but the company claimed that she had tried to alight before the train stopped and the jury accepted its version, probably helped by medical evidence that she had been drinking spirits.[43]

In addition to clearly exaggerated claims there were instances of downright fraud. Miss Harris, a young woman of about nineteen whose father kept a beershop in Whitechapel claimed concussion of the brain and spine as a result of the New Cross collision, causing hysteria, sickness, loss of appetite and other symptoms 'to which it would be impossible to allude here'. People who had been in her father's employ said she had taken to her bed and openly stated her intention of making up a case and was in the habit of making herself sick by putting fingers down her throat. Her case took more than two days to complete (very unusual then) and the verdict, for the company, was given so late on the third day that it was not in time for the following day's paper. No evidence of action against her was found; it seems that she was regarded more as an object of pity than a criminal.[44]

Less fortunate was Matthew Burton, a weaver living near Nottingham, said to be earning 25s per week. In December 1868 he claimed to have been injured in a collision on the Midland near the junction at Mansfield; there were no immediate serious effects and initially he accepted £10. However, as time went on he felt much worse and claimed for higher damages. When his action came to trial at Westminster in June 1869 he was apparently in a deplorable state, only able to answer in whispers; he had to be carried into court and lay in an armchair covered with blankets while one man held his head, another his heels. Various medical men said his illness was a genuine result of spinal injuries. Burton received £750 damages plus £213 taxed costs. The Midland paid but as a result of information received they had him watched: he was seen climbing to the tops of omnibuses without effort and larking about on the beach at Scarborough. The result was a retrial at which Burton maintained the genuineness of his injuries but was ordered to repay the damages; this he claimed unable to do because he had spent it. The Midland then prosecuted him at Nottingham Assizes for fraud and perjury. Burton claimed that he was medically too weak to understand what he was doing but the jury took less than half-a-minute to convict him. The judge sentenced him to fifteen months, adding, with some reluctance, that since he had undoubtedly suffered somewhat, it should be without hard labour.[45]

An even more blatant case was that of Dickeson, aged 32; allegedly he was a travelling draper but prosecuting counsel argued that he had no proper occupation. He had received £250 damages though he had not even been on the train hit at New Cross. A number of people of dubious background had helped him and his failure to provide one of these with her promised share caused his downfall. At his criminal trial he was able to produce one witness who swore he had seen Dickeson at Crystal Palace on the day involved, but he had disappeared when the judge tried to call him back at the end of the trial. The final reward was two years with hard labour.[46]

Passengers were not the only ones to benefit from compensation cases. They made much work for lawyers – the Chairman of the Brighton company claimed that 20% of cost of the New Cross accident had gone on legal fees. He also said that some lawyers had apparently been touting for business, and one had been behind as many as thirteen or fourteen claims. This could explain the apparent ease with which people of limited means were able to sue large companies.

The medical profession gained because there was much need for expert witnesses, who usually managed to provide conflicting opinions. One called more than once was Sir William Fergusson, Professor of Surgery at King's College, London.[47] No information was given about the fees he received but he seems to have been prepared to give his opinion rather lightly. He appeared for Matthew Burton and also for Mr Statham, who claimed 'large' damages for injury to his nervous system in a New Cross case; under cross-examination Fergusson admitted that he had not personally examined Statham but based his opinion on what he had been told by Docking, whom he had believed to be Statham's doctor but was not. The jury awarded one farthing and Statham's appeal that this was inadequate was later rejected.[48]

Some doctors also seized their chance to profit, though it was then common for doctors to operate a rough and ready health service, subsidising poorer patients by charging larger fees to the wealthy – and railway companies were clearly seen as very wealthy. In Miss Harris's case Dr Budgett of Commercial Road claimed £220 expenses for his ministrations. On 24 June he had charged £2 8s, including 5s and 7s 6d for visits. At this point the judge intervened and demanded to see his fee-book; this showed that he usually charged the poor 1s 6d per visit, including a powder, and tradesmen 2s. Mr Keeper, also involved at New Cross, was attended by Dr Pryce (a specialist?), who charged three guineas for each of 13 consultations, and Dr Swire (a local practitioner) who claimed £45 for visits and medicines to the end of December; the judge said that allowing for medicines this worked out at about 120 visits at 7s 6d each.[49]

The most obvious result for railway companies was the financial loss, the brunt of which was borne by shareholders. The Brighton's chairman claimed that but for the accident they would have been able to give a dividend of 22s 6d for the second half of 1869 instead of the 10s actually given; it had also set back the company's recovery from its financial problems of a year or two before, when no dividends had been paid. At least one company found a way round this: in two weeks in August 1851 the Midland deducted two days' wages from all employees to cover the damages paid to Mrs Blake whose husband was killed in an accident at Clay Cross. No distinction was made – clerks as well as porters were 'docked'.[50] One would have expected criticism from shareholders but no letters along these lines have been seen in The Times though those criticising alleged general financial mismanagement were common and there were instances of shareholders demanding (and sometimes getting) committees of enquiry into directors' handling of finances. The reported versions of half-yearly meetings point the same way: the cheers at the LY's meeting were not an isolated response.

There were suggestions that such matters should be put before a specially selected tribunal. The Regulation of Railways Act of 1868 did allow the Board of Trade to appoint an adjudicator if both company and claimant made a written request but this seems rarely to have happened – there is nothing to indicate that this provision was not to come into force immediately upon the passing of the Act in July 1868 yet no instances of its use before the end of 1870 have been seen.[51] Several chairmen also argued that compensation ought to be linked to fares paid: if a well-to-do person travelled second or third-class (which some then still regarded as an undignified practice, if not downright theft) then he should receive damages appropriate to that class.

It is possible that the introduction of cheap workmen's fares was held back by this issue. Some railway officials publicly said that unlimited compensation was a barrier to providing cheap trains, but this might have been an excuse for not providing services they opposed anyway. When a Bill was before the Commons Watkin said that if it was not passed he would have to withdraw workmen's trains since he had found 25% of the 100,000 using them were not those for whom they were intended, so they were losing revenue. The Metropolitan had been obliged by Parliament to provide these but the LCD did so of its own free will, from 27 February 1865, having first taken the precaution of obtaining a special Act to limit compensation to £100 and to have the amount decided by arbitration, an arrangement *The Times* considered provided a reasonable balance.[52] This had been considered, though not always favourably, at a number of meetings held by groups seeking to promote the cause of workmen's trains. On 23 June 1870 it was reported that a Bill including a maximum of £100 compensation had passed the Commons.

As a result of representations by railway companies, a Commons Select Committee looked into the whole issue. Its report later 1870 said the limited workmen's compensation arrangements appeared to be working well, though one wonders whether they had been in operation long enough for a fair verdict to be given. Their opinion was that that trial by jury was unsatisfactory for other cases and recommended the setting-up of a special tribunal whilst retaining unlimited compensation. However, if juries were retained, they suggested setting limits: £1,000 for first, £500 second, and £300 third-class. Nothing came of this.[53]

One way of ensuring compensation was by insuring for death or injury. On 5 January 1849 *The Times* reported the formation of a company to provide insurance at a trifling premium, affordable by all. Another scheme began on 1 August 1849 on the LNW and LY. For a single journey, irrespective of distance first-class cost 3d (£1000 compensation to dependants if killed), second-class 2d (£500), third-class 1d (£200).[54] In 1852 insurance was advertised for Easter excursions by The Railway Passengers' Assurance Company at the same rates.[55] This was in addition to any compensation due from railway companies but was not applicable to children under twelve because there was then a fear, as with other life insurances, that hard-up parents might try to dispose of their offspring at a profit.[56] At the tenth half-yearly meeting of the Railway Passengers' Assurance Company in September 1854, the chairman provided some details of its operations. The previous half-year's income had been £5,094 (a 26% increase compared with 1852) and they had paid out £1,802, including £370 and £350 to people injured in a previous half-year. He commented that August seemed to be the worst month for accidents – though this should not have surprised him since it was the peak of the excursion season. The Company had also had good luck: it had issued 70 tickets to passengers on an excursion from Dover but at Ashford this had been divided and most of its patrons had been in the first part, which had reached Crystal Palace safely, leaving only seven in the second part, involved in an accident.[57]

Damage to clothing and possessions also led to claims. In September 1843 'TW', writing from Peckham, had been a third-class passenger from Folkestone to New Cross and his clothes had been materially damaged by fire from the engine and he had applied by letter to see if he could get any recompense. The reply was 'no' – if you travel third, you take the risk.[58] Lost luggage resulted in many claims, with varying degrees of success; their usually complicated nature makes it impracticable to deal with them in detail here.

Other questions cropped up from time to time but they were reported only sporadically and it is impossible to say how far, if at all, they set binding precedents; matters are cloudier still because some were made in Scottish courts. In 1843 there was what *The Times* called an 'Important legal decision'. The Glasgow & Ayr followed the normal practice of issuing tickets at intermediate stations with the proviso that issue was conditional on there being space. Normally there was ample room but a passenger bought a ticket at Irvine for Ayr on the last day of Eglintoun Park races and there was no room. He declined either to take his money back or wait for the next train but hired his own carriage and sued the company for expenses. The Sheriff, after a full investigation, found against him with costs.[59] More successful was another Scottish passenger in January 1849. In the Sheriff's Small Debt Court in Edinburgh the 'pursuer' got 2 guineas damages and 1 guinea and 1 penny costs against the North British for failing to stop a train due, according to the timetable, to stop at Portobello, thus causing him to walk to Edinburgh.[60] A case against the GSW was brought at Glasgow small debts court on behalf of John M'Nab, a boy living at Milliken Park who had a second-class season to go to school in Glasgow. The company had withdrawn the second-class carriages and told him either to go third or pay the difference for first. The Sheriff said the company could alter the time of a train or withdraw it completely but were in breach of contract if they altered it in this way though nothing was said about damages or other redress.[61]

Some were able to receive compensation for delays they had suffered. In 1853 T Raikes wrote that he had received £20 from the LBSC for a delay after an accident at Redhill on 1 November 1852; he included copies of letters from his solicitor to the LBSC and their reply, saying he had been treated fairly by the LBSC but felt it was in the public interest to publicise his case. One suspects he was trying to persuade all to claim, thus making companies more careful but he was a rich banker and not all could afford to take on railways.[62] Later that year, though, it was reported that a working man had recovered £5 from the South Wales Railway in compensation for loss of time owing to the irregularity of a train in arriving at Chepstow.[63] The following year a civil engineer recovered £6 from the Oxford, Worcester & Wolverhampton after one of its trains had arrived late at Stourbridge and then stopped to take in a gang of workman, causing him to miss the London express at Dudley, preventing him from attending a meeting in his professional capacity.[64] In 1865 a commercial traveller, Mr Brent, claimed five guineas compensation against the LNW for detention in the Dudley area. The company claimed it was protected by its disclaimer but the judge said this could only be applied in case of an accident and the jury awarded three guineas.[65]

Not all were so fortunate. Major Grey had had urgent business at Barnard Castle in 1855. The Stockton & Darlington time-bill said a train left Stockton 6.30 pm, arrived Darlington 7.10. On 3 May this was 5 minutes late arriving at Stockton and further delayed, reaching Darlington at 7.30 so he missed the connecting coach and had to hire a special carriage; he claimed for the cost of this. The judge decided the company had carried him within a reasonable time so he lost, though each side had to pay its own costs.[66] Mr Lankester, wine merchant and wholesale grocer of Stourmarket, Suffolk [Stowmarket?] lost his case in 1860. He had been a passenger on 2 January from Ipswich; they should have left at 8.17 but were delayed to wait for a connecting train from East Suffolk. As soon as the telegraph told them the latter had been derailed, his train was sent on, leaving at 8.57. He arrived late, missed appointments and sued. The defence was that they had done all they reasonably could to forward the train to time and the judge agreed: as long as they exerted themselves to keep to time they were covered by the disclaimer in the timetable.[67]

One even took on a company over the vexed question of overcrowding. In December 1857 a solicitor residing at York brought an action against the NE. He had taken a second-class return from York to Scarborough on the evening of 21 November and come back the following Monday morning. As far as Flaxton there was only one other in his compartment but there the door was unceremoniously thrown open and ten other persons, principally servants and labourers rushed in. They had caused the plaintiff considerable annoyance by behaving in a rough and coarse manner. He claimed the company had contracted to carry him in a comfortable manner, free from annoyance. The seats were made for four each side; even if they had been made for five, it would still have been two too many in the compartment. He won 1/- damages.[68]

One wonders what would have happened if all so inconvenienced had acted thus; presumably this did not happen because most would not have felt it worthwhile and a solicitor would have been capable of handling his own case.

Chapter 21: CRIME

Railways were a great boon to criminals as well as travellers. Even before lines were in public use, ceremonial openings with all their attendant hullaballoo provided opportunities: an item headed 'GLASTONBURY FESTIVAL' dealt with the ceremonial opening of the Somerset Central from Highbridge to Glastonbury on 17 August 1854:

> Amongst the vast concourse of strangers at the 'Railway Opening Festival' we regret to learn that several persons were made the victims of 'the light-fingered fraternity', having had their pockets picked of various sums, though happily, to no great amount. One lady of about 30s; another of 9s; another of a smaller sum; and a fourth of a sum not divulged. A gentleman also, of his watch. We are sorry to add the thieves escaped undetected in every instance.

This appeared, identically worded, in the *Wells Journal* 26 August, *Western Flying Post* 29 August and *Bridgwater Times* 31 August.

Most crime against passengers was unspectacular. The only murder known before 1870 was on the North London in 1864 when Muller murdered a bank clerk to take his watch and chain but closed compartments made many fear serious attacks. A case originally treated as murder occurred at Cottingham in 1853. Mrs Duffill, an innkeeper's wife, had visited Hull, and was left alone in a second-class carriage with a man who tried to rob her as the train left the station. Originally it was reported that she had been thrown out by the robber but in the following week's paper, by when she had died, the evidence suggested that she had jumped. The coroner's jury brought a charge of manslaughter against the villain, whose name had evolved from William Hillyard to David Halliday over the course of the week.[1] In February 1858 a gentleman was found in the last train of the day when it stopped at Littleborough; when he recovered, he said the only other passenger in the carriage had drawn a pistol, robbed him and left him as he was found. It was assumed the robber alighted at Walsden.[2]

One whose family was well known in the Channel Islands was about to go to India in 1855 and wanted to visit his mother. At Paddington he happened to show there was money in a pocket book he put into his breast pocket. He was followed into a first-class carriage by a gentlemanly-looking and respectably dressed man and after some polite conversation the other took out a flask and glass and had a drink; he was about to put it away, then apologised for his rudeness and offered the first man a drink. He accepted, fell asleep and woke up at Swindon. His pocket had been cut open and he had been robbed of £69 – but a larger sum remained safely hidden. It was assumed that the flask was a double one, part holding ordinary, part drugged sherry. The thief wore large whiskers and moustaches [genuine?].[3]

Much crime was carried out by people dressed respectably and able to merge with their surroundings, travelling first-class, rather than by Artful Dodger types. Pickpockets thrived and were often well-organised, crowded stations giving the best opportunities. Two women of elegant appearance and manners (calling themselves Ann Loft and Sarah Smith) were caught at Bristol in June 1847. Mrs Barnard, from Cheltenham, waiting in the Bristol & Exeter booking office for her train to Weston after missing the previous one, was jostled by them. Since they looked so respectable, she made nothing of it but when it happened again and they hurried off, she checked and found that her purse with £25 was missing from her pocket. She immediately informed the police, who found them in the GW booking office; they threw away the purse but were caught, found guilty and sentenced to 12 months hard labour; it was believed they had been responsible for many thefts on railways and steamboats.[4]

In September 1852 three notorious characters (George Taylor, Elizabeth Barnes and Mary Calloway) were finally caught, at Bristol, their favourite haunt. Their method was to force their way through crowded booking-offices or platforms, creating disturbance and distraction and picking pockets; one would indicate targets to a second, who would steal and pass the goods to the third. The authorities had been after them for some time but until then they had been too clever for them; this time a victim's niece saw them in action.[5] One, whose reward was three months' hard labour, was even daring enough, and careless enough, to try his trade in 1855 in the booking-office at London Bridge when Her Majesty's Ministers were about to depart for Dover; a vigilant constable saw him.[6]

Once inside a train, people with outside pockets were particularly at risk. Two examples of the way pickpockets were organised were reported in 1844. In January a carpenter who had been left £110 went to London to collect it from the solicitors and then had drinks with a couple of strangers. He went to the station, where two people took seats opposite; they left at Reigate. When he got home to Brenchley, near Maidstone, he found the gold in his pockets had been replaced by about 2/- in coppers, tied up in paper. He believed the change occurred in Merstham Tunnel.[7] A few months later a lady and her niece left Manchester in a first-class carriage; shortly after two gentlemen got in, and at the next station a third, all enveloped in large cloaks. Both ladies went to sleep. The elder thought she had been poked by an umbrella as she woke. The men alighted at the next station and on arrival at Birmingham she found three sovereigns had been taken from her pocket but they had not taken the roll of notes tied to her garments.[8]

In November 1852 a party of pickpockets, including a woman, came by the north mail to Teignmouth, where they robbed one lady on the platform, returned to the train and robbed three more at Newton Abbot; they were not caught.[9] A Miss Day was robbed (of five sovereigns and four shillings) between Yatton and Bristol in 1855, by a female sitting next to her. The thief and a male accomplice moved to another carriage when the train stopped at Nailsea but they were identified and arrested at Bristol. The Bristol & Exeter went to considerable trouble to prove the case, even tracking down one witness from London, whom they were able find because she had been travelling with a parrot. The pair had been seen travelling up and down the line regularly so others had probably been robbed without realising until it was too late to work out where and when it had happened.[10] 'JM' told the story of a young lady who had travelled first-class in a LNW carriage from Liverpool to Bristol on Christmas Eve 1862. At Birmingham her carriage was attached to a Midland train, leaving at 4.40. It was getting dark and there was no light in the carriage though one had been requested; it was again refused at Worcester and Cheltenham but eventually provided at Gloucester at 7 p.m. In the dark her purse had been taken, which she only discovered when the thief had gone; repeated applications to the railway authorities had elicited no more than formal promises to inquire into the matter.[11]

There were also opportunistic thefts. In February 1843 a 'flying stationer' called John Riley, a cripple, left a large bundle of books in the carriage at Stockport (now Heaton Norris) station while he got out and then found that they had been stolen. He saw that Bridget Hanley of St Peter's Gate was advertising new books for sale; he was able to identify her as having been in the carriage with him and the books as his. He recovered his books and she was sent for trial.[12]

Gambling became a leading topic in 1854. 'Clericus' had travelled from Birmingham to Worcester and found himself in a carriage with a party of gamblers. One was playing a game like thimble-rig, using four cards; the other three betting on which was coloured – he assumed these were accomplices, hoping to tempt travellers into the game. When the train stopped, they moved to another carriage, as did two others; on complaining to the railway authorities he was told that under the present state of the law they could do nothing about it. 'HBC' wrote shortly afterwards about his experience of about six months previously when he had been in a LNW second-class carriage and the man next to him invited those present to buy a dressing case. All refused. Next he offered to raffle it; again 'no'. Then he turned to cards; a dirty little man opposite selected the right one and wanted to bet. Others were also inclined to do so but he said he would tell the police at the next station and that stopped the game. At the next station the pair went into another carriage. At Wolverton he told the guard; his reply was that there was no harm in it and he had no orders on the subject – indeed, the directors allowed a board and packs of cards to be hired at Euston-square. In a P.S. he claimed he had been told that the early morning express from Manchester to London was frequented by card-sharpers who made a good living out of rich business-men. Next day there were more letters. 'A traveller' had gone from Worcester to Ashchurch and at Defford an expensively dressed man but with large and dirty hands (many rings) got in. At Bredon he looked out intently and just before the train left another, shabbily dressed and almost certainly an accomplice entered. The newcomer suggested a game of cards (2 plain, 1 picture, pick last); the expensively dressed one played and first lost 2/6, then won 2/6. Both urged a farmer to join in; by the time he had left the train the farmer had lost 2/6, then a sovereign. He had complained to the guard but no action was taken. 'A lucky fellow' had recently travelled from Carlisle to Liverpool third-class, in a carriage where seats were 'fore and aft' [lengthwise]. A knot of fellows of dubious respectability were at one end but apart from large amounts of foul cigar smoke, there was initially nothing to complain about. After Preston they were travelling in the dark; one of them pulled out a candle and lit it, cards were taken out, the probable accomplices played first, then others joined in. At the first station he shouted for the guard; immediately the candle was extinguished and the ringleader jumped out of the other door and bolted down an embankment. Immediately below there was a letter from Mark Huish denying that gambling was permitted on LNW trains and enclosing a copy of a notice, exhibited at stations, warning that there had been several instances where passengers, especially second and third-class, had been induced by strangers to gamble and lost large sums of money and asking passengers to notify the guard at the earliest opportunity.[13]

Next year JDL (Inner Temple 21st) warned about the activities of a gang of card sharps on excursions to and from Aldershot Camp.[14] In that year the Glasgow & South Western was so concerned that it sought an extra bye law to stop gambling; it claimed every railway company in Scotland had tried to put an end to the practice but had not received any help from the authorities, who argued that they had no powers to punish offenders because they were on fast-moving trains travelling through a variety of jurisdictions. After some legalistic to-ing and fro-ing over the wording, the Board of Trade finally sanctioned a bye law that imposed a maximum penalty of £5 and allowed the offender to be removed from the Company's trains and stations at the first opportunity. Thereafter the topic disappeared for a while.

In August 1865 'A Foreigner' alleged that organised gangs of card-sharps were active on SE trains from Dover, apparently targeting foreign visitors; he had not played himself but knew of several cases where losses had been up to £100.[15] In December at Port Glasgow George Thomson, who had 'fleeced' an Irishman of £55, was charged with gambling in a railway carriage. The case seems to have been tried in a light-hearted way, the bench saying that anyone losing had only himself to blame – the Provost said, 'This poor Irishman left his wits at home, but took his purse with him'. The accused pleaded guilty and was fined 40/- plus 80/- expenses; he paid promptly, took out three cards and asked if there was any possibility of getting enough to take him to Glasgow but he was told the walk would do him good.[16]

Luggage provided a tempting target. One pair of thieves gained particular notoriety in the mid-1840s. The active one was Daniel Garrett or Garratt who had been employed by various of the nobility as a butler and thus knew how to pass himself off amongst first-class passengers; he blamed his troubles on drink and claimed he had not intended to make a career out of crime but had found it too easy. His partner was Charles Maynard who was described by *The Times* on his first appearance as 'Mr C Maynard, estate agent of 19 Howland-street' but soon became Charles Maynard, alias Gregory, who had been sentenced to transportation in 1816 for stealing from his employer, a hosier, but served his sentence in the hulks and so was released in this country at the end of it; in the course of the case he was also revealed as a bigamist. The pair were assisted by various people whose role seems to have been to hide stolen property; it was also almost certain that they received inside help from railwaymen but only one porter was brought to trial and he was acquitted.

Garrett had use of rooms at several addresses and could spread his captures around. The scale was revealed when a coach-load of apparel was taken from the place where he was arrested. Some items were identifiable and the evidence given by their owners showed the methods used and the wide area over which he had operated. Dr Daniels of Bath had arrived at Paddington in the dark and there was much confusion as the luggage was unloaded. He saw a man he was able to identify as Garrett call to a porter and claim a portmanteau which he thought was his. He approached Garrett but believed he was the one who had made the mistake when Garrett assured him it was his and only realised the truth when his own failed to appear; by then it was too late because Garrett had jumped into a cab and driven off. Mr Winter had lost his luggage on arrival at Waterloo from Barnstaple and Mr Bedingfield, a commercial traveller, lost his there on coming from Gosport. One from Huddersfield lost his after seeing it arrive safely at Euston, and another his at Wolverton while he was booking for one train and it was grabbed by someone jumping into another train as it moved off. The Brighton and Dover lines had also been targeted.

Their downfall resulted from an attempt at repeating a trick which had paid off handsomely in the past, when Mr Hartley had lost a writing-case containing railway shares and other non-negotiable papers reputedly worth £40,000 to himself. His solicitors, Bush & Mullens, advertised in *The Times*, offering a reward of £100 for its safe return, provided a satisfactory explanation was given. The proviso seems to have been put in as a face-saver since there was no attempt to enforce it. The outcome was a letter directing them to work via coded notices in *The Times*. One such, after Mr Bush had received a sample, appeared on 26 May 1845:

> PASCEOLI – first instalment received, terms accepted and confidence may be given without reserve. None but principals will interfere.
> Address, marked private, B esq., only.

They then met Maynard and let him have £150 since he claimed he would receive none of the £100.

On 7 July that year Mr Vaughan Prance, a solicitor from Nether Stowey, between Bridgwater and Minehead, caught the night mail from Paddington. He wanted to keep his writing case, containing bills of exchange to the value of £2,000, with him, but a porter persuaded him it would be safe in the luggage van. When he arrived at Bridgwater it was missing. On 12 July he received an anonymous letter saying his case was safe but those holding it would need a liberal reward; contact should be made via coded messages in *The Morning Post*. He handed this to Mr Seymour Clarke, the GW's Superintendent, who passed it to Mr Charles Nash, chief manager of Maples, Pearse & Stevens, solicitors to the GW, giving him a free hand and promising to support him.

After various exchanges, Prance and Nash met Maynard at the Guildhall coffee house, where he was arrested by Superintendent Collard of the GW's police. Garrett, using the alias of 'Mr Smith', visited Maynard at the Giltspur Street Compter, and it was presumably then that they organised the hiding of incriminating evidence, principally a writing-case containing pawnbrokers' tickets for stolen items. This was lodged with a publican by Wareham, one of the lesser members of the group but some partly-burnt scraps of paper relating to the Hartley episode were found in Maynard's grate when his house was searched. Nash expected Hartley's solicitors to cooperate in prosecution but initially they denied all knowledge and then Bush got Mills, a GW director friend of his, to have the Hartley incident dropped from the charges; this was done without consulting any other director. Prance's protest in court was supported by the magistrates and public pressure resulted in a full prosecution, four companies eventually taking part. Garrett's part had become known and he was eventually arrested on 12 September after being followed for some weeks. The two main culprits were eventually sentenced to 14 years transportation.[17]

Some railway authorities were clearly not pleased at their lack of public spirit being exposed and they gained their revenge by failing to support Nash in various matters arising from the case. At one point he had had Wareham arrested, in the belief that further incriminating evidence would be found and this would probably have happened but for Mills's sabotage. This enabled Wareham and his wife to sue for wrongful arrest. The jury awarded ¼d in damages, clearly believing that the Warehams were rogues but technically in the right; more serious were the costs involved, which effectively ruined Nash.[18] He and Collard, and their female relations, were also subjected to threatening letters, so much so that at one point Nash tried to withdraw from the prosecution on the grounds that there was enough evidence without him, but the magistrate would not allow him to do so. The police found what they believed to be convincing evidence about the perpetrator but Nash could not afford the expense of bringing the necessary witnesses from Birmingham and Edinburgh and had to let the matter drop. Others were rewarded, including Hartley, even though he had had to be compelled to give evidence. In September 1847, 'at the suggestion of some Gentlemen of high standing in the Railway World' a public appeal was launched to compensate Nash; Captain Huish of the 'North Western Railway' signed this but he was not joined by any GW functionary. This appeal was a failure financially, the money raised going straight to Nash's creditors.[19]

Needless to say, that was not the end of thefts. In 1846 John Farr, alias Farmer, received three 'several' sentences of transportation for very similar crimes. Dr Roberts of Baker Street lost a portmanteau between Folkestone and Bricklayers Arms; others lost belongings on the SE and LNW. Many stolen items were found amongst the belongings of Mary Anne Newland, with whom Farr lived and she received six months with hard labour. The survivors of Garrett's circle continued their depredations but some soon ran out of luck and were brought to account, as will be described later.

Luggage thieves could come in all shapes: George Thomas, described on his first appearance in 1851 as 'a respectably-dressed young man of somewhat sanctimonious appearance', tried to steal a carpet bag and portmanteau at Shoreditch. At his trial his counsel said he was of high character, studying for holy orders and had taken the bag by mistake and the rector of St John's Clerkenwell gave him a good character. The evidence allowed no doubt, though it did show that he was an incompetent thief, having drawn attention through his suspicious behaviour in looking at luggage on the platforms. The jury recommended him to mercy; the judge sentenced him to four months' hard labour.[20]

George Logan, 30, a well-dressed man was accused at Doncaster in April 1864 of stealing a clock, value £10, on the GN. On a Monday night Mrs Maxwell and three children under her charge, Miss Price and Mr Robertson, MP were in a first-class carriage from Newcastle to York. Mrs Maxwell had a travelling clock and various other items with her. At York, she got out for refreshments; when she came back she found her seat occupied by Logan, the bag and clock missing. She told Robertson, who beckoned the guard and station-master; a search was made, the bag was found but not the clock. The station-master advised Robertson to look after his own luggage and said that five or six of the swell mob of London were down, hinting that Logan might be one of them; he would telegraph Doncaster to tell the police to be on the look-out. Robertson advised Mrs Maxwell to do nothing; he pretended not to suspect Logan, engaged him in conversation and soon discovered he was not the gentleman he looked. At Doncaster, Robertson occupied the window, summoned two guards and told them to bring two police. They came and he gave Logan in charge for stealing the clock; the policemen were reluctant but the station-master was now present and Robertson gave his name and said he would take responsibility. On arriving in London, the guard brought two superintendents of police who made a search and found the clock in Logan's carpet bag. Logan was identified as a man recently released from prison and committed for trial.[21]

The Great Western was the victim of two spectacular thefts by men posing as passengers. In January 1848 a box containing £1,200 in gold and £300 in silver, destined for Badcock's bank in Taunton was stolen by six men of apparently respectable appearance. The box had been put under the seat of a locked second-class compartment free of passengers. The thieves occupied an adjoining one, removed a panel under the seat in their own, pulled the box through and cut through it with a circular saw. By the time the theft was discovered the culprits had gone and it was not known where they had alighted.[22]

Even more daring were thefts from the night mails, 1st and 2nd January 1849. The two men directly involved were Henry Poole, an ex-railway guard, sacked for misconduct, and Edward Nightingale, a horse-dealer from Hoxton who initially refused to give his name and was only identified as a member of 'the swell mob' when a detective from London came to identify him. They took a first-class compartment next to the mail van on the London-bound train and between Bridgwater and Bristol one of them climbed out, made his way to the mail and robbed it, though some of their victims had taken precautions against this – Badcock's had divided the notes being sent to London and sent the halves separately. At Bristol the thieves alighted and either handed the proceeds to a confederate or hid them. Almost certainly they would have avoided detection had they not been undone by their greed and a miscalculation – they expected the guard to stay with the train to London, but he moved to the Plymouth one at Bristol. They now joined the west-bound mail and repeated the trick but a guard, whose suspicions had already been aroused by their strange behaviour, found at Bridgwater that the mail had been tampered with; the train was sealed and searched at Exeter where the culprits were found in a compartment where they had tried to hide the proceeds and various items of disguise. At Exeter Assizes in March they each received 15 years transportation. Also widely believed to be implicated was Frederick Manning, another ex-railwayman, dismissed because he had been a guard on several occasions when thefts had occurred. At the time of the robbery he kept the White Hart Inn in Taunton; though questioned no charges were brought against him, but the pressure of public opinion caused him to move to London. There he and his wife murdered a customs official for his savings and were hanged at Horsemonger Lane Gaol in November 1849; this was a particularly popular execution and was witnessed by Charles Dickens, who then wrote to *The Times* attacking the idea that public executions were any sort of deterrent. Various evidence quoted in the press made it likely that most, if not all, of those concerned had been associates of Maynard and Garrett and had been responsible for many other railway crimes, including the overnight theft of takings from a booking-office at Paddington.[23]

Railway employees were thus not always to be trusted. In 1848 a number of serious depredations committed by one of the superintendents of Preston station of the North Union, was brought to light. John Hetericks had been in the employ of the company but had been dismissed a few weeks previously for disobeying directors' orders. A portmanteau had been lost and after he had been dismissed, suspicion fell on him so his house was searched and it was found that he had been stealing for some considerable time. Articles already found were worth £150 to £200 – including 3 dressing-cases, 1 small bookcase, several portmanteaux, carpet-bags etc, numerous umbrellas etc, a richly embroidered black velvet shawl (very valuable), 6 bottles of otto of roses and wearing apparel in abundance – the names/initials on some of these were quoted.[24]

It is now time to consider the crimes committed by passengers directly against railways.

Information sent to the Board of Trade illustrated the variety of offences that were committed in the latter part of 1842. Henry Simmons continued his journey beyond the destination for which he had paid on the Bolton & Leigh and was fined 20 shillings, plus costs. Mark Turner stayed on board as far as Hartford, having only paid the fare to Warrington, was fined 20/- and costs 8/- and in default of payment committed to Chester Castle for one month. The Manchester & Leeds prosecuted four for not paying any fare: one was fined 10 shillings and two went to prison in default but Mary Sutcliffe, who had her son with her only had to pay their fares and a 5 shilling fine. The last offence was committed on Christmas Eve, and dealt with on the 26th – were the magistrates in compassionate mood? One who travelled second-class with a third-class ticket, and refused to pay the difference, was fined 5 shillings and had to pay the difference. A drunk and disorderly, in a third-class carriage, was fined 12 shillings, and paid up. There were three cases of assault, only one of which was specifically reported as against a fellow passenger; Philip Kershaw was responsible for that one and one other (within a fortnight) and paid fines of 20 and 25 shillings.[25]

There were more sophisticated ploys. James Patteson bought a second-class ticket from Liverpool to Rainhill for 1 shilling and altered it to one for Manchester (fare 3 shillings). This was discovered by the ticket collector, because Patteson had been careless (or ignorant?) enough to call it 'Mancester' and use larger type than the official version. When searched he was found to be carrying printing ink and type, for Sheffield as well as 'Mancester'. He was initially charged with forging and uttering a receipt, which led to a legal debate on whether a ticket was a receipt. Since no fare was stamped on it, the judge decided it was not a receipt and ordered the jury to return a verdict of not guilty. He was then immediately charged with 'forging a printed paper, purporting to be a passenger-ticket of the London and North-western Railway Company'. This time there was no escape and he received six months for what the judge described as 'a very gross fraud'.[26]

Two frauds on the Bristol & Exeter were reported in the same paper in 1855. One passenger, described as an agent to a Bridgwater corn factor, had travelled from Taunton to Bridgwater, where a guard caught him trying to get out of a window on the wrong side. When he was challenged, he produced a ticket with the date defaced and claimed that it had been issued that day; the booking-clerk was able to produce the 'train-book' which showed it had been issued several days before. He was fined £1, with £1 15s 6d costs, to be paid within a week or suffer a month in prison. The other concerned a Taunton commercial traveller who had been under suspicion for some time. He had been seen going around the tail of trains to avoid the ticket-collector and had several times been caught without a ticket and paid double the fare. Authority had clearly had enough and decided to make an example of him; the Cullompton magistrates did not believe his involved story and fined him the maximum, 40s plus costs. His willingness to pay double when caught would suggest that, up to this point at least, he had avoided detection often enough to emerge in profit from his activities.[27]

From time to time cases of misuse of excursion tickets were reported as companies sought to make examples. In 1851 the GW had suffered frauds for some months. People intending to stay some time had been buying them, selling them to others wanting to return that day and relying on being able to buy in a similar way for their return. One who had been caught was fined 20/- plus costs or 3 weeks in gaol.[28] Ten years later at Brighton five people were charged with disposing of and purchasing excursion tickets marked 'not transferable'; all were found guilty and each fined the maximum 40/- plus 12/6 costs or one month in prison.[29] A variant on this was openly admitted by 'A Caledonian', who wrote in 1865 that at Lowestoft he had bought a single for 28/9. In the waiting-room the 'coolie' who carried his luggage asked if he had got his ticket. He showed him and was told he could have had a return for 25/-. He went back and changed it, getting 3/9 change, the clerk saying it was not his duty to tell of a cheaper ticket. At his hotel he had given the return half to a waiter and hoped he got something for it.[30]

Some fiddles clearly needed collusion between railwaymen and passengers, though in an early case the jury eventually acquitted the accused in a case which, at this distance, seems reasonably clear cut. It may be that some of the jurors were showing their disapproval of railway companies and their practices and the others just anxious to get home.

> Some of the guards employed by the Grand Junction Railway Company were charged at Kirkdale on Monday last with having cheated the company of certain passage money for carriage by the railway. Two policemen gave evidence to prove that the prisoners had taken up passengers and carried them to their destination for half-price and had put the money into their own pockets. The jury, after consulting together in the box during about an hour, begged permission to retire. They remained for some time when the Court adjourned. Several messages were sent, and it was decided that the jury were to be locked up all night, as it appeared that they were as far from concord as ever. Just as the bench was nearly deserted, the barristers disrobed, the desks locked, and most of the candles extinguished, the jury returned, having suddenly made up their minds to agree. They acquitted the defendants.[31]

Some misdeeds provide evidence that guards could be crafty defenders of their employers' interests. In 1845 a Brighton tradesman tried to repeat an artful dodge; he took a third-class ticket, rode in a third to Hassocks, then moved to a first until New Cross, when he went back to third but he was caught by the guard, who ushered him back into a first and forced him to pay extra at London.[32] On a Saturday afternoon in August 1846 a train left Bath at 2.50 pm for Bristol and near Twerton tunnel the engine driver saw two men waving a red handkerchief so he thought there was danger ahead and reversed his engine. He explained the stop to the guard, who went to the men; they said they had no money and wanted a lift to Bristol so the guard gave them seats in the van and handed them to police at Bristol where they received the choice of a 40/- fine or one month in prison.[33]

Vandalism was reported from time to time. The superintendent of the Eastern Union said in 1846 that someone had written obscene remarks on the windows of first-class carriages with a diamond, between Ipswich and London so they had had to remove several panes; they offered £20 reward for information.[34] The LSW offered a reward of £50 in June 1855 for information about damage by cutting and mutilation of cushions and other fittings to several of the company's carriages.[35] In 1849 W Bletchley was fined £2 or one month in prison for throwing stones at the carriages in Highbridge station. He chose to go to prison – was this his way of getting a month's free lodging?[36] Inevitably there were oddities. In October 1869 the General Manager of the SE sent a circular warning station staff to be on the look-out for a woman who had apparently been stealing fenders from stations.[37]

However, there were honest people. In December 1841 there were instances in which sums of £7,000 and £6,000 had been left behind in Brighton railway trains by passengers; they had been carefully secured and faithfully restored to their owners.[38] Not all those who had lost property restored were as grateful as they might have been, an example of which was reported in 1846. When a train arrived at Rugby from London, an inspecting officer found a travelling bag on a seat and was unable to find its owner. He took it to the station-master who opened it and found £270 in sovereigns; it was tied, sealed and put in the station-master's desk. It was claimed by a passenger who arrived by another train two hours later and was able to describe it accurately: he had taken a ticket at Euston and had the bag put on a seat but failed to catch the train. He only said, 'It's all right thank you; had I lost it I should have been ruined', and left.[39]

Charles Lambert, who gave his address as Charleston, South Carolina, 4 July 1851, was a passenger from London to Cheltenham on 27 March 1851. He was about to leave the station when guard Connor asked if he had lost anything; he said 'no' but the superintendent asked him to check and he then realised a pocket book with £80 and other monies was missing. The guard gave him back the book and was offered £10 but refused it. He hoped the GW directors would see this. (It would have been double honesty – handing in lost goods and refusing a tip – but should an American dating a letter 4 July raise suspicions?)[40]

Railways could provide both the opportunity for theft and the means for catching culprits. This story seems rather far-fetched but footplates were bumpy places at the best of times and would have provided precarious footing for someone unused to their ways, especially at full speed. A grazier going from Derby to Nottingham to attend Lenton fair fell into conversation with someone claiming to be going to the same place. Soon after he reached Nottingham he missed three £10 notes and immediately suspected his companion; he then found that the latter had boarded the train which had just started back to Derby. He agreed to be strapped to an engine which chased the thief's train and caught up with it; the thief was identified and the stolen money found on him.[41] Less spectacular was a case in May of the following year: a forgery suspect had taken a train from Gloucester to Birmingham and an engine was sent in pursuit. The train was overhauled, the suspect taken off and later returned to Gloucester. An interesting insight into the actual and potential speeds of the engines of the day is that the train had set out an hour before the pursuing engine, though one must take into account the much heavier weight of the train and the time it would have spent at various stops.[42]

Chapter 22: WAR AGAINST THE EASTERN COUNTIES RAILWAY (1846)

The Eastern Counties, which also operated other companies' lines, was a favourite target of critics. At the start of 1846 it provided services to Cambridge, Ely, Norwich and Yarmouth on one line and to Colchester on another; during the year the latter was extended to Ipswich and Bury St Edmunds. That year it had more than 40 letters of complaint against it published and was the target of several pungent editorials in *The Times*; its recently-begun connection with Hudson probably gave an extra incentive to pillory it.

A blast by 'The Passenger on the Truck' on 14 October 1845 provides a good introduction. The day before he had come from Romford by the 11 o'clock which had reached Romford with every seat occupied; there were no spare carriages so upwards of 20 waiting passengers had the alternative of waiting two hours or stowing themselves away in various parts of the train. A few found admission into carriages already containing more than their allotted number, some seated themselves on top of a carriage, others were allowed to ride on the tender, some packed up in the luggage-carriage with baskets of fish and two others besides himself were seated on a truck. They arrived safely but on the way they passed several footpaths and one carriage crossing and he saw only one policeman between Romford and London though one crossing near the schools at Ilford was used by many children at the very time morning trains were running.

'ER' called attention to the irregularity of its trains on 19 March 1846. On Monday he had intended to catch the 8.20 from Brentwood but there was no train until 9.45, half an hour after the advertised time of the second train of the day; about 10 they got under way and reached town at 11.10, two hours late, which was not just occasional but something regularly occurring. 'A commercial traveller' wrote from Chatteris on 1 April that that day they had professed to accelerate all trains and in proof thereof the 10.15 up from Yarmouth (on the still-independent Norfolk Railway) was only about ¾ hour late in reaching Ely where began the boasted Hudson management. They were just 1 hour 16 minutes covering 16 miles to Brandon; twice they came to a dead stop for several minutes, the engine labouring to go but not able to, though there were only seven or eight passenger carriages and two luggage vans.[1] A fortnight later 'A Sufferer' claimed that the day before the line had exceeded itself: the train which should have been at Chelmsford at 2.49 p.m. arrived at 4.16 and was 1 hour 43 minutes late at Shoreditch; he had been told not a single train ran to its time by half-an-hour that day. On the same day 'A proprietor in the E C' protested against the acceleration of trains since the company was not fit to compete with the speeds of others and by trying it was endangering passengers' lives.[2]

On the 17th 'Medicus' had joined in. A few evenings before he had waited 1 hour 20 minutes at Tottenham for the 8.11, in company with about 50 others, though the train had only started from Hertford, 18½ miles away. When it arrived, he was told there was no room; however, many were allowed to occupy laps of fellow sufferers and a few travelled outside with the guard. His own dignity was too shocked for this or to accept the kind offer of a horse-box for himself, so he waited for the next, which came within a quarter-of-an-hour of its professed time. He also commented on the clocks: that at Stratford had shown 8.15 for 10 days; another had been at 1.15 for a long time.

'JC' added other complaints. On Sunday 31 May [Whit Sunday] he had intended to go to Chelmsford. According to the time-bill, times would change on 1 June but they had changed that day so when he went for the 8.30 a.m., he found it had left at 7 and many others were caught. Since there was no other train until 6 p.m., he went to Brentwood by the 9.45, then on the best way he could, in the heat with no conveyance of any kind. The train to Brentwood was more than half-an-hour late: the engine and carriages were ready to go on, but there was only accommodation for half those wanting to go, so the engine was detached, another carriage attached and soon filled and this was repeated five or six times. What were third-class carriages yesterday were second-class today, causing all sorts of squabbles and annoyance; what an hour before had been pig trucks were now thirds.[3]

'ADVANTAGE OF A SPECIAL TRAIN' was the heading of an item on 7 July which described events with a slapstick touch. The Governors of Christ's Hospital had engaged a special train from Shoreditch to Hertford which left at 9.30 and a creditable speed to Broxbourne promised an early arrival but at the junction with the Hertford line (then single) the driver decided he had to wait for the 10.45 from Hertford and nothing could induce him to move. The clerk at Hertford had received orders not to despatch the 10.45 until the special had arrived so two trains were stuck at either end of the line, both fearing a collision if they moved. After a while, horse and rider were despatched to Broxbourne to find the cause of the delay; eventually the special went on its way, arriving about 1.30. Two trains were waiting to leave for London and eventually left joined together. The Governors were doubly unlucky: they were delayed at Broxbourne 1½ hours on the way back by the bursting of a tube in the engine.[4]

Four days later 'E.A. Hullah' described his Friday evening journey. The mail due to leave at 8.30 left at 9 and after passing Ingatestone it was brought to a dead stand by the 'breaking' of the engine. Passengers were left to amuse themselves by conversation inside or smoking outside the carriages while the unfortunate stoker, lying on his back under the engine, took three-quarters-of-an-hour to repair the damage. At Chelmsford they were delayed for another half-hour while engineers hammered and porters caused confusion by rushing every five minutes to tell passengers to get on, which they did, only to find all except the last were false alarms. They arrived at Ipswich at 1.45 a.m. instead of 11.49 p.m.

'RB', a daily passenger who had suffered much from late running, contributed three letters detailing a check he had made by sending a clerk to make an accurate record at the London terminus. According to this, from 30 July to 4 August inclusive 60 trains had been late in starting, 69 in arriving.[5] There followed a stream of letters giving examples of late trains and ridiculing Hudson's effort at 'spin' by saying that the average was only three-quarters-of-a-minute per passenger. A Sunday evening train which carried 'JLH' from Waltham Cross at the end of August brought forth more criticism. It was due at Shoreditch at 9.10 and arrived at 10.10, taking 2 hours 5 minutes over 14¾ miles; furthermore, hundreds of passengers had been left at intermediate stations since there were no carriages for them. 'AEF' had been on the same train: people at intermediate stations were frantic to get on and some carriages were crammed with double the proper numbers of passengers so there was much struggling and foul language. At Tottenham it really appeared that the train had at last been taken by assault and remained for some minutes in hands of an irritated mob. He admitted he was no saint: he had twice threatened to knock down anyone else who tried to enter his overcrowded carriage. He had deserted his parish church to enjoy fresh breezes on the banks of the river Lea, but others had probably deserted pubs and skittle alleys for the same reason.[6]

'FO' wrote about his experiences in October when, with about 20 others, including ladies, he had taken first-class tickets at Ware for the 'express' leaving Hertford at 9. There were no firsts on the train at Ware. All seconds were already full so they had to travel in a third whose seats were dripping wet; one of the porters did his best with a cloth but they were still damp. They were only 35 minutes late and got a partial refund of fares after only 20 minutes wait.[7] Complaints grew fewer as the year approached its end but all was not yet right. On 5 November 'A Traveller' reported that a Saturday train, the 8 p.m. from Yarmouth, due London at 10 p.m., arrived at 1.15 a.m. Sunday morning, which he put down to a 'broken-winded engine'. A faulty engine was also the reason 'HRC' gave for a journey just before Christmas when he left Cambridge at 3 and reached Shoreditch at 7.40 – a loss of more than 2 hours on journey supposed to take 2 hours 20 minutes. His indignation was increased (as was that of various others) by the nonchalance of the railway servants who expressed no surprise or concern and took the delays as everyday events; they seem to have been told to say or explain nothing.[8] By this stage, letters frequently said complaints were met with jeers by railwaymen accusing them of learning them from *The Times*. One who received this treatment was 'Viator' who, after various other delays, had been held at Shoreditch for another eight minutes while tickets were collected and had had the temerity to say that this could have been done during one of the earlier delays.[9]

In 1845 Hudson had been brought in as Chairman in a desperate bid to improve the finances of this struggling company. He was then believed to be the miracle worker who could create prosperity out of any organisation; most of his dubious methods lie outside the scope of this book, but one of his strategies was to cut costs. He had used this on the North Midland, thus precipitating the labour problems considered in an earlier chapter. An editorial in *The Times* on 7 August made it clear that the shareholders were at least as much to blame as Hudson:

They have got a king of their own choosing – a monarch of vast pretensions and singular renown ... In return for an undivided throne the new sovereign guaranteed a 10 per cent constitution. ...

Some excuse, however, may perhaps be urged for His Majesty's conduct. It is possible that he may only represent the impersonated rapacity of his subjects, who have shifted on his shoulders the responsibility of exacting and amassing a certain amount of tribute ...

The speech from the throne yesterday afternoon will be perused with some interest, and we hope our readers will attach full weight to the rather novel defence of unpunctuality which it contains. According to King Hudson, 4,448 trains had only been detained on the average three-quarters of a minute per passenger per train. Perhaps by the same law of distribution, His Majesty will show that 24 stokers have only been damaged at the average rate of a broken finger per man.

Another page included a table designed to show that Hudson's lines, which included the Midland and other East Anglian lines run by the Eastern Counties, charged the highest fares.

Three days later *The Times* copied a piece from *The Examiner* ridiculing Hudson's claim that until a very recent accident only one passenger had been killed on the line, three had had legs broken, one a dislocated shoulder and '17 others injured in a way not worth mentioning' so there were no grounds for complaint. He had also taken no account of the railwaymen killed and maimed, apparently regarding them as not worth a mention. Late in August the editor commented on the official accident statistics. Between 1 January and 20 July the 66 railway companies between them killed and wounded 157, averaging, in the Hudson fashion, about 2 3/8 victims each. The Eastern Counties, far from being average, had been responsible for more than a quarter of the total – 4 killed and 41 wounded. In 15 accidents they had killed or injured 31 passengers, 13 servants and 1 trespasser. Hudson had misled people by cutting short his account before the worst accident.

On 14 August the paper gleefully quoted an item, 'KING HUDSON', from *Punch*: 'It is rumoured that His Majesty is so disgusted with his railway kingdom, situated on the Eastern Counties Railway, that he intends, in imitation of Napoleon at Fontainbleau to abdicate. The Isle of Dogs is spoken of as his Elba'. The rumour was premature.

In July there had been a serious accident at Stratford when a goods train ran into a stationary passenger train, injuring about 20 people, one of whom died soon after. The signal that should have provided protection was on Halle's principle and consisted of a fan-like arrangement in four sections, painted yellow, green and red (the bottom two). There it always showed three sections, as a warning to slow down; the fourth was lowered to tell drivers to stop. Tests showed it was easy to draw up the fourth section but much harder to pull it down; its shortcomings were so blatant that immediately after the accident it was replaced by an upright post 20 to 30 feet high, with arms painted red and raised or lowered as needed, with a red light attached at night. It was being operated by an 18 year-old hired for errands and odd jobs because the regular signalman was attending to a goods train. The engine-driver, Clare, who had lost the sight of one eye some years before, was only a fitter and occasional driver, and his stoker only a labourer; neither had been supplied with a full copy of the rules, which stated that no fitter was to take a train out of a station. The train hit should have been in London at the time of the accident. The Company tried to get the Board of Trade to prosecute but it passed the buck back to the company and the magistrates committed Clare and his fireman for trial, acquitting two other employees. The inquest jury gave a verdict of manslaughter against the driver and declared the culpability of the company in not ensuring rules were obeyed, fit people employed, and so on. The press comment now was that it was but another Hudson testimonial; the outcome would be the trial and acquittal of Clare since the jury would not blame a servant for the company's failings.[10] The prediction was accurate and the jury took about five minutes to acquit Clare; as well as the defects already mentioned several drivers had complained about the difficulty of seeing and deciphering the relevant signal and nothing had been done.[11] However, that was not the end: Clare was sent back to Essex Quarter Sessions on a charge of committing a misdemeanour in running past signals at danger but the company's counsel said they had decided there was no point in proceeding so he was again acquitted, as was his stoker, whom they had not tried the first time because his driver had been cleared. The verdict was greeted with a burst of applause, immediately suppressed.[12]

In this case there had been one letter of slight mitigation for the defence. 'JAR', writing from Kent, said he had applied to the directors on behalf of two parishioners injured in the accident and they had immediately, in the kindest manner, sent a 'check' for the whole amount.[13] It is unlikely that this resulted in widespread forgiveness.

Clearly there was no immediate improvement. Samuel M Page, Chaplain to Ipswich County Prison travelled on an excursion from Ipswich to London and back on Monday 14 September which carried upwards of 1,000. At Brentwood they were one hour late, and going rapidly downhill about two miles further on they came across some men with a trolley working on the line. The driver reversed his engine; he and an inspector alongside him jumped off since it was impossible to avoid a collision but luckily the engine remained on the rails.[14] On 15 October there was a brief item that since a collision on Saturday, there had been two more minor derailments. In the year as a whole six collisions and two derailments were reported in the Board of Trade returns (which do not tally with press reports); in addition a woman had her arm broken when a porter told an engine driver to start before the guard had said they were ready.

For a while *The Times* had been prepared to accept that the directors were trying to mend their ways but on 17 October the editor returned to the charge:

It is with mingled feelings of exasperation and despair that we revert to the abandoned career of the Eastern Counties Railway. Barely six weeks have elapsed since we welcomed with ready forgiveness the first appearances of repentance and reflection which these obdurate directors have ever been known to exhibit. ... Confident announcements stated that observations of 'Won't do', 'Must pull up', were in circulation throughout the august assembly, and that a murmured apprehension of 'cutting it too fat' had been heard to fall from the lips of Royalty itself. We held out the hand of fellowship to these returning prodigals ...

Now we really do not know what to do with this unnatural corporation. They are hard at it again. From Shoreditch to Yarmouth their whole line is a scene of that wild merriment and frantic adventure conventionally characteristic of a rover's cabin. Cambridge trains go to Hertford, and Hertford trains go off and are never heard of again. We do predict with the utmost confidence that there will in a few years be a veritable country tradition of some lost Parliamentary train plying about Ely and Brandon, like the Flying Dutchman around the Cape, with phantom stokers and ghastly passengers, and perhaps a director on the tender condemned in popular legends to a doom like that of the Wild Huntsman of Saxony. Our paper last week conveyed almost daily notifications of catastrophes or delays. ... East Anglia is demoralised. A sentiment analogous to that most fatal effect of servitude which makes the slave hug his fetters is rapidly developing itself throughout this devoted district. Men declare they *like* travelling on the railway. They snatch a fearful joy from the romantic and hazardous character of the expedition, and would regard it as a spiritless and unstimulating incident if they were taken to the right station, with entire limbs, and in proper time. ...

It was long ago remarked that ['Boards' have] neither souls nor bodies ... But railway boards are the worst of all boards, and the Eastern Counties board is the worst of these. Like that well known specimen of the menagerie which 'kindness can*not* conciliate nor hunger tame', it is inaccessible to remonstrance as to rebuke, to amity as to anger. ...

Soon after he delivered another broadside, relating to Clare's acquittal:

For a great portion of the mischief created in the world, that notorious nonentity called 'NOBODY' appears to be responsible. This incorrigible malefactor is a most useful adjunct to the staff of the Eastern Counties Railway. The number of mistakes and casualties, to say nothing of the amount of manslaughter and mutilation occurring on this unfortunate line, must be allowed to be more than mortal man can bear the *onus* of. ... It is true that there is now and then the semblance of an intention to give up some substantial culprit to justice. A stoker or other subordinate of the company is indignantly surrendered by the Board to be dealt with according to law, but an acquittal ensues, and we are compelled to revert to our old friend, NOBODY, as the delinquent. ... There was abundant evidence of gross mismanagement, which endangered the lives of the public for the sake of niggardly economy.[15]

Luggage also suffered. Robert Southee went from London to Bentley, where he discovered that his carpet-bag had been taken out at Manningtree. There it had been broken open, for which considerable force had been needed. No loss was involved, except for the broken lock. He was assured it would be investigated immediately and he left it to be forwarded to the principal officer at Colchester but when he saw the latter he found he knew nothing about it.[16] There were also complaints about delayed and mislaid parcels, and traders at Billingsgate and other London markets complained that perishables were arriving too late for market and they were not receiving the compensation they had been promised when the railway had taken over from road carriers who had provided it. 'JF' included a charge that, if true, helped to explain some of the general problems of the line: on one day the fish had arrived at 9 a.m. instead of 3 a.m. and on enquiring, was coolly told 'no coke at Ely' so the driver had had to burn everything he could get hold of, including wooden railings along the line [yet more stray cows?], to get his train moving at all.[17]

Outwardly, at least, the company was unrepentant. On New Year's Eve 1846 the directors gave a dinner to all in their employ who could attend; about 1,600 were fed in the carriage repair workshop and 400 unable to attend received an extra day's pay. Hudson was absent so D Waddington, the vice-chairman, deputised. The speeches were belligerent: Waddington said he treated press criticism with contempt and Mr Sheriff Kennard claimed it was the best-managed line in the country. After dinner light refreshments were served during entertainment that included the wives and female friends of the company's servants in 'mazy dance'.[18]

If 'A Constant Reader' (Cambridge) is to be believed, there was improvement. In the course of a letter complaining about fare increases in August 1847 he asked for the paper's help in reversing this – 'We are mainly indebted to your exertions for the comparative security and punctuality with which we are now able to use this line'. How far it had been brought about by *The Times* would seem to be questionable; certainly the supply of letters had dried up – or was it that the editor had had enough of this issue for the time being?[19] However, as will have been seen from earlier chapters, the line was far from perfectly run. Indeed, at the beginning of 1860 *Herapath* reported that this 'unhappy company' had suffered a collision at Forest Gate on the first day of the year.

BIBLIOGRAPHY, NOTES and REFERENCES

Main references:

If just a date is given, it means that the item was derived from *The Times*; it should be clear from the text whether it was a news item, a letter to the editor, an editorial or a notice put in by a railway company. If it is ..../ *another newspaper* it means that *The Times* acknowledged the other as its source. Note that these are all the dates of <u>publication</u>, not of the event itself.

'*The*' is the first word of the title of many newspapers cited; it is omitted from the notes below.

LNW Officers' Minutes – *RAIL 410/585 on* – at Kew (The National Archives, previously The Public Record Office).

MT = item at Kew catalogued *MT* ....

RAIL = item at Kew catalogued *RAIL* ... . The first 770 odd deal with individual companies; higher numbers more general information.

RCHS Journal = *Journal* of the Railway & Canal Historical Society.

RM = *The Railway Magazine* – the periodical of that title whose series began in 1897 and is still in being.

Taunton = *The Taunton Courier*. If it is *Taunton / another newspaper* it means that *The Taunton Courier* acknowledged the other as its source.

All material concerned with accidents and inspection reports should be assumed to be derived from the annual Reports submitted to Parliament by the Board of Trade (briefly replaced at one stage by the Railway Commissioners). Much of this has been taken from originals owned by the writer (and thus no reference to sources publicly available is known); otherwise the source will be either the *RAIL 1053* series at Kew or the *Parliamentary Papers* series at the House of Lords Record Office.

Works that might be of further interest to the reader.

Many of the works listed below devote only a small proportion of their space to the period covered by this work; those used for compiling this book (which are only a tiny fraction of the works available) are identified in the notes by the surname of the author(s) only, unless ambiguity could result, and are asterisked below. Some titles have been somewhat abbreviated. A few books devoted to early lines and general topics are also included.

P Bagwell & P Lyth, *1750-2000: Transport in Britain from Canal Lock to Gridlock*, Hambledon & Lindon, 2002.

*Barnes, *The Rise of the Midland Railway*, P Kay reprint.

G Biddle, *Great Railway Stations of Britain*, David & Charles, 1986.

*G Body, *Great Railway Battles*, Silver Link, 1994. [Inter-company quarrels].

*Bill Fawcett, *A History of the Newcastle & Carlisle Railway 1824 – 1870 ...*, North Eastern Railway Association, 2008.

*G Gabb, *The Life and Times of the Swansea and Mumbles Railway*, D Brown & Sons (Cowbridge), 1987.

*A Gray, *The South Eastern Railway*, Middleton Press, 1990.

*Herapath = *Railway & Commercial Journal* (title varied over the years); a journal devoted to railway matters, principally aimed at investors.

*P Holmes, *Passenger Traffic on the Stockton & Darlington Railway*, author, 2000.

*AA Jackson, *London's Metropolitan Railway*, David & Charles, 1986.

*ET MacDermot, revised CR Clinker, *History of The Great Western Railway*, Ian Allan, first 2 vols, 1989 reprint.

*D Martin, *The Monkland & Kirkintilloch and Associated Railways*, Strathkelvin District Libraries, 1995.

*MC Reed, *The London & North Western Railway*, Atlantic Transport Publications, 1996.

*CJA Robertson, *Origins of the Scottish Railway System*, John Donald, 1983.

*LTC Rolt, *Red for Danger*, David & Charles, fourth edition, 1982 [accidents and safety].

*R Sellick, *The West Somerset Mineral Railway*, David & Charles, 1970 edition.

*J Simmons: I – *The Railway in England & Wales, 1830 – 1914, The System and its Working*, Leicester University Press, 1978;

II – *The Railway in Town & Country, 1834 – 1914*, David & Charles, 1986;

III – *The Victorian Railway*, Thames & Hudson, 1991.

*J Simmons and G Biddle (editors), *The Oxford Companion to British Railway History*, OUP, 1997.

*RHG Thomas, *The Liverpool & Manchester Railway*, Batsford, 1980.

*WW Tomlinson, *The North Eastern Railway*, David & Charles, 1987 reprint.

*J Howard Turner, *The London, Brighton & South Coast Railway*, 3 vols, Batsford, 1977/8/9.

*NW Webster, *Britain's First Trunk Line* [Grand Junction], Adams & Dart, 1972.

*F Whishaw, *The Railways of Great Britain & Ireland (1842)*, 1969 reprint, Augustus M Kelley, New York. This was a contemporary description of many of the early railways, mostly derived from personal inspection – or so the author claimed.

*RA Williams, *The London & South Western Railway*, David & Charles – vol I 1968, vol II 1973.

*J Wrottesley, *The Great Northern Railway*, 3 volumes, Batsford, 1979-81.

David & Charles published a series of Regional Histories, 14 volumes covering England, Wales and Scotland.

Col M Cobb, *The Railways of Great Britain, A Historical Atlas*, Ian Allan, 2003, is the best atlas available.

In the very early days a number of volumes giving large-size engravings (some coloured, others black and white) were published. Amongst them were the following, with the publisher of a modern reprint (originals are rare):

Bourne's London & Birmingham, and Great Western, both David & Charles;

A. W. Tait's Manchester & Leeds, printed by Fletcher & Sons of Norwich;

Bury's Liverpool & Manchester, Hugh Broadbent of Oldham.

For exact dates of the opening and closing of stations see: ME Quick, *Railway Passenger Stations in Great Britain, a Chronology*, Railway & Canal Historical Society, 4th edition, 2009.

Notes to chapters.

Chapter 1.

1 – 24, 25 June 1839; 2 – Acworth p 38, Rolt p 30; 3 – 27, 28 June 1870; 4 – also see RCHS *Journal* May 1960/ *Railway Times* 31 March 1860; 5 – also see RCHS *Journal* March 2009 for text of a Ballad that bears a suspicious resemblance to this story; 6 – 29 May 1847; 7 – 10 November 1860 / *South Eastern Gazette*; 8 – 11, 12 January 1842.

Chapter 2.

1 – *Taunton* 22 September 1847; 2 – *Kinross-shire Advertiser* 13 March 1858; 3 – Holmes p 9, 14; 4 – *MT6/1/280*; 5 – *Herapath* March; 6 – 30 April 1839/*a Montrose paper*; 7 – *Taunton* 9 October 1839; 8 – 12 March 1847/ *Globe*.

Chapter 3.

1 – *Trewman's Exeter Flying Post* 17 June 1830; 2 – Gabb; 3 – Holmes; 4 – Robertson p 87-8; 5 – Whishaw, p 60; 6 – 15 October 1840; 7 – Tomlinson, p 366-7; 8 – *Royal Cornwall Gazette* 19 July 1834; 9 – company's Day Book, *RAIL 57/10*; 10 – company minutes *RAIL 57/3*; 11 – 10, 13, 14 September 1866 / part *Carnarvon Herald*; 12 – 13 March 1867; 13 – Sellick; 14 – D Joy, *The Lake Counties*, volume 14 of the David & Charles Regional series, 1983 edition, p 146; 15 – 12 October 1858; 16 – 8, 14 December / part *Tyne Mercury*; 17 – *MT6/1/120*; 18 – *RAIL 384/22*, 12 March; 19 – notices 3, 5, 23 July 1845; 20 – half-yearly report 21 August 1850; 21 – *Tewkesbury Register* 21 May 1864; 22 – *Salisbury & Winchester Journal* 10, 17 June; 23 – MacDermot I 239-61; 24 – Body 40-66, MacDermot I 177-204; 25 – 1 June 1857; 26 – 4 March 1858; 27 – 10 April 1838; 28 – 24 April 1839; 29 – 21 October 1841; 30 – 3 September 1841, MacDermot II p 73; 31 – 7 November 1840 / *Birmingham* Advertiser; 32 – 29 December 1846; 33 – 14, 17 September 1841, MacDermot II p 73; 34 – 23 September

1839; 35 – 28 November 1870; 36 – also see A Dow, 'An iconclastic word ...', RCHS *Journal*, December 2007; 37 – 4, 13 October, Body 139-48; 38 – 23 August 1859; 39 – 14 September 1858; 40 – see Wrottesley I, plate 14 , *Times* 31 January 1861. 41 – *RAIL 981/226*; 42 – *Taunton* 27 January 1841; 43 – *Taunton* 27 February 1839; 44 – *Penzance Gazette* 31 May 1843; 45 – P Scowceoft, RCHS *Journal*, March 1991; 46 – notice 13 July 1840; 47 – notice, *Manchester Guardian* 29 April 1843; 48 – 4 June 1868; 49 – Robinson's Time and Fare Tables 1841; 50 – 9 July 1868; 51 – notice 6 April 1864; 52 – notice 25 August 1870; 53 – 12 January 1852, 1 June 1868; 54 – notice 9 September 1867; 55 – notice 13 May and half-yearly report 20, 26 August 1852; 56 – 3 November 1849; 57 – 15 April 1843; 58 – 12 August 1844; 59 – reported in *Railway Times* 20 November 1847; 60 – *Taunton* 19 January 1848; 61 – J Latimer, *The Annals of Bristol in the Nineteenth Century*, W & F Morgan (Bristol), 1887, pages 253 and 326; 62 – *Taunton* 24 May 1840.

Chapter 4.

1 – *RAIL 667/9*; 2 – company minutes, *RAIL 667* series – note that this station was provided much earlier than the 1848 date given by most works in print; 3 – notice 5 February, copy of report 8 February 1844; 4 – 12 July 1848; 5 – 21 October 1842; 6 – 29 September 1846 / *Sunderland Herald*; 7 – 24 October 1848; 8 – report of accident on 3 August 1851; 9 – RA Cook, RCHS *Journal* July 1973 / *Halifax Courier*, on opening of replacement; 10 – 24 April 1840; 11 – 10 May 1844; 12 – 5 January 1867; 13 – *Times* 24, 31 August and 15, 22 September and articles by N Bowdidge in the Great Eastern Society's *Journal* July 1989, July 1996; 14 – *Westmorland Gazette* 21 February 1857; 15 – 15, 18 September 1869; 16 – 5 August 1841; 17 – 2 November 1843; 18 – 31 July 1845; 19 - RCHS *Journal* July 1978 / *Railway Times* 9 January 1869; 20 – 10 September 1843; 21 – 8 January 1842; 22 – 9 September 1869; 23 – 7 October 1858; 24 – D Martin, RCHS *Journal*, July 1983; 25 – MT6/1/171; 26 – notice *Leeds Intelligencer*, 3 October 1840 and CR Clinker RCHS *Journal* April 1955; 27 – K Belsten, RCHS *Journal* January 1971 / *Jackson's Oxford Journal*; 28 – Simmons & Biddle; 29 – e.g. 1 September 1867; 30 – vol I, p 75-6; 31 – 29 August 1842; 32 – 9 July 1846; 33 – 4 September 1867; 34 – 19 October 1843; 35 – 24 July 1845; 36 – 30 September 1851; 37 – *RAIL 410/142* – *LNW Traffic & Coaching Minutes*; 38 – 13 November 1849 / *Leeds Intelligencer*; 39 – 15 September 1851; 40 – 18 August 1867; 41 – D Martin, *Monkland* ...; 42 – Simmons vol III, p 245-6; 43 – 14 April 1870 / *Exeter & Plymouth Gazette*; Simmons & Biddle 212; 44 – 1, 9 November 1838; 45 – A Hasenson, *The History of Dover Harbour*, Aurum Special Editions, 1980, page 130; 46 – 30 September 1842; 47 – 19 August 1845; 48 – 8 September 1843; 49 – 30 October 1851; 50 – 28 July 1869; 51 – 5 October 1855; 52 – 7 March 1843; 53 – 26, 29 July 1856; 54 – 18, 19 September 1863; 55 – *Taunton* 26 April 1865; 56 – 21 August 1869; 57 – 20 September 1843; 58 – 18 January 1845 / *Globe*.

Chapter 5.

1 – Tomlinson p 127; 2 – notice, Webster and timetable for 15 February 1841 in *Freeling's Companion*; 3 – CR Clinker, RCHS *Journal*, April 1955; 4 –6 July 1840; 5 –

notice 29 June 1840; 6 – 15 October 1840; 7 – *RM* July 1898, p 13; 8 – 15 February 1844; 9 – 4 July, 1 October 1844; 10 – 7 & 8 Vic cap 85; 11 – notice 19 October 1844; 12 – 21 September 1854; 13 – 25 June 1850; 14 – 24 August 1850; 15 – 30 May 1841; 15a – 24 July 1843; 16 – Reference under General Acts in Report for 1855; 17 – item, 28 January 1852; 18 – 2 December 1858; 18a – 12 March 1845; 19 – *Taunton* 18 July 1849; 20 – RCHS *Journal* March 1959; 21 – *Herapath* January; 22 – Simmons & Biddle p 437; 23 – 11 January 1847; 24 – 21 April 1851; 25 – *Taunton / Morning Adveriser* 2 July 1851; 26 – Simmons III p 325; 27 – 14 April 1852, RA Williams vol 1 p 223; 28 – 9, 15 October and 2 November 1861; 29 – *RAIL 667 series*, Holmes; 30 – 13 August 1853; 31 – 17 February 1865; 32 – RCHS *Journal* July 1957; 33 – Jackson; 34 – 10, 14, 17 February 1865; 35 – 12 November 1870; 36 – Thomas p 190-1; 37 – *Herapath / Manchester Guardian* July, – trip by 7 p.m. on 14 June; 38 – *RAIL 667/32*; 39 – 12 March 1845; 40 – 29 March 1845; 41 – 3 April 1845; 42 – 26 February 1846; 43 – MacDermot I, p 347; 44 – Gray p 288, RA Williams I p 242, Wrottesley I p 195.

Chapter 6.

1 – 27 June 1853; 2 – 29, 30, 31 January and 1 February 1867 and Barnes, p 180; 3 – 2 September 1867 and also see Jackson; 4 – 22, 24 June 1837; 5 – 11, 12, 13, 17 May 1842; 6 – 8 June 1842; 7 – 23 June 1842; 8 – 14 August 1845; 9 – 13 June 1865; 10 – 8 June 1865; 11 – 31 July 1865; 12 – 17 August 1865; 13 – 20 August 1868; 14 – 21 August 1861; 15 – Board of Trade; 16 – *RAIL 384/22*, 13 May and 10 June 1842; 17 – 5 November 1846; 18 – 17 October 1839; 19 – 12 November 1849; 20 – 1851 Report, Appendix 65, reference under General Acts; 21 – 28 September 1850; 22 – copied, *Taunton* 17 May 1854; 23 – 8 July 1862; 24 – 5 January 1839; 25 – *Taunton* 8 May 1844 / *a Liverpool paper*; 26 – 1 July 1843; 27 – 7 November 1843; 28 – 13 December 1843; 29 – 29 June, 2 July, 5 September 1844; 30 – 26 September 1844; 31 – 1 October 1844, and 21, 23 January and 3 February 1845; 32 – 23 December 1845; 33 – 2 February 1846; 34 – 2 May 1848; 35 – 1 February 1845; 36 – 4 March 1854; 37 – GO Holt, RCHS *Journal* October 1955, based on letters in *Herapath*; 38 – 25, 27, 31 December 1841 and MacDermot I p 334; 39 – 14 October 1846; 40 – 11 July, 24 September 1862; 41 – 29 October 1852; 42 – 29 January 1845; 43 – 18 October 1853; 44 – 3 September 1847; 45 – 18 April 1854; 46 – 15 May 1857 / *Northern Express*; 47 – RCHS *Journal* January 1861, and *Times* 16 January 1862; 48 – 11 December 1862, *Simmons & Biddle* p 75; 49 – 11 August 1864; 50 – 28 May 1868; 51 – 27, 28 December 1870.

Chapter 7.

1 – 28 January 1847; 2 – 21 January 1847; 3 – 22 July, 10 November 1845; 4 – *Taunton* 7 April 1847; 5 – 29 October 1861; 6 – 6 September 1846; 7 – 6 January, 6 February 1865; 8 – 1 January 1866; 9 – 15 June 1867.

Chapter 8.

1 – Tomlinson p 374; 2 –*Bristol Times* 23 November 1839; 3 – *Herapath* March / *Birmingham Herald*; 4 – 1 March 1842; 5 – *Caledonian Mercury* 16 March, *Scotsman* 26 March 1842; 6 – Tomlinson p 374; 7 – *Weston-super-Mare Gazette* 9 April 1846; 8 – 16 April 1846; 9 – 9, 17, 25, 31 October 1850; 10 – *Bridgwater Times* 24 August 1854; 11 – *Daily Scotsman* 19 July 1856 / *Border Advertiser*; 12 – *Railway Times* 30 January 1858 and 5 August 1865, quoted in RCHS *Journal* March 1958 and October 1965; 13 – 13 August, 18 September 1850; 14 – 8 July, 5 and 5, 6, 10 August 1851; 15 – 4 April 1856.

Chapter 9.

1 – 1 May 1826; 2 – 6 October and 27 December 1830, 19 October 1831; 3 – 14 August 1840; 4 – 24 May 1839, 14 August 1840 / *Renfrew Reformer*, 19 August 1840 / *Glasgow Argus*; 5 – 19 July 1842; 6 – 12 June 1844; 7 – 25 May 1857, 7 May 1860; 8 – 10, 15 June 1865; 9 – 26 February 1850; 10 – 26 September 1838 / *Northampton Mercury*; 11 – 18 September 1840 / *Derby Mercury*; 12 – H Paar, RCHS *Journal* March 1983; 13 – Wrottesley vol I p 167; 14 – 14 April 1846.

Chapter 10.

1 – Simmons & Biddle p 427-8, MacDermot I p 349-52; 2 – 15 September, 22 December 1845; 3 – 7, 9 August 1865; 4 – 5, 9 September 1865; 5 – 9, 11 March 1863; 6 – *RAIL 384/22*, minutes 11 March and 10 June; 7 – 14 April 1846; 8 – JN Charters, *The Brampton Railway*, Oakwood, 1971 and B Webb & DA Gordon, *Lord Carlisle's Railway*, Railway Correspondence & Travel Society, 1978; 9 – GS Hudson, *The Aberford Railway*, David & Charles, 1971; 10 – Tomlinson p 374, *MT6/1/171*, *Bradshaw*; 11 – Robinson's Time and Fare Tables 1841; 12 – 13 April (paper said weekly but *Bradshaw* fortnightly); 13 – 17 July 1865; 14 – 10 October 1844; 15 – 15 October 1846 (*Times* said Cross Lane but BoT report Windsor Bridge); 16 – *Trewman's Exeter Flying Post*; 17 – JM Clarke, *The Brookwood Necropolis Railway*, Oakwood, 1995; 18 – M Dawes, *London Railway Record*, October 1999 and Friends of National Railway Museum *Newsletter*, Summer 2000.

Chapter 11.

Many items not individually noted come from companies' advertisements in *The Times*, others come from Board of Trade/Railway Commissioners material.

1 – Simmons III p 272; 2 – *Royal Cornwall Gazette* 20 September 1834; 3 – Tomlinson p 374; 4 – Simmons III; 5 – Simmons III p 273-4; 6 – 1 October 1842; 7 – *Taunton* 7 June 1854; 8 – 14 August 1844; 9 – *Taunton* 1 September 1852; 10 – 26 August 1840; 11 – 9 September 1840 / *Leeds Intelligencer* and *Sheffield Iris*; 12 – 7, 17 September 1844; 13 – 13, 16 June 1848, latter from *Globe*; 14 – 10 April, 29 May, 8 & 13 August 1849; 15 – 3 September 1844; 16 – 2 June 1846 / *Globe*; 17 – 14 May 1845 / *Sun*; 18 – 27 May 1850; 19 – copied by *Taunton* 3 September; 20 – 7 August 1851; 21 – 10 September 1851; 22 – *Kinross-shire Advertiser* 28 July and 11 August 1860; 23 – 19

June, 30 September, 8 July, 30 August 1851; 24 – 23 October 1858, 22 August 1861, 20 and 27 August 1863; 25 – *Taunton* 28 May 1856 / *Weston-super-Mare Gazette*; 26 – *Taunton* 6, 20 August 1856.

Chapter 12.

Most of the special events were found from companies' advertisements in *The Times*, usually included several days running, just prior to the event.

1– 5 & 6 Vict c 55 s 20 and 7 & 8 Vict c 85 s 15; 2 – 6 August 1860; 3 – *Ormskirk Advertiser* 1 November 1860; 4 – 9, 13, 14 August 1866; 5 – 21 September 1867; 6 – *Taunton* 30 May 1849; 7 – *Taunton*; 8 – *West Briton* 29 July, 5 August; 9 – copied *Taunton* 13 August 1851; 10 – *Taunton* 28 May, 4 June, 23 July, 17 September, 1 October 1851; 11 – *Stroud Journal* 13 September 1856; 12 – 8 January 1862; 13 – 16 June 1868; 14 – 16 March 1858; 15 – MacDermot I p 353; 16 – notice, *Taunton* 9 July 1842; 17 – 17 June 1864; 18 – advert Times 21 June, description *Taunton* 2 July; 19 – 14 October 1848; 20 – P Scowcroft, RCHS *Journal* November 1983; 21 – 20 September 1858; 22 – *Taunton* 25 August 1852; 23 – S Bragg, letter, RCHS *Journal* November 1986; 24 – 26 May 1860; 25 – A Gray, RCHS *Journal* July 1985; 26 – G Guilcher RCHS *Journal* July 1986; 27 – *Chepstow Weekly Advertiser* 6 June 1857; 28 – *Tiverton Times* 5 November 1867; 29 – Fawcett, p 155; 30 – RCHS *Journal* March 1958, Simmons & Biddle p 151; 31 – RCHS *Journal* September 1960; 32 – 1, 7, 9, 28 May 1867; 33 – 30 September and 9 October 1867.

Chapter 13.

1 – many letters from *The Times* that were originally considered for this chapter were discarded as suspect; 2 – 9 October 1866; 3 – 12 December 1844, 21 September 1847; 4 – 26 September 1857; 5 – 3, 4 July 1861; 6 – copied 25 August 1869; 7 – 8 September 1854; 8 – 22 November 1858; 9 – 30 November 1870; 10 – 2 October 1844, 10 January 1848, 9 September 1851; 11 – 23 January 1847; 12 – 20, 22 July 1863; 13 – 14, 27 September 1867; 14 – 10 September 1862; 15 – 15 February 1866 / *Pall Mall Gazette*; 16 – 19 October 1844; 17 – 20, 26 July 1864 (case, as identified in letter, was Castell v Bembridge); 18 – 2 November 1854; 19 – 2 April 1863; 20 – 7 January 1846; 21 – 27 August 1869; 22 – 29 May 1841; 23 – 24 September 1852 / *Ayr Observer*; 24 – 20 November 1845.

Chapter 14.

1 – 6 July 1840, 15 October 1863; 2 – *West Briton* 5 April 1844; 3 – 29 September 1838, 25 October 1844; 4 – 15 January 1841; 5 — 2 February 1846; 6 – 11 June 1844, 2 November 1850; 7 – 2 August 1844; 8 – 21 January, 17 May and 27 May 1847 and 3 May 1848; 9 – 23 September 1854; 10 – 19 February, 12 March 1855; 11 – 20 June 1862; 12 – 1 January 1845; 13– 9 October 1862; 14– 8 May 1868; 15– 9, 16 September 1863; 16 – 11, 13 September 1869; 17– 11, 19 August 1851; 18 – 7 August 1845; 19 – 13 June 1865; 20 – first report 5 August; 21 – 23, 26 March 1852; 22 – 20 October

1843, 17 November 1846; 23 – 17 February 1852; 24 – 3 January 1845; 25 – 5, 6 June 1860; 26 – 4 November 1868; 27 – 3 October 1851 / *Kilmarnock Journal*; 28 – 1, 3 July 1846 (in first report paper called her 'Mrs Burtonshaw').

Chapter 15.

1 – *MT6/1/171*; 2 – 12 May 1838; 3 – 28 August 1846; 4 – 2 January, 3 February 1849; 5 – 12 December 1849; 6 – 24, 26 September and 1, 8 October 1863; 7 – 1 October 1863; 8 – 31 August and 2, 7, 8, 9, 10, 11 September 1868; 9 – 31 May, 5 June, 14 August 1860; 10 – 27 December 1841 / *Wilts paper*, *Taunton* 28 November 1855; 11 – 18 February 1846; 12 – 2 August 1849; 13 – 9 August, 26 December 1855; 14 – 10 June 1853 / *North British Daily Mail*; 15 – *Fifeshire Journal* 23 September 1858; 16 – copied by *Times* 12 August 1840; 17 – 6 December 1843; 18 – 9 September 1846; 19 – 7 June, 29 September and October 1866 (bulk of letters 3 – 11 October); 20 – 17 October 1868; 21 – 16 April, 21 November 1870; 22 – 18 April 1870.

Chapter 16.

1 – 29 July 1837; 2 – 24 July 1845; 3 – 20 October 1840; 4 – 22 October 1844; 5 – 11 November 1856; 6 – 29 March and 29 August (company half-yearly) 1849; 7 – see MacDermot II, especially chronology at the back; 8 – see notices included on preceding days; 9 – 3 July 1862; 10 – 28 November, 4 December 1866; 11 – 6 July 1870; 12 – Fawcett; 13 – BoT Report, references under General Acts and ER Mountford & RW Kidner, *The Aberdare Railway*, Oakwood, 1995; 14 – 26 October, 6 November 1855; 15 – 16, 17 July 1855; 16 – 29 October, 2 November 1856; 17 – 14 February 1868; 18 – 16 October 1858, 14 February 1859 (LNW half-yearly); 19 – 3 April 1868; 20 – 22 December 1845; 21 – *Taunton* 20 January 1841; 22 – final account 8 January, rest dated in text; 23 – 24 October, 1 November 1848; 24 – 19 January 1853; 25– *Taunton* 17 November 1852; 26 – from report of accident on 26 November 1852; 27 – 19 June 1853; 28 – 15, 17 August 1857; 29 – 3, 8, 10 September 1866; 30 – 10 January 1838; 31 – 25 December 1846; 32 – 10 February 1847; 33 – *Taunton* 25 May; 34 – 4, 5, 6 January 1854; 35 – 24 December 1859; 36 – 19 January 1867; 37 – Reed p 41; 38 – MD Greville, RCHS *Journal* January 1962; 39 – 15 April 1850; 40 – 19 August 1850, also see RS Joby's *Eastern Counties Railway* p 170 on; 41 – 26 August 1850; 42 – copied by *Taunton* 8 January 1851; 43 – 26, 29 March 1867, also see Turner II p 277-8; 44 – 29, 30 March 1850; 45 – 30 August 1837; 46 – 5 March 1846; 47 – 3, 6 November 1837; 48 – 5 October 1837; 49 – 22 February 1838; 50 – *Taunton* 24 April 1844; 51 – *Taunton* 6 March 1850; 52 – both 1 November 1856; 53 – 14, 18 November 1867; 54 – letters 7 August and 3, 4, 20 September 1851; 55 – 23 March 1847; 56 – 30 January 1850; 57 – 9 December 1857; 58 – 14 September 1865; 59 – letters 15, 27 November; 60 – 31 July and 1, 2 August 1867; 61 – 28 December 1852; 62 – 19 August 1853; 63 – *Kinross-shire Advertiser* 6 June 1857; 64 – 1 August 1838; 65 – 13 September 1842; 66 – 25 October 1850; 67 – 24 April 1856 and see J Marshall, *Biographical Dictionary of Railway Engineers*, RCHS, 2003 edition; 68 – 1 August 1839; 69 – 5 November, part from *Manchester*

Guardian, 70 – company minutes, *RAIL 250/125*, 18 March 1847; 71 – P Scowcroft, RCHS *Journal* December 1973; 72 – 17 February 1868; 73 – LNW Officers Minutes, 4457, 14 July 1869.

Chapter 17. For technical aspects see Rolt; where no source is given, assume was Board of Trade report.

1 – *Taunton* 31 October 1838; 2 – 10 January 1842 / *Examiner*, 3 – 28 March 1846 (not traced in BoT returns though paper said there had been 'contusions'); 4 – 3 & 4 Vic., c. 97; 5 – 13 November 1840; 6 – 9 September 1861; 7 – 16 December 1846 / *Globe*; 8 – 25 August 1865; 9 – 16 January 1861; 10 – 16, 17, 18, 19 January 1867; 11 – 14 February 1868 / *Bureau Veritas* of Paris; 12 – 19 July 1859 (correcting earlier information); 13 – 17, 21 October 1840 (former from *Globe*); 14 – 9 June 1865; 15 – 18 June 1855; 16 – *Taunton* 27 January 1841; 17 – *MT 6/1/280*; 18 – 14 August 1860; 19 – 3 June 1846; 20 – 13 August 1840 (W Wilkinson); 21 – *RAIL 384/22*, minute of 26 November; 22 – 6 January 1841 / *an Essex paper*, 23 – 17 August 1867; 24 – 23 August 1867; 25 – 4 May 1840; 26 – *Taunton* 3 June 1840 / *Morning Herald*; 27 – 12 September 1847; 28 – 16 October 1848; 29 – 18 August 1863; 30 – 27 October 1839 / *Berkshire Chronicle*; 31 – 15 April 1840; 32 – 9 December 1847; 33 – 12 October 1857 and BoT report; 34 – item and letter 9 January 1868; 35 – JR Whitbread, *The Railway Policeman*, Harrap, 1961; 36 – 'Infelix' 1 December 1845; 37 – 26 June 1847; 38 – 20 July 1846; 39 – 13 February 1850; 40 – 28 October 1845; 41 – 12 September 1837; 42 – 21 July 1840 / *Manchester Guardian*, 43 – 16, 21 September and 17 November 1840; 44 – 3, 4, 5, 6, 11 September 1861 and Rolt p 51 on; 45 – *RAIL 1053/2*; 46 – *MT6/11/91*; 47 – 6 August, 20 September 1851; 48 – 4 and 22 March and 26 September 1867; 49 – 20 April 1835 and Thomas p 211; 50 – *Taunton* 2 April 1851 / *Gloucester Journal*; 51 – 28 October 1863; 52 – 5 September 1860; 53 – 12 October 1857; 54 – 10 September and 22 October 1840; 55 – *Cardiff & Merthyr Gazette* 7 January 1854; 56 – 14 July 1837; 57 – 17 February 1845; 58 – 28 February 1867; 58a – 16, 17, 22 December 1868; 59 – 16, 17, 22 December 1867; 60 – 26 August 1840; 61 – 13, 14, 16 November and 3 December 1840; 62 – *Taunton* 25 December 1867; 63 – C Emsley, *The English Police*, Longman, 1996 (2nd edition); 64 – 1 August 1851 / *Globe*; 65 – 20, 22, 25 October 1853; 66 – *RAIL 384/22* 11 November 1841; 67 – *RAIL 384/22* 10 February 1842; 68 – *MT6/1/280*; 69 – *Taunton* 8 May 1844; 70 – 13 November 1834; 71 – 11 November 1839 / *Wigan Gazette*; 72 – 12 August / *Aris's Birmingham Gazette*, 13 August, 26 August / *a Worcester paper*; 73 – 3 January 1843 / *Caledonian Mercury*; 74 – 27 February 1843; 75 – 17 October 1843 / *Berkshire Chronicle*; 76 – 14, 15, 18 April and 12 May 1845; 77 – 2, 10, 14, 16, 18, 19 June 1851 and Rolt p 133; 78 – 16 October 1857 / *Bury & Norwich Post*; 79 – 4 February 1863; 80 – 28 September 1863; 81 – 31 October 1867; 82 – 31 August 1865; 83 – 25 October 1840; 84 – 31 January 1851 / *Maidstone Journal*; 85 – 6 August 1863; 86 – 17 June 1839; 87 – 10 July 1868; 88 – 6 July 1836 / *Macclesfield Courier*; 89 – *Taunton* 1 June 1853; 90 – 12 August 1839 / *Sheffield Iris*; 91 – 19 February 1839; 92 – 22 July 1840 / *Essex Herald*; 93 – 22 July 1840 / *a Preston paper*; 94 – 25 January 1845; 95 –

27 January 1845; 96 – 23 November 1864; 97 – 9 January 1866; 98 – 31 December 1867; 99 – 14 December 1855; 100 – 30 December 1863; 101 – 7, 8 July 1869; 102 – 22 February and 17 November 1838, 12 October 1850; 103 – *Taunton* 13 January 1841; 104 – 27 June 1841, 21 August 1861; 105 – 9 August 1845; 106 – 12, 19 November 1844; 107 – 19 July 1860.

Chapter 18. Again, much from official returns is not individually sourced.

1 – B Wright, *Insurance Fire Brigades*, Tempus, 2008; 2 – 23 November 1840 / *Leicester Chronicle*; 3 – 15 November 1840; 4 – *RAIL 384/22*; 5 – 1 January 1841; 6 – 5 September 1845 from *Tyne Mercury*; 7 – 2 February 1846; 8 – 8 May 1846; 9 – 7 October 1846; 10 – 1 June 1852 / *Spectator*; 11 – 12 October 1852; 12 – 10 April 1852; 13 – 13 July 1847 and GO Holt, RCHS *Journal* January 1957; 14 – 18 August 1848; 15 – 26 July 1852; 16 – 7 March 1853; 17 – 10 February 1859; 18 – 1 February 1849; 19 – 15, 17 January and 30 March 1848; 20 – 5 July 1851; 21 – 15 January 1851; 22 – 28 August 1852; 23 – 3, 4, 6, 7, 9, 11 September and 24 October 1861; 24 – also *Times* 4 February 1841.

Chapter 19.

1 – 26 October 1857; 2 – 23 November 1844 / *Nottingham Mercury* and *Nottingham Journal*; 3 – 6 August 1845; 4 – 20 July 1846; 5 – 17 March 1847 (report that she had returned home); 6 – 5 November 1846; 7 – 12 May 1848; 8 – *Taunton* 21 February 1849; 9 – *Taunton* 23 October 1850; 10 – *Taunton* 13 August 1851; 11 – copied *Taunton* 27 August 1851; 12 – 25 November 1851, letter Walter Cooper; 21 September 1854; 13 – 21 September 1854; 14 – 26 September 1857 / *Nottingham Telegraph*; 15 – letters 17, 22 August 1857; 16 – 1 November 1858; 17 – 3 September 1861; 18 – 6, 7 April 1863; 19 – 13 April 1863; 20 – 8, 9, 10, 13 June 1865; 21 – 28 September 1865; 22 – 1, 2 July 1867; 23 – 22, 24 (description), 27, 28, 29 June 1870; 24 – 15 August 1857; 25 – 25, 27 August 1857 (often 'Reigate' and 'Redhill' were then used loosely for the same station).

Chapter 20.

1 – 21, 28 August 1840; 2 – 14 (from *York Courant*), 6, 18, 23 November 1840; 3 – 7, 10 January 1842 and Rolt; 4 – Thorne v LBSC 25 December 1869; 5 – Roocroft v LY 15 December 1869; 6 – Blackman & wife v LBSC 3 May 1869; 7 – Warren v GN 29 June, 1 July 1869 (both *Examiner* and a piece copied from *Railway Times* in the RCHS *Journal* March 1978 said jury made the award but it would seem that the matter was settled before they had a chance to have their say); 8 – Ody v GW 1 April 1869; 9 – Bratt v LY 24 December 1869; 10 – Farr v LNW 15 June 1869; 11 – Sagar v LY 20 March 1869; 12 – Chadwick v LY 6 August 1869; 13 – Milne v LNW 15 December 1869; 14 – Foster v LY 6 August 1869; 15 – Colmer & wife v LCD 9 December 1869; 16 – Everett & wife v LSW 7 August 1869; 17 – Onions & wife v LNW 16 March 1869, Bennett & wife v LY 6 April 1869; 18 – Cooper v LBSC 11 August 1869; 19 – Outen v LNW 26 January 1869; 20 – 27 February 1847; 21 – 17 January 1849; 22 –

Maycock executrix & another v GE 28 February 1869 and 21 June 1869; 23 – Bradley v LBSC 10 December 1869; 24 – start of inquest (adjourned) 14 August 1869, civil case 23 June 1870; 25 – *Taunton* 31 August 1853; 26 – 5 December 1868 (from BoT reports); 27 – figures from BoT accident report (LBSC chairman said 600 on train, 360 claims); 28 – Squires v LBSC 14 January 1870; 29 – 16 February 1860; 30 – 14 August 1869; 31 – copied *Times* 5 July 1869; 32 – Dunford v LBSC 12 February 1870; 33 – 3 August 1869; 34 – 11 August 1869; 35 – copied 25 August 1869; 36 – Penver (infant by a friend) v Cornwall Railway 7 December 1869; 37 – Sims & wife v GW 10 February 1869, Praeger v Bristol & Exeter 5 November 1869; 38 – Trowbridge v Met 14 December 1869; 39 – 5 November 1869, 17 November 1869; 40 – all v LBSC 1870, Scott 21 January, Johnson 9 July, Fenton 11 February; 41 – Wilson v LBSC 24 December 1869 and 29 January 1870; 42 – Plank v LBSC, retrial 13 January 1870 (original not traced); 43 – 30 January 1851; 44 – Harris v LBSC 4, 6, 7, 8 December 1869; 45 – civil actions 24 June, 6 and 24 November 1869 and criminal 30 July 1870; 46 – criminal trial 13 January 1870 (LBSC chairman said he had received £330 – included expenses?); 47 – paper did not give his position – reporter clearly thought readers would know who he was; would seem safe to assume he was the Sir William Fergusson thus described in the Concise DNB (on one occasion he was reported as 'Sir J F…'); 48 – appeal 4 June 1870; 49 – Keeper v LBSC 6 April 1870; 50 – 21 August 1851 / *Lincolnshire Chronicle*; 51 – 31 & 32 Vic cap 119; 52 – 14 (item), 17 (notice) February 1865; 53 – text in *Bradshaw's Shareholders' Manual*, 1871; 54 – 7 August 1849 (advert); 55 – 9 April 1852 (advert); 56 – *RM* vol 4 p 257 on; 57 – *Taunton* 20 September 1854; 58 – 9 September 1843; 59 – 16 June 1843; 60 – 27 January 1849; 61 – 5 January 1859; 62 – 7 January 1853; 63 – 13 October 1853; 64 – 4 January 1854; 65 – 19 August 1865; 66 – 18 October 1855; 67 – 20 February 1860; 68 – 16 December 1857.

Chapter 21.

1 – *Taunton* 2, 9 February 1853; 2 – 13 February 1858; 3 – 9 December 1855; 4 – 24 June and 9 July 1847; 5 – 29 September 1852; 6 – *Taunton* 5 September 1855; 7 – 26 January 1844 / *Maidstone Gazette*; 8 – 4 May 1844 / *Birmingham Advertiser*; 9 – 6 November 1852; 10 – *Taunton* February 1855; 11 – 14 January 1863; 12 – *Stockport Advertiser* 24 February 1843; 13 – 21 September and 1, 2 November 1854; 14 – 24 July 1855; 15 – 9 August 1865; 16 – 5 December 1865 / *Glasgow Herald*; 17 – preliminary proceedings and criminal trial in 1845 spread over 6, 13, 18, 30 August, 18 and 29 September, 1, 2, 18, 25, 29 and 31 October, 1 and 4 November; 18 – 13 June and 3 December 1846; 19 – *Railway Record* 5 December 1846, pages 1288-9 (*Z PER 3/10* at Kew) and *HO 45/2370* (1847-8) at Kew; 20 – 23 June and 12 July 1851; 21 – 7 April 1864; 22 – *Trewmans* 13, 20 January; *Times* 19th; 23 – *Taunton* and *Trewmans* almost every issue January to November; *Times* 13, 14 November, support for Dickens and contrary opinions following days; 24 – 15 April 1848; 25 – *MT6/1/280*; 26 – 27 March 1854; 27 – *Taunton* 28 November 1855; 28 – 10 September 1851; 29 – 21 August 1861; 30 – 26 August 1865; 31 – 7 November 1839; 32 – 8 November 1845; 33 – 20 August 1846; 34

– 14 October 1846 / *Ipswich Express*; 35 – 15 June 1855; 36 – *Taunton* 18 July 1849; 37 – RCHS *Journal* November 1977; 38 – 21 December 1841 / *Sussex Express*; 39 – 24 August 1846 / *Warwick Advertiser*; 40 – 8 July 1851; 41 – *Taunton* 1 July 1840 / *Lincoln Gazette*; 42 – *Bristol Times* 8 May 1841.

Chapter 22 (all 1846 except last two).

1 – published 6 April; 2 – published 15th; 3 – 4 June; 4 – from *Herts Mercury*; 5 – 3, 4, 6 August; 6 – 1, 3 September; 7 – 13 October; 8 – 24 December; 9 – 29 September; 10 – 4 August / *Examiner*; 11 – 26 September; 12 – 24 October; 13 – 4 August; 14 – 17 September; 15 – 26 October; 16 – 20 August; 17 – 27 March; 18 – 1 January 1847; 19 – 10 August 1847.